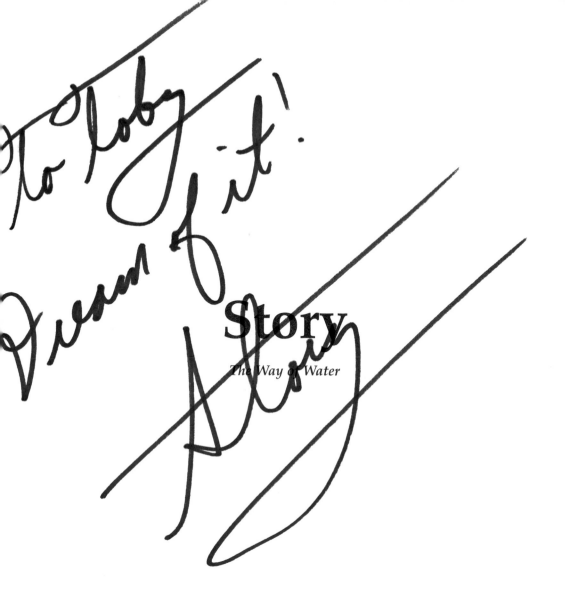

To Toby
Dream of it!

# Story

*The Way of Water*

*By Anne E. Lenehan*

National Library of Australia
Cataloguing-in-Publication data:

Lenehan, Anne, E. 1967- .
        Story : the way of water.

        ISBN 0 9752286 0 9.

        1. Musgrave, Story.  2. United States. National Aeronautics
        and Space Administration.  3. Hubble Space Telescope
        (Spacecraft) - Maintenance and repair.  4. Astronauts -
        United States - Biography.  I. Title.

        629.450092

First published in the USA and Australia in 2004 by
The Communications Agency
PO Box 1674, Hornsby Westfield NSW 1635, Australia.

Printed in the USA
by The Maple-Vail Book Manufacturing Group.

Cover design by Anne E. Lenehan.
All theme page quotes are by Story Musgrave.

**For Story.**

# Contents

| | | |
|---|---|---|
| **Foreword** | *By Story Musgrave* | ix |
| **Prologue** | *A Passionate Life* | 1 |
| **Childhood** | | 9 |
| | *The Child* | 11 |
| | *The Farm* | 37 |
| **Nature** | | 51 |
| | *Experiences in Nature* | 53 |
| | *Nature: A Philosophy* | 71 |
| **Mechanics** | | 89 |
| | *Lifelong Mechanic* | 91 |
| | *Marines* | 95 |
| | *The Road to Medicine* | 111 |
| | *Flying* | 139 |
| **Space** | | 177 |
| | *Space Flight* | 179 |
| | *The Richness of Space Experience* | 239 |
| | *A Philosophy of Space* | 271 |
| **Death & Life** | | 293 |
| | *Death in Life* | 295 |
| | *A Philosophy of Death and Life* | 315 |
| **Body, Mind, Art** | | 329 |
| | *The Body* | 331 |
| | *Spacewalking Ballet* | 347 |
| | *Art and Literary Influences* | 375 |
| | *Communicating Through Art* | 393 |
| **Journey** | | 411 |
| | *Lasting Impressions* | 413 |
| | *Self-Reflections* | 429 |
| | *The Way of Water* | 443 |
| **Acknowledgements** | | 457 |
| **Photo Credits** | | 460 |
| **Medical Research** | | 461 |
| **Missions** | | 463 |
| **Select Chronology** | | 466 |

# *Foreword*

This is a magnificent biography, a work of art, an impression born in the heart, grown in the heart and of the heart. It is very rich and very readable. Anne has produced a verbal portrait, a character that comes alive in the mind of the reader, page after page. More than a chronology of what happened when, or what was done when, it is who this character is, how he came to be and even why. It is an expression of the major themes, the operating principles that constitute the person, that drive this being.

It is molded out of a multiplicity of penetrating content: media appearances, published interviews, personal interviews, in-person encounters, visits to places of geospatial significance, notes in the margins of books, flight logs, private journals never intended for public consumption, and the personal experience of a life shared with the subject over several years. It is an objective expression of a massive amount of very subjective content.

I do love this piece; as I look into Anne's mirror I not only relive my life, but I get to know Story in ways that I had never experienced before. I have a greater understanding of the world that he came into and how he evolved along with that world. I know better who he is and who he is not. I now see the past with a richer perspective, a more complete and clearer vision; the future with more meaning and more hope.

*Story Musgrave, May 2004*

Through your eyes I've seen the earth
in colours so profound,
And tasted her delicious shades
through subtle light and sound.
I've soared above her desert sands,
cast ripples on her lakes,
And danced around the twilight
to the rhythms she creates.

Across great sweeps of rich terrain
of every shape and hue,
Across the changing oceans
'til I drowned amid the view,
And out beyond the limits
of our precious earth and sun,
I found a sense of freedom
in the things I'd never done.

Because of you, I learned to float
where few have learnt to fly,
To savour every moment
as we drift through earth and sky,
To balance on the edge and ride
with passion where you lead,
To breathe of earthly visions
and on star-turned thoughts to feed.

For through your eyes I've found a way
to share what you have seen,
To capture what it means to live
and never fear to dream.
To look about the universe
for what my place might be,
Reflecting on the things we've shared
and what they mean to me.

*Anne Lenehan*

# Prologue: A Passionate Life

The seeds of clover were sown
the kernels of my soul were grown.
Grew I through food and fear
through Nature's land far and near.
Grew I, rooted in hill and vail
till uprooted, born by road and rail.
Among the mountains and the streams
in and out of all the earthly seams,
up and down the heavenly beams,
melted, molded I by myriad steams.
Sculptured by the seasons,
listening to Nature's reasons,
Grew I, rooted in the ether.

*Story's Prelude*
*Story Musgrave 1988*

In October of 2002, Story and I travel to New England and arrive in the midst of a spectacular Fall. In the cooler weather, the leaves have turned into a multitude of colors and during our stay they reach their peak beauty. Word has spread and visitors are arriving in their hundreds. Hillsides glow in shades of red and yellow, and everywhere underfoot is the sound of crunching leaves.

We are in Stockbridge, Massachusetts and I have come to learn about one of Story's worlds. Certainly, few biographers have had the opportunity to be led so literally through their subject's life like this, but here we are. I am going to be shown, first hand, the details, as well as the overall picture of the land into which he was born. As it turns out, our visit to Massachusetts is very significant. The more I learn about Story, the more I realize how important the physical world is to his experiences and how critical his childhood is to his perception of the world. This is where it began almost seven decades ago.

My first impressions of Stockbridge are of a delightful town with well-kept houses and a lively main street. There are several churches in the town center, a variety of small shops and cafes catering to out-of-town visitors, a library and, of course, a grand old inn – the Red Lion.

Story leads me into St Paul's Episcopal Church where his parents were married. It is an old stone church, dark inside but with wonderful stained-glass windows. Story's family for several generations were patrons of this church, his great-great-grandfather having made a considerable donation in memory of his wife. Outside in the garden is a statue of a lady which Story loves to admire on his visits. Unidentified by inscription, she wears a queenly crown, as well as a beautiful, serene expression.

We leave the main street as a light, steady rain settles in and drive along the narrow roads of town. We are surrounded by a rainbow of overhanging branches which sometimes brush the windows as we pass. Story knew the autumn colors would be compelling for me and they are. He is passionate about color and it is easy to see why, when you come from a place like this. His descriptions of the earth from space are enhanced by these experiences.

We pause along the road beside the Housatonic River. We will see it from a number of angles as it weaves its way around town, but this time, we stop by a little bridge. Story spent a lot of time here as a child – the sloping bank of the river was the launching ramp for his raft. We are upstream from Linwood, his childhood home, and a decent distance by river for any adventurous five-year-old. Right nearby is a long, flat stone wall, the front boundary of another property along which Story used to ride his bicycle. It is a great looking wall and I sense that, even now, Story would find that a fun thing to do.

We head on towards Linwood, following the Housatonic from time to time. Story points out a familiar curve in its trajectory, an island where he used to play and his favorite part of the river. Everywhere are trees: we are traveling beneath them as we continue to wind our way along the road.

To catch the ambiance of the trees, we stop a while and venture into a pine forest which Story loved as a child. Nothing much has changed here: the trees are just as tall, the forest floor a soft, sponge-like bed of pine needles and the sunlight still filters through the branches to reach the open canopy beneath. It is comfortable and inviting here – a child's paradise. We walk the length of this playground, stopping occasionally as Story remembers a particular view or a familiar tree. Pine trees are Story's favorite trees. He touches the trunks of the trees, describing how he used the moisture on the shady side to navigate through the dark. Both the smell of the pines and the sound of the wind through the pine needles are powerful. Story played here; sometimes slept here.

Continuing further down the road we reach Butler Bridge, named for the original owner of Linwood, Charles E. Butler. It is a stone and wooden bridge which crosses the Housatonic, but it is now closed to vehicles. This was once the traditional entrance to Linwood, leading to the front gate and a long, sweeping driveway to the house. A group of enormous pine trees mark the entrance. Story loves those trees; he wanted to show me this perspective.

To reach the house, we drive back along the road and enter the property from the other side, beyond another impressive line of planted pine trees.

It is through the formal garden that I gain my first glimpse of Linwood. It is large; its stone walls rise above the massive evergreen hedges. It is not what I was expecting – it is far grander, yet somehow unpretentious in the way it is situated among the trees and garden. It's creator obviously had impeccable taste.

This was Story's home for the first ten years of his life; this is where he played out those formative times. Seeing it for real is somewhat stunning. This beautiful dwelling – one of the most outstanding of the Berkshire Cottages – was the setting for his father's violent tirades, his parents' unhappy marriage and separation, and finally, his father's suicide. The contrast between the physical and the emotional worlds is great.

Some years after the death of Story's father, the Linwood house and property, which passed to Story's stepmother, Josephine Cary, was purchased by Norman Rockwell's trustees. They converted the site into a museum – now one of the most popular destinations in the area. The house was retained for mostly administrative activities while a new building was constructed nearby for the museum itself. Eventually, Rockwell's studio was also relocated to the property.

The scene around the house is different from the way Story knew it as a child. Gone are the farming activities, the dairy cows and haying, and in their place are visitors by the dozens who come to pay homage to the spirit of Norman Rockwell – one of America's most renowned artists and iconographers. A political and cultural commentator through his art, Rockwell moved to Stockbridge in his middle years and would frequently visit Linwood to dine with Story's father and stepmother, who maintained a social standing within the Stockbridge community.

These days, Linwood is generally off limits to the public, however, when we return again the next day, the museum staff allow Story and I to enter. They are fascinated by its former occupant and eager to learn as much as they can about the dwelling's history. Story leads us from basement to attic, from room to room, each place evoking a comment or a detail. Most of the original furnishings are gone, but he finds a familiar sofa, the original kitchen stove and even a Grecian urn sitting just as it used to on a windowsill. The staff ask about a particularly interesting wall papering in the stairway – an oriental-style bamboo design. Story remembers it as part of the décor of the 1940s and also notes that the glass conservatory which extended from the library has been removed, as have a few of the large shrubs outside the main entrance. All in all, for Story there is little sentimentality or emotion attached to the house itself, for it was the nature outside which provided him with a real home.

Afterwards, Story and I walk through the garden with its valley views and winding river. I am drawn to the beauty of the world in which Story immersed himself as a young child: the original pines trees and thick maples groves are still there. During the time Story lived at Linwood, the farm consisted of over 1000 acres. He spent his time outdoors in the fields, in the woods and in the distant hills. Amazingly, as we inspect some of the larger trees, Story finds remnants of his old maple syruping activities – an odd nail for the bucket, or the long-healed hole in the trunk for the spout. He is so excited to be able to show me: it is a tangible link with his childhood. More than fifty years have now passed.

With sweeping gestures, Story explains the farm's layout as it was back then. He points to where the hay grew, where the cows grazed and where the pigs and chickens were housed. Back along the road he points to the scene of an accident which was just another fact of farm life – the memory flashes upon him in all its detail. So too, the places where Story and his older brother raced their cars, or rounded a corner too fast and left the road.

The next day, Story and I take a walk around Stockbridge Cemetery, which, like everywhere else, reflects the season. The cemetery is full of history and old blood, and we enjoy reading the epitaphs on the various graves. In a newer section we come across the rather large Musgrave family headstone, which was installed by Story's father Percy. Some people consider it rather pretentious in its size, given the relative social status of its occupants. Story also seems to agree and is waiting to capture my reaction. Percy and his second wife Josephine are buried here, but although both of Story's brothers and the date of their deaths are listed, neither of them lie beneath. Like Linwood, the headstone is a status symbol which is more in line with how Percy hoped to be perceived, rather than how he really was by those who knew him well.

Other memorable highlights of our stay in Stockbridge include a meal at the Red Lion Inn, the drive to the Mahkeenac Boat Club with the autumn reflections on the lake, a visit to the Plain School which Story and his brothers attended, and meeting with some of Story's cousins.

What I take with me from all of this is a sense of time, a sense of the family history, but above all else, a feel for the physical world to which Story was born. And in a way, every part of Story's life gets back to that: he is so passionate about it. In the pine forests and maple groves he touches the trees; around the old farm he picks up handfuls of soil. Wherever we go, Story points out the smells and the sounds.

*

Story and I return to Linwood again at the end of our week long stay in New England. The sun is shining now, the leaves are even redder, and we stroll down to the river to enjoy the solitude.

Story mentions the crows. I do not even notice the crows, they are difficult to hear, but Story hears them. I have to concentrate hard, but then it becomes clearer – a continual chorus, but extremely faint. Story loves crows because they are associated with his childhood.

We find a log and sit down together along the river bank. Although I have traveled to Linwood with the adult, it is the child who now sits on the log beside me, the child of the 1930s, enjoying the moment and the memories, enjoying nature. That is what it gets down to; that is what this book is about: a human life in touch with the world. And Story found that world through this one.

There is an odd duck upon the river, but otherwise nothing stirs. It is one of those rare moments of peace in Story's busy life. We do not need to speak, it is before us.

A short time later we are joined by a visitor to the museum, obviously drawn to the beauty of the scene. I am somewhat bemused, having to bite my tongue really hard, when he unknowingly turns towards Story and remarks, "Nice place, isn't it?"

Story simply looks his way and smiles.

# Childhood

"Childhood – that boy got me here – now what am I going to do with it?
Loyalty to Story, what he fought for, what he did to get here."

# 1. The Child

Story, alone in the middle of the back seat of a 1938 Roadmaster, sat on the very edge of his seat, grasping the front seat firmly with two little hands, and resting his chin and his mind in those hands, vigilantly watched the road and the landscape reel from the future to the past...

He watched the road and the landscape weave a drunken pattern back and forth across the front windows, wondering which past had placed him here and if any future would place him anywhere. He saw the oncoming headlights in the distance and desperately hoped that the mindless, random searches of the Roadmaster would by chance let them pass clear. Mindless and random as they were, he tried to look into his future, tried to see his fate weaved before the windows, tried to predict the weave at the point the oncoming car would pass, or would not pass. Mindless and random as it was, the prediction was terrifying. As the horn screamed in dread, the tires screeched in vain, Story dove for the floorboards, slammed his little back tight against the front seat, and braced it there by wedging arms and knees against the base of the rear seat. The horn approached like that of a train, the time stood still, the horn disappeared into the past like a train gone by, the Roadmaster weaved on. Story, alone, crawled back to the edge of the back seat, firmly grasped the front seat with two little hands, placed his chin in those hands and vigilantly watched the future reel into the past. The mindless Roadmaster drifted onto the shoulder, back onto the road, then deeper into the shoulder, back onto the road, and again toward the shoulder. The pattern was no longer random, Story dove again for the floor boards. The Roadmaster departed, rolled along the shoulder, rolled through the ditch, rolled along the side of an incline, rolled over on its back, and slid to a halt. The acorns rolled gently down the incline, the leaves descended to the earth with a final whisper, the birds sang of fall and coming winter as they departed. Story still wedged between the seats, but now on the ceiling boards, worked to free a leg to let himself carefully down from his perch. The smell of gasoline was strong, sickening, and terrifying. "Mom!" "Mom!" "Please Mom, you've got to be OK". "Don't die Mom". The air in the Roadmaster was thick with gasoline and smoke. The doors were crushed shut. Story, with little sneakers, pounded out the remains of a front window and crawled out. He turned around, planted two little sneakers on either side of the front wind screen and slowly dragged his mother free of the Roadmaster. He knelt on the ground, holding her head on his knee, his tears washing the blood from her face. A siren rang its way along the road, and soon Story could see its spotlight scanning the roadside. He bent over and kissed his mother – "Good-bye Mom, I love you", and crept up the incline and into the trees. He watched the light find the Roadmaster and then his Mom. He watched them bundle her up, carry her off, and listened to the siren fade into the past. Story walked down the incline, to the Roadmaster, and putting his hand softly on it – "I'm sorry, God I'm sorry, I hope you will make it OK. I wish there was something that I could do, but I know that you understand. If they knew my Mom had a twelve-year-old they would take me from her or her from me. Somehow we'll get you back on the road. I love you." Story walked far enough so as to not be connected with his Mom, and then hitch-hiked home.

*"The Roadmaster" by Story Musgrave, 1988*

Living life strongly in the moment, Story Musgrave has a positive view of his past. As far back as he can remember, the child defined who he was, gave him an anchor in the world. Fundamentally, Story does not believe either he, or that, has changed:

Story stands on himself, on his childhood, who he was from the beginning.[1]

For a college paper in 1990, Story wrote: "For better or worse, I am one of the 'introverted creators who are able to define identity and achieve self-realization by self-reference, that is, by interacting with their own past work rather than by interacting with other people'. My interaction happens to be with the person that I was as a child."[2]

Story's early childhood was remarkable for the unhappy and often violent family situation, and the way in which it propelled him into an exceptional relationship with both himself and the world around him. He built resilience, determination and self-reliance: characteristics which would resonate throughout his entire life.

While preparing for his final space flight in 1996, Story again referred to the importance of his childhood. In his journal he wrote:

Childhood – that boy got me here – now what am I going to do with it? Loyalty to Story, what he fought for, what he did to get here.[3]

Filled with strong emotions sixty years later, Story continues to celebrate and explore the past, for it has made him the person that he is today.

\*

The New England state of Massachusetts was the setting for Story's childhood – a place to which his ancestors emigrated almost four hundred years ago.

The name Story was originally a family name, belonging to ancestors on Story's maternal side, such as Elias Story who arrived in America in November of 1620 aboard the *Mayflower*. Elias was one of the first of Story's distant ancestors to reach America – both sides of the family having a long and established history on English soil. Among the original one hundred and two passengers who set sail from Plymouth, England, in September of 1620, Story can claim several other ancestors by different family names. Massachusetts, therefore, became the starting point for much

---

1. Handwritten note in Story's copy of *The Denial of Death* by Ernest Becker: New York, Free Press, 1973. This book won a Pulitzer Prize in 1974.
2. Story was quoting and agreeing with Anthony Storr in *Solitude: A Return to the Self*: New York, Free Press, 1988. The college paper was titled: *A Personal and Scholarly Look at the Process of Creativity*.
3. Journal 19, page 9; Date: 20 February 1996.

of the family's growth in America.

There were many prominent Storys in the lineage. Joseph Story, born in Marblehead, Massachusetts, in 1779, was appointed an Associate Justice of the Supreme Court at the age of thirty-two. Joseph's son, William Wetmore Story, born in 1819, also became a lawyer of note, but his real interest lay in sculpture. In 1856 William left his legal career behind and moved permanently to Rome – his most famous work being an elegant marble sculpture of a contemplative Cleopatra. So highly regarded were his artistic skills that during his lifetime William enjoyed the patronage of the Pope, who arranged transportation of Cleopatra to London for exhibition.

If not as distinguished, Story's maternal grandfather, John Butler Swann Snr, born in England several generations later, was certainly entrepreneurial. According to Story's first cousin and family historian Clover Swann, "Apparently, he went to Costa Rica to manage a coffee plantation which he had a shares in. Well our version, is that he went to look for gold, because he heard that there was gold in Costa Rica, but in fact he was managing a coffee plantation, because I have pictures of it. They were digging up holes in which to put coffee plants and they were running into Mayan artifacts. And so he had quite a collection by the time he left Costa Rica in the early 1900s.

"He then heard that there was gold in Alaska, and he thought, 'I must go there'. So he starts towards Alaska. In the process he brings back to America the Mayan artifacts collection and thinks that maybe he can sell it, but finds that there's no market for it at all in 1906. I believe he then donated it to a museum.

"So he heads over to Alaska and takes a good look around and then he decides that what the miners really need in Alaska are horses, and he happens to be extremely good with horses. So he and a friend travel to Arizona, rope and capture wild horses, break them, train them, get them to the ferry at San Francisco and get them transported up to Alaska. Once there, he's trying to sell these horses and nobody will buy. And then winter sets in and there's no hay. And he happened to really love horses and he had to sell them for horse meat and he was really devastated."

After that, in an attempt to encourage John to settle down, the family decided to buy him a horse farm in Virginia, however, he wasn't home for long. "They had no idea he would immediately train for a polo team and start taking them up and down the East coast, going to polo matches, which was a very high-end, ritzy sport," explained Clover. He would soon meet his end dramatically in a polo tournament accident in Rhode Island around 1910 when his youngest child, Story's mother Marguerite, was just one year old.

On the paternal side of the ancestral charts, Story Musgrave's father, Percy

Musgrave Jnr, was a descendent of the Musgrave family of Eden Hall, a stately residence situated on the banks of the Eden River in the Cumberland district of England. The estate, which came into the family during the reign of Henry VI, became famous for one of its antique treasures – a goblet known as *The Luck of Eden Hall*. This precious cup survived numerous ordeals for over five hundred years, bearing a legendary fairy curse: "Where'er this cup shall break or fall, Farewell the luck of Eden Hall." Although the original Eden Hall was demolished and rebuilt in 1882, *The Luck of Eden Hall* is alive and well and still remains the property of that family today.

Across the other side of the Atlantic, the Musgrave family established itself well in New England, with many distinguished graduates of Harvard University and some seven generations of surgeons, including Story's grandfather, Dr Percy Musgrave of Boston. Dr Musgrave served with the British Expeditionary forces in England and later with the American Expeditionary forces in France during the First World War.

Story recalled, "There was a big string of doctors back there, very well known surgeons, Chief Surgeons at Massachusetts General Hospital."

Of particular importance to our present narrative, these two distinguished family histories were to merge during the 1930s, with the marriage of Story Musgrave's parents, Marguerite Swann and Percy Musgrave Jnr, on 10 October 1931.

The marriage was lauded in local newspapers as the "leading society event of the fall season." The bride was portrayed as "upper crust" of Milton, while the groom was noted as a Harvard graduate and the grandson of the late Dr Charles Burnham Porter of Boston and Mr and Mrs Thomas Bateson Musgrave of New York.

The ceremony took place at St Paul's Episcopal church, Stockbridge, which had been built with a generous donation by the bride's great-grandfather. The bride, wearing a simple silver gown and carrying Lilies of the Valley, was attended by her maid of honor and nine bridesmaids. Following the service, the bells of the town hall rang for half an hour to mark the occasion. Details of the family, the ceremony, the guests and subsequent festivities were covered by a large number of newspapers, including the *Boston Evening Transcript* which, on October 17, published a double page photo spread of the extensive wedding party. As Percy and Marguerite Musgrave headed to Europe for their honeymoon aboard the luxury cruise liner *Europa*, it appeared in every way to be a picture of domestic bliss and societal privilege – the handsome young businessman and his beautiful and well-connected wife.

At the time of their marriage, Percy had, for four years, been employed by the banking firm of Stone & Webster and Blodgett, Inc, where he continued for a further two years. Then, in 1933, Percy and Marguerite were offered a rather extraordinary opportunity by a relative of hers, a Mr Charles Stewart Butler, to purchase Linwood farm near Stockbridge for the small sum of $10,500. Having lived in Boston since their marriage, the couple took advantage of the offer and moved to the thousand-acre dairy farm with it's stylish English residence – a forty-room, five-story house with formal gardens – in the foothills of the Berkshire Mountains.

From the commencement of his agricultural career, Percy Musgrave strove to portray the image of a gentleman farmer. Patricia Musgrave, whom Story married in 1960, vividly recalled her first impressions of Linwood and its master.

"Stockbridge, Massachusetts, is just beautiful – mountains, streams, dense with forests and trees. We came into a long driveway, a dirt driveway, and I am saying to Story, 'Where is your house?' Finally we go up a hill and we park in front of the house. And out of the front door comes Story's father. He has a cap on, an English cap, a tweed-looking jacket, riding pants, boots, rifle under his arm – I mean classic English. He comes out of the house and I meet him. He is very English and very, very formal. And Story showed me around. It's a stone home – elegant, country-English-style. And there were carriages, dating back to the 1800s. They had three carriages – their mode of transportation before cars came along. They had formal gardens, rose gardens and hedges – an English setting. It was just beautiful."

On 26 July 1939, *The Berkshire County Eagle* Dairy Section ran a feature on Linwood Farm, describing it as "one of the outstanding farms which furnish milk and farm products to the 121,000 residents of Berkshire…Linwood's milk is distributed by the Pittsfield Milk Exchange." The farm was stocked with pure Guernsey cattle.

The early years of Percy and Marguerite's marriage appear to have been relatively happy ones: if otherwise, it has not been documented in any detail. They produced three sons: Percy Musgrave III, born 5 September 1933, Franklin Story Musgrave (known as "Story"), born 19 August 1935 and Thomas Bateson Musgrave, born 28 May 1939. At Percy's insistence, Marguerite took her confinement in Boston for each of the births under the care of well-respected doctors. In a letter written shortly before Tom's birth, she spoke of the privilege she felt in bearing Percy's sons: "Feeling wonderfully rested and relaxed in preparation to produce your third son… It is, to me, a tremendous privilege and joy to be allowed to produce your sons."

The marital relationship, however, would soon enter a rapid decline. Clover Swann shed some light on the situation, based on family letters. She suggested a disappointment in Percy's expectations – that he probably believed his wife to be wealthier than she really was. In an attempt to increase the family wealth, Percy had wanted to represent the Swann family as their investment manager and, with the support of Marguerite, who wrote to her siblings pleading with them to trust her husband, he succeeded.

From as early as three years of age, probably not long after Tom's birth, Story could remember the deteriorating family situation. In an interview with Barbara Burgower Hordern in 1997, Story recalled that his earliest memories were of fear. According to Hordern, "His father often lashed out violently, usually targeting Story and his mother rather than his brothers. Yet even at age three, Musgrave had a strong sense of his own worth. "I distanced myself from the family," he explains. "I looked at it and said, 'This is a sick world.' But I was not causing it, and I was not a part of it. I was a survivor.""[4]

Story explained: "I had an incredibly harsh, malicious father; a violent, physical, terrorizing father with an incredible temper. You get the sense that he was hugely frustrated with the life that he had, just dissatisfied with the whole thing. His presence pervaded the family influence – he was the key dynamic. I mean, there was absolutely no other influence that mattered. When you're dealing with a tank in your face, it doesn't matter that there's a bicycle there. The tank is the tank and, when you've got the gun in your face, nothing much matters. Mom was very loving and a passive person and it didn't play well with him. In other words, she didn't stand up to him."[5]

According to Clover Swann, "It was very hard for Dad[6] to try to watch what was happening to his younger sister so fast with this man. He managed to get control of Linwood and then it was obvious that he was torturing Marguerite; he was just brutalizing her. And he didn't make a lot of friends as far as we can tell. One day he came over to talk to Dad about something and they got into fierce argument. Percy jumped into his new truck in a fury and drove away and somehow managed to run into one of the posts on the little railroad crossing – how on earth Percy managed to run into one of those posts is ridiculous. Then he had to go back to Dad to have Dad's tractor pull him away from the post."

Marguerite would later testify to the courts what life with Percy was like. As Clover recalled, "Part of it was that when the children were small, Percy did not want to eat with them. I guess he'd already spent her money so they didn't have any help there particularly – so Marguerite was supposed to cook the meals for the children, and feed them, and then she was supposed to serve dinner to Percy who, every night, whether they had visitors, guests or any other dinner companions, would be in the full tuxedo and Marguerite would be the servant. The picture I got from these particular papers was that he would be sitting at the dinner table, by himself, in full tuxedo, and she would serve the dishes. And that the children had to be absolutely

4. The article was titled *Rocket Man* and appeared in *Biography*, July 1997.
5. Interview with author for this book.
6. Story's Uncle Jack; his mother's brother.

silent, they could not be calling their mother or their father to their bedrooms. Everything had to work like clockwork. And part of the dynamic when she was giving this report was if the vegetable was a little cold, he'd fly into a rage and scream at her. And that at any little thing, such as if she spilled a drop of wine, he'd fly into a rage and scream and berate her. The emotional abuse was really intense. So Percy ate late and then he would go out on the town, by himself, in full tuxedo, without Marguerite."

There was one particular incident at the dinner table, Story recalled, when his father flew into a rage, smashing his fist into the table as an act of war. He smashed not only the mustard cup, which was directly beneath the incredible blow, but his hand!

Story abhorred his father's behavior and called it what it was: "My Dad was a son of a bitch. I knew he was a son of a bitch and it didn't matter that he was my father. I didn't understand the concept back then of 'That's your father so you can't feel that way about your father.' At the age of three, I had absolutely no problem in recognizing that and thinking, 'That's how I feel about my father.' And that never changed until the day of his death. And so in a way, that's very simple, very straightforward: I built upon self-reliance."

Story's brothers were, of course, also caught up in the unfolding drama. According to Story, "My brothers were, in some ways, companions on the journey. I had a much closer affinity with my younger brother. I had huge empathy for my younger brother and, of course, he was rather young in this process. I had been young in this process too. We had sort of been through the journey together in a way. But my older brother simply went along with the whole process with Dad and he bought into what was going on – it was an easy way to do it – whatever Dad did, that was fine and he took that attitude all the way through. He just sort of went along with it, became a 'yes man' to him and that was that."

Influenced by these circumstances, Story maintained a close relationship with his younger brother Tom throughout their mutual lives, however, he was never able to establish the same kind of relationship, built on mutual understanding and experience, with his older brother Percy.

While living in Stockbridge, Story, along with his brothers, attended the Plain School. His grades were more than satisfactory, being placed first or second in the class most of the time. The school appreciated Story's vivid imagination and his ability for storytelling, often asking him to share stories with more senior classes.

Story also used his imagination as a means to escape the uncomfortable family life at home. He wasn't a loner, but circumstances forced him to get away from intolerably bad situations and to live in his own creative world. At Linwood, he made a stage for himself using a window seat with retractable curtains, arranging chairs in front of it and inviting "guests" to his performances: usually, his mother was the only person interested in being entertained. Story would spend the majority of his time outdoors with the farm animals and machinery or in the surrounding pine and maple forests, where nature became his friend.

In January of 1946, after almost fourteen and a half years of marriage, Marguerite took herself and her three sons away from Percy. In a letter to her husband she wrote: "I am leaving and taking the boys… as far as I am concerned it is an intolerable situation that gets progressively worse… it is having its effect on the children who are strained and … obviously scared to death of you… I am willing to agree to anything that is reasonable that will solve a hopeless situation."

Story was ten years old at the time. He recalled, "We went to New York City for two weeks. I was out picking blueberries that day and Mom met me when I was heading home. I don't know how she knew I was out – I suppose she saw my picking buckets and she knew – 'Aah buckets, where's he going? He's going to go and get blueberries out there. Well I know where that is!' – and so she met me, I remember that. She met me in the car and she said, 'We're leaving' and, of course, to me, that was wonderful. So all these kids and Mom, we went to New York City, to the Wellington Hotel… two weeks in New York and then we went to Boston. We lived in a hotel – the Bostonian Hotel. We were there for a year and I went to Dexter School, a private school.

"I liked the city and, of course, I had a new world to explore. So at the age of ten, I was out in the city of Boston by myself – that's the way it worked. I was as much at home in the city as in nature. I used to choose a restaurant to go to and I would choose some nightclubs, not knowing that there was a difference. I would go in there and I couldn't believe it! A ten-year-old was in this place to have something to eat. I didn't know it's the city, right, and so, of course, after I ate I didn't have enough money to pay the bill – and they knew. They took what I had and that was good enough. But I enjoyed the city and I explored the city and I went for miles at the age of ten.

"The hotel was nice 'cause there was a social dynamic. It was a dynamic kind of place and we had a little two or three bedroom suite. The hotel is still there – it's an art school now. But over that year my mother got no support from her relatives to leave my father. The relatives – her brothers and sisters – they did not help in this whole process. Dad was a malicious son of a bitch – and they knew because they were prohibited from visiting us [at Linwood]. Once in a while they would get the courage to come over. Once in a while my Uncle Jack would extract me from the place to do something real – the only time I ever got to go to a movie. I used to build my own ski jumps and my own trails but the only time I was ever taken to the ski lift – maybe once a year – was when my Uncle Jack took us. We, as a family, didn't do that kind of thing, ever. We simply didn't do that."

Rosaly Bass, Story's cousin and another of his Uncle Jack's children, recalled the situation at Linwood. "We were sort of told that the father was the devil incarnate and we weren't invited and we didn't want to go."

Years later, Story wrote in his journal:

> Playing little league baseball – the rare few times that I could – I sprained an ankle – worst fear was whether I'd get beat up by my father because I got injured![7]

Of his mother, Story said, "She had the courage to get up and leave and the family should have said, 'You've done the right thing and don't you dare go back'. [But] they were of the old mentality of what a divorce was, what a family split was and that you didn't do those kind of things. Dad was attempting some kind of reconciliation and saying he was going to become good or whatever, so they encouraged her to go back. They did not support what she was doing."

According to Clover Swann, "We were brought up that you don't get divorced, you just have a large enough house that you don't have to run into the person too many times. When my parents talked about difficult marriages, they didn't talk about physical or emotional abuse."

Linwood farm had presented a number of financial difficulties and personal strains for Percy. In a letter to her husband shortly after their first separation, Marguerite wrote: "You say you like farming. Your word about what you like is the best. However, it seems to me (outside of your winter lumbering) it has presented, on the surface, more of a strain than anything else. … the milk outlet has always been a problem in regard to satisfactory price, the worry you have and the actual troubles in the summer – to do with haying and crops… In any event, the decision concerning the farm has got to be yours. … If you still want to continue farming, I will consider it your privilege to do so. .. I would prefer to live at Linwood rather than anywhere else, whether or not I am separated from you. If we remain separated, however, and you wish to farm, I will live elsewhere... As you agreed, I do not feel that the 'financial situation' has been more than an incident in the past in regard to our general incompatibility."

Percy confirmed in a reply: "The Linwood situation, without going into details, appears to be approaching difficulties and it may be necessary to approach banks with some of its problems in the not too distant future."

During that initial period of separation, Marguerite's difficulties with alcohol were highlighted. She had admitted to drinking heavily in the past, said that she had

7. Journal 15, page 28; Date: 19 April 1994

been on the wagon for two years, but also claimed in one letter that she had a hangover. Percy then approached his doctor for advice. There is no indication in Marguerite's letters as to why heavy drinking was an issue for her, but one could assume that the unhappy home situation and disappointment of young hopes were a major factor.

Through much of the early part of 1946, Percy, through a series of letters, pleads with Marguerite to return home with the children. He attempts to persuade her and the boys to join him over the Easter break, saying that he has changed and will do his utmost to make her happy. Their return to Linwood is contingent upon a few conditions of Marguerite's own: she expects greater independence in all matters.

The outcome was rather straightforward. Story says, "She went back for Summer; nothing had changed, so she left a second time."

This time the family was physically divided in a different way. Story said: "When Mom finally left, my older brother optioned to stay with my father and that was that. My younger brother left with us because Mom took him, but in a few days he wanted to go back home. He was threatened by the fact that we had left the home – that great big 1859 stone house and the hundreds of acres around it. My younger brother was only seven then, but he was threatened by the split and he was threatened by having been taken from home and, of course, he wanted to go home. In a threatening situation you want to go home – but home meant to go to Dad… She should not have let him go. That ended up being his demise, but she let him go back, that being her nature.

"Mom could have stayed in the house and legally, of course, had Dad thrown out. However, as violent as things were, I don't think that was an option. I think in communicating to him that she was leaving, I think the only way you could safely communicate that was to be out of there."

Story's father demonstrated a distinct favoritism towards his eldest son, Percy III, and, at the same time, a neglect towards Story. It was a subject which Marguerite felt compelled to mention in a letter to her husband during their separation. Of Story, she wrote: "I wish you would 'pat him on the back' whenever you see fit to do so. He has this essential reassurance from me and he knows it, but I think he feels an essential lack of satisfaction and trust on your part, his father, which is, in my mind, the most important element of all for him to have. In my mind, it will benefit him enormously to feel you have great confidence in him… Story does not know how much you think of him, because, I am guessing, he has never been convinced. Story is amazingly free of jealousy in regard to his brother Percy or anybody else (you remember I have always said this). He has no resentment against Percy, but I think he feels that you expect much more of him in view of accomplishment than you have of Percy. He has mentioned the fact that when Percy got a "fair" [school] report in

Stockbridge, it was, by you, all right; but when he, Story, got a similar one, it was not all right… You felt that because he was judged to be very bright when very young, that he should live up to this ideal.… I do not believe I prefer him to the others, but I do recognize that he has missed having from you the confidence and support that, in my mind, he should have in view of his qualities and the lack of any serious misbehavior or character defects on his part."

From a very young age, Story had an incredible love for his mother whom he affectionately called "Sweety". He was totally devoted to her, but recognized her limitations.

"Mom was quiet and Mom was serene and I perceive her really as pretty much the same person throughout. She was an immense support and she remained that throughout my entire life. She accepted me for who I was and was non-judgmental. Mom was Mom. And she was fantastically comforting; Mom was a friend. But I've struggled over the years with, to the extent that, you know, if Mom was that wonderful, was she the anchor in my life or was I the anchor? But the best I can come up with is that I was the anchor. If it had been Mom and I alone, if I'd been raised alone with Mom, she probably would have been my anchor; she could have been who I was. It would have been a different scenario. But obviously in the total picture, Mom was caught up with Dad in that relationship. She could have been my anchor, she could have been my identity if she and I had been alone from the start, but it wasn't that way."

Patricia Musgrave remembered the spontaneous nature of Story's mother. "Sweety was a really warm, loving person. She was not great on Christmas and Easter and all those holidays – she didn't send packages, Christmas presents and everything – but her heart was very much with our children. One time when we were living in Kentucky, I got this big box from a very famous store in New York City. She had sent me a beautiful winter coat – out of the blue, just sent it to me. She was walking by the store on Fifth Avenue, it was on the model, and she thought, "That's Patricia's coat." And it was like Joseph's coat – a plaid coat, multi-colored. Doesn't sound beautiful, but it was absolutely gorgeous. And I loved that coat. And that was my gift from her. She just did that out of the blue. She just had an overwhelming passion to buy that coat for me."

The major issue which Story had to deal with as he formed a new life alone with his mother was her growing alcoholism. He said, "She was drinking before the separation but it was different because, I think, we didn't understand the process and we didn't have the opportunity to see it. But it became very evident when I was living alone with her.

"After she left Dad, most of the time she couldn't get off the floor. She couldn't even get to her hands and knees. It became very bad. The fact of the matter was that she was on the warm whisky as soon as she got up in the morning. I didn't know what alcoholism was; I didn't know what being drunk was. I wasn't sure just what this was until I saw her drinking, until I saw her pouring warm whisky out of a bottle in the morning and that really brought it home... and all I ever wanted was to come home and have her sober, that's all... The relationship was all right except she was a really, really severe alcoholic at that time.

Story later alluded to his mother's alcoholism in a poem called *Summer of 47*, when he wrote about their first seaside holiday together. In the opening lines, the situation unfolds:

> Forgotten son stranded on a sand bar;
> his mother stranded in a Cape Cod bar.
> Summers passing twelve and forty seven,
> now drinking oceans and Seagram's Seven.

According to Story, "The really hard part about the drinking was the driving. I thought I was going to die. I would ride in the back and, you know, it's easy to ask, 'Why did you do it?' Well, when I had to go somewhere further than I could ride on a bicycle, I had no option, I had to get in the car. So that was the really hard part. I'd ride in the back seat; I'd have my chin kind of on the seat and I'd have my hands grabbing the seat and I'd be like a chipmunk in the back seat watching the road come."

Years later, during his studies of creativity at the University of Houston, Clear Lake, Story wove the short narrative at the beginning of this chapter, *The Roadmaster*, based on his memories of that precarious period of his life.

Story commented: "When the sirens were coming I had to leave 'cause they would have taken me away from her. If she's drunk-driving with a kid, Dad is going to get [custody of] me. So that is why whenever these things happened, I saved what I could and then I departed. When the authorities came they wouldn't know there was a child with her. They'd take her off to jail or wherever she had to go and I'd simply go home. They didn't know that I was at home, so I got to stay with her."

The alcoholism continued for several years. Story tried to help his mother by attempting to institutionalize her. "I tried to put her in an institution when I was twelve. I'd tried to institutionalize her but what does a twelve-year-old know about an institution? I knew nothing about hospitals or mental institutions. I didn't know what they were but I did know something had to happen... I just don't know what's going on... a twelve-year-old kid is a twelve-year-old kid, he doesn't know what's going on in the world. But I remember the day when I probably knew [that she was an alcoholic]. My Dad used to call it alcoholism and it was coming up in their divorce in the courts. He was making a case that she was an alcoholic and, of course, I was defending her that she was not – but I didn't know. I should have picked up on it earlier but I did not. Then all these words in court ... just like a bolt of lightning.... it was that image, that picture: she got out of bed and she's got a whisky bottle and the glass. And I thought – 'Mom is an alcoholic'.

"So then I knew what I was dealing with – and so I dealt with it. I tried to institutionalize her but her brothers and sisters would not support me. I took it to the school; I'm looking for help. I can't put her in an institution because I'm a twelve-year-old. I said my mother has got to go to an institution because she needs help.

"The brothers and sisters wouldn't do it. They could have done it, they could have put her in an institution and they would not. They said, 'It's okay.' Well, it's not okay! So, to this day, I have due respect for what I did. I was trying to institutionalize her and no one would go along with me, like somehow it was all okay – but it wasn't okay.

"But she got better. It's amazing, but she recovered and after she recovered she might have one or two setbacks – just one bad episode – but she recovered very nicely and I think she recovered on her own. I don't think she did it with professional help."

An even bigger issue of the separation began to emerge during 1947: the fight for custody of the children. It was a war that was to stretch out over the next ten or so years until all of the children came of age.

For the first couple of years after the separation, Story and his mother moved into the gatehouse on his Uncle Jack's estate, which was just a couple of miles from Linwood. Rosaly Bass recalled the lengths to which Percy went to entice Story to return to the farm. "Story's father kept trying to figure out ways to keep Story there. For instance, he gave him a horse, but he wasn't allowed to ride the horse off the place. So he couldn't ride his horse over and see his mother, for instance. So there were all kinds of little things like that, that were not very nice."

Removed from his father's domineering influence, Story did enjoy the company of his cousins in the new environment. It was during this time that Rosaly, her brother Mark, and Story, who were all similar in age, became close. Rosaly recalled, "I remember things like we would put on these circus shows where we would do all these tricks in this enormous beech tree. And Story would be sort of directing us on what things would look good. We would collect an audience – my father and mother and anyone we could grab to come and watch us. It wasn't too difficult to collect people to watch 'cause my parents always had people to tea and people would stop in and there were always a lot of people around, so we could usually get a reasonably-sized audience, even though the performances were very impromptu."

The threesome also went to great lengths to procure and to store candy. Rosaly explained, "Somebody would be elected to go downtown and buy a lot of candy. And then we had this room that was in a lumber shed, and there was no entrance to it. You had to sort of climb around the side of the building to get up to it - which we felt was very safe and we kept our candy stashed up there."

Rosaly recalled how calm Story was as a child. "There's one incident which shows how cool-headed he was and is. When I was about eight and my brother Mark was about five, he had a dog who fell through the ice in our pond. And Mark thinks Story told us to go get him, but I don't think he did. What happened is my brother, who is the youngest, couldn't stand seeing this dog struggling to try to get out and so he went and tried to help the dog and went through the ice. And then I'm not going to leave my brother with a dog coming over him, and not only that, he couldn't swim, so I went to try to get him out and I went through the ice. And Story was very cool. We were all sort of struggling in this icy water with a dog trying to climb out over us and pushing us under, and Story stood there and told us what to do. I mean he could have ended up in the pond too, but he didn't do that. He stood there and he said, 'You know, I think the ice is thinner, I think you can break the ice if you go the other direction.' And so he stood there while we broke the ice and I pulled Mark along 'cause he couldn't swim and the dog didn't follow us fortunately and we got out. But it was really a bad situation; we could have died. And I think it was very good that Story didn't come in, and I thought it was very good that he stayed there and observed this situation that we had not figured out. [Most other people] would either have ended up in the pond or run for help and that wouldn't have been good either. That's the way Story is; he's not inclined to panic and is very clear-headed."

The family situation continued to deteriorate. The bitter divorce of Story's parents became the focus of both their lives – a battle which pitched the children at the center and tragically left its mark on all of them. According to Story, the actual cost of the legal proceedings added up to hundreds of thousands of dollars, which, in the 1940s and 1950s, was a staggering amount of money. It does, however, reflect the intensity and determination of both parties. The divorce became final on 17 April, 1947 on the grounds of "the cruel and abusive treatment of the said libellant [Marguerite] by the said libellee [Percy]" – as stated in the divorce decree. These words also appeared in an announcement in the local newspaper at the time.[8] The article stated that "Mr and Mrs Musgrave agreed not to prejudice the children against either parent."

Percy stepped up his efforts to win custody of Story and employed detectives to follow Marguerite during their summer holiday. According to a brief prepared by Marguerite's lawyer and presented in the probate court for Berkshire county, "Percy

8. I have been unable to identify the source.

Musgrave, Jr, … by his own admission … commenced gathering evidence even long before the divorce was granted, and since then he has employed three detectives to follow his wife and make minute reports on her activities. She has had to live either in a little cottage on her brother's place, or when her husband's conduct drove her from Stockbridge, in public hotels, while her husband has maintained himself on the estate of Linwood – to which his only claim is through his wife – where he kept himself and the children largely secluded and from which he has barred both his wife and others. Yet in spite of the protection which has surrounded him and his activities during almost all the period in question, since April 17, 1947, and in spite of the searching and hostile scrutiny to which her every act has been subjected, the evidence against Mrs Musgrave is relatively slight while the evidence against him is truly extraordinary… all that could be found… was a mother who took good and tactful care of her child while he [Story] enjoyed her company as a vacation companion."

The document goes on to say, "At the date of the divorce, Percy Musgrave Jr had all he could possibly ask and more than any sane man with a sense of justice could demand: the estate of Linwood for life if he wished it, with all its luxurious furnishings and its background of wealth and family heritage – to which he would have had no possible right of his own but for his marriage to his wife. He had the farm property of Linwood for life if he wished it, with the whole of its income, the occupation of a gentleman farmer and, it now appears, ample financial assurance from his family if he should need it [from his sister and an aunt]."

The previous owner of Linwood was called on by the court to explain the transaction of Linwood. He advised, "This was not a sale – it was a family arrangement between Marguerite Swann Musgrave and myself, she and her husband expressing their desire to live in Stockbridge and run the farm at Linwood and I having a large country place on Long Island, which I was running as a farm… As my grandfather and my aunt, Miss Helen C. Butler, had both expressed the desire to have Linwood remain in the family as long as possible, it seemed to me a very excellent idea to have Mr and Mrs Percy Musgrave own and operate Linwood. And realizing as I did that Linwood was a very valuable asset to anyone obtaining it and living there, and enjoying it, we came to a mutual understanding that I should take certain articles of personal property from Linwood – from the house and from the farm…I was particularly interested in Marguerite owning Linwood, and of course Percy was to share in that ownership – but merely as Marguerite's husband."

This piece of information adds to a sense of injustice with the fate of Linwood many years later when Story, as the only surviving son, was unequivocally excluded from his father's will and the possibility of inheriting his childhood home.

In the early days of the divorce, Marguerite's lawyer focused on Percy's behavior in trying to prejudice the children against their mother: "He handicapped the schooling of the two oldest boys by constant visits and telephone calls, placed the oldest boy at a disadvantage with his schoolmates by frequently taking him away from school, and so disturbed the boys by his vicious accusations against their mother and by the situation he brought about that even Story [who joined his brother as a boarder at St Mark's School, Southborough, in September of 1947] broke down on occasion and young Percy had to be sent to a psychiatrist for help."

Marguerite's lawyer acknowledged the increasing difficulty of the situation for Story in an earlier letter dated 16 December 1946. "Story's adjustment to the new situation is naturally not easy, but he is an exceptionally intelligent boy with unusual perception and a good deal of both human understanding and humor."

By September of 1947, Story's lack of enjoyment of his new school became increasingly evident. Every Sunday the children were compelled to write a letter to their parents. Story's letter to his father on September 22nd is very blunt. "I hope I don't have to come here next year. I hate it! I don't like sports at all. And the food's awful."

A teacher's letter, addressed to Percy in October of 1947, seems to reinforce the young Story's unhappy situation. It states: "As you can see from his grades, he is doing fairly good work in all his studies on the whole. Most of his masters seem to think, however, that there is room for improvement. The boy seems to be a little inattentive at times and in some cases gives the impression of a slight attitude of indifference."

Story recalled recently, "I didn't really want to go to boarding school but for some reason there was a momentum there; it was with Dad principally. I was not happy there and it did not result in any good."

Story's older brother Percy, by now fourteen years old, was also unhappy at boarding school. He appeared to continually struggle with variable grades and was terribly homesick. On one particularly unhappy day, he wrote to his father: "Please don't write or call me because it makes me more depressed than I am."

Story's memories of St Mark's over the years include the mercilessly cold winters and freezing dormitories. Angry at the lack of humanity and care which he perceived in the school's management, Story would smash frozen towels to pieces in defiance. Students were also expected to attended mealtimes in the medieval-style dining room with its regimented rows of tables, rigorous punctuality requirements and compulsory role call – not something which went down very well with Story, who detested the restrictive boarding school environment.

In his journal, Story later recalled his feelings when returning from a school summer vacation to Florida:

> Thinking back to the platform at the train station in Daytona –
> the dread, the sickness of going back to St Mark's! The loneliness,
> the sense of separation and loss.[9]

During their years at St Mark's, Story and his older brother both maintained a steady correspondence with their parents – albeit by the school's enforcement. This regular communication has, in the process of describing the early period in Story's life, provided rich biographical content. It serves to illustrate the way in which the children were caught up in the ongoing conflict between the parents, as well as Percy and Marguerite's lack of understanding and empathy for their children's plight in an unhappy school situation.

Story believes his parents never really moved beyond the divorce. "The divorce was fantastically angry and aggressive; that was a war. Unnecessary, but two people simply couldn't get it together and they made it the focus of their lives… They never got over it themselves. She 'lived' him for the rest of her life; she never ever recovered to herself and to her own sense of being, her own serenity. The rest of her life was in reference to that – which was very, very unfortunate and she put that on us for the entire time. I guess I ended up feeling bad for her that she couldn't get beyond it and she never did. Never. Neither did he.

"And so, did I ever get upset or angry the way things were? Not really, no. I accepted it the way it was and I went forward, did my own thing."

Within days of the divorce being finalized, Story's father remarried and again partnered himself with a woman of means. Supposedly struggling financially with the farm finances and with the children's private school education, he was seen driving a new car while the Linwood home was being refurbished. In June of 1949, Percy finally settled an amount on Marguerite for her share in Linwood. At the same time, she rescinded all claim to her family's former home.

Towards the beginning of Story's fourth year at St Mark's, he finally found one teacher who could inspire him: his biology instructor, a Mr Frederick R. Avis. The students participated in some very innovative surgery for its day, with the artificial insemination of animals.

Story recalled, "Once in a while I'd get a mentor who understood me and, of course, I shined. When I got a mentor I shined. I shined in biology; I shined in taking care of the animals. I was the animal caretaker for an experimental biology program.

"At the level at which I excelled there, it did show that if I had the right mentor, I had it in me to excel. But it points out the extraordinary importance of the mentor – having the right teacher and the right mentor. That if you have the right mentor you're going to excel. But in school I did not have the right mentors – he was one of

9. Journal 15, page 24; Date: 23 March 1994.

the rare exceptions. I did not have great teachers, I did not have a great environment to pursue intellectual kinds of things… so he was a teacher that did get the most out of me. He was my coach in football as well and I was captain of the team, a quarterback."

Mr Avis wrote to Marguerite about Story's progress. "Of course, as perhaps Story has told you, he is keenly interested in biology and doing a grand piece of work. It is a pleasure to have him in class. I am very fond of Story and want his life at St Mark's to be successful and happy."

Story also enjoyed wood working classes at St Mark's and the opportunity to work on his own. "It was wonderful that they had a course in 'shop' for the first year or two. But I continued to go to shop my whole school career and that was really a highlight. You could go to shop and just build things on your own, not as part of the course."

Of his early teenage years Story said, "I don't think I changed at all during puberty and adolescence. I sense the continuous trajectory from early childhood on through; I perceive a constant trajectory from the age of three. I cannot see any change in personality or any change in stream of experience or stream of consciousness – that sense of self.

"School [St Mark's] did not work well because they may have had a high standard of book learning and I was simply not into books in the classroom. I got into loads of trouble because of my exploratory tendencies – always leaving the school, leaving the school at night. There was about a five-story building and, of course, I could traverse every roof. I had a set of ropes and I was always climbing, always departing the school out my window."

During daylight hours, Story would also find legitimate means of 'escaping' from the school by training for various sports, which somehow necessitated a great deal of long distance running on the picturesque laneways around the local area of Southborough.

The real downward spiral in Story's high school life came at the beginning of October 1951 when he was ranked 33rd out of a form of 40 students. His report card read: "I have received several unfavorable reports on Story's work during this first month. Assignments have been turned in incomplete or not at all and Story has been accused of sporadic effort. Story is a slow worker and he undoubtedly has been pressed for time. The deficiency in time will be 'ironed out' and I trust he will apply himself with greater vigor and consistency this next month. This is an inexcusably bad start. Dave Coe [teacher] has Story in hand and I am sure there will be a different 'story' from now on."

Marguerite wrote a letter of encouragement to Story in response to the report: "I am sorry you have lost interest and not done very well in some of your studies, but don't worry about it. Just try to do the best you can in the time given and I am sure things will turn out well enough. I remember it being said that the fifth form was the hardest all around – and it must be plenty hard!"

Story's father reacted strongly when disciplinary action was taken against him for possessing a radio which, incidentally, he had built during one of his physics classes. Percy wrote: "Sorry to hear that you were caught with a radio in your room. However, you certainly deserve such punishment as has been metered out. I beg you not to do it again or it might mean suspension or expulsion. It just isn't worth it and you are old enough to realize it."

Around the same time, Story had devised a way to bring electric lighting to his room after the 'lights out' enforcement by wiring a light to the basement several stories below. According to Story, lots of other sympathetic students would visit him in his room – another reason why not much work was getting done.

Story's father again vented his frustrations at his son's lack of discipline: "I plead with you to buckle down to work and not to be 'Puck's Bad Boy'. There is no question at all that you have the ability to produce, of that I am sure. Therefore please dig in and try to settle down to hard work and good behavior."

Infuriated by Story's lack of progress and concentration, Percy instigated legal proceedings to gain custody of him. Marguerite responded in a letter that "I should think you must be sensible enough to realize that a sixteen-year-old boy, and one who has never been weak, will be in the custody of the parent whom *he* chooses. This is as it should be and would be endorsed by the court."

Indeed, the truth of this statement was later demonstrated in court as Percy put forward his case for custody of Story, despite written assurances to his son that he would never seek to take him away from his mother.

At the end of the school year, in June of 1952, the school master reported on Story's academic situation. "I feel that I have been unsuccessful in reaching Story this year. I could not shake him out of his lethargy this spring and in general he was not responsive to my suggestions. However, the stages of growth, both mental and physical, in young men are most variable and we may see an entirely different pattern during his last year at St Mark's."

A successful final year did not eventuate for Story. The year began with a serious road accident in which the car Story was driving collided with a truck at an intersection. He suffered major injuries, some of them life threatening, which prevented him from attending the first month of his final year of school.

At around the same time, Percy was gearing up to sell the farm portion of the Linwood estate. An advertisement in a major newspaper on 30 October 1952 stated: "Linwood Farm Sale – Complete Dispersal by Auction of Farm Implements and Guernseys. Linwood is 2 miles west from Stockbridge. Closing-out sale of the entire herd, not one animal will be retained." The Linwood home and garden, with a small acreage, would remain the residence of Story's father and his stepmother Josephine.

At the end of December 1952, Story wrote to his father: "I have spent a dreadful month here at school. It does not matter how much work I do, I still go to bed with lots more work [to do]. Right now I have ceased to worry about it. If I don't make it, I don't, and that is it. I wasn't expecting [the doctor] to say what he did, but I see that I should have as the truth does come out eventually. I do have faith in Dr Colby more so than any other doctor... In opposition to Doctor Colby, I have my own attitudes on life. While I am alive I am going to really live. I may only live three or maybe one hundred years more but while I am alive I am going to really live. A year full of activity is better than five in bed."

Unfortunately, Percy passed this letter back to the school. The head master replied: "I am afraid his outlook ties in with what you told me of his activities last summer. He is a hard-headed kid, but perhaps somehow we can get him to change his thinking during the next six months. Certainly I will try my best. This philosophy can lead him only to tragedy if he does not change."

The school's concern for Story behavior continued into February 1953 with only months to graduation. In a letter to Story's parents, the school wrote: "I am sorry that it is necessary to report to you on such a poor record. However, the damage has been done and now we must see what we can do about it. It seems to me that there are two factors, possibly more, that have largely contributed to Story's unusually poor record. One of these is his carefree attitude or philosophy of living and the other was his disappointment with the restriction on his wrestling. During the past two years, it has become increasingly evident that Story has adopted the philosophy that enjoyable living is the best way of life. He seems to delight in talking about, and possibly doing, those things which are daring, risqué and 'off color.' I believe a certain amount of his time is consumed in talking about his exploits or planned exploits with those boys who are sympathetic to his ideas... Part of his attitude can be associated with growing up and its appeal will gradually diminish, but in the meantime it has hurt his school work. Story was visibly upset and possibly more so inwardly by the decision to prohibit him from wrestling. I am sure that his work suffered because of this sane medical edict. His interest in wrestling, and the importance he attached to it, overweighed the more important aspect of school life – the academic work. I don't know what the outcome of this year will be. Story is fully aware of his precarious position and I think he means to do something about it. It will be necessary for him to achieve a fairly high average during this second semester to offset the low marks of the first half year. This he can do but it may take more will-power than he anticipates at the moment to accomplish this end. We shall do all that can be done to help Story during the remainder of the year and I trust that he will overdo himself to gain a diploma."

Story described his sense of futility during that final year of school. "The key thing, the thing that really brought it down was that I had an automobile accident in the Summer before my final year and I missed the first few weeks of school and I never caught up. I couldn't catch my grades up. That was something that I was not very appreciative of. When I came back to school, no one gave me a break to catch up. I had to take exams when I had missed the first month of school. The school refused to acknowledge that after having been there for five years, I had had a severe automobile accident and came close to losing my life.

"So when I started out, my grade average was in the twenties. I couldn't ever recover it because I had a grade that stuck – it's in the record books at twenty, even though I did catch up as time went on. So my overall grade average would start in the twenties and thirties and as the year progressed would try and creep up towards a passing grade. A couple of them never made it to a passing grade and so I could not have graduated based on those grades but it didn't really matter anyway because I was in discipline trouble all the time – continuously, basically for six years. I had a disciplinary session on Wednesdays and then on Saturdays and I never checked to see if I was on the list because I was months in the hole. I had so many hours it didn't matter. I could beat that for years and not work off all the hours. So I just went Wednesdays and Saturdays and did what I did and actually accumulated more hours for misbehavior during the time out periods. I got more hours than I worked off.

"But the culminating thing was that I was already on probation for various activities and then I got caught going out on a date. It was very unfair the way I got caught. I had been very spiritual my entire life from the age of three. I was spiritual at school too and I would always serve at communion. I was one of the acolytes that would help in the religious services you know, a lead acolyte despite my sins. And there was a communion before breakfast on Sundays and the acolyte [for that day] had gotten sick [the night before]. So the minister, of course, goes to find another acolyte. Well, I wasn't there; I was not to be found. It's not that I got caught – I wasn't there. I came back the next morning and the school was waiting for me. I came up over the roof and down the roof of my room and got inside, got in bed and no one saw me get back in. They never saw me leave and they never saw me come back. And so I'm in bed when the [wake up] alarms go off and I went to breakfast. And this wonderful man – one of the few that had any empathy – said, 'Good morning Story.' I said, 'Good morning Sir.' And he said 'Where have you been?' So I said, 'I just climbed out of bed sir'. Then he said, 'You're probably not aware of it but we've been looking for you all night.'

"I thought that was the end anyway. I would not have graduated because I was already on multiple probation. Whether or not I had been able to raise my grades from the auto accident, that ended my high school diploma."

There was one staff member at St Mark's who, over the years, did understand Story's predicament. His name was Mr Gacon.

Story recalled, "He was the 'de facto' principal – he was probably just the house master – but he was the head and heart of the school. He defined what the ideal could be, as a humanist. That's what he was; the others were not. And he was kind of the hope – he was held as this is what it might be. In him, you saw what it could be and was not. So he was an inspiration.

"He was there the whole time, he was there for decades. He lived in a room in the dormitory and I used to go in and have early morning tea there before all the bells rang. He understood that I was not a criminal. He understood that I was doing what I had to do; he could walk all the edges. He had to do what he did within the school, being the house master, but he also understood that I was not necessarily a discipline problem. He understood that I was doing, in a way, what I had to do. I would have tea with him before all the bells would start ringing – that was really one of the few relationships I had at St Mark's."

Story has no regrets in looking back at his childhood or, indeed, his time at school. He said, "School didn't work; nothing worked there. I did not approve of the culture that was there. So in a way I made a statement – the lack of family, the lack of girls, the lack of humanity, the lack of empathy and companionship and attitude of the faculty and the entire ambience and the culture, I disapproved of. I paid no attention to books. An occasional mentor would bring me back into the fold within just that course. And that's kind of it for school I think; I was a misfit there. On the other hand, the things that I rebelled against and the rules that I did not obey – that particular school today has changed everything to the visions that I had – to where it's co-ed, to where there are pastel colors. Of course I go back there all the time. I go back there to visit myself and so I have a fantastically good relationship with the school. I have no regrets and I have no animosity; it's just the way it was. I needed that to get me to where I am.

"My entire childhood, whether it's father or mother or schools or whatever, I have no regrets because it brought me to here and one of my philosophies is this: your view of the past is conditioned by your view of the future. And so, if you have immense hopes for the future, whatever it took to get you where you are is marvelous. And so that's why I celebrate the past, no matter how bad it was. I don't regret it; it had to happen to get me to where I am today and I like the possibilities I have today.

"I went forward and so my greatest strengths in life right now are the worst things that happened back then. The hardest things that happened back then, that's where my strength is today. My child is my hero. People ask me 'What's the greatest thing you ever did?' Well it's the childhood that I had back then and being able to push through it to who I am now and loving every minute of it."

# 2. The Farm

Not a tie holds me to human society at this moment—not a charm or hope calls me where my fellow-creatures are—none that saw me would have a kind thought or a good wish for me. I have no relative but the universal mother, Nature: I will seek her breast and ask repose… I looked at the sky; it was pure: a kindly star twinkled just above the chasm ridge. The dew fell, but with propitious softness; no breeze whispered. Nature seemed to me benign and good; I thought she loved me, outcast as I was; and I, who from man could anticipate only mistrust, rejection, insult, clung to her with filial fondness. To-night, at least, I would be her guest, as I was her child: my mother would lodge me without money and without price.

*Extracts from "Jane Eyre" by Charlotte Brontë, 1847*

Eager to avoid the often violent and unpredictable family situation, Story Musgrave discovered meaning in nature. He explored the external world around him, which became a powerful way of distancing himself from the inhumanity to which he was exposed.

From a very early age, Story would leave the house and immerse himself in the woods, the fields and rivers which formed part of Linwood Farm and its surroundings.

He recalled, "The sense of solitude, the sense of confidence, the sense of absolute faith that I am totally secure out there. I'm not secure at home; I'm afraid at home, I don't know what's going to hit at home. I am fearful, very fearful as to what's going to happen in the house. In the middle of the forest, I'm at home; nothing can happen to me, I'm at peace. It's peace and it's quiet."

In the margin of a book, Story once wrote:

> Story – always, since age two or three has looked to the universe versus humanity, nature versus humanity.[1]

Importantly, though, being on the farm meant being in touch with the earth: feeling the soil between your fingers and living among the elements. The experience was fundamental to Story's future. In his journal he noted:

> The fact that you are so rooted in earth (Linwood) is an interesting and RICH contribution to your perspective on space![2]

Story inherited his mother's sensitivity, her gentleness; he interacted emotionally with everything. Perhaps it is these characteristics which nurtured his ability to relate to the world in a special way, even as a young child. Without a doubt, Linwood was key to his development.

Unhesitatingly, Story said, "Linwood is nature, my nature: the roots of my nature."

\*

Story's home for the first ten years of his life, was Linwood, in Stockbridge, Massachusetts. For nearly a hundred and fifty years, the well-positioned stone dwelling has sat at the top of a gently sloping hill, surrounded by rolling grass fields and rows of large pine trees. From the house, the view is panoramic: the Berkshire mountains, hillsides laced with maple trees which burst into myriads of warm color around the second week in October.

The Linwood garden runs down to the river – the Housatonic – a quietly meandering beauty which is seldom disturbed by human presence. In winter, the river

1. Story's handwritten note in his copy of *The Denial of Death* by Ernest Becker: New York, Free Press, 1973.
2. Journal 13, Page 27; Date 9 July 1992.

might be covered with ice, but at other times it is home to numerous birds, both local and migratory.

In this part of the world, the seasons are well-defined. Story recalled, "The basic geography was of course New England. It had short seasons. It had very cold, *very* cold winters with lots of snow, very short summers, but of course a very powerful spring. Because you'd done winter for so long, spring would break and that change of season was incredible."

The town of Stockbridge, formally established in 1739, is typical of New England towns with its prominent church steeple, its narrow, tree-lined country lanes and undulating geography. From spring right through until late autumn, it is a picturesque and popular retreat from the fast pace of modern life in the great bustling cities of Boston and, of course, New York.

Linwood was built as a summer residence in 1859 by Charles E. Butler, a relative of Story's mother. Covering five levels, including basement and attic, the house is decidedly English and elegant – with stone walls made of hand-cut limestone blocks from a local quarry, decorative wooden window shutters, and slate roof shingles interwoven in three shades. Overall, the effect is one of moderate grandeur.

The interior of Linwood is beautiful. The ceilings are high and ornate; the floors inlaid with timber or tiles. A graceful center staircase links the levels and the forty or so rooms which include ten bedrooms, servants quarters and a large, well-lined library.

Charles Butler filled Linwood with antique furniture and ornaments. According to an appraisal and inventory compiled in 1924, the vast majority of the books in the library dated from the nineteenth century. The collection included many first editions, including works by authors such as Scott, Tennyson, Austen, Eliot, Browning, Spenser, Pope, Dickens, Emerson, Stevenson and Byron.

By the 1920s, the Linwood estate comprised of the main residence, an ice-house, a storage building, a garage and stable with accommodation, various sheds and barns for livestock and feed, as well as two other nearby residences: Grove Cottage and Farm Cottage.

One thing Story doesn't remember about Linwood is the view from the windows. From an incredibly young age, he spent as little time as possible in the house, avoiding his father's pervading presence. Sometimes he would even sleep outdoors.

He explained, "The forests were the most powerful thing and the pine trees for whatever reason. And I love crows. Most people don't love crows, but crows are very powerful in my life today because the crows were there with me. The crows were in the pine forests, so that's purely a sentimental thing that I love crows."

The striking landscape provided much needed stimulus for Story's socially devoid childhood. He recalled, "[Nature] was my home. It was the home in which I found myself, instead of interacting in social situations. As is well known in the child development world, most children define themselves, find themselves and develop a personality, in social interaction. I had no social interaction. None."

Part of the magic of Story's world came from his ability to bring everything around him to life. He said, "I animated everything. I animated all the trees – they were persons and I talked to them. They were beings and so I had my "people" out there – that was my social interaction. I was an absolute magician with animals, I'd do anything with animals. I had a total rapport with animals and I still do today, but that was my interaction. I animated machinery as well; I talked to machines and had a relationship. I touched machines, I kissed machines and I still animate machines. I have difficulty nowadays because I animate machines and when I need to do something to a machine which you wouldn't do to a person, sometimes I have difficulties. So I animated everything – the soil, the trees, the machines, the animals. I talked to the trees and I still talk to trees; I feel their presence. Some trees have a presence – you crawl underneath them and you feel them. I have a spirituality about them, always will."

The pine forests were a wonderful place for a child to explore, with soft beds of pine needles and an open playground below the canopy. To Story, the trees were majestic: "Pine trees, today, still touch me in ways that no other tree does. I was listening to the way the wind moved through different leaves. I could tell what kind of tree I was in by the sound of the wind passing through the leaves, the frequency of the song they sung. Pine trees and the pine forests were of deepest meaning to me."

At night, Story would weave his way between these giant friends, feeling the trunks to determine the direction in which he was traveling. He said, "I immersed myself in it and even in the middle of the night in the forest I could tell direction by feeling the bark. Bark that has been exposed to the sun is different to the bark that's never seen the sun. In the dark I'd just grab a tree trunk and go in one direction. I might wonder why I'd get lost, but I'd just grab another tree and then go off in that direction: eventually I got to where I wanted to go. I wasn't exactly sure where it was going to take me, but once I'm out of the forest, I know where I am. I had that kind of unbelievable intuition."

Story took to the river the same way he did to the pine forest: with great enthusiasm. He rarely saw anybody else, probably because the smell of the water was too strong. Waste from numerous paper mills and other industrial activities would travel downstream, but it wasn't enough to deter Story.[3] To him, the river was "enormous", as everything tends to appear to a young child. As he appropriately termed it, the Housatonic was "his Mississippi"! With his bicycle, Story would drag his raft or kayak to a place upstream and drift back down the current to Linwood.

---

3. The nation's first paper mills were established in Massachusetts, along the Housatonic, during the 1800s, culminating in almost thirty mills in the Berkshire County before the end of the 19th century. Source: Housatonic Valley Association website: http://www.hvathewatershedgroup.org

Story contrived his first raft at the age of six. He said, "I just used logs and I'd go rafting down the river. I'd do multi-layers. I'd put the first layer of the logs one way and then cross them the other way and tie them together with something, maybe a few nails. But I'd go down the river in a raft and, of course, without a paddle. I got on it and shoved off, so you don't need a paddle. You get on and shove off, and where it goes, it goes – and that's kind of life too."

Linwood's maple groves were another memorable part of Story's life on the farm. They were important for their beauty, especially during the fall when the leaves changed from vibrant greens to striking yellows, oranges and reds.

Story explained, "The red leaves, the bright red leaves of the sugar maples, were hugely powerful. I ate the leaves, I did the leaves with my hands, I did the leaves with my feet. And so the leaves under feet is what it sounds like. I did the leaves all the ways that you could do the leaves. They smelled just delicious and I watched the leaves come out of the trees and the path the leaves took down to the ground. So at that young age, I really didn't know what fall foliage was, but I was absolutely immersed in the maple groves."

As Story grew older, the maple groves provided another outdoor activity: maple syruping. He found little difficulty finding buyers among those who happened to be passing along the local roads. In 1988, for a college paper,[4] Story captured the ambience of his surroundings and the romance of the activity:

He was surrounded, possessed by, a grove of massive, majestic maples. Their trunks, three to four feet across, branched symmetrically again and again until they had formed a cumulus-type billowy overhead. In the fall they too would be a fiery orange-red but now, at least outwardly, they appeared barren, if not dead. Dead they were not, the sun of spring gave life to them, made their blood run. Story looked over and down the hillside at all this spacious splendor. Each of these giants had a little aluminum painting-pail hanging on its south-facing side, the side exposed to the fire of the sun, the side in which the sap would run like the Housatonic in spring.

Toward the bottom of the hill, amongst the trees, Story's little syrup mill was barely visible... The day warmed, the sap ran, Story ran, and Story warmed, warmed to the work, to the fire, to the nature and the process all about him. The fire in the West dimmed and died. Story chopped on, stoked on, and kept his fire going late into the night. Finally, having filled the pan with sap, the furnace with wood, his body with a long day's work, and his mind with the serenity and beauty of the grove, he crawled into his soft burrow, radiant with heat, and lay on his back watching the shimmering red steam drift into the night sky and disappear among the stars.

Linwood was very much a working farm. As a thousand-acre dairy operation, supporting about two hundred Guernseys, there were plenty of farm animals and

4. Titled *Sweet, Delicious, Warm, Fire*, this piece was written by Story for a creativity course at the University of Houston, Clear Lake.

machinery to fascinate a young boy like Story. The animals, in particular, were his companions: he befriended them, understood them, worked with them. He was especially fond of a pair of draft horses which had a role in the farm's day to day activities.

He recalled, "I was riding the draught horses at an extraordinarily early age. They were probably a ton a piece. My father was not happy with my riding the draught horses but I continued to do that. He was not happy with my riding the cows. I rode all the cows and I rode the dogs: we had Great Danes and I'd ride them.

"The draught horses I'd ride without a saddle or a bridle. I was right at home riding a ton of horse without a bridle or a saddle. I got a smacking every time I did that but I didn't stop. A four-year-old's not supposed to be on a ton-sized horse, without a bridle or a saddle, galloping down the road! You can't run into a fence 'cause they'll go right through it! There's no leaping over. That was so powerful and I didn't have any idea of what I was doing really.

"I couldn't climb on their backs so I had to shove them up against a fence, you know. You can't believe how big a draught horse is; you cannot believe how big they are; they're immense... But I had this old tea kettle. I'd fill it full of cut corn and get the horses to come running to the fence. And then I'd move down the fence, hoping that as they moved they would go sideways to get their backs and their butts up against the fence so I could jump on.

"But if that didn't work, I used to shove on them – you know I'm four years of age and they're a ton! And so I'd get in their legs and put my shoulder into their legs to try and move them. They would look down between their front legs at this "fly," but they knew they couldn't move, they knew they had to take care of me. But I'd be down there shoving on them, thinking they'll move their leg if I push hard enough. And I'm shoving them trying to get so I can leap from the fence onto their back.

"And so somehow I'd climb up the fence, you know, five or six feet, and talk at them so they wouldn't move. If I wanted to leap, I'd land with both feet on them. If they moved, I'm six feet under the ground, so I'd land with both feet and they wouldn't move. I'd always jump on the rump 'cause that's big, that's like an aircraft carrier! I'd land both feet, right or wrong and then I'd walk up by the withers and I'd get me some hair and then away we'd go!"

The New England soil contains copious amounts of rock and plowing the fields would invariably bring them to the surface. Rock was a fact of life for farmers in the region and something that is illustrated by both the landscaping and the literature of the times. As Story got a little older, one of his jobs was to ride a team of draft horses which were towing a toboggan-like cart, or stone boat as it was called. Made from solid oak and curved steel, large rocks could be rolled onto the stone boat as it moved through the fields.

According to Story, "If you look at all the New England walls, if you look at Frost's poetry and mending walls, that's all New England rocks and horse drawn carts and the stone boats."

A team of people would work the stone boat – one person driving the horses and the others rolling the heavy stones. On one occasion, as Story was guiding the horses from behind, the heavy oak pallet carrying the stones fractured from the steel which was harnessed to the horses.

Story recalled, "It broke loose, a gap opened up and I went underneath the boat, was run over by the boat. I went down through the hole and I was underneath the boat and all the stones. And all it did was just shove me down into the ploughed soil.

"So when I came out the back end, all the soil was smooth and I was smooth too! Except for abrasions, I didn't get hurt, yet I had tons on top of me. There were no rocks to push me against, so there was no hard point. I just got shoved into the soil. But that's what the farms were about. It was life and death. People were impressed when I came out the back end and dusted myself off! They were impressed!"

There were other memorable moments with the draft horses. One involved near-disaster when the horse-drawn wagon, loaded with a hundred bales of hay – roughly eight thousand pounds in total – came out of a meadow and headed up a steep incline. Two farm workers had gone ahead to block traffic while Story was to bring the wagon up the hill. Unfortunately, when the horses hit the road, they lost traction.

According to Story, "We knew the outcome but we stopped thinking; we quit thinking about this process. It was going to be close whether they could make the hill anyway, so we weren't doing the right thing. The tractor by itself couldn't do it, so they stopped the tractor and I got a team of horses going. I was on one of the horses and we did all right, we were making it until they hit the pavement. When they hit the pavement, they had no traction. Horse on a pavement? There's nothing to dig into. They were digging into the ground, they were digging into the soil to get up on ahead to the pavement.

"So we hit the pavement and now they have absolutely no friction and now you've got a wagon that's on the steep part of the hill and going backwards, and so the horse I'm on went down; she just couldn't do anything. The other horse dug in; she wasn't going to get dragged back so she dug her hind feet in, but she couldn't hold a load, so she went over backwards. This is a horse that weighs a ton and she went over backwards in the harness and broke the harness. [The other horse was] being dragged down the hill on her belly. I have a ton with each horse, I have eight thousand pounds of wagon, all going backwards down a hill. And so we cut them out of there and we jumped on their heads, trying to stop them from flailing. If you get hit with that you're dead. She's flailing and you've got to try and jump on her head and cut her out of the harness. That's where it is, but anyway they survived that one. This is what farms are about; this is what I didn't like, but this is what I did."

On another occasion, Story's favorite horse wasn't so lucky. The two draft horses, with wagon attached, were resting beneath a tree when something spooked them. Story said, "We were in the hay field when they broke, so there was nothing we could do. They just flat broke and something must have got in their mentality – I don't know what – I don't know why they'd do that.

"As they went down the hill to go into the barnyard, they couldn't make a corner. They were going too damn fast to make the corner and there was a rake, a hay rake sitting right there. And [snagged by the rake], they got run over with this big wagon. It wasn't full but they got run over – pulled over with the wagon behind them. One horse got [an axle through it] and died. Just like that, died. They of course destroyed the rake. They destroyed the whole thing but the axle went right through her and she was dead. She was my favorite horse too.

"That's life and death. Everything on the farm is life and death. There are always things being born, and things die in the cycle of life."

Milking was the primary activity of Linwood Farm. According to Story, "Milking defined dairy farming and was the principal reason that dairy was so much more work than other types of farming. It was ever present, had to happen and happen on time; it scheduled and drove all else. Taking care of the cows and feeding them was the other major task – personal care of the animals – and you knew each one by name. We brought the milk to the dairy every morning; that had to happen. The rest of the work was care for the farm: grounds, buildings and equipment.

"We had to produce grazing fields for the short summer and enough hay and corn to last the long winter. Both the grazing fields and the harvesting fields, hay and corn, were produced by plowing, harrowing, seeding and fertilizing. The corn would need to be planted every year; the grass when it wore out."

"Winter was milking and feeding because there were no pastures to graze and it was rather harsh outside. We continually fed everything that breathed. Winter was not as busy as summer so we did lots of maintenance then and other work such as logging and getting the summer's ice out of the frozen lakes."

In winter time, a team would go out and cut blocks of ice from a nearby lake to store in the freezer room or 'ice-house' as it was known. The room had insulated walls two feet thick with sawdust and the ice would last all summer. Story explained, "You want ice cubes? Get the pick and hack off some ice. Get a block and put it in a tray in the wooden 'refrigerator' in the kitchen."

Story spoke of the large vegetable garden which was cultivated for household use. It was located in a quadrangle behind the rows of pines and spruce trees. As he recalled, trellises of roses adorned a walkway through this section of the garden. Story's diet was naturally determined by what was available to him on the farm.

In his journal he wrote:

Childhood: poached eggs and toast for breakfast. Whole unpasteurized milk by the gallon. Drank milk from a steel cup in the dairy barn; raw vegetables from the garden. I ate clover, grass, hay, ensilage (corn). I ate muck, dirt – i.e. soil from the earth. I used to eat soil from the fields. I ate grain which we fed the cattle. I licked the salt blocks which were put out for the cattle – I loved salt blocks – would kneel and lick them along with the cattle. The salt blocks were pink in color and had smooth grooves from the tongues of cattle and Story. Apples from the orchards were a favorite. Wild blueberries from the mountain were my favorite fruit.[5]

On a practical level, the farm gave Story an introduction to the world of machinery. He learnt to operate tractors and other farm implements, and to repair them at an early age. He developed a way of understanding mechanisms simply by looking at them. It was literally a hands-on approach, without an instruction manual and without a tutor. Machines were exciting to a young Story and they still are today. His understanding of mechanisms would play a vital role throughout his various careers – from the Marines, to medicine, to spacewalking and the Hubble Space Telescope Repair Mission and many worlds beyond.

At a very young age, Story had developed a love for machinery and fixing things. When he was five years old, his father purchased a combine (baler), which required lots of attention. Prior to this, the hay-gathering activities had been done manually with a pitchfork.

According to Story, "I rode the baling machines at the age of five. The bales come out and you're working with the machines that tie the knots and seeing if the knots get tied. You're pulling on the strings to tighten up the knots so that when the bale falls off, the knot will hold. I would see Dad or a farmhand on the tractor ahead of me while I'm riding after them to bale."

Story did far more work on the farm than either of his brothers – his older brother Percy wasn't as interested in the work and his younger brother Tom was only nine years old by the time their father sold the dairy operation. But Story wanted to become a farmer, and so, when young, made the most of being part of the working farm.

"The power – when you're very small you know – when you're driving these machines; you give a ten-year-old that kind of toy – it's a present! You're in your own little playground but it's a big toy you have. And so other kids had model airplanes and model fire engines. I had big machines that I got to run.

"By the age of ten, I got to be really a kind of a magician at fixing things and making things work on my own. It's a wonder I still have all my arms with the moving machinery and the rest of that. It was of course extraordinarily hard work – very, very long hours."

Riding large farm machinery sometimes posed difficulties for a young eleven or twelve-year-old Story. "I had tractors get away from me. I couldn't reach the pedals

5. Journal 9 Page 14; Date 16 September 1990.

and if I wasn't careful, the tractor would get going down a hill and I couldn't stop it 'cause I couldn't get to the pedals. I did that a few times. I couldn't stop it because I got off balance. You're trying to hang on but you're also trying to get to the pedals, get to the brake and so you're like a monkey just climbing around. It's not like you're sitting in a seat and you just reach out and push the pedals – I couldn't reach the pedals. I had wooden blocks positioned on the pedals so I could reach them, but if I got off balance doing other things on the tractor and it started to get away, I couldn't get seated and then get to the pedals.

"I'm thinking of one notable runaway and I wasn't at all happy with that one! I had a wagon behind me and I went to the bottom of the hill. I couldn't get to the brake. So then the fact that I was too small for the machine at times caused problems.

"No one sat me down nicely and gave me an instruction of what all the levers did. They should have but they did not. They would tell me, 'Here's this [tractor], plough the field, okay?' They didn't teach me all the levers and they didn't teach me technique."

The level of danger in operating farm machinery was high, although it wasn't something of which Story was particularly aware. "It's very fortunate I'm still alive. The danger was just inches away where you could have your whole hand come off. No one taught me about that. Danger was everywhere and that happened all the time. People just simply had their whole arm taken off and all they did was ask the doctor when they could get back to work."

The fact that Story was brought up on a farm, and on this particular New England farm, is significant to who and what he has become. The farm brought him into contact with nature for the first time – the trees, the animals, the freshly ploughed fields, the river, the seasons. It was the source of his spirituality and of his relationship with the universe. Later on, Story was able to bring this into the world of space flight and experience space in a very unique way. To him, space was an extension of nature and a place where he could reflect deeply on creation and evolution, about life and death.

Story thought a great deal about his childhood while in space. Childhood has always been the root of who he is as an adult, his main source of identification. In some ways, he continually looks to the child that he once was for approval.

"At age three, I became my own anchor and my explorations out to nature were how I defined myself. It was not only my world out there but it was how I found out who I was. It's what you interact with and what you take into yourself to build a character, to build a personality. It was my explorations out into nature and those little journeys is how I defined myself. That's how I tested myself, that's how I found out who I was."

Mia Liebowitz, who many years later worked with Story at the Kennedy Space Center's Astronaut Encounter program at the Visitor's Center, commented: "It's very important for him in every show to mention that the reason he is who he is, is because of his experiences on the farm. Very key to who he is and he always says it. And he encourages kids to go after what makes them tick, their passion, to play with things and to take things apart and to go out and experience nature. It's very key. And you find that there's a common thread in a lot of astronauts like that. A lot of them come from the farm. I think exploration on earth is key to exploring space.

"He says some people want to go out there and conquer space; he says I don't think that's it. I go out there to let space conquer me. I experience space, I invite it to do things to me. He lets space experience him. I think that comes from his nature background too because he was out there, and he didn't go out there to conquer nature, he invited nature in and let it conquer him. And that's why I think he has such a great handle on space. I think that's why people appreciate space from him so much.

"He always emphasized that he was born on a farm and he always says it like this – I fixed tractors, I fixed people, I fixed Hubble, if you're not careful that's what's gonna happen to you! It's very simple in his mind that image. Fixed tractors, fixed people, fixed Hubble. And so he really emphasizes that kids should follow their heart and do things that they're interested in and then whatever you do you'll be good at it, 'cause you're interested in it. He'll rarely ever mention the many degrees he has. Rarely does he ever mention them. He'll say he was a doctor but he'll never ever talk about himself in terms of how many masters degrees he has. In fact, if you mention it, he kind of disregards it and says 'yes, but that's not the important thing. The important thing is that I was born and raised on a farm and that I went out into the woods when I was very little, at three, and my parents were OK with it 'cause they knew that that was who I was.' So that's something he really wants people to know. For as complex a man as he is, the simplicity, in his mind, is that he was a guy from a farm who happened to become a doctor and who happened to fix Hubble. It's just so clear. So simple."

Of his childhood, Story said, "I did not think about my future and I don't recall ever thinking about the future. I lived in the moment, I lived for the now. Didn't know what the journey was but I think I was living in the moment, even then.

"I had self esteem at the earliest point that I can remember. I was the anchor and it was about me, that I had to run my world. I was the reference point because, honestly, I had no human world then that I could use as an anchor or a way of learning about the world and things.

"I think I've never gotten away from myself as being the anchor. And I think that when I need answers I tend to turn inward; I had no one to talk to back then."

In the margin of a book, Story once wrote down these thoughts about his childhood and the characteristics of the child which he continues to carry with him:

> Story – courage to be on the edge. Going it alone. Not antisocial, not anti-cultural, but self-reliant, making MPH [metaphysical] decisions and the courage to live with them. Self reliance, self-determination. Story – a child, but a child alone, abandoned to the world.[6]

6. Story's handwritten notes in his copy of *The Denial of Death* by Ernest Becker: New York, Free Press, 1973.

# Nature

"Nature is sacred for me, and when you look at nature, you're looking at God."

# 3. Experiences in Nature

To see the World in a grain of sand
And Heaven in a wild flower
To hold Infinity in the palm of your hand
And Eternity in an hour.

*William Blake*

There is arguably nothing more powerful in Story Musgrave's life than his relationship with nature. That is a significant statement, given all that he has experienced, his many careers and achievements, as well as his numerous passions.

But Story was at home in nature from his earliest recollections – it was, in ways, the only thing which made sense for him. He developed an acute awareness of the natural world and his spirituality was firmly established in the wonder of universal creation.

He said, "My way, my exploration was to go out in the rivers and especially the forest. So that was the key thing: it's very Romantic and it's nature. It's so Emersonian.[1] I had that kind of expansiveness early, like the Lake Poets,[2] so that's what I was doing, not knowing it, of course.

"I was after the winds through the trees and I was after the rubbing of my hands and getting a handful of pine pitch you'd never get off – but I didn't need to get it off; it just smelled incredibly delicious. The feel of the soil. All of this is an aesthetic kind of sense. And so the body here is very important."

There are times, in fact, when it is difficult to distinguish Story from nature; it is a unique synthesis. Although he loves human communication and interaction, it is in nature that he is most at home. Nature is a world free of external demands, prejudices and conflict, and rich in form and beauty.

According to Story, "Looking to nature is sort of an internal thing too. It's a feeling; it's an inward turn also."

In his journal he wrote:

Hungry for solitude, hungry for nature.[3]

*

Five miles along a dirt road in Central Florida, in fact, not far from some of the state's most popular family entertainment parks, lies a small piece of paradise. It consists of a moderate home surrounded by approximately a hundred acres of uncleared land – a mixture of mainly rainforest and desert terrain.

The weather in Central Florida is spectacular for at least seven months of the year. Temperatures hover in the seventies and eighties during the day, with mostly cool nights and beautiful crisp mornings. It can get a little cooler around Christmas time and occasionally freezes overnight in the early part of the year, however, pleasant blue skies and strong cumulus clouds dominate the majority of days.

1. In reference to Ralph Waldo Emerson 1803-1882, American writer.
2. A group of English poets of the Romantic period who lived in the Lake District of northwestern England. William Wordsworth was among their number.
3. Journal 8, page 36; Date: 24 June 1990.

This is where Story Musgrave has made his home since leaving NASA. In fact, he moved there the very next day!

Daughter Holly Musgrave recalled her father's move from Houston to Florida. "With thirty years at NASA, he said the day after I retire I'm out of here, I'm gone, I'm moving. And he did, exactly the day after. He talked about it for about a year and a half; it might have been a couple of years. And sure enough, the day after, me and my sister were going – 'Huh? He's doing it!' He just packed up and started leaving. That was that."

Florida has been special for Story since he was a teenager. In similar fashion, the very day he left high school, his mother took him to a bus station in Massachusetts where he boarded a bus for Florida. What attracted Story most to Florida at that time were the palm trees, the beautiful beaches and the extensive warm weather.

Again, shortly after joining the Marine Corps, Story was stationed in Jacksonville, Florida, for a couple of years. On weekends he traveled to Daytona Beach to enjoy its thriving social scene.

More than ten years after this, Florida became a focus for a different reason. Story spent a good deal of time at the Kennedy Space Center and surrounding areas during his thirty year career as an astronaut. He became familiar with the Central Florida coastal region, extending from the Patrick Air Force Base, to Cocoa Beach, Merritt Island, the Banana River and, of course, Cape Canaveral. Again, he was attracted by the beauty of the beaches, the ocean, the sunrises, the palms and the enormous stretches of wildlife reserve which surround the Space Center's activities.

In his Journal, Story wrote of Cocoa Beach:

> Sunrise on the ocean, cumulus clouds raining into the sea, the sun behind a cloud radiating beams skyward, no sound except the waves and the birds…. the smell of the ocean … a cruise boat coming home, birds fishing, girls on a morning run! A cloud forming just off shore to shade the risen sun.[4]

Florida, therefore, was not an unusual choice of home base for someone like Story. What he really wanted was acreage where he could surround himself with nature and spend time working the land. It is by no means an exaggeration to say that he was looking for somewhere which was spiritually uplifting; somewhere to appreciate beauty. And he was able to purchase that, and an existing home, within a reasonable distance of an airport.[5]

According to Story's son Todd, "He wants to achieve aesthetic beauty as well as getting physical exercise. Surrounding himself with beauty at home, or wherever he

4. Journal 26, page 2; Date: 23 March 2000.
5. Story's current life comprises a great deal of travel.

spends a significant amount of time, is an imperative rather than a passion or objective. It is an absolute necessity for him to function creatively. Listen to him talk about how gracefully a vulture flies, the sounds of an owl hooting, the beautiful palm trees, the smell of flowers, the sounds of frogs. Nature is consistent and it is ordered by unwritten rules. If nature is not consistent with its surroundings, then it will cease to exist. Nature does not have the propensity to force itself, or conquer its surroundings, such as humans do."

Holly Musgrave spoke of her father's great love of nature. "He's always been a land person, a nature person – that's really who he is. Even though he goes into space, space is actually nature, a whole other environment to explore; it's part of creation. Instead of nature, you could say creation. He's really exploring and enjoying creation and discovering it like a kid does, you know. But growing up on a farm, he's always liked to have land; he's always liked to be surrounded by nature. I don't think he admires architecture as much as he admires nature."

Even in Houston, Story needed to be as close to nature as was logistically possible. He said, "I lived on a golf course and so I didn't live in the country. I could have done an hour-and-a-half commute to work but it's tough. You know, I need to be effective, so I didn't live in the country in Houston but I lived on a golf course. My backyard opened into nothing but green trees and grass, there was nothing else there – so I had the country, I was out there in terms of what you saw. And I insisted I would not have lived anywhere else other than on a golf course. I went running and walking on the golf course in the evenings as well as at sunset. I have the expanse, I have the trees. And the trees I grew, I plucked them out of the sidewalks in Houston – a little one inch or two inch tree trying to make a go of it in the cracks of sidewalks, lifted out. I put it on my plot and there they are, today, fifty, sixty feet tall."

Story's Florida acreage requires extensive care and vision. Much of it was covered with strangulating vines which needed to be removed by hand. Without this, many of the mature trees – stunning oaks, pines, cypresses and maples – would have died and fallen over. For Story, it has been a race against time to save as much as possible from biological destruction and to restore the land to its natural beauty.

Former neighbor and friend Doug Warner witnessed some of those initial efforts. He believes it took great will power and fortitude for Story to cut out the vines and pull them down by hand. Sometimes he would see Story work at it for twelve to fourteen hours a day, but the results were stunning. He said that for a man his age, Story does incredible things physically: "He gets all these projects going – drops them for a month and gets going on another one. He's got so much going on, there's no end to it. He wants to beautify everything here. If he had his choice, Story would work on the land all day; just be here!"

Life on the land has also allowed Story to return to his love of farming and farm machinery. Doug said, "Being on his property with his equipment is like Christmas for Story whenever he gets back home."

The equipment consists of four tractors, an excavator, two dump trucks, a compact loader and numerous other farm implements. These are the tools which allow Story to achieve his goals for the place. Doug recalled Story's undying enthusiasm for his land. "He would be out at 7am working. In winter when it's dark, I could see the lights on the tractor!"

Friend Rob Corum believes Story likes the relative isolation of his property. Rob met Story while renovating the pool in the home's central courtyard. "When I first came out here, Story was saying that I was the only [pool contractor] who had actually come out because he lives so far out. And I said 'Yeah, we call this place the G.U.D.' because not a lot of people want to come this far out to make money. And he goes 'G.U.D.?' and I said, 'Yeah, it's called Geographically Undesirable.' After I'd said it, I thought, 'I've just met him and I probably shouldn't have said it – it's probably an insult for somebody who lives there.' Well, Story stopped for a second in the conversation and looks up and goes, 'Hmm, geographically undesirable – good! I like that! I might use that again.' So I immediately started apologizing and he goes 'No, I like it." And it took me another six months to understand that he probably does like it. We were able to put the context of where he lived in a couple of words that he thought described it well. So it went from an insult to describing where he wanted to be!"

Since that time, Rob and his two sons, August and Cooper, have enjoyed getting to know Story in the context of nature. Rob said, "Sometimes I look at him when he's standing on the tractor or hooking up the chain and I can't see the astronaut. I see the farmer, I see the guy that's passionate about animals and plants and the earth that is revolving around. He'll be standing there, filthy, hooking up a chain to pull up a palm tree – which wouldn't make a difference to hardly anybody that it's going to get moved to somewhere else – and I see a farmer and I don't see an astronaut.

According to Rob, "He's completely in tune with it all. And I found that out one of the first times I came out here. Story likes to say provocative things. We were standing with a couple of people who were doing work out here and we were talking about the vultures [which roost locally] and he says, 'You know they're magnificent.' And he uses that word all the time about nature – 'magnificent' – which means he's in awe of so many different things – with the swan which lives on the pond, the palms, the way the wind blows. So we're standing with these people and I said to Story, 'Every time I come out here I see the vultures circling and I check to see if you're not laying under the tractor or something.' And Story says, 'Well, if I am, don't worry about it, because it's a meal for them.' And he says, 'If I die in my house, I hope I can just crawl out and let them feast on my bones. From that point forward, it's nothing more than organics.' And so I've got these two guys standing here that have just met him. I'm going, 'Ok, yeah, this is my friend Story, and he's OK and we're just kidding' and I changed the subject real quick. Because I *know* he's *not* kidding!"

Confirmation of this can be found in a journal note. Story wrote:

> If I become acutely, mortally ill, will go outside so my friends, the vultures, can cremate me![6]

Rob continued, "Story is passionate about everything in nature and somehow he is connected to nature and feels a bond. You've got to walk through the woods with him, like I have, and spend time looking at little things coming out of the ground. He loves pointing things out about nature. He was recently traveling on business and got four or five thousand palm seeds to plant at his home. He has the time and the patience to water them and watch them grow. And this is where the passion comes in because most people expect results and he doesn't expect anything. He waits for things that may not be today or tomorrow: he sees in terms of years. A lot of us are momentary; we talk about what we think and feel at this moment. But he's walking through, looking at his palms and thinking five, ten, twenty years down the road. He's sat up for hours and watched the ducks with the binoculars and he has no sense of having to be anything for anybody else. He really enjoys these things."

The palm farming is central to Story's activities on the land. He spoke of the great enjoyment it gives him. "I have hundreds of palms germinating after having been planted a year or two before. My entire front yard has seeds in it from around the world – they are about five inches tall and I'm potting them. Potting takes lots of care – the soil, ashes, compost in the pot – and mulching the surface with oak leaves and cypress slivers to prevent weeds is very critical. I don't wear gloves – I love the feel of the earth, ashes, mulch and stuff, and get great pleasure working it with my hands. I have been outside long hours, working hard and effective, yet something tells me I should not be doing so much out there – but I do it anyway; it is what I love doing."

Collecting palm seeds is a large part of the passion of this activity for Story. Whenever he sees a great palm tree or an unfamiliar species, he's either reaching up to loosen a bunch of fresh seeds, or crawling around on the ground gathering the seeds which have already fallen. And it's wonderful to be there to assist in the process. At the Kennedy Space Center's Visitor Complex one day, he had the grounds staff eagerly climbing up ladders and using extension saws to obtain the treasured bunches of seeds. More than a dozen staff were caught up in the excitement of Story's quest.

As they reach a certain stage of maturity, the cultivated palms will be

6. Journal 31, page 23; Date: May 2001.

transplanted to various locations on Story's hundred acres, according to their aesthetic qualities. It is part of a much-loved dream to create a beautiful arboretum within his personal paradise.

Filmmaker David Grusovin visited Story's home in the summer of 2002. He explained, "He took us on a walk through his backlots and a lot of the time he spoke of these grand visions and plans that he has for these lots. He'd say, 'I want to landscape this, and I want to kind of move this area here, push it aside and create a little walkway bridge.' We went deeper and deeper into this lush rainforest, just fifteen minutes off the track, with a compass because it was just so disorientating. It was just so lush and rich in nature in there. And we just stood there – there's a great power in the unspoken word as well – we didn't have to talk a lot. We walked through and we stopped and all eyes went up to the heavens, in a way, because of the light seeping though the canopy.

"He's totally at home, immersed in every second tree, the shape of plants and the curves in nature and he's always pointing that out. He seems to just relax and his shoulders seem to drop away. He's absolutely at home, content and very happy within that tropical rainforest; he's in another state. I think he's much more relaxed because there's no stress and when he walks up the road, he's dragging his feet! Now that was a very different walk; that was a really different walk to how I'd seen him walking in all the other places. He's just dropped away; he's in absolute bliss."

Story concurs with the power of the rainforest. "Out there in the untouched part of the land where you have the powerful forty, fifty, sixty foot trees everywhere – the big cypresses and the palms and the cedars and all the rest of it out there – that's when I feel it the most."

According to David, "He's building a nature thing around him so he's surrounded wall to wall. And he's got his little palmettos [a small variety of palm], which he calls his little 'aliens', which, when you see the whole collection of them, looks like an alien party!

"On one night we came home in his truck – we'd been out to dinner – and Story just peeled off the side of the road at night with his big headlights and we started thumping through one of his lots. He's saying, 'We're going to check this out in the morning.' He's so proud of this vast nature wonderland that he's got. I'm not surprised – it's fantastic. Even the landscaping of the lake that he has – when the sun sets, you see it channel right down the middle of the lake."

Indeed, one of the things which Story loves to do is to take a canoe on the pond at sunset and enjoy the beauty and tranquility of a Florida evening while gliding around the small palm islands.

Story also enjoys a special relationship with the wild animals on his property. He loves to be surrounded by them, to observe them and interact with them. He wrote:

> There are four turkey vultures that are getting very tame – four to five feet away – they got their confidence up from the other birds. The two hawks followed me around while I worked and the black vultures just act like dogs now. They follow me around in the hopes of some morsels, but they also hang out and talk with me even when there is no food: I sit on the step and we 'talk'. At one time I had four turkey vultures, two ducks, two hawks and multiple black vultures, not to speak of the squirrels, doves, cardinals and so on. The migratory geese were overhead in flocks today!

A couple of years earlier, Doug Werner recalled that Story would hand feed the raccoons and the foxes, and found endless enjoyment in a goose which took up residence for a while on the lake. If Story returned home after being away for a period of time, the goose would see his car coming and fly a circuit around the house and lake, sweeping low over the roof of the car. It was the goose's way of welcoming him home. In fact, the goose was a great watchdog and would announce the arrival of any human or animal.

Doug recalled an incident which Story related. "One day Story was talking to the goose and it was making a big racket. And when Story turned around, there was a cow! He ended up patting the cow for an hour! He just loves animals.'

When Story had finished relating the incident to Doug, he paused for a moment, then asked, "Doug, should I get a cow?" It was a serious question!

David Grusovin recalled Story's particular interest in the vultures: "He locks his focus up in those birds. I remember one day he looked up and said, 'Look at the altitude. Look at them fly' – because there were about forty-five vultures on this one day; I counted them, up high in the sky. It was like something out of Hitchcock's *The Birds*. Story would almost cock his hands a little bit to partly imitate them – he wouldn't raise them up to create a shape of himself like a bird, but he would say, 'Look at those fingers, they're working every finger'. And you do look closely at those vultures, and they do extend [their wing tips] out like five fingers."

Story's love for the birds is undoubtedly enriched by his appreciation for flight. David recalled, "Vultures are absolutely awesome to watch because they're not fliers, they're soarers. And the way they're hovering, finding and hitting the currents – they just dance on the currents like a glider, and they try to weave their way up higher or bring themselves down. Story watches with a really acute eye. You're certainly aware of this intense focus he has when he's watching what's going on. He just admires the concept of flight.

"Of course he's thinking of himself up there. In his imagination and his thoughts he has put himself in that context, amongst the birds flying. So even now on the ground when he's watching them, he's in great envy of those birds, that they're doing what he had done. He's looking at those birds and going 'wow.' And he's got an enormous smile because he realizes the buzz that it gave him. It's empathy because he knows how they feel. I mean, how close is he to thinking how they're thinking!"

Story also enjoys feeding the vultures. According to David, "They come in like clockwork to be fed. Story's world stops, or he stops everything around him when they come in. What I found was that it's part of the cycle of life with Story. In the morning the vultures come, and in the afternoon they come back. They arrive in the morning to be fed and then they take off if all the conditions are right. They'll come back in the evening and sit in the trees. Like the clockwork of life, that's what happens. And Story's come to expect that. Story questions when they're not there – 'I wonder where the birds are? They haven't gone up today.'"

The daily activities of the vultures represent an exciting and bustling airport for Story and he often refers to them in that context. He wrote:

**I have an airport here; I have my own air show all the time!!**

Story takes such an interest in the birds that it causes him grief if he has nothing to feed them, especially after being away from home for long periods of time. On one occasion he expressed his feelings to me about this: "The vultures were so loyal, after so long. They saw me and came home in huge numbers, spent the night and were all over the place in the morning. I had no food – I will not do that again! They are so caring and so loyal and I had nothing for them."

Holly Musgrave spoke of her father's love for animals. "I think he has a lot of appreciation for animals. He loves animals, he likes to take care of animals, even though the animals are in the wild. He likes to be nurturing – I think he senses the frailty of life in taking care of animals because there's a certain helplessness, they're out in the elements and even though they're programmed to survive, they have a pretty rough life."

Such is Story's respect for all animals, that he is known by his neighbors for his tolerance of snakes. Whenever they wish to remove one from their property, they know they can bring it and release it into his woods.

Perhaps one of the most touching relationships which Story has had with animals in recent times was with a beautiful white swan which came to live on his lake. Story would walk to the water's edge to talk with the swan, whom he had affectionately named "Goose", and the swan would come to him with great speed. Face to face, with Story bent down on one knee, he and the swan would communicate their friendship, the swan making tremendous nasal sounds while rubbing its long graceful neck against Story's famously bald head. Sadly, the swan was to die of natural causes a year later. And, as you would expect, Story was devastated.

Story's relationship with nature began at a very early age and has continued throughout his life. Nature was an escape from the unhappy human world which surrounded him at home as a young child and later on at boarding school.

While studying at the University of Houston, Clear Lake, Story wrote about some of his night time adventures during his time at St Mark's school. A delightful piece of creative work, these excerpts from *Mud, Dreams and Coca-Cola* highlight the wonder of nature in his life and the pleasure it gave him. Story gives the name and personification of himself to a female character in the biographical narrative:

Ahead of her the landscape in the distance began to croak and crawl, softly at first but shortly as a roaring chorus. She sat on the banks of the pond to remove her black sneakers and black socks. The pond was alive, alive with croaking bullfrogs, jumping fish, slithering snakes, clicking beetles, and every form of creature. Its life gave life to her. Her body and soul mingled and moved with the pond. With glee she slogged out into the dark mud and slime, sinking into the delicious mire almost to her knees. The pond sucked at her every step, tried to hold on, but Story, delighting in each effort, slogged on. With each step she hoped that none of the wiggling creatures she felt underfoot would be hurt or imprisoned in the mud. She reached into the muck for a handful and marveled at the amount of life she held – tadpoles, minnows, and all sorts of things in different stages of growth, wondering where she might fit in this handful. After one final revelry in the living mud, she crawled out of it and put her black socks and black sneakers onto her now black feet.

Later, the character heads for the beach:

Hair flying, rope flying, heels flying, and spirit soaring, Story flew out of the forest across a clearing and onto a beach. Gathering her breath she looked out over the ocean, saw her moon rising on the horizon, felt the breeze caress her hair. Without breaking her gaze, she took the rope from about her neck and coiled it in the sand, removed her black sneakers, black socks, black pants, black shirt, and then so deliberately, so slowly, so ritually, slipped out of her pastel pink pajamas. Her naked, moonlit silhouette joined her body at the feet and followed them toward the sea.

Story, still looking out over the distant sea and the shimmering moonlight, walked into the water. It climbed and caressed her knees, her forming hips, her narrowing waist, her pointing breasts; it burned and soothed the rope marks on her neck as she continued into the sea. She tasted it, swallowed it, breathed it into her nose, smelled it, opened her eyes to it, opened her soul to it and as it passed the last strand of floating hair, she relaxed and gave all herself to it. The ebb and flow of it returned her to the beach where she lay on her back, looking at her moon, her stars, her universe. The sea careened, crushed, crashed, caressed by her, over her, onto her, and into her. She rose above the water, above the beach, flew by the clouds, watched the shoreline shrink, the continent shrink, and accelerated on toward the heavens. But as she ascended, a thin line of red light on the horizon brought her rapidly back to earth. Daylight was on the horizon; day was on the way.

According to Story, "It's in touch; it's being in touch with that stuff. 'Mud and blood', it's poetic [see the poem *Nature Walk* at the beginning of the chapter on 'Philosophy of Death'] but in that mud, of course, is life. There's all those creepy crawlers in it but it's also the minerals that I have in my blood. It's the minerals of earth that you know that you can't live without – that's what mud is. Mud is life, blood is life and, you know, reaching into the muck – I did that all the time. I used to walk barefooted through the ponds; they were all mud. I did that all the time and no matter how mucky, it never bothered me. I love mud!

"Earth makes blood and earth makes you. I am totally of earth; I know that. Every single molecule in my body is of earth, it's provided every molecule in my body, every one of them and it'll go back. That's the relationship, that mud is earth and blood is life. And it's also ashes to ashes. That's not said in here but that's implicit in here."

Story said of his childhood in nature: "It was that exploration that made me, as opposed to the usual child development things, where, through social interaction, they find out who they are. This is the first time I've said this: it was the relationship of my body to the world that was defining me. I'm in a bodily place, I'm in a severely cold place, I'm in the leaves, I'm in the forest. It's my body that perceives the environment; it's not a social situation with facial expression and talk. No, my body was my relationship to the world which I was getting to know. Everything I do now, listening to my body – the body and mind being all the same thing for me – that's very important and that's where it came from. I had to have my body to find my identity. I couldn't have done it without my body because of how I was doing it out there.

"And so in terms of who I am and how I got to be like that, I had to have my body there to do this job. And so it wasn't my mind, the facial expression and words; I got this through my body. And, of course, it's a very bodily place – all the sensations and whether it's the cold or the wind through the trees or anything else like that. But it was, of course, always in beauty – the beauty of the wind through the trees, the beauty of the leaves, the beauty of watching the world go by, the beauty of watching the motions of the limbs overhead when I floated in the kayak, the beauty of being rock'n'rolled by the boat, the kinesthetics. That's not scientific information coming to me, it's beauty. My relationship to the world back then and the only way I could know my world, the only way I could find my world, the only way I could find out who I am was through beauty; the beauty of nature.

"As far back as I can remember I had a transcendence about myself. I'm in the forest in the middle of the night, I transcended all that [the home situation]. I'm in deep, dark ponds, I'm in some other world now. I have transcended my local environment through those kind of experiences and so I had always had a sense that there's something beyond the current existence and I was always reaching for it, I was always trying to be there."

The seasons are incredibly important to Story and always have been. He loves the changes from one season to the next, the turn of the leaves, the migrating birds, the changing shadows. The subtle changes are very important as part of the cycles of nature, and of Story's own life.

He said, "It's very powerful to me to look at the shadows and know the time of day and to know where the peak sun is and when the sun has crossed it's zenith. That means a lot to me and I feel the body respond to that. But it's the same business, it's the cycles of life, the cycles of life and death."

"The migration is very important to me, again, for all the same reasons. It's in touch with what is going on and the process that's going on. Every time I hear the geese overhead, I am going outside. Night or day, whether I can see them or not, it's very powerful.

"When the migratory ducks go through my pond, you can see them. It's very important to me to know that this is the time that they're heading south. It just sinks you in what's going on; it's seasonal. So migration then – that's just creatures' response to the law of mechanics. It's the cycles of the sun, it's the cycles of the moon, it's the cycle of the seasons and biology. Biology's the message and so here is life responding; it's that simple. Life is responding to these seasons but it's very important to me, just like it's important to tell the time by the shadows. But migratory geese – it makes my evening if I hear them go by at night time when I can't see them. I go out and listen to them going by.

"The seasons are very powerful to me now. My being in sync with things, I notice all these little variations."

Story recalled the intensity of seasons during his childhood in Massachusetts. "Spring was hugely powerful because it broke. We had very long winters, very snowy winters and when the spring breaks and the blooms are coming out, it is a very powerful season, so the seasons got embedded in me.

"And, of course, the wonderful summertime. You had the harsh, cold, very cold winter which I loved as well, but the summers were incredible crisp air, warm afternoons and cold nights. Even in summer you're forty, fifty degrees at night.

"The falls were fantastically powerful; that was my favorite season by far. I viewed myself in life as being a 'fall' person and even at a young age I should not have; I should have been late winter or early spring, but I always identified with fall and, of course, I still do."

For Story, spring has a different feel altogether. He wrote in his journal:

Spring as a source of motivation and energy.[7]

Story believes we have a lot to learn about nature from primitive societies. "You need an attitude like the primitives. Being in touch is listening. The primitives were in touch because they had to be in touch; their life depended upon the seasons, they had to know how nature was going. The cold would come and there would be no food."

People often wonder if Story has changed as a result of his space flight experiences. He already had a rich and spiritual background in terms of nature and so what he saw and experienced from space was a new perspective of nature, ultimately a reinforcement of what he already felt and knew. But in terms of who he was, in terms of his character, however, that did not change.

Story explained, "I don't think anything changed in my life due to the space program. I was already there at the age of three and so as the one continuous person all the way through. The only thing about space was that it expanded my horizons and put me into a new relationship with nature, a new view, a look into the big picture. I could see the whole forest from the air. Clearly, the love of earth is part of it and so space flight is getting the mission done in zero-g;[8] it's what you see out the window and so earth is greatly powerful. It's just looking at the universe unfold before your eyes; the child grown up in space looking at the heavens and earth from a different vantage point. It's probably given me a more powerful feel for evolution, cosmic evolution, biological evolution. I'm a huge evolutionist, that's the way I work, that's the way I think. I'm into change, I'm into birth, I'm into death, I'm into process, I'm into the journey."

Astronomical observations have always been important to Story – looking at the night sky for familiar stars and constellations or following the daily progression of the moon: "I have my own favorite old stars and things – like The Milky Way. I do relate to it. I have my own little relationships with the things out there – I like to look at Andromeda and Magellan clouds. I like to see galaxies; I love the Southern Cross – I just adore it! I don't know why, I just do.

"The planets and the stars – I know where they all have to be in the sky and I know what they all have to look like and I have a geometric understanding of things.

7. Journal 15, page 16; Date: 25 February 1994.
8. Zero-gravity.

I know the planets personally. I can look and see them and know which one it is. I know how bright they are, I know where they have to be in the sky.

"I didn't know the planets as a child; I was never taught – they were just bright stars. Now, the planets are very, very important to me; they stop me in my tracks. If I'm going somewhere and I look up and see a planet, I have to stop. I stop and take it in. It's stunning to just stop and take it in, just wonderful, you know.

"I know when it has to be a full moon or a crescent moon. I know what it has to be and I know how it's going to change tomorrow; I know where it's going, what it will look like then. I don't look in a book you know. I don't read in a newspaper what kind of moon you're going to have; I know what kind of moon I'm going to have.

"So I have a geometric view of all this: where I am on earth, and where these things are and where they're going to go."

In terms of geography, Story does have some favorite places on earth; places which are beautiful and spiritually uplifting. The desert, for example, has provided some of his strongest experiences of nature. Story loves the beauty of the desert, to fly in the desert – places like White Sands, New Mexico, or Washington State. He has taken hundreds of desert photos from space – especially 'sand art' as he refers to it, or patterns created by the wind and sand. Story calls it beauty for the sake of beauty: "You don't want to buy it and have it in your home; it's totally disinterested. Other astronauts go to eat lunch when the deserts are coming up!"

In his copy of *Wind, Sand and Stars*,[9] Story wrote:

> Immensity expands one's horizons, one's soul – Sahara, Pacific, Antarctica or Australia. Sahara brought on that mood of silence, even here. Story – love of the sand! Love of the black velvet [of space] is like one's love of the desert. Desert [is like] space: empty, full of spirit. Space – searching the void, if for nothing except some desert-like mirage.

Story said, "I love the desert sun, I love the desert heat and I usually go out midday in the desert. But it's a matter of feeling the heat penetrating; it's a matter of being penetrated to the bone by dry heat. So since you're not pouring out anywhere near the sweat you are in the humid weather, you get the penetration to the bone, so I like that a little better."

In California, Story loves to climb the Verdugo Mountains. The steep, slippery terrain is no obstacle – rather a challenge. Filmmaker David Grusovin recalled walking

---

9. *Wind, Sand and Stars*, by Antoine de Saint-Exupéry: first published in French in 1939 under the name *Terre des Hommes*. My copy was translated by William Rees and published in London by the Penguin Group, 1995.

with Story among the mountains, particularly the way he attacked it. "It's this relentless drive for the top of the hill. This wasn't any casual walk – it's like a drive to the top. He was always ahead of us, he led the drive. He was lurching up that hill at this incredible pace – phenomenal the physique and the whole drive of him."

David also shared a couple of visits to another of Story's great loves: The Huntington Botanical Gardens in Pasadena, California. The Huntington's enormous cactus garden, in particular, is one of Story's favorite retreats from his busy business life in Los Angeles. According to David, "Story would say, 'It's like being on another planet.' And he's quite happy in expressing that view; it's wonderful. He's looking at all the shapes....Places like that are so powerful 'cause you walk into that specific cactus garden and you go quiet. Sometimes it's more powerful not to say anything than to try to put it into words. When you walk through The Huntington, it's the sort of place that envelops you. And between what sporadic words we spoke as we walked through, you just smile. Story is a great observer. He'll be walking along and he'll just pull you up and point out a shape or a curve in something."

Of his experiences at the Huntington, Story says, "It's getting away and it's getting a fresh start. It's an escape, but it clears the mind of everything it is working on – just immerses you in nature. I use it as a creative retreat; I take my creativity out here and I see how it works out here.

Without a doubt, the Huntington's desert garden is the most creative for Story. "I think the desert garden is the most powerful because of the forms.[10] Everywhere you look, you have mandelbrots or fractals. It's an other-worldly place and so you're not in your own world. It's incredible being able to animate these things into other creatures and other forms. It's dry out here, in fact it's like the desert, and that makes it other-worldly too. Beauty, of course, is always at work; there's beauty in the forms as well. The powerful beauty and the powerful patterns – everything has a marvelous structure to it, so you're in the middle of art here. If you look at the way evolution is done here, you have spectacular creativity in different forms – the power of evolution. It's also the fact that [the plants] have to survive in the desert and that you get this spectacular structure where there is no water."

Story has traveled the world extensively since leaving NASA. Some of his favorite experiences have been in the blue waters of the Bahamas or the volcanic islands of the Pacific Ocean. He is particularly attracted to the beauty of these places. Of the Cook Islands he wrote to me: "The visceral beauty and the associated deep sinking relaxation is spectacular."

An excerpt from Story's poem about the Bahamas, written during his studies at the University of Houston, Clear Lake, reflects the wonder of color:

10. A spectacular range of cactus and other succulents.

> Oh Bahamas – Islands of the Sun. Tropical trees:
> beached with fine grains of soft sand,
> bathed with waves of light blue ocean,
> buoyed in an ocean of deep dark water,
> born in streaks of wispy white clouds.
> Oh Bahamas – Jewels of the Sea. Delicate strings of
> Emerald:
> bounded with rims of gold,
> touched by tides of turquoise,
> surrounded by seas of sapphire,
> streaked with strings of pearl.

The Hawaiian islands are another of Story's favorite destinations: his eldest son Scott has lived there for over a decade. Story loves the blue waters, the white and black sand beaches, the enormous telescopes on Mauna Kea and the colorful marine life of the coral reefs. Again, it is beauty which attracts him.

Two things stand out about Story's relationship to nature: his awareness of all the little details; and the simplicity of his emotions when these things delight him. It could be the shape of a leaf, the sounds of the insects or the texture of the soil. He takes the time to stop and reflect, to enjoy it all.

Frankie Camera, a restaurant owner in Houston, has known Story and his family for a long time. His restaurant, *Frenchies*, has been a popular eatery for people within the space program for decades. According to Frankie, Story is like "a breath of fresh air." He reminds him of the words of German poet Goethe, who wrote that walking alone in the woods, he was not looking for anything, when, in reality, he found everything:

> I was walking in the woods
> Just for the heck of it.
> And to look for nothing,
> That was my intention.
>
> In the shade I saw
> A little flower standing
> Like glittering stars
> Like beautiful little eyes.
>
> I wanted to pick it
> When it said delicately:
> 'Should I just to wilt
> Be picked?'

I dug it out with all
Its little roots.
To the garden I carried it
At the lovely house.

And replanted it
In this quiet spot;
Now it keeps branching out
And blossoms ever forth.[11]

This is a fitting description of a man whose journey through life has been inextricably entwined with nature; who has found profound meaning, spirituality and solitude among its depths.

# 4. Nature: A Philosophy

Wisdom and Spirit of the universe!
Thou Soul, that art the Eternity of thought!
And giv'st to forms and images a breath
And everlasting motion! not in vain,
By day or star-light, thus from my first dawn
Of childhood didst thou intertwine for me
The passions that build up our human soul;
Not with the mean and vulgar works of Man;
But with high objects, with enduring things,
With life and nature; purifying thus
The elements of feeling and of thought,
And sanctifying by such discipline
Both pain and fear,–until we recognise
A grandeur in the beatings of the heart.

*William Wordsworth*

Like one of his favorite philosophical writers – the American, Thomas Berry – Story Musgrave leads us back to a Romantic vision of the earth through communication. It is not just to make us aware of the continuing devastation of our planet, but more importantly, to propel us, as a species, into sustainable practices which will ensure the earth's future and, consequently, our own.

This approach demonstrates the biological and spiritual relationship between ourselves and the earth as part of a cosmic, creative process – one which grabs our imagination and fills us with awe. For as Berry says, "There must be a mystique of the rain if we are ever to restore the purity of the rainfall."[1]

Story has communicated his own personal relationship with the cosmos through his poetry, his performances and numerous interviews. It is an intimate relationship, even a primitive one, in which the most complete experience is only to be found in total surrender. He wrote:

Immersing oneself in nature – increasing the elasticity of one's mind.[2]

Human relationships, such as those between mother and child, or between two lovers, become metaphors for how Story interacts with the natural world.

In the midst of some of our greatest technologies – perhaps even because of them – Story's relationship with nature only seems to intensify. He has photographed rocket launches through the trees, supersonic jets flying into the sunset and spaceships in the early morning fog.

In the context of Story's philosophies, nature encompasses the universe. It is all one cosmic process by which the earth, its living creatures, including human beings and their scientific and spiritual processes, evolved. And everything is sacred.

According to Story, "My world is sacred. Nature is sacred for me and when you look at nature, you're looking at God. God may be a lot of other things as well. *This* is God; it's not just a creation of God, the sacred is *here*, he's not just out *there*."

Like the transcendentalists before him, Story goes out into nature for direct revelation.

∗

Story's personal creed is the result of intense observation and study, both at a practical and philosophical level. He is incredibly sensitive to processes and changes in the natural world and passionate about discoveries in our universe. All of these things are central to his deep sense of spirituality.

Story is careful about describing this relationship: "If you tell [some people] that I'm a pantheist, they think you're saying I'm a pagan and a non-believer and it's not

1. *The Dream of the Earth*, by Thomas Berry, San Francisco, Sierra Club Books, 1988, page 33.
2. Journal 18, page 8; Date: 18 September 1995.

true. There are different levels of pantheism. You have the different levels – for example, that the earth is sacred but it's not God; or at the deepest level you can say the earth is God and that's where I am. If I have to pull out one ethnic cultural group that's spiritually the closest to what I have arrived at, it's the North American Indian. They are at the highest or deepest level of pantheism in that the earth and the creatures are not only sacred, it is God you're looking at."

Story has been spiritual since he was a child. Looking to the stars was always very important and being involved with the Hubble Space Telescope has carried that forward in a special way.

He explained, "I was always talking to the heavens. Oh you can say, oh I'm talking to God; I'm talking to whatever's out there. I'm always talking to the heavens, looking up there, talking to him.

"If Hubble did anything it gave me more evocative images of what I know through life and death here. It's evolution. The images from Hubble immersed me in evolution – cosmic evolution, biological evolution. It's the birth and death of stars, that's what it is. It's the birth and death of planets. It's change. It's birth, growth and death and it's getting living things from dead things. It's like being in the forest. The dead trees feed on the live trees. So for me, Hubble is the forest but on a cosmic scale. It lets me feel it, it lets me see it – that's what it is, that's the link I make. It hasn't changed me – it's given me a different scale."

The Romantic writers and poets – also known in America as transcendentalists – have been incredibly important in terms of expressing the relationship which Story has with nature. He has studied them for decades and brought their relevance into his own thinking and writing.

In a college paper he wrote:

> It has been about two hundred years since the nature poetry of the continent and about a hundred and fifty years since the American Renaissance and the transcendentalists such as Emerson, Thoreau, and Whitman. The return of an interest and ability in nature poetry and literature will provide for the expression of one of the major aspects of humanity's experience in space – man's new point of view and relationship with the universe.

Story told Nina L. Diamond, "I always ran out into nature. As a child I could be more at peace in the middle of a dark forest at night than anywhere else. There was an unbelievable amount of chaos and suffering around me, so I headed for nature. Later, studying the humanities, I saw the roots of my experiences in nature in the American

3. Interview for *Omni Magazine*, by Nina L. Diamond, August 1994. Reprinted by permission of Omni Publications International Ltd.

Renaissance – in Emerson, Thoreau, Whitman, Melville, Hawthorne. And in the English Romantics – Wordsworth, Coleridge, Byron, Blake, Shelley."

But Story was by no means limited to these writers. Of Charlotte Bronte's work *Jane Eyre*, he concluded:

> Correspondence in themes with Emerson[4] and Whitman[5]… that the spirituality of humanity must be in part derived from humanity's relationship to nature.
>
> Jane Eyre was rooted in nature, not in humanity or in divinity. Jane achieved her self-identity, received her spirit through her relationships with the physical universe: the earth, the moon, the planets, the sun and the stars.

The similarities with Story's own life are undeniable. He continued:

> Humanity alienated Jane; she then turned inward to herself and outward toward nature. As expressed by the transcendentalists, nature is the link for Jane between humanity and divinity. [6]

Story likens his world to that of Henry David Thoreau's *Walden*. Thoreau built himself a cottage in the woods beside a pond and lived there for two and a half years in order to immerse himself in nature, re-evaluate his own life and discover the essence of humanity. It is a nice coincidence that Walden lies in Massachusetts, in the land which bred Story Musgrave. Thoreau wrote:

> Both place and time were changed, and I dwelt nearer to those parts of the universe and to those eras in history which had most attracted me. Where I lived was as far off as many a region viewed nightly by astronomers. We are wont to imagine rare and delectable places in some remote and more celestial corner of the system, behind the constellation of Cassiopeia's Chair, far from noise and disturbance. I discovered that my house actually had its site in such a withdrawn, but forever new and unprofaned, part of the universe. If it were worth the while to settle in those parts near to the Pleiades or the Hyades, to Aldebaran or Altair, then I was really there, or at an equal remoteness from the life which I had left behind, dwindled and twinkling with as fine a ray to my nearest neighbor, and to be seen only in moonless nights by him… I went to the woods because I wished to live deliberately, to front only the essential facts of life, and see if I could not learn what it had to teach, and not, when I came to die, discover that I had not lived. I did not wish to live what was not life, living is so dear; nor did I wish to practice resignation, unless it was quite necessary. I wanted to live deep and suck

4. Ralph Waldo Emerson
5. Walt Whitman
6. College paper for the University of Houston, Clear Lake: *Nature, Humanity and Divinity: A Thematic Interpretation of Jane Eyre.*

out all the marrow of life, to live so sturdily and Spartan-like as to put to rout all that was not life, to cut a broad swath and shave close, to drive life into a corner, and reduce it to its lowest terms, and, if it proved to be mean, why then to get the whole and genuine meanness of it, and publish its meanness to the world; or if it were sublime, to know it by experience, and be able to give a true account of it in my next excursion.[7]

In essence, this is Story – living life to the fullest and paying great attention to the world around him while looking for what it means to be human.

Story wrote of this important work:

Walden brought an American Romantic face to face with nature and a life symbolic of the primitive life. Walden challenged the American Romantics to define their spirituality, brought them physically and morally face to face with nature... An American Romantic stood for innocence, individuality, nature, rebirth, and cultural and religious freedom. The American Romantic also had more than one root – in the church and nature, the woods and the library, ... all other places and peoples where the search might lead... Thoreau carries me back to my childhood on a New England farm, because he encourages me to wonder and to see with innocent eyes, causes me to be vulnerable and yet to take the risks of direct experience.[8]

Looking out over my Walden... As Walden was to Thoreau, the world is to Story; space is to Story.[9]

Story considers himself to be a Romantic. "A Romantic is a realist but a Romantic is more. The Romantic is very interested in how the individual reacts to nature. So the realist just paints the picture of nature without the human element in it. The Romantic portrays how nature moves the individual, and paints the human responding to nature. So I'm a Romantic out there in nature, but it's basically an inward turn because you're looking at the human response to nature and what part nature plays in all of that."

Story feels an affinity with the poetry and essays of Emerson. "Emerson was a philosopher as well, so he expressed a kind of pantheism where not only is nature sacred, but nature is God – and that was true for me as far back as I can remember.

"Emerson tells us, there is no past, only a present and a future, possibility and promise, and a responsibility to do something with the opportunity."

Story wrote a college paper about the *American Renaissance in Literature and Space*

7. *Walden*, by Henry David Thoreau, 1854.
8. College paper for the University of Houston, Clear Lake titled: *Thoreau – An American Adam*.
9. Journal 2, page 10; Date: not stated, but between September 1987 and April 1989.

for his studies at the University of Houston. In it, he talks about the role and relevance of the American transcendentalists in terms of humanity and its relationship to nature.

> Space gave humanity a new start on its relationship with nature, an opportunity to do this one right, as humans, showing to ourselves what the human essence is. From the point of view of the transcendentalist, space as a human experience, is a grand opportunity for the exercise of a Romantic epistemology, how is earth viewed by humans, what does history mean when its actions can be seen in one glance? What new truth is held from the viewing of the childhood beaches of Cape Cod, the landing place of the Pilgrims, and a New York medical school in a single scene? It's useless to leave this earth unless you know what it's like to be in it. The literature of the American Renaissance is a great way to know what it's like to be of and on this earth and is extraordinarily relevant to being of and out of this earth.

Story admires the creativity, the flow and sheer volume of what he refers to as Walt Whitman's catalogues of nature and humanity, and continues to devour Whitman's *Leaves of Grass* on a regular basis. Of all the American poets, Whitman is perhaps the most powerful for Story. According to Story, Whitman makes you appreciate the sensuous nature of things.

> And you O my soul where you stand
> Surrounded, detached in measureless oceans of space,
> Ceaselessly musing, venturing, throwing, seeking
> the spheres to connect them.

> *Walt Whitman*

Story studied Whitman's poetry in the context of the space experience. Much of Story's own poetry is undoubtedly influenced by Whitman's work and spirit. Reading poetry like this enabled Story to communicate his experience of space – in particular, the earth from the spaceship window – in the same way that the transcendentalists viewed the earth from the ground.

> Space is a unique way to redefine Whitman's matter, a new sensuality and self-awareness to immerse us in the Truth. It is a unique way for Whitman to examine what it is to be human as a product of evolution. Space is an environment which may not have been working in the evolutionary scheme, as an example, gravity was very much a part of the human's evolutionary design, now we have the chance to look at humans without it. Whitman can look at us in an environment that was not in the game. For the Whitmans, to whom Earth is the source of life and death, one is able to look at Whitman's earth, not only from a different perspective, but at most or all of it, and someday, hopefully soon, be able to form

another of Emerson's truth's by viewing an earth, not just any earth, but one understood in Whitman's terms.[10]

Story has made a habit of reflecting upon universal themes as part of his daily life. He has the ability to focus on both the details at hand and the bigger issues affecting humanity. While observing a total lunar eclipse in 1989 he wrote:

> Total lunar eclipse. Took some photos 1600 ASA. Looked with binoculars. Looked at shadow on the moon and felt and saw myself. Held my hand out to make a shadow on the moon. Thought of the primitive people and what it would mean to them. I felt the eclipse. What goes on in the cosmos is important to people. It is not just science, it is our identity, ourselves. It is not just reason and empiricism. The object is the eclipse, the subject is the human effects and significance of the eclipse. The moon in eclipse looked more like a planet and I was there, in the vicinity. I felt as if I was away at the planets. The moon turning red as it passed into total eclipse. Red, probably because lit by light passing through so much atmosphere. A circular sunset around the whole earth. I envisioned myself being on the moon and looking toward earth. Would have been spectacular show – earth seen from the moon.[11]

Exploration of cosmic evolution is perhaps the underlying theme of much of Story's personal philosophy. He does not like to categorize things, but prefers to think of everything as coming from the same source: a universal source.

He says, "That's what makes it all work: we all came from the same place, it's all part of the same process; the big process. We are part of that process. That's what links everything. That's what dissolves all human categories, that's what dissolves science and religion. That's what dissolves cosmology, philosophy, theology, astronomy and the whole thing. They're very human categories but, at that level, it's all one thing. Religion and science are the same, they're just human categories. Humans say 'this is religion'; humans say 'that is science'. Of course you look at technology differently – that's a human enterprise – but humans are also nature: human nature."

In his journal, Story expressed these things on a number of occasions:

> I look to the cosmos to find God in myself.[12]

> God is all, God is the totality of all the principles that run this place, those elements of this place that have always been and always will be... [13]

10. College paper for the University of Houston, Clear Lake: *The American Renaissance in Literature and Space.*
11. Journal 6, page 5; Date: 16 August 1989.
12. Journal 23, page 33; Date: 13 August 1997.
13. Journal 23; Comment added afterwards; date not specified.

We are God's co-creators, part of evolution, we effect evolution, creation...
As storytellers, we determine the direction of evolution on earth and eventually
elsewhere. The cosmos speaks its meaning through us.[14]

Plants grow toward the light, humans could learn from them![15]

Nature is not impersonal; lives by the same rules that I do. Volcanoes, earth
quakes, hurricanes and all that we call 'violence', created an environment in
which life could arise and supported life. Nature is nature, physically energetic,
not violent. Cosmic processes involving all star birth and death are 'violent', [as
well as] planetary formation – process of creating and destroying order –
nothing is created or destroyed – changes found + energy. [16]

Story took the paradigms of evolution into space in order to view the earth.
Earthly exploration, as viewed from space, can also be seen as a metaphor for
exploration of the universe:

I feel earth...Earth shaped humanity... Earth formed us in order that we might
look at earth... Earth is that soft dark velvet, like an orchid in the desert. Seeing
the route of the explorers from space – now I am one. Seeing the frontiers on
earth and now looking to the edge between air and space. Egypt – five thousand
years of history in the window of a modern spaceship.[17]

The work of Teilhard de Chardin is also critical to Story's thinking on cosmic
evolution, particularly, *The Phenomenon of Man*.[18] He said, "This is another one of my
books which is in the top twelve – it's his philosophy. What he does is link cosmic
evolution and spiritual evolution – that's very nice – the way the cosmos works and
the way spirituality works. So for him, he links the physical with the spiritual and in
terms of philosophy, I am right there with him, all the way. It's very important stuff to
me; it's evolutionary, That's my philosophy, that's the link between cosmic and
spiritual evolution – they're all the same to me."

According to Story, there is a certain irony in human categorization:

Physical, chemical, biological, mental, spiritual – same process, same source. No
matter how advanced the science and technology, we still look to the heavens for
direction.[19]

14. Journal 23, page 13; Date: 11 August 1997.
15. Journal 17, page 42; Date: 7 August 1995.
16. Journal 17, page 45; Date: 10 August 1995.
17. Story's handwritten note in his copy of *The Spell of New Mexico*, edited by Tony Hillerman, Albuquerque,
University of New Mexico Press, 1976.
18. *The Phenomenon of Man* by Pier Teilhard de Chardin (1955): translated by Bernard Wall, New York, Harper
& Row, Publishers, Inc. 1975.
19. Journal 5, page 43; Comment added later; date not specified.

There are other themes woven into Story's experiences of nature from space. One of the more significant ones is beauty.

> We have been designed to perceive the beauty of earth and heavens. It is part of our constitution, a means to survival! Response to beauty is organic, mind and body – physiological.[20]

> Oh Earth, you are only what you are! Nature is beauty, the original beauty.[21]

> Magnificence of earth – magnificence of maker... Abyss upon abyss...[22]

> It is the sensual experience and observation of the earth that propels Story into space. Sunset and death in the ocean, then launch into the heavens. And the launch producing a sunrise... Curve of the horizon – geometric beauty. [23]

> Earth blossoms, earth as a flower. Image of earth on a stem.[24]

> My earth, my moon. Looking at earth – eye music. Music of the breeze, music of space... Harmony, universal desire, hunger.[25]

Human relationships are often used as metaphors for Story's relationship to earth; for humanity's relationship to earth. It is a context which enables us to view the earth with sensitivity and respect. Earth's nurturing and guidance are recurring themes in Story's journals:

> Children of the earth – if we all returned to the earth, we would be one...Earth putting on an aspect of welcome... Earth as home – re-entry... Earth – as a home – airy, roomy, convenient, sensuous.[26]

> Your earth – belongingness.[27]

> Earth nurtures! Supports! ... Appreciation of the earth as a work of art. Drink the earth.... Satisfaction and replenishment by earth, nature.[28]

> The sound of a sunrise sweeping across the earth at 1000 mph... People have been given the earth, given the stars to find their way.[29]

20. Story's handwritten note in *Principles of Literary Criticism* by I.A. Richards 1925.
21. Journal 3, page 5; Date: 1988.
22. Journal 3, page 44; Date: 2 November 1988.
23. Journal 3, page 44; Date: 2 November 1988.
24. Journal 3, page 45; Date: 3 November 1988.
25. Journal 3, page 46; Date: 12 November 1988.
26. Journal 3, pages 23-24; Date: 19 September 1988.
27. Journal 3, page 46; Date: 12 November 1988.
28. Journal 1, page 4; Date: 1987.
29. Journal 1, page 7; Date: 1987.

> Dark float [looking at the night-time earth from space, with the Shuttle lights turned out] – the womb of the mind, the womb of space. Swimming even deeper within the womb of mind... Life – womb to tomb... Earth [is both] womb and tomb.[30]

> Develop personification of earth as woman – beautiful, warm, caring, cuddling, and independent and strong.[31]

Story's childhood is a recurring theme in his journals – his sense of adventure and exploration of the world, and the associated awe and wonder that a child experiences. This enables him to relate to nature on the highest levels.

> Like being on the raft in the river – the world flows by! ...The power and the majesty... my eyes can't see it, my mind can! ... [Like] Huck on the river, faster and higher, but oh the power and majesty of this – my eyes can't see the raft.[32]

> Stop the world – I want to get off. Or would like to stop life here a moment, stop the velocity... Story's life is similar to spacecraft's path.[33]

> I want to have the earth that I had as a child.[34]

> Walking barefoot in ploughed fields. Thoughts grown in the soil.[35]

> How does one best maintain the primitive amidst overwhelming technology and information? How does one maintain awe and wonder, realizing that drowning in data we know and understand almost nothing?.. What attitudes and actions will raise humanity to its highest levels and values?[36]

> Maintaining the highest level of appreciation of nature, [with] awe and wonder, takes energy, Romanticism; it is work and energy to maintain highest level of relation to nature.[37]

Experiencing the earth, nature, space, the universe – for Story, it's all about surrendering to the experience, surrendering to the environment and immersing oneself in it. Story believes we will not experience it all fully if we try to impose ourselves upon it. The writing of Emerson expresses this powerfully for Story:

30. Journal 6, pages 6-8; Date; 17-20 August 1989.
31. Journal 3, page 45; Date: 3 November 1988.
32. Journal 1, page 8; Date: 1987.
33. Journal 1, page 17; Date: 1987.
34. Journal 26, page 7; Date: 24 March 2000.
35. Journal 3, page 24; Date: 19 September 1988.
36. College paper for the University of Houston, Clear Lake: *Classic Texts in Future Studies*.
37. Journal 21, page 21; Date: February 1997.

Beauty through my senses stole;
I yielded myself to the perfect whole.[38]

Story wrote of the underlying influence of Eastern philosophies in Emerson's work, especially that of the Japanese aesthetic and culture:[39]

> [Both Emerson and the Japanese] want to experience their bodies, art and nature rather than to control and conquer such. They wish to experience by being open to experience, by yielding to it, by giving themselves over to it. They are more sensitive, more sensible, and more responsive. Their aesthetic experiences are deeper, richer, and result in an art which is itself more open and richer in its pluralities and possibilities.

> The importance of giving oneself over to the world in order to gain the real truth of it is expressed more strongly, as one would expect, in *The Poet* than in any other of Emerson's writings. 'It is a secret which every intellectual man quickly learns, that, beyond the energy of his possessed and conscious intellect, he is capable of a new energy (as of an intellect doubled on itself), by abandonment to the nature of things...by unlocking, at all risks, his human doors, and suffering the ethereal tides to roll and circulate through him: then he is caught up into the life of the Universe...the intellect released from all service, and suffered to take its direction from its celestial life...' (*The Essays of Ralph Waldo Emerson*, Alfred Kazin ed., 1987, page 233).

Story elaborated, "It's a primitive attitude but it's surrender and let go. Surrender is the key because you've got to listen, not control. That's the key thing, you have to listen. Being in touch is listening.

"The correct revelation is you're going out to get at the answers directly and to be sensitive to listen to nature and to the universe, which is very important as opposed to picking up a human document and saying, 'Here it is'. I'm not against the human documents. I think they have lessons too, but I think in addition to reading books to get the answers, the human answers, I think if you listen to your body – the architecture that came through millions of years through genetics; you have millions of years of experience in nature that it took to form the DNA. It really is evolutionary genetics. You can listen to what is in your subconscious; you can listen to your body, listen to the cosmos by letting your body respond to things and letting those archetypes come out."

In his journal Story wrote:

---

38. Ralph Waldo Emerson - *The Essays of Ralph Waldo Emerson*, Alfred Kazin ed., 1987.
39. College paper for the University of Houston, Clear Lake: *Similarities in the Aesthetics of Emerson and of the Japanese*.

I look for revelation, I believe what God and nature and everything reveals to me. I do not accept or reject other people's beliefs. I am on a quest, a search, a pursuit, a pilgrimage! It is the search that matters. For you, I accept your beliefs; for me, I neither accept or reject your beliefs – God reveals itself to me directly, in part through you, in part me, in part nature.[40]

According to Story, "Again, it gets down to the key word of surrender: surrender and listen. If you surrender to things totally, you can listen in a pure kind of way. Surrender also means [leaving] personal baggage behind – all the things that you have learnt and all those human things which happened to you which cloud your view of the universe, which cloud your view of direct revelation. So, surrender is important: you get rid of the baggage.

"The native Americans were critically successful at that. They'd been here thirty thousand years. They were totally sustainable."

Story referred to this again in a college paper entitled *Sensitivity to the Unconscious*. Not surprisingly, nature and the universe were pervading themes of Story's essays as he looked for ways to express his own relationship to them, and to confirm his personal philosophies concerning humanity's.

> Acceptance of the primitive mind reaffirms man's emotional ties with the universe, with "Father Spirit" and "Mother Earth". The new intellect tends to dominate, to conquer Nature, not to bond to her. The primitive mind hears the melody of life played in harmony with the archetypal rhythms… reason is but one approach to Faith, the unconscious mind offers another…. Acceptance and sensitivity to the primitive mind causes one to be in touch with, in harmony with, one's self, others, nature and with the nature of humanity.[41]

For Story, it is imperative to know the universe both physically and spiritually. He observed:

> Freeing the inner allows one to perceive the expanse and other dimensions of external space including infinity… One needs inner development and spiritual growth before one is willing or able to comprehend what space is… Experience your universe, not just know it… Universe/Cosmos – nature is an anchor, a ship in the middle of social/cultural chaos and change. Universe – evolution, change, but guided by principles![42]

> Until we establish oneness with the cosmos, we will never get meaning. Surrender to the cosmos/nature: kneel before God! Culture is alienated from

40. Journal 13, page 22; Date: 12 June 1992.
41. Course: *Cause and Effect*; Date of paper: June 26, 1988.
42. Handwritten note by Story in his copy of *Transcendence*, Edited by Richardson and Cutler, 1969.

nature/cosmos! We exist for nature, we are a process of nature, the direction of the species, our motivations, our ethics are and must be driven by nature! We use nature as a tool, a utility, not as a guide or an ethic. Belong to nature, exist for nature, meaning must come from nature…Get face to face with God. I surrender to this, can't know it – joy that I can't, it is the quest, the journey, and a deep faith in the hope and meaning of it all – I go forward.[43]

During STS-80, Story shared Catholic communion with crew member Tom Jones during a night pass of the earth.[44] It was a deeply moving occasion for both of them, and for Story, one of the highest points of his physical and spiritual experience of the universe. Some time later, in his copy of *Wind, Sand and Stars*, Story wrote:

Total surrender of body, soul and being to that eternal spirit – that which has always been and always will be.[45]

Sustainability is a theme which is central to Story's appreciation of nature. It is a subject which is dealt with in a wider context in the chapter *Philosophy of Space*, but needs to be mentioned here in the context of nature. On a visit to Arizona in 1991, Story wrote about the sensitivity which enables humanity and nature to co-exist in the world of the native American Indian.

Presence of (native/American) Indian spirit is overwhelming – I'm captivated by their spirit, their dead, their images. I see images of them, living the way humans ought to live – ecological – *with* nature versus against. Free individual spirits.[46]

Story's views on sustainability are closely aligned with the philosophies and spirituality of Thomas Berry. Again, it can only be achieved by having a special respect for nature, immersing oneself in nature. According to Story, "Immersion in nature? Yes. It will do all kinds of things, it really will, it's the Thomas Berry thing. It's sustainability. It's looking to the future, it's living within the resources [of the earth]."

*The Dream of the Earth*, is a key book in Story's library – one which he has read and absorbed many times. In it, Berry also expresses Story's appreciation of the Native American and their relationship to the earth. Story explained, "*The Dream of the Earth* is fantastic writing. I think it's emotionally driven too. The clarity is such, the clarity of what he says, the rationality of what he says is extraordinary. His ecology, his spirituality, which is really related to his ecology and his sense of sustainability and sustainable behavior, I totally agree with and that's where I come from. He expressed

43. Journal 23, pages 11-12; Date: 11 August 1997, additional comments added later.
44. Viewing the earth at night time from the darkness of an unlit space shuttle cockpit.
45. *Wind, Sand and Stars*, by Antoine de Saint-Exupéry: first published in French in 1939 under the name *Terre des Hommes*. My copy was translated by William Rees and published in London by the Penguin Group, 1995.
46. Journal 10, page 18; Date: 25 January 1991, Sierra Vista, Arizona.

it so well – the behavior of human beings as a species on earth and the non-sustainable course they're currently taking."

D. H. Lawrence, another of Story's favorite writers, also wrote of sustainability. Lawrence was speaking of the spiritual power of New Mexico – of the American Indians who dwelt there – and the apparent path of Western development. Of his experiences, Lawrence observed:

> There it is: the newest democracy ousting the oldest religion! And once the oldest religion is ousted, one feels the democracy and all its paraphernalia will collapse, and the oldest religion, which comes down to us from man's pre-war days, will start again.[47]

Story said of D. H. Lawrence's remarks: "He saw it and he expressed it as powerfully as anyone – we, seventy-five years later, see it but deny it, and on we go down into the spiral of death and destruction. The natives knew it then, and we as individuals know it now, but as a culture, a global civilization without checks and balances, we are unable to respond or to take action even as we approach the abyss; we helplessly ride our machines over the cliff. As an earthly creature, I will suffer for all those creatures who will suffer, especially for all those who had nothing to do with it. As a cosmic creature, I will not suffer, I will follow the path, wherever it goes, smiling and laughing, swimming in the supreme irony that, in an evolutionary sense, *intelligence* turned out to be a dead-ended survival strategy. I, as a cosmic creature, will know and accept that I am a creature, no better and no worse than any of the other creatures and with that, I will, with faith and hope, journey on."

In Story, there is a hunger – a hunger for the universe, for nature, to be part of it, to immerse himself in it and to be fulfilled by it. His approach is appropriate to the desired result, which is to gain a greater understanding and appreciation of the world around him:

> Immerse, metabolize, surrender to the natural world – you came from it, you are it, the metaphysical answers are in it – listen to god! Direct revelation versus a human product![48]

> God's trying to talk and we are on another channel. [49]

> Receptivity to all earth, heavens, space, universe, soaking it all up. Space-ocean: drowning, drinking in the ocean, reveling in the consumption and consummation.[50]

47. *The Spell of New Mexico*, edited by Tony Hillerman, Albuquerque, University of New Mexico Press, 1976, p36.
48. Journal 23, page 24; Date not specified.
49. Journal 23, page 25; Date: 12 August 1997.
50. Journal 2, page 20; Date: between September 1987 and April 1989.

Do you feel a sunset, taste the ocean, talk to the trees, melt in the desert sun? Are you instinctually compelled to migrate with the seasons, to see, to smell, to touch, to fall and die with the frosted leaves? Are you swept in and out by the tides of urgent earth? Do you sleep, not upon nature, but within nature? If so, or mostly so, you are sensitive to, touched by your unconscious self. You let its primitive pure spring bubble to the surface, slake your thirst for the depths, and run with the mountain stream to the ocean....A sensitivity to the unconscious tends to cause one to be: unrepressed, healthy, accepting of one's self and others, in harmony with the spiritual, and with nature, and appreciative of the complexity and plurality of humanity.[51]

It gets back to Story's photo of the child on the beach which he exhibits in his performances – the eyes and ears tuned to the world, the whole body exploring the universe. It is also the inward turn – self-discovery and revelation – as we look to the outer world.

This image, perhaps more so than any other, reveals Story himself. It was Story on the beach or in the forests – hands in the dirt, whole body in the dirt, tasting the dirt, face down in the streams drinking the life-blood of the cosmos. Delicious nature, so serene and welcoming.

As always, Story tries to see things from the child's point of view – with curiosity, awe and wonder; innocence, imagination. A child has not yet learnt to categorize things, to look at them from a cultural point of view – that will come later. For now, the child sees, touches, tastes, listens and smells in a process of discovery. The child's whole being is absorbed in the experience, has surrendered to the experience.

If there is one phrase which captures the essence of Story Musgrave's message, his philosophy of nature, it is, as he tells audiences:

Reach out and touch your universe; and let *it* touch *you!*

51. College paper for the University of Houston, Clear Lake titled: *Sensitivity to the Unconscious.*

# *Mechanics*

"I love the motion and I love big engines that make the right kinds of sounds. I got into that; I got into engines and the hum of machinery."

# 5. Lifelong Mechanic

Sound and smell of diesels:
have always loved machinery.

*Story Musgrave*
*Visit to England, March, 1993*

Story Musgrave's fascination with machinery began at Linwood Farm, his family's thousand acre dairy operation in western Massachusetts. It was working in the fields from a very young age, teaching himself to use the tractors, harvesters, bailing machines and other farm implements.

Naturally enough, young Story dreamt of being a farmer one day. He loved the hard physical work, the sweat and the grime, the contact with nature: "It's not just the machinery, it's what's associated with the machinery and so it's all that business – there's some grease involved too. I'll never forget the body – the dirt and the sweat. I was into dirt. You're in a machine where you're just sweating like a hog! I mean you're so filthy that you take the dirt off with a shovel. You don't bathe it off – you scrape it off first!

"It was the immersion in work, in hard work and in sweat and making a body do what it's got to do and just a total immersion in that kind of physical world. It's the wonder of work and just enjoying incredibly long days of just sweating like a hog."

Story also loved the motion of moving parts and the noise of machinery: "The visual mechanics was very important back then. I love the motion and I love big engines that make the right kinds of sounds. I got into that; I got into engines and the hum of machinery. You get addicted to the hum of machinery. And even now if I hear a machine I have to go and listen to it. If I hear some good boulder train or truck, I have to go listen to it. I just love good sound; I love motors."

The decision to enter the US Marine Corps was less to do with machinery and more to do with expanding one's horizons by traveling to exotic places. However, when choosing an occupation within the Corps, Story wanted to drive heavy machinery – it was what he knew and loved.

Instead, as it turned out, Story learnt the world of airplanes in the military hangar. Although he had informally flown an airplane before joining the Marines, without a high school diploma he could not be trained as a military pilot and was relegated to ground-based duties. That, in itself, was to enrich Story's future relationship with airplanes and to increase his appreciation for the ground crews who looked after him during his thirty years with NASA.

After discharge from the Marines, Story pursued studies in mathematics and business, which led him to UCLA and, at the time, the biggest computer in the world. His fascination with that machine was passionate and consuming. It led him to wonder about the human brain, the workings of which were reflected in its design, and so again, Story leaped off into other disciplines, with interests in artificial intelligence, neurophysiology and the mind. It became the study of the mechanics of the body and the brain.

It was in Kentucky during the mid-1960s, while he was completing post-doctoral Fellowships in medicine, that Story's private pursuit of flying really began. From that point onwards, he owned a variety of airplanes, including sailplanes, and took up instructing and charter airplane flying as a means to finance his flying interests.

By the time Story joined NASA in 1967, he was an exceptionally qualified aviator. He flourished in the world of the T-38 supersonic jets, which were used by the astronauts for proficiency training. During his career with the space agency, he accumulated the greatest number of flight hours in that airplane by any astronaut, completed the most functional test flights[1] and spent more than 2000 hours as a T-38 flight instructor. But this was not about accumulating flight hours or records: Story Musgrave loved machines, loved flying and above all else, enjoyed discovering the world around him, and his relationship to it, in yet another physical and spiritual way.

The world of space flight, whilst it does belong in part to the world of mechanics, was a significant new dimension to Story's life. In that world, Story continued to develop personally on many different levels. It was a world of technology, of flight and exploration, of psychology and physiology, of nature and spirituality. And so, thematically, it deserves its own place.

Nature was never really absent from Story's mind in the midst of technology. When asked about the relationship between nature and technology, he said: "I think the sailplane metaphor puts it as close as I can to nature and technology. It just allows you to have a sailplane and soar with the winds; it allows you to soar with the hawks. It's an extension of yourself that allows you to become a bird.

"Whenever I can, I put the machinery in perspective of nature. I attempt to do that and I don't think I ever take photographs of the technology alone and find them that great. In my performances, I'm always showing a photo that's truly technology and then following it with one that has [the nature] perspective – the whole audience – you can just hear the breath go out of everyone!

"You'll see a Space Shuttle launch which is nothing but the power: the rocket engines and the plume are just that. And then you show a photo with the Shuttle and all the palm trees silhouetted, you see the moon and you see the glow of the rocket engine in the water. And you see the birds flying and then you say, 'Oh there it is!'"

Story's home in Florida is a perfect example of the relationship between machinery and nature. Machinery is the tool to beautify the landscape. But it's also the fun of driving tractors, maneuvering the excavator and the satisfaction of fixing various pieces of equipment when they break down. That is something Story has been doing for nearly sixty years. It's sitting back then and enjoying the beauty. It's gathering the palm seeds, raking them into the ground and watching them germinate. But the machinery has sculptured the ponds, it has maintained the soil and the grasses, and invigorated the soul of the farmer.

Above all else, the lifestyle Story wove around mechanics – the farm machinery, the computers, the human body, the worlds of aviation and space flight – were filled with the human dimension and personal quest.

---

1. A test of an airplane after it has undergone major mechanical work.

# 6. Marines

I loved the airplanes, loved the flying,
and passionately pursued every form
of flight from then till the present.

*Story Musgrave*

Story Musgrave is a highly independent person, both by nature and necessity. That's definitely an asset when joining the US Marine Corps! And having led a very restrictive life until his late teenage years, he was more than ready for some kind of new environment, some way to broaden his experience.

He said, "The home life and the school were fantastically narrow. And so I was looking to go out there and go do something – I felt the urge to expand my horizons and to see the other worlds. So I think, number one, that is why I joined the Marines – it was an adventure, it was a journey and it was a way out."

As a Marine, Story ventured across the Pacific to the exotic Far East and came into contact with vastly different cultures for the first time. Life was fairly simple, with the basic necessities provided and genuine opportunities for self-improvement through additional training and study.

In all, Story was with the US Marine Corps for two years on a full-time basis, although he would continue in the active reserves for a further three years. Much of the first year was taken up with basic training and further qualification as an aircraft electrician and instrument technician. With that accomplished, Story headed for Korea and the first taste of another life. He spent a year away from the United States, also stopping in Japan and Hawaii.

During those first two years, Story was able to indulge his love of machinery through the world of the airplane maintenance. He also enjoyed the excitement of being flown aboard military airplanes and ferried across the Pacific on the enormous aircraft carrier, the USS Wasp.

For the young teenager from Massachusetts, life as a Marine in the 1950s did, in many ways, expand his horizons.

*

Before Story joined the Marines, he had an idea of what that life would be like.

He said, "I had this vision, which I always have – this imaginative vision, this tape that plays that sees me in the future, that sees me in the new role. I always have these – I guess it's my imagination – that I can play this film that I see unfolding. And I was driving bulldozers on some kind of paradise, I was constructing runways and buildings, but I was driving heavy machinery in some exotic, romantic, foreign land.

"And so that kind of vision was absolutely too compelling. I did have a push – in terms of escaping the two environments of my childhood – the push to go beyond them, to get ahead of them, to get them behind me – and I had the pull of the Marines itself. I did know I had to get out there and get a worldly experience. But I also did have this fantastic image of myself running big machinery. I had machinery on the farm, but I was after bigger stuff. Bigger machinery and exotic land!

"I had the view of myself, you know, boots and coveralls and green T-shirt, just sweating like a hog out there in the hot sun, which I loved. Just physical work for twelve to fourteen hour days; that's what I wanted and that's what I knew.

"I tried to get there in time for the Korean War, but I missed it. The Korean War was still on – technically, I'm a Korean Veteran – but the fighting had stopped."

Story left high school behind in 1953. The very day he left St Mark's school, his mother drove him to the bus station in Boston where he headed for Florida with a friend by the name of Fred Harvey. Fred accompanied Story for the first ten days, while Story continued in Daytona, forming a friendship with a contemporary by the name of Gerald Raymond.

According to Story, "The summer of '53 was important in that the day that I did not graduate I got on a bus. The bus led me back to the first paradise I had ever known – and that was Florida. That summer of '53, I traveled over a good part of the United States with Gerald. We had a ford pickup truck and it was just going out and really seeing the world for the first time."

After several months of traveling, doing occasional part-time work and covering some thirty states, Story returned home briefly to New England. He formally entered the US Marine Corps on 30 December 1953 and was sent to Parris Island, South Carolina, for basic training.

Story and his family exchanged a great deal of correspondence during the subsequent two year period. The letters home expressed Story's thoughts and feelings about his time with the Marines, giving us colorful insights into the type of existence he was leading. They also move us superbly through the chronology of his studies and active duty.

Early in basic training, Private Franklin Story Musgrave was given an aptitude test to help determine a suitable occupation within the Corps. On the 10 January 1954, he wrote to his father Percy and stepmother Josephine at Linwood, the family farm in Massachusetts:

> I got 135 on my important classification test. All you have to have to go to officers' training school is 120, so you can see I did fairly well. I decided not to become a 90-day wonder because it ties you up for more than I have enlisted for. I asked them to go to a crane, shovel, bulldozer etc ground. The interviewer, quite horrified, pushed me up the line to higher office. At this point I thought I had better ask for something more technical so as not to perturb the next interviewer. I came half way up the line technically and still horrified my second interviewer. At this point I was pushed to the top interviewer who, hearing the story, gave me no choice and assigned me to a school called Aviation Engineering Electronics. This, he said, was the most technical and highest paying school in the Marines. It's all to do with guided missiles, radar, navigation equipment, rocket launches etc. The best thing about it is that the school is stationed in Jacksonville Florida. Daytona Beach, my traveling friend and other interesting friends I have,

are only a two hour drive away. While in school, weekends can be taken almost all the time.

More than fifty years later, Story still recalled his initial disappointment with his military career path: "My civilian job counselor would not allow me to do bulldozers or heavy equipment. Unfortunately I did too well on the tests – that was what precluded my doing that. He has to match up test scores with the occupation that the Marine Corps wants you to do, and so I did intellectually too well on the test scores to get sent to heavy equipment school. I was disappointed not to get that – I struggled with the occupational counselor, but my drill instructor spoke to me. The job counselor talked to my drill instructor and my drill instructor told me what I really wanted. So then I had the answer – that's what I really want. So then I signed up for the aviation. Of course I love machines, I love airplanes – they're not only great machines, they also fly. So that was my introduction to military flying."

Story was to be stationed in Florida for the next nine months – from April to December of 1954. In a letter to Linwood on 12 April 1954, he wrote:

> After this month of mess duty, I'll go to a general aviation school for two months. This consists of physics, math and working with hand tools (sheet metal, threading bolts etc). There is no question that I'll do well in the former two since I've had a tremendous amount of experience in both. I also should be set with the hand tools due to tinkering around with things and manual training at St Mark's. After these two months of general school, I'll go to a technical school for around five months. If I do quite well in general school, I get my choice of any technical school I want... One of the two schools here in Jacksonville is Aviation Electricians School. Another credit to it is that it would probably be very helpful to have a knowledge of electricity on a farm or another phase of civilian life. The electricians school I was originally slated for is in Memphis and probably isn't useable in normal civilian life.

In May of 1954, Story mentioned in his letters that he was saving for an Oldsmobile and also building a house with his friend Gerry down at Daytona. He recalled, "From Jacksonville I'd usually go down to Daytona, three out of four weekends: I had duties on the fourth weekend. The free weekends, I went on my little motorcycle, down to Daytona almost all the time."

Story relished the weekends of freedom. He wrote to Linwood:

> My weekends at Daytona, even though haunted with having to be back at the base by 11.00 o'clock Sunday, are almost perfect. I've gotten to know every little street, every little bar and any other things of interest in the town. .... I've been renting a triumph motorcycle over the weekends for cheap transportation and added excitement. I don't yet go in for this hundred miles an hour stuff, but for

dragging out at lights and hot-rodding on the beach, it's ideal... A triumph is as quick and as flashy as any motorcycle. This one is a '53 and is cheaply rented from a friend over the weekends so he can catch up on his payments for it ... Am thinking seriously of buying one temporarily while in this outfit to save traveling expenses and avoid the usual bus routine.

At the beginning of July 1954, Story graduated from the preparatory school in Jacksonville. Several days before, on 29 June, he wrote to Linwood:

I'm graduating from this preparatory school this coming Friday and yet am not too excited since I'm finishing this school just to start another advanced school which lasts twenty-two weeks. At my interview with the civilian counsel last week, I had, at that time, a 94 average so was thereby given the choice of any advanced aviation school I wanted. For practical reasons on my future farm and also because it is the second longest school in the USMC and I want as much as possible, I chose aviation electrician school which also is located here in Jacksonville. This school will take me up until Christmas when I hope to take a thirty-day leave and land a job somewhere... It's not definite now, but the odds are much in favor of my going to El Toro, California, or Kaneohe Bay, Hawaii, after finishing aviation electronics school. From either of these two bases I'll either go to a base in Indo-China, Korea, or on a Pacific fleet carrier. Everything in the future seems quite honorable and is just what I want.

Story recalled, "The preparatory school[1] was about two months and that was an introduction to aviation and to what airplanes are. The prep school was for everyone, whether you're going to be a sheet metal worker, a mechanic or whatever you're gonna be. After that was Naval Air School, Florida, and that was the specialty school of aviation, electricity and instruments. I was responsible for all the electricity – the batteries, the starters, the generators, all the lights. I had responsibility for every instrument – you look in the cockpit – I had every switch, I had every altimeter, airspeed, every instrument you see. So I was both electricity and instruments."

Over the next few months, things went more or less according to Story's plan. By early January 1955, he was stationed at El Toro, California, awaiting transportation on a troop ship to a foreign destination. On 9 January 1955, Story wrote to the family at Linwood:

January 28 seems to be the determined point that I'll go beyond the seas, so to speak. Am not too enthusiastic about it though, since I'm treated more like a human now than ever before and then, too, California is almost like Florida, which I do love very much. I still do want to go since this is the only way Asia would

1. Naval Air Station, Jacksonville, Florida.

ever be seen, since I'd never travel in that direction if a civilian. There are a pile of hotrods around this place, even more than California's reputation for them. They all sound like jets and are driven just that way.

Story's brother Percy responds to this letter, excited about an MG he has been borrowing to drive around town while "sitting next to a damned good looking Harvard Junior." Fast cars provided a topic for discussion which Story and Percy enjoyed very much. In his letter of 23 January 1955, Percy wrote to Story:

> I have decided that my dream car (when I make my first 1 million) will be a Mercedes Benz 300SL...What a car!...We will have a lot of fun 'dragging' around when you get your car in 1956... I sort of envy you, heading for a foreign country, while I am cooped up in Cambridge.[2]

Story is still unsure whether his overseas destination will be Korea or Formosa (Taiwan). In any case, he is leaving the United States at the end of January. He writes to Linwood:

> I have to get up at 1.55am in the morning to square away my gear, clean up the barracks and eat, and then board a train for San Diego where I'll get my ship. ... When we board the train tomorrow, a USMC band will be there to say goodbye, so it's quite an affair. Right now I'm looking forward to it very much and, being in the USMC, wouldn't want to do anything but this as I chose.

It is rapidly determined that Story's destination will, in fact, be Korea. He is to board the USNS *Gen. Brewster* in San Diego for a three week voyage, with a stopover in Japan.

On 3 March 1955, Story wrote to his father and stepmother:

> My trip over here was not very pleasant but lots more so than most of the boys since I don't seem to get seasick... The second day we hit a small storm which caused the bow to rise high in the air and then go way down to where the water was coming over it and sent a shudder through the whole ship. Almost everyone was horribly sick but somehow it didn't bother me much although I could have felt better. I spent three weeks on that tub and had had all I wanted by the time debarkation occurred.

He elaborated a little further in his letter of March 13 to his brother Percy, who intended to join the Navy:

> The ship ride here was not very pleasant to say the least. You'll probably find it

2. Percy was referring to college life at Harvard University, Cambridge Massachusetts, where he is an undergraduate.

> different, though, since you'll be an officer and have a private compartment. I don't
> seem to get sea sick which was a blessing to me on the trip. The food was worse
> than I'd ever seen before and I wouldn't even have put it in front of Toper[3] had I
> been home. The ship was only five hundred feet long and there were three
> thousand troops aboard, so sardines had nothing on us. The second day out we
> hit fairly rough seas, at least rough enough to cause the bow to rise way in the
> air and then crash down to where the water would be rolling over it. At that
> point, a shudder would run the length of the ship as if it were breaking in half.

Despite the rough ride, Story recalled his excitement at finally being at sea. He said, "Twenty something days on that thing…living so many floors down. But I would get out there and I'd look at the green and the blue water, I'd watch it for hours, the green and blue roll by. And the clouds – and watch the birds follow us all the way across the Pacific. And so even a troop ship was incredible. In terms of habitability, it was from some other world, but I still enjoyed that. It was an adventure – where is this thing going? I know intellectually that it's going eventually to Korea, but what is Korea? I mean I don't know what that place is.

"We landed at Inchon like a lot of other Marines: there were some famous Inchon landings. But that day was probably the coldest day of my life. I don't think I have ever been colder in my entire life. It was so cold you wanted to die. They didn't issue us the warm clothing until we got to the base, but we had, however, many miles to cover in an open trailer truck. We laid down on top of each other like sardines just hoping to get some warmth. It was so cold you couldn't go to the bathroom – you had to, but you couldn't. But it's an open bed trailer truck that's scooting along at forty miles an hour in the cold. We finally got there, to the air base, and I loved Korea. It was an adventure; it was learning another culture which I'd never gotten exposed to. And I loved the living conditions – people just left you alone, they just wanted you to work on the airplanes and so people didn't mess with you. There were no parades, they didn't come into your quarters and inspect your bed and your bureau and everything. They never came in there. You'd take care of the airplanes, that's what you're there for. Good job on the airplanes, you're like a professional. So I really enjoyed that part of Korea."

Story spoke of his new role to his brother. In the same letter of 13 March he wrote:

> My job here is of an aviation electrician on prop-driven fighters called ADs. As
> you probably already know, they can and do carry more of a bomb and rocket
> load than any other navy or marine fighter and are the mainstay in supporting the
> ground troops. They can carry twelve rockets and two bombs or a load of

3. The family dog.

fourteen smaller bombs. They also have four 20mm cannons in them. The reason I stick up for them so much is the fact that most civilians nowadays think that jets are the only good fighters. I'd much rather work on jets since they are simple and easier to work on.

On 16 March, he wrote excitedly to his mother, Marguerite, about his newly acquired flying experiences:

Due to my own persistent begging, asking, inquiring, etc I have been doing quite a bit of flying in various sorts of aircraft. Up until today, I'd never ridden in a jet fighter, but today after days of looking for a pilot etc to go to the trouble, I got a hop. The plane was a TV-2 which has two seats, one in the back of the other with a set of instruments and controls for each pilot. Usually two pilots go up, but I went instead of one pilot. It afforded odd circumstances which otherwise would not be possible. At one time today I was traveling upside down, another time I weighted 760 lbs and another time was going around 500 miles per hour. As you know I've always treasured the idea of experiences and this little flight adds around ten to my list. ... Also, have been flying in double rotor helicopters, which is another thing quite different from the normal routine of life.

Story laughed as he related how he came to be given those first exciting airplane rides. "In the Marine corps you ran the engine up before you gave it to the pilot. And you ran through a very, very detailed checklist. The pilots did not pre-flight the airplane – it sounds like heresy in the flying world, but no, you just assign responsibility to the crew chief to do the pre-flight. And if something goes wrong, it's not the pilot's error, it's the mechanic's error.

"You've got a young kid with 33 hundred horse power! I would run it full bore – at least the highest pressure I could at sea level – that's a technical thing. I'd run at the maximum pressure I was allowed to run at, but that is one big roar. And, of course, I'd back it off and there's no mufflers. You've got 33 hundred horse power; it just makes an outrageous noise. The pilots are drinking their coffee, waiting to fly and they see this young kid out there. He doesn't just run it up and check – everyone else is finished with the airplane – but I'm just taking endless time just roaring, you know. So they said, we have to fly this kid or he's going to wreck our airplanes!"

Korea was to be Story's base for only a month. By the middle of March 1955, he was already heading for Japan. On 16 March 1955, in a letter to Linwood he wrote:

Despite my love for this base and the Marine Corps [in Korea], I decided to continue my ever-present pursuit of adventure and volunteered for some sort of special detail and tomorrow am being flown to Japan for future transfer. After a couple of weeks there, the carrier WASP will take me to the permanent duty station. Don't know exactly where it will be, but since the WASP is in the seventh fleet, it most likely will be on or about Formosa. Hawaii is another possibility but quite remote and a little too good for my luck. ...Am flying in all sorts of aircraft and adding many experiences to my odd list. ...As you can probably disseminate from the general spunk of the letter, I feel in the best of health mentally and physically. Between experience, am trying to think of plans, goals, etc for the future.

On 10 April, 1955, almost a month later, Story was able to confirm his future in Hawaii. In a letter to his father he wrote:

The special detail landed me in Hawaii for several months I guess, but then, too, I expected to be in Korea several months. On the sixteenth of March we were flown to Japan where I expected to stay for longer than I did. The ten days I was there were days of complete freedom, except to check in once a day... I have been accepted to several colleges and will definitely be in college from January to June this next year... Can't wait to get out [of the Marines] in December and start something constructive, instead of ramming around all over the place.

The USS Wasp had carried Story from Japan to Hawaii. He described it impressively as "2400 men, 40,000 tons of steel, cruise at more than 32 knots, with power plants, complex telephone system, soda fountain and cobbler's shop, ship's stores and library plus dozens of other facilities."

According to Story, "I enjoyed Japan; I saw a little bit of Japan. And I liked that culture; I enjoyed meeting another culture, another bunch of people. And the WASP, the carrier, big machine that was! We went off to Kaneohe Bay, Hawaii, on the other side of the island there from Waikiki.

"I was at Marine Corp air station on the windward side of Kaneohe Bay and that was an attack squadron. That means, for the marine corps, the airplane is attacking the ground, as opposed to an airplane attacking another airplane fighter. The role was to attack things on the ground with bombs, rockets and cannons."

Story, as usual, found time for adventure outside his official duties. "Hawaii, of course, was paradise. I had a little motor cycle and I'd get a boat from what you'd call 'special services' and I'd go across Kaneohe Bay in my little boat, little outboard. Like Robinson Crusoe, I'd go across the bay in a little row boat!"

Shortly after his arrival in Hawaii, Story sat for the Military Test Report (High School Level). This was a GED or high school equivalency diploma, which he passed with stunning results. The test results stated:

Correctness and effectiveness of expression – 98 percentile
Interpretation of reading materials in the social studies – 88 percentile
Interpretation of reading materials in the natural sciences – 99 percentile
Interpretation of literary materials – 84 percentile
General mathematical ability – 99 percentile

In a moment of self-reflection, Story had written to his mother, Marguerite shortly before the examination. The letter was dated 10 May 1955:

> I am definitely going to college as soon as possible after being discharged. This is definite. I will have a Massachusetts State high school equivalency diploma shortly as I am just awaiting test results now. Also I will send a list of the colleges to you that accept this diploma. I am also told by officers that I can pass a two year college equivalency test and receive a certificate for it. This is equal to two years of college education and would get me into the Freshman class of almost any college. The test is coming up shortly.
>
> I want the college to be on the east coast and probably near home. I am going to get married in the summer of '56 or '57 and bring an end to this shifting, indifferent, no-interest, unconstructive, worthless, no-security, not-give-a-damn, miserable life that I have been living for the past seven years and nine months. It has been completely my own fault and I'm sorry you have had to be with me while I lived such a life but it's going to end with marriage, something to be responsible for, a goal in occupation and building a home etc!!

Meanwhile, Story continued to enjoy his time in Hawaii. He had purchased another motorcycle – a Triumph 650 Twin of English make – and had great fun riding along the mountain roads and the beaches.

Story's jet flying, however, had come to a temporary halt pending further safety training. He wrote to his father and stepmother on 29 May 1955:

> They are much more particular on safety precautions. I have to be blasted out of cockpits and [taught] the general procedure on the whole for bailing out of a disabled plane. These jets are so fast that you can't climb out of them and jump as you can in most planes: you simply eject the canopy and then pull two triggers on the seat you are strapped into. This sets off an explosive which blasts you out of the plane and about sixty feet above it. From here you unbuckle yourself, step off the seat into space and then pull the rip cord for the parachute. I also have to be tested for different changes in gravitational force called positive or negative "g" units. Can't wait to get back into the air. If I could become a jet pilot I would undoubtedly make a career of it but, fortunately, for a lot of things, my eyes prevent me from doing this.

Admittedly, I am building some sort of character out of my self with various experiences, but in what direction the building is going towards, I am not sure. If it builds much more I'll probably be too eccentric to even live with. Well, time, as always, will bring about the unpredictable future.

In June 1955, as he had mentioned to his mother, Story sat for the second set of exams – the Military Test Report (College Level). Again, his results were very satisfactory:

Correctness and effectiveness of expression – 74 percentile
Interpretation of reading materials in the social studies – 75 percentile
Interpretation of reading material in the natural science – 95 percentile
Interpretation of literary materials – 81 percentile

This was good news, indeed, as Story began to prepare for life after the Marines – in college. On 7 November, 1955, he received a Certificate of Admission from Syracuse University, Syracuse, New York, which stated:

I am happy to inform you that you have been admitted to the college of Business Administration for February 1956. You have been allowed the following 19 entrance units: 4 English, 3 French, 2 Latin, 1 and a half Algebra, 1 Plane Geometry, half Trigonometry, 1 Civics, 1 Biology, 1 Chemistry, 1 General Science, 1 Physics, 2 other electives. This record is based upon credentials on file in this office.

Meanwhile, on 10 November, Story wrote to his brother Percy of an accident while undergoing jet ejection training:

I had my first frightening experience in aviation just recently and it happened not in a flying jet, but in a training device on the ground. The training device is a simulated cockpit of a jet with a very long extended track for the ejection seat. It is meant to train pilots and qualified crew members on ejecting themselves from a crippled jet. After the usual emergency procedures, one pulls the face mask down and is blasted out. Instead of into the air, though, you follow a track until hitting the top and come gradually down. In my unfortunate case, the power charge blew out the bottom of the chamber and spread burning powder throughout my cockpit. The powder was burning like hell and also the cockpit caught fire. The smoke was so horribly thick, I couldn't possibly breathe, so held my breath and it started to get hotter than hell in there. I couldn't unstrap myself from the seat and get out because at any time the seat might blow out with the remaining powder burning in the chamber. By the time my breath was out and my trouser legs were on fire, they started pumping $CO_2$ at a freezing temperature into the cockpit. This immediately put out the fire and cooled me off, as well as pushing the smoke out. In an hour or so the chamber was replaced and the cockpit cleaned up, so I climbed back in and blasted out in the usual manner.

Story spoke of the high fatality record among the Marine pilots at his base. "We were losing people left and right, and we were losing people often. We lost six out of twenty-two pilots – this is on the base at Hawaii – and so death kind of came home. We lost more than a quarter of the pilots to various flying accidents.

"We, as the enlisted people, never learned any of the facts. None. And it would leak down to us, but there was a difference in the Marine Corps between officers and enlisted men. There's a lot [of things] that didn't cross that barrier. We didn't live together, we didn't talk together, we didn't socialize together. The marine corps in those days was total separation.

"You would know, indirectly, that some were missing – they would become missing. We would launch every single airplane we could possibly get airborne, so we knew that they didn't have the body, or the airplane. They told us, 'Launch every single airplane that you can get airborne'. When they told us to do that and told us that we had to do it now, you know, you go in the hangar and throw pieces together. You just get everything in the air you can. So we knew it was a search party, we knew people were missing. When you saw all the other squadrons down the line launching every airplane they had, it was a search party. But then, of course, you'd read the newspaper too. That was kind of rough; it wasn't going to war but it was a lot of people dying.

"Airplane quality was very good. This was not the airplane's fault, that we know of. We have no evidence, we don't know, it could have been the airplane's fault. But the airplane record gets frozen when the airplane doesn't come back – all those things you've signed off to say this is a flyable airplane. But there was no evidence.

"Going to the funeral with the spouses there – you know, a twenty-two-year-old spouse – is grim. All these pilots are in their twenties. And especially when we kept having deaths, it must have really shaken the spouses, 'cause they'd know… With each subsequent one, they had to know the risks that were involved."

By early December 1955, Story's Marine Corps tour was coming to an end. By mid-December, he wrote to his mother and to his father and stepmother at Linwood, saying that he was back in the United States and stationed at Treasure Island in San Francisco Bay. He expected to be discharged by the end of the year.

Story's official discharge from the US Marine Corps came on 3 January 1956. His plan was to head directly to Lansing, Michigan, to pick up his new car – an Oldsmobile Super 88 Convertible, which he had just purchased.

Story explained, "I found it through a very nice man that lived in Palo Alto, California. I don't know what his connection was, but we got word that this man could get us cars for under buy-at-cost from the factory. He came and met me there and we did all the paper work. I still don't know who this man was; I don't know how I got onto the man except that it went through squadron at the Marine Corps: here are the prices this man will offer these marines."

Story recalled the train journey to Michigan and the hospitality extended to a wandering Marine.

"From Treasure Island, I got on the Santa Fe Super Chief; it was great. I remember the Super Chief 'cause it was a heck of a day. It was the day in the transition between my life in the Marine Corps and the next life; it was an incredible day, a euphoric day, a transitional day.

"I had me a Rocket 88! But that was spectacular: you know I came out of the Marine Corps an enlisted man, then that was a great journey, back when trains were really trains. It was an incredible ride from Santa Fe to Lansing; just glorious. I'm getting out of the Marine Corps and I don't know what's happening next, but I'm going forward, I'm going to Lansing in Michigan to pick up my new car. You know what I mean? – you leap off! Where's the trail next? Don't know where the trail is, but I'm on a super train in the dark, going to pick up my Rocket 88 and head East – I'm not sure where, not sure where the car will take me, but I'm on the way.

"So I get to Lansing and I get off the train. I'm looking around for a while – what do I do now? I have to get to the factory – I don't know where the hell I am or what I'm doing or how I get there or when. And this family came running up and said, 'You look a little lost.' I said, 'Yeah I am.' So they said, 'Why don't you come home and get your feet on the ground and then find out what you got to do?' They just took me home! That's what they did to Marines in the old days; they took you home. No matter where you went, they took you home. Military's different like that. They had a nice daughter too and they, the family, took me and the daughter out dancing. Well that's the way things worked, I guess!"

Story spoke of his time in the US Marine Corps from the distance of fifty years. At the time, like many young men, it was about adventure and it was about joining the war effort, in this case, the Korean War.

He said, "I didn't know anything about war, I had no idea. A seventeen-year-old, what do they know? What do I know about war affairs? But on the other hand, I was the kind of person who, simplemindedly enough, if there was a war on, I'd have gone off to war. If I'd been aged seventeen and WWII came along, I'd have gone off to war. I think at that young age, you don't really know what you're fighting about and who the good guys and bad guys are; it's not very clear – you go to war. So I would have gone to war if I'd had a war to go to and I would have gotten [to Korea] earlier if I could have."

The romantic memories of that life have endured, despite the fact that a harsher reality intruded on a daily basis during those military years.

"I enjoyed the camaraderie, I enjoyed the discipline, I enjoyed an efficient, effective outfit. I enjoyed that way of life if your purpose is to go off to war. I enjoyed the travel, the training, getting to learn aircraft, the flying. I enjoyed pretty much the spirit of things."

The rougher side of the Marine Corp life was not something that was talked about, although Story finds himself questioning those values today.

"It was rough, but I did exceedingly well. I was extraordinarily adept and adaptable, and I was a survivor and I knew how to survive; I knew how to work in a hidden way, how to work my own agenda, and I was fantastically hardy, given the two environments that I came from. I had learnt the ropes!"

Story was referring to the hard physical treatment and dealings with virtually all the enlisted, something which was accepted at the time as part of the process.

"At the time, I thought what was going on was a rational process, because you have the starting point here, and in three months, you will be a Marine. There are people whom the judge has told – you go to jail or you go to the Marine Corps. It was used like that in those days. So you get a very heterogeneous group that, in three months, must become Marines, ready to go to war. And so for me, I saw the process, I saw what came in the pipeline, and I saw what exited. I understood the process and I accepted the process – and of, course, did very well in it.

"But as the years have progressed, I have looked at means versus ends morality and I do not accept what went on then. They were rough in basic training and basically pretty rough from there on, but they certainly do create a war machine. If you go to war and the person next to you is a Marine, they're going to go and kill out of anger for what they've been through – they're gonna take it out on the enemy!"

"But anyway, philosophically, I don't think the ends justify those means, so it was kind of a rough life. But even in basic training, I had a very good life, so I came in there equal to everyone else without having any particular station. And I did exceedingly well – I was exceedingly adaptive, I accepted the process as necessary to have a three month production line, with heterogeneous people from all walks of life, including people that were criminals, and you had to come out the end with someone that you would go to war with, and I understood that. And I saw the people that came out the other end and said, yeah, if I've got to go to war, those are the people I want. And so my attitude at the time was far more positive than now – I accepted it, and I was proud that I was there, and I went through it. And so it made me a Marine. I accepted it, but at this late current age where I am now, I look at the people who went through and I look at the people who didn't make it through. So I look at the entire process."

So what did Story carry with him through life, as a result of having been a Marine?

He said, "I think the most important thing, like everything else, is I carried myself. And so if you look back to my childhood, I don't know how influential that environment was on forming me – it was my memory of how I did in that environment. I was always my own anchor, my self-anchor.

"And so what I carried forth from the Marine Corps is how I went through that – the memory of what I was as a Marine and my own identity there, as opposed to the environment."

# 7. The Road to Medicine

Surgeons must be very careful
When they take the knife!
Underneath their fine incisions
Stirs the culprit,—*Life!*

*Emily Dickinson*

When Story Musgrave enrolled at Syracuse University in 1956, he had difficulty deciding which department to join. Fortunately, math was of interest – the beauty of mathematical equations – and beyond that, he thought business studies would provide a useful background to whatever lay ahead in his career, whether it be farming or otherwise. So Story decided to join the School of Management.

He said, "I liked playing with numbers so majored in math, multi-variant statistics and probability theory. What really appealed to me in those disciplines was the sense of mystery and the uncertainties inherent in both the problems and the solutions, despite the medium of mathematics."[1]

Story's interest in computers grew during his time at Syracuse and after completing his studies there, he sought the best computer education center in the country. At that time, it was at the University of California, Los Angeles (UCLA).

He recalled, "That was before the era of the personal computer, when large computers and punch cards took up whole rooms."

For Story, the passion for computers went deeper than the desire to learn the technical side. A computer was a machine, and just like all the other machines in his life, he animated them: "There was a romantic notion. The computer was a being for me… I animated the computer the way I animated everything… I programmed, but mostly I would go there and sit and look at it, just mesmerized by the size… this huge box of tapes, just doing their little motions to find the right place you know on the track… it's zipping up and down and all the lights… I'd sit, watch and listen and … it had nothing to do with computers. I animated the thing but I had more excitement doing that than my technical work in programming."

However, Story quickly found a greater interest beyond his fascination for computers. As always, it was the human aspect which attracted him: "I got into [computers] and I instantly had to get to the human brain… I had to get back to the body and the human being."

According to Story, "Operations research and computers in Graduate School at UCLA, led me into the fields of artificial intelligence, neurophysiology and the mind."[2]

It was the writings of W. Ross Ashby, Claude Shannon and Norbert Wiener that helped Story leap from computing to the brain, motivating him to continue his college studies, this time within the discipline of medicine. He applied to a number of universities, including Columbia University in New York City, and hoped to combine the study of neurophysiology with a career in neurosurgery.

Story explained, "I'd always done that – that is, reached a certain level of proficiency in one discipline and then seen the bridges and looked at ways where it would lead to the next step."

1. Written by Story for St Mark's School, Southborough, 50th Anniversary publication of the class of 1953.
2. As above.

That was true again when, in 1964, as Story was working through his medical internship in Lexington, Kentucky, NASA announced it would fly scientists in space. That was exactly what Story wanted to do! Space flight would enable him to combine just about everything he loved – mechanics, medicine, flying and computing.

In order to improve his chances of selection, Story threw himself into post-doctoral research in physiology and took on biophysics and pharmacology courses towards achieving two further degrees: a Master of Science degree and PhD.

In an interview for *New Texas*, he told Kyle Swanson: "[NASA] almost didn't take me because they said I was so over-trained that I might not be comfortable. I had about six earned degrees at that time, and everything else that I was doing in life, and an active laboratory, and a surgical practice and all these other things going on."[3]

But for Story Musgrave, a career in space flight did lie beyond the road to medicine. And, as it turns out, through the convergence of all of these paths, he was a perfect fit.

*

Story wrote: "I shall be forever thankful to Syracuse University for opening its doors to a Korean Veteran without a [high] school diploma."[4]

For some time, Story had contemplated Syracuse University in New York state as the place to continue his education. It was, in fact, one of his Marine Corp associates who encouraged him to think of Syracuse. He recalled, "A pilot told me about Syracuse, about all the nice things there, even though he went to Pennsylvania State University. I don't know why he recommended Syracuse, but he did. He painted a picture and I said, 'I'll look into that.'"

Before leaving the Marine Corps, Story wrote to his father and stepmother:

> I am still very interested in agriculture but do not and will not, for quite a while, have the capital it takes to go into farming. In the meantime, I will have to pursue another occupation – unknown as of yet – along my interests and aptitudes.[5]

Story arrived at Syracuse University at the beginning of 1956 and delved heavily into mathematics and business courses. He worked hard and achieved good results, settling well into the routine of college life.

On 5 February 1956, Story wrote of his new experiences to his father and stepmother at Linwood:

> Although Syracuse is quite a ways further than Boston, it is naturally a much easier trip in both time and effort. The town of Syracuse is of course large, having a population of over

---

3. January 2002, feature on *Passionate Careers*.
4. Written by Story for St Mark's School, Southborough, 50th Anniversary publication of the class of 1953.
5. Letter dated 30 October 1955.

220,000 and is spread out all over the place. All the university streets and buildings are familiar to me already and most of the important streets downtown are known well enough to navigate to and from the university and to the Olds[6] garage, nightlife, movies etc. The university is completely separate from the city and doesn't have the city traffic running right through the middle of it. It is quite large because of 13,000 students but any of the buildings can be reached on foot in ten minutes. The campus is extremely beautiful with typical elms and lawns everywhere. I have moved my spirit de corps from the Marines to Syracuse, so have a lot more pride in my college than most students who don't quite know what the word means yet.

The College of Business Administration has a whole assortment of interesting majors which interest me greatly. My whole four years here will probably be in that same college. Three of the majors that seem quite interesting and develop directly into good jobs are production management, real estate and business law.

Syracuse has almost as many girls as boys here which is exceptional for any university… There is so much to do and so many pleasant people to do things with that studies aren't going to get much of my time, but we can hope enough. Veterans[7] in the Freshman's class are permitted cars and all other upper class privileges. I have complete freedom except just to pass all my courses …

The courses this year are fairly stiff. As Bun[8] will know, economics isn't easy to integrate and is quite complex. Accounting is a striking combination of math, logic and English. The others are English, zoology, business administration and physical education. I elected to take wrestling as my Phys Ed so I should get a good mark there. I have around 12 hours of classes in the afternoon during the week so I don't think I'll be able to work in wrestling this year except for two classes a week. The food is naturally much more appetizing than it was at the USMC… Everything is quite well here and I couldn't be having a better time.

One particular teacher at Syracuse who influenced Story during this time was Morris Boudin. Story recalled, "Dr Boudin taught statistics, probability theory. There were about five of us who would simply take everything he taught, just to be in his class. We did statistics a little bit, but mostly we just talked about life. And so that was what his course was about: he just kind of taught us about life. We liked to watch his mind think and liked to watch his perspective. And so that's why we did that. So it was both him and about five of us. You loved to have a class in which you have students who are really on the edge and thinking. If the students are all dead in the class, no matter how good the professor, you can't make a class out of it. And so it was not only Morris Boudin, it was the students – the real thinkers of the business school that liked to just go in there and plain old think."

One noteworthy fact about Story's academic life at Syracuse was that he

6. Oldsmobile
7. Story is a Veteran of the Korean War.
8. Story's older brother Percy was often referred to within the family as "Bun".

completed a four year Bachelor's Degree in just two and a half years and was on the Dean's list three years in a row. According to J.P. Goldman, of the *Syracuse Herald American*, "School of Management officials today can't recall the last time a student completed the rigorous degree requirements in less than 3 years. Musgrave roared through the School of Management curriculum."[9]

Story took day classes on the main campus, night classes at the University college, and summer courses – sometimes accumulating 24 credit hours per semester.[10] He worked incredibly hard to achieve these results but still found time for other pursuits. He became a varsity letterman in wrestling and also participated in jazz, jitterbug and swing, winning several all-university dancing competitions from 1956 to 1958. Story said he enjoyed physical, gymnastic dances with a good, strong beat. He had learnt to dance while stationed in Florida with the Marines, back in the days when Elvis played at the local movie theatres down there. Stylishly dressed and confident, Story was never short of a dancing partner.

Significantly, during this time, Story met his first wife, Patricia van Kirk, of Patterson, New Jersey, who was also a student at the University.

Patricia Musgrave laughed as she recalled their first meeting: "I was in the cafeteria and my back was to Story. I had this long, long hair – it was down my back, straight – and he saw that hair, and thought, 'Oh, I've got to meet her'! He didn't see my face, he saw my hair! So he came over. He was in wrestling at the time, so he had this big plate of spinach. He was trying to get down to 145 pounds or so – he was in the lightweight college wrestling – and so he came around and sat down at the table and we talked. I enjoyed meeting him and I thought – how curious, he's just eating spinach! So he would look for me and we would meet in the cafeteria. Then he called and we started going out and seeing each other, but it was very low key, you know.

"I remember we bought shirts that were the same, plaid shirts, and so we had a lot of fun times together. When I broke my ankle, he came over every day to the hospital. It was a bad break – they had to put a pin in. I was a dancer and had studied dance – ballet – and I could no longer continue that, but we jitterbugged at Syracuse University. In the 1950s it was the jitterbug, that was really *the* dance. And we played around with the Charleston – only because I could really do a good Charleston. But our favorite was the jitterbug; we loved it."

Of his studies at that time, Story recalled that he was "good, but not a thinker yet." He enjoyed philosophy courses, he was methodical. However, he believes the real intellectual explosion came in Graduate School while taking business problems and moving them into the mathematical world.

---

9. *Syracuse Herald American*, 3 April 1983. Article titled: *Astronaut Roared Through SU* by J.P. Goldman. Reprinted with permission.
10. As above.

To this day, Story retains a great fondness for Syracuse University – for providing him with the opportunity for education. He was quoted in the *Syracuse Herald-Journal*, saying: "I have tremendous affection for this place. This is where it all began for me." During his first space flight, STS-6, Story demonstrated this by flying one of the University's banners.[11]

Before commencing graduate studies, Story spent the summer of 1958 as a mathematician and operations analyst for the Eastman Kodak company in Rochester, New York. During August of that year, he wrote to his father and stepmother of his experiences:

> I have enjoyed my work with Eastman Kodak Co. very much. It could not have possibly been a better job. .. I have my own little office with a private telephone and my own calculator etc. This summer I have been developing a new inventory control system, so I have been on my own most of the time. ... The research I am doing has to do with programming inventory control for the IBM705 electronic computer system. When this is completed, the machine will tell you how much of each of hundreds of thousands of items are in stock.[12]

In September of 1958, Story headed to graduate school in California to begin a Master of Business Administration degree in operations analysis and computer programming at UCLA. He settled comfortably as a boarder in a private residence not far from the University Campus. Upon leaving Syracuse, Story had purchased his first Corvette and driven it west to California. In a letter he wrote:

> Got it up to 142 miles per hour on the Santa Ana freeway one night. That is about as fast as it will go. I had three white stripes painted down the center of the car. ... this really makes the car look like the racing machine it is... As you can see, my studies are not reducing me to an academic intellectual – which they never will. I'm not cut out for that!"[13]

Story enjoyed a very active social life in Los Angeles, attending parties and escorting some well-connected young women to various society events about town. During this time, however, he continued to correspond with Patricia, for whom he had had very serious intentions.

Patricia explained, "I just didn't want to get married right away; I just couldn't settle down. And so we went our ways when he graduated from Syracuse, but he kept in contact with me."

In fact, it was the death of Story's eldest brother, Percy, in a Navy accident,

11. November 10, 1983.
12. Letter dated 15 August 1958.
13. Letter dated 4 February 1959.

which was instrumental in reuniting Story and Patricia during 1959. According to Patricia, "Everything changed when Bunny [Percy] died. It was spring break, my last year in college, and Story called me up and said, 'Can you come and see me, I lost my brother.' And I called up my folks and I said, 'You know, I don't know if I should do this.' And if I didn't, we probably wouldn't have married.

"But when Bunny died, I did go to see Story at his Mom's house in Pittsfield 'cause he was suffering so much, and that's what put us back together again. We got married shortly after."

Story explained the main reason for moving to California. "I'm looking for the most advanced computing center in the world – and that was at UCLA.

"I had gotten into operations research and computers at UCLA. The operations research part of that study was really more important to me, more exciting to me than the programming aspect of what I was doing. I was enamored by the personality of the computers; I animated them. I was fascinated by the tape motions and this idea of a building-sized thing being a thinking machine."

While working with computers, Story became interested in the human brain. This would, inevitably, change the course of his career: "As is almost everywhere, my principal inspiration, motivation and the thing that formed my foundation, the thing that led to me leaping off into a different discipline, did not happen to be the people that I was there face to face with. And so, of course, the people I was face to face with would be teaching computers or teaching business – not leading you astray into other areas. But the real inspiration there was the reading that I was doing; reading that was beyond the coursework – like *Design for a Brain*, by [W. Ross] Ashby; communications theory by Claude Shannon [*A Mathematical Theory of Communication*]; and Cybernetics by Norbert Wiener [*Cybernetics: or Control and Communication in the Animal and the Machine*].

"Gray Walter had these little robots running around, but it was those people, and the earliest computers called the Eniac and the Brainiac, that were built somewhat after the understanding people had of the nervous system – I read about them. So that was the key thing there; it was reading the neurophysiology and reading the people who were walking the two different worlds with one leg in each world.

"But that's pretty much true of my entire life. The real inspiration, the mentors, the motivators, the people that formed my foundation or that built the bridges for me to go from one place to another, were not so much the people I was in day to day contact with, but they were people who were on the edge and doing the writing and all.

"But it was, as always had been characteristic, that for whatever book I had in class, I would read another three or four as kind of corollaries. But I started reading,

I'm not sure why, but I got interested in – here's a human brain hardware thing that does some functions like a brain. So I got interested – I had no idea how the brain would do the same things. And so I started reading books like Walter Ashby's *Design for a Brain*, and Grey Walter's early work – he built robotic tortoises; he built little robots, even though he was, by occupation, an electrical encephalographer. I started reading Claude Shannon's communications theory; I started reading Norbert Weiner's *Cybernetics*, which was the earliest sort of a philosophical look at what computers might mean. I was fascinated with the early computers. So I'm not sure why, but I started reading about the fields that interconnected – what we knew of the relationship between brains and computer hardware, and I was fascinated with that. It turns out that a lot of the early computer architecture came from what little was known of the brain, and so the people who were trying to design computers were looking at that area to try to get some things."

By the time he graduated from UCLA, Story knew that he wanted to study the brain, preferably at a college in the eastern states, so he headed back across the country, stopping at Marietta, Ohio, along the way. It was then that he decided, almost immediately, to begin premedical studies at Marietta College, being totally captivated by both the town, the educational facilities and college staff. In order to boost the number of credited studies for the course, Story enrolled in summer school at Syracuse University in June of 1959 and spent a few months there before returning to Marietta in September to begin his Bachelor of Arts degree in chemistry.

Story's mother, Marguerite, joined him for that year of study, which he later described as "a wonderful year with Mom." They both loved Marietta. "It was the ambiance, it was the elms, the brick streets and the rivers really that formed the place," according to Story.

The college atmosphere at Marietta suited Story and he did well in his studies. Somewhat ironically, he believes that one of the most important courses he took at that time was a speech course.

He recalled, "The speech course I took was fairly instrumental. I wasn't sure quite what speech was, but, of course, I ended up doing it my whole life. And I almost instantly recognized the importance of speech and communication: if you can't communicate what you've got, well you're not going to go very far. You got to be able to communicate in whatever medium you decide to work.

"So it turned out that the speech course was the most important course, probably, that I took in my entire college career. It gets down to human communications and it gets down to what I do right now – and that is communication: taking the experience and moving it into some art form. I won contests and that kind of thing, but what I learned there was what I do now, basically.

"Ronald Loreman[14] – I've kept up with him over the years – I had a very nice time with him, despite the fact I was in a premedical curriculum with a major in chemistry."

The summer of 1960 brought about further changes in Story's life. After graduating from Marietta, he married Patricia van Kirk and relocated once again to begin his medical studies.

Story and Patricia were both excited about the move to New York City. It was a place far removed from their previous experiences and full of its own culture and diversity. Story had had big city experience before, having lived in both Boston and Los Angeles, but that was somewhat different to the sea of skyscrapers and fast-paced living of the great eastern metropolis. And Patricia had spent most of her life in nearby New Jersey, without really experiencing what New York was all about.

"It's just a huge place any way you want to look at it, but we did not in any way find it overwhelming; we just found it fantastic. It was entertaining; it was wonderful all the way around. That experience was just very, very rich," Story recalled.

Story and Patricia established their home in a fifth-floor, one-bedroom, walk-up apartment, just a short distance from the University[15] – on West 173rd Street, right by the George Washington Bridge. They had little money and lived in the middle of the city for less than $1800 per year, including their $100 a month rent. During those four years in New York, the three eldest Musgrave children were born – Lorelei Lisa, Bradley Scott and Holly Kay.

Story said, "We lived on [the remaining] $600 a year, five of us, and so we lived on nothing. But the wonderful thing about New York was that you did not need money to have a great time. The subway was unbelievably inexpensive and to go to the parks, to go to Times Square and sit on a bench, it costs nothing. And we had very young children – we went to New York for four years and one of them arrived every spring – and the young kids had a grand time there; just a fantastic time."

Patricia remembered: "They were good years. My mother would come in once a week to baby sit and I would go to the museum, I would go do something fun. She loved to come in and take care of the grandchildren, of course, and she brought in the pork chops and steaks for us 'cause we lived on fifteen dollars a month for food. I sewed the children's clothes. I continued to sew the children's clothes when we went to Kentucky, so they had matching dresses and whatever. We also had a couple on our floor – a police officer and his wife – and she took care of the children for a couple of

14. Ronald Loreman conducted the speech course which Story attended at Marietta College.
15. Columbia University, New York City, where Story would complete his Doctorate in Medicine.

hours while I would go grocery shopping, so that helped a lot."

Patricia, who loved swimming, became a lifeguard at the medical school's swimming pool and also took art and cooking classes. Her social life, like Story's, revolved around the medical fraternity. She recalled, "The medical students – Story's friends – became my friends. They came over on Wednesday nights and we would watch *The Untouchables*. Someone would bring the beer and I would make a cake. And we would just sit down and watch *The Untouchables* and laugh and that was our relaxation in the middle of the week. You know, two hours or so. And we'd have cake and beer. Great combination!"

Patricia recalled that when she was almost due with her daughter Holly, her new friends gave her a baby shower. "The fellows gave me a baby shower! I didn't have any girl friends there – my friends were in New Jersey and everyone was scattered anyway – and so the fellows gave me the baby shower. It was really good!"

The College of Physicians and Surgeons (P&S) at Columbia University has a unique history. It was founded in 1807 in the City of New York and, in 1813, merged with the medical department at Columbia College, the second oldest medical school in the country – formed in 1767 as part of King's College, as it was then known. The combined entity continued to use the name P&S, and in 1928, when it joined with the city's Presbyterian Hospital, it became the first combined academic and medical center in the country.[16]

Story had considered several universities in which to commence his medical studies – including John Hopkins, Harvard and George Washington – but was completely won over by the atmosphere at Columbia. As always, Story listened to his emotions, his bodily reaction, when making a decision of this magnitude:

"I selected Columbia just out of pure emotions and when I saw it, it was all over – I cancelled all further interviews, everything. I turned down the acceptances that I'd had to other places and that was it.

"I don't know what I *liked* about it – I *loved* the place! It's hard to say but it's a feel for a place and it says, 'this is my place.' And, of course, it was absolutely immense; it was huge and it was in the middle of the city. But it was a powerful place; you sensed that this is a going place in terms of research, the number of hospital beds. Every single department has a huge building – the Department of Neurosurgery has its own building, the Neurological Institute, and so you just look around and you say, 'Wow, this place is humming!'

"And so, this place is humming and the city's humming and it just looked alive

16. *Source:* The Neurological Institute of New York, Columbia University, website: http://www.healthsciences.columbia.edu/dept/neurology/

– looked very big and very alive – but it was also personable. I liked the people that I spoke with, I liked what they said about the school, but it gets down to your intuition, your intuitive feelings.

"When I got done with the interviews there, that was it. I had other interviews the next few days, but I simply cancelled them. But on that day, even though it's not a written commitment and they don't really say in hard words that you are accepted, I told them, 'This is it, I want to come here.' And so I got the expression from their faces and got the indirect communication that I was 'in'.

"And so that was it. And, of course, I have loved that decision ever since. P&S had extraordinary teachers; that's what it was noted for. It's a fantastic research institute, one of the greatest medical research centers. And I adored the medical school, I loved the medical school and I love it more and more every year; every time I go back there. I adore that place; it has really solid, fantastically good memories."

As a medical student in a big city, Story was exposed to a wide variety of clinical experiences – both with private and public patients.

He recalled, "The opportunities with teaching partnerships that Columbia had with hospitals all over the city was extraordinarily rich. It also took us to different parts of the city and to meet with really diverse cultural backgrounds.

"We did clerkships, which means that you're functioning as an intern: you have all the responsibilities that an intern has. You take the history of the patient, you do the physical exam and you actually write the orders for the care that is needed. You're a clerk but you're functioning as an intern, taking orders and directing patient care because you're in your third or your fourth year and you have had quite a bit of experience, especially in a big city and a medical school such as this.

Parallel to Story's general medical studies, he became involved in neurophysiology with the mentoring of a brilliant neuroscientist, Dr Dominic Purpura, who is world-renowned for his work in this field and later became Dean of the Albert Einstein College of Medicine.

Story explained, "At medical school you didn't major in anything. But within months of arriving at Columbia, I was working on the nervous system – I had a job in the Department of Neurosurgical Research. The name of the department does not reflect what they did; they did fundamental neurophysiology although they might do some neurosurgical research. But I saw that title on the door on the way to class and I said, 'Well, I'll go in there.' And so I went in there and that was that.

"I had my own experiments involved with epilepsy. I created epileptic lesions in the cerebral cortex of animals and studied the process of epilepsy – that was my research. But I started pulling electrodes for the other team who were studying the behavior of individual cells."

Dr Purpura recalled Story's time in the laboratory. "We were probably the only group at Columbia that was doing some physiological studies on the cerebral cortex. And that, of course, was intriguing to him, since, to this day, forty years later, it remains the great frontier of the inner space.

"Story quickly became very skilled in preparing animals. We used cats in our studies and he very quickly picked up the neurosurgical skills to prepare the animal for some detailed studies. We were doing rather pioneering work in recording with very, very fine electrodes inside nerve cells in the living animal, which was an extraordinarily tedious task. And I must say that more than once, Story's energy carried the day to continue working, almost without fatigue, in trying to get impalements of cells in the cerebral cortex that we could then activate by appropriate stimulation."

Story remembered, "I did get rather good at pulling electrodes – and they'd have to be one micron or two across. That's very, very small; that's less than a red blood cell. And you fill them with potassium chloride and you record inside a cell without hurting the cell. But I got so I could look in the microscope and tell which electrodes were going to be effective, which electrodes would get you the information and not hurt the cell. And that was a visual intuitive kind of thing. I built my own relationship between what I saw in the microscope – looking at the cell tips and how they perform. So in a way I was becoming sort of an indispensable part of the team."

It was not unusual for Story to work long into the night to achieve results and carry the experiment forward. Dr Purpura recalled one particular episode: "It must have been about 8 o'clock at night, at the end of a long day. At that point, my feeling was that I was going home! I'd had enough of trying to get some impalements and Story said, 'No, I think there's more to this animal. I'm going stay on and see what I can get'. Well I've got to tell you, I walked in the next morning about 9.30am and Story was still with the cat! Although it hadn't been terribly rewarding, he was extraordinarily persistent to see whether he could get some more cells and he had some. And to me it was absolutely amazing that he'd had the energy to continue. I had really felt, at that time, that maybe we should dispatch the animal, but Story went ahead with it. I think that's an extraordinary example, to me, of just Story being 'Story'. I didn't make it as a command or an order, but I made it clear that I didn't think from my experience that much more was going to happen. But since we weren't in the marines and we didn't have a chain of command, we accepted Story in the laboratory like any other faculty member – the students were part of our family and, as such, had almost equal opportunity to express themselves."

For Story, it was not only a challenge, but a remarkable opportunity to be working and gaining experience in this laboratory: "I got to where I was running the experiments. I was doing my own surgery for my own stuff, but then I started doing the surgery for the other team. And so I would come in at 4 or 5am and do the surgery – and here I am a freshman or a sophomore doing surgery!"

Dr Purpura described the work they were doing as quite significant. "It was a very, very remarkable year we had. We published a paper which has become very classical in the field – on Cortical Intracellular Potentials. We were studying two very important types of responses that reflect the character of brainwaves and looking at the ways in which different cells responded to these. And this work has, over the years, been recognized for defining two major kinds of pathways to the cerebral cortex. That's not terribly important – but it is important to indicate that Story played a very important role in the back-breaking and difficult task at that time to study these cells."

Story's own satisfaction was evident. "Dr. Purpura was generous enough to make me a co-investigator. Through that mechanism, I got to publish some very good papers as a medical student within the branch of neurophysiology. I was getting established in brain research even as a medical student, so all of that went exceedingly well. It was publicly funded research, but it was not part of the medical school curriculum. Nothing I did in that lab was formally part of the medical school curriculum – I did that in addition to medical school.

"I was not a theoretical genius, nor did I know neurophysiology that well, but I was a pragmatist – I knew how to make things happen. I was, again, just good with my hands: the physical world of pulling electrodes and looking with the eyeball at electrodes and making the relationship with what worked and [how it] looked. And, you know, my surgery and that stuff, it was sort of back to the physical again; it was sort of back to what you can do with the hands. So it was mostly what I did with the hands that put me in those positions. My own work on epilepsy,  I had to know the literature and I had to write that up and present those things."

"I published quite a few papers once I got into my post doctoral Fellowships, in the realm of aerospace medicine. My papers were the neurophysiological ones that came out of Columbia as a medical student and the ones I did in physiology and biophysics as a Post Doctoral Fellow and in the aerospace physiology field."[17]

Dr Purpura enjoyed working with Story and found him to be very personable and always enthusiastic. "It was to our advantage [to have Story's participation]. The advantage was that he was an energy dynamo to really keep that particular work going. Like I could walk in the next morning and see him just as bright as if fifteen hours hadn't gone by; it was amazing.

"I noticed another thing: I never found him depressed as some students would

17. A list of research papers, authored or co-authored by Story Musgrave, appears at the end of this book.

get during the time they're doing research. There's a certain smile that he always has and I think I've seen that continuously, even when we met a couple of years ago over dinner together. He was the same Story – the guy hadn't changed in forty years. And I went back and I told my wife that Story's still 'Story.' Back then, we had a home in New Jersey and we would have parties where all the students were invited. And my young kids hadn't seen a bald-headed guy like that. More importantly, we hadn't seen anybody getting so involved with children the way he did.

"Part of his whole persona was the continuously happy sort of guy, ready to take on any kind of mission that I gave him, which sometimes was extremely tedious. He didn't seem to get bored with tedium, that's for sure."

A jovial atmosphere pervaded the lab. According to Dr Purpura, "We all had fun. If we didn't have fun, what the heck were we doing? We weren't making any money! Story, myself and a couple of others – we really enjoyed the day, even when experiments went badly, which many did. So I think Story was a very positive part of that."

As Dr Purpura reflected on those times, especially Story's persistence through the night, he did wonder a little about his motivation. "I must say, there was one reservation I had about it all. Why didn't Story let that animal go? What was he doing with an animal that wasn't going to give us very much more, and to stick it out during the day and over the night until the next morning when we had to dispatch the animal and start on a new one? I've always had that in my mind – was there something there that even if someone tells him to do something, if he's got a different idea about it, then it's gonna come through? I mentioned this episode at a NASA meeting where I gave a little talk. Story was there and a number of people in the program were there – at the Washington headquarters – and I said, 'One thing about Story is that he didn't like to obey orders!' – and that led to a big roar in the crowd!"

Dr Purpura spoke of the importance of physical fitness in Story's life and his decision to enter the space program: "When he got into the space program there were two things I knew about him – his physical fitness and his desire to use physical fitness as an important part of his lifestyle, very early on. In the sixties, nobody ran or did the things that a Marine did as he got out of the service. But Story's physical fitness and his interest in exploring things beyond the horizon – it was a natural, I believe, for him to go into the [space] program."

Story's enthusiasm for parachuting, which he began in New York, did surprise Dr Purpura at the time. "I thought it was absolute insanity in 1963. Now, of course, it has become a big sport. But he was pioneering in that too, of dare devilling kinds of things which we thought would be crazy for anybody with a family to do!"

Of the physical aspects of Story's career with NASA – the spacewalking, T-38 flying world and all – Dr Purpura observed, "I think Story enjoyed showing that he had built a machine, namely his body, that he could rely on. He had a certain reliance on his capabilities. And once you get that kind of confidence, I don't think you can be afraid of doing anything – as long as you examine the full parameters of the danger, understand it, know what you have to give to it and what you expect your body to do."

When asked what he would remember most about the Story Musgrave of the 1960s, Dr Purpura replied, "I think his persistence and his energy, and more importantly, a dedication to getting done what he thought was right to get done – that's the best impression I have of his laboratory experience with me. And, of course, a guy that is insatiable for new kinds of physical and emotional stimuli – like he hasn't explored the full range of human stimuli that can effect his nervous system!"

Dr Purpura mused about Story's future – had he continued to pursue neurophysiology and neurosurgery for forty years, instead of joining the space program. He put it this way: "He could have been highly successful as a neurosurgeon or even in neurology, or wherever he decided. But I think the practice of medicine, in final pictures, would have been too dull for him and maybe he would have gone off to set up new programs or new therapies – being rather adventurous and that. But in medicine, that can get you into trouble [career-wise] since medicine is really peer review, all the way.

"To be a neurosurgeon there's a personality type – that you can't be licked by adversity. It's too punishing sometimes with tumors and aneurisms and you've got to have a sort of a feeling [with patients that] first of all, you didn't put [the medical problem] there, and secondly, you've got to do something because something has to be done. So I think he would have been a very courageous surgeon and, at the same time, I think he might have been a little too overzealous. So he would either have been the greatest neurosurgeon or tar and feathers! One or the other," he laughed.

Another close friend at Columbia was Dr Edgar Housepian. Story recalled, "Ed did research in the same lab and we knew each other very well. He was a Professor of Neurological Surgery the entire time that I knew him."

Dr Housepian has kept up with Story for forty years. He said, "He's taken up just about everything, that's what's so incredible about him. He seems to be sort of six paces ahead of himself. He's really moving and off to something else while you're trying to catch up with what he's been at!

"My first introduction to Story was when he came to the lab – I was a Fellow in Dr Purpura's lab. Little by little, we learned about his accomplishments already – not only was he married with several children, but he also had a couple of degrees. Obviously had an immense capacity to absorb things and a tremendous interest and intellect.

"He has had so many different interests, and I don't think he got bored with them, but he wanted a new challenge, it seemed. And then he'd get into something totally new. The only continuum in his life was flying. The impression I got is that he'd rather fly than anything else. If he wasn't flying he was skydiving, and if he wasn't doing that, he was teaching flying."

Dr Housepian recalled Story's visits to Columbia University during the 1990s and the way his enthusiasm and passion still pervades everything he does. "He came up here and he gave some lectures. The lectures were a little hard to follow 'cause they were almost poetic in their scope! He showed incredible pictures of the universe and the galaxies and all. There was almost more poetry than science – not that he didn't know the science – but he was really sort of carried away with the enormity of what's out there. He wants to communicate many things."

Of Story's pursuits, Dr Housepian observed, "Whatever he's done, he's done well, by putting in a lot of hard work. And that's true of most things – you can be inspired and brilliant and still take some hard work.

"Is he a genius? I think so in view of his relentless quest for knowledge. There must be many kinds of geniuses. He has the capacity and he has exercised it. He's gone and built on his experiences to go onto other frontiers and then has built on that to go farther. So I think that takes something extraordinary."

Story celebrated the caliber of teachers and professors at Columbia University: "There was Dr Donald Tapley[18] – he was representative of what I call 'the Classics and the Greats' – they had the grace, they were magnificent, they had the nobility, the majesty – they were simply giants in the practice of medicine. Tapley was one of them, but there were many others at the College of Physicians and Surgeons. And so they were my inspiration. They had posture, they had presence, they did things quietly. It wasn't only their professionalism, though – it's what they stood for. They stood for greatness and they were champions. I kept up with Donald Tapley for many years and at the last commencement address I did there, a couple of years ago, I dedicated that to him."[19]

*

The blue grass of Kentucky held a powerful attraction for Story. He had encountered it in his youth, on his first real adventure across America before joining the Marines. Lexington, with its manicured horse farms and lush green pastures, was a place Story felt very much at home – much more so than in the New England to which he was born. He had always hoped to return one day to this picturesque, farming paradise.

Story recalled, "My love affair with Kentucky, and particularly Lexington,

18. Dr Donald Tapley became Health Sciences Dean at Columbia University, New York. He died in 1999.
19. Story dedicated the commencement address which he gave in May of 2000 at the College of Physicians and Surgeons, Columbia University, to Dr Tapley.

started as a teenager. Lexington had spectacular farms – the most outrageously beautiful horse farms, and this was not only farming, this was *gorgeous* farming – the animals and the countryside. This was nirvana; this was it! It was a different place in the universe! And so you get a kid off the farm who wants to be a farmer; you look at this country and it's heaven. This was my heaven. And so that set in motion that I'm going to get back to Lexington when I can; I am going to end up in Lexington; I'm coming 'home.'

"It was fantastically powerful when you want to be a farmer and you see this kind of beauty and grace, and you see thoroughbred racing horses – it was the thoroughbred racing capital of the world, by far. And you see that whole scenario; you see the incredible barns and the fences and the bluegrass and all of that, and road after road after road of incredible horse farms. And you say 'this is where the farm is going to be.' Not necessarily my farm – maybe I'll farm for someone else – we don't know how we'll do it, but we are going to come *home*. I said that as a teenager."

The fact that Story was now progressing rapidly towards becoming a doctor and surgeon did not alter that goal. Completion of his medical studies at Columbia University opened the way for a change of scenery – an opportunity to carry out his medical internship through a different university.

According to Story, "Although I'm not going to be a farmer anymore, it doesn't matter. And so now, finishing medical school and selecting an internship – wow, I can go to Lexington! They have a good school there and I can do a great internship there. So here is the first time that, yes, I can get home to Lexington and continue on the trajectory that I'm now on.

"I did do other interviews; I wanted to get a solid internship. I wanted to go back to Lexington, but if I had not had good interviews and not been happy with the department of surgery, I would have gone elsewhere. The opportunity might not have happened that would allow me to go to Lexington. But it turns out it was a perfect fit. I just had wonderful interviews and there was a brand new medical school. It was more than acceptable; it was marvelous – so that was that."

At the University of Kentucky, Story met and was interviewed by Dr Ben Eiseman, who, at the time, was Head of Surgery. It was to be the beginning of a long and rewarding professional relationship, a solid friendship, with each developing a healthy respect and affection for the other.

Dr Eiseman recalled Story's interview process at the University of Kentucky: "He came down to Lexington, Kentucky, as a medical student to be interviewed by us as to whether we would give him a surgical internship and residency. He, along with the others, was interviewed for say thirty minutes by each of the four or five of our faculty. And then all the other applicants, as usual, left. But Story came to us and said,

'You know, I want to stay for another day or two.' And that absolutely knocked us off our feet, 'cause he said he just wanted to get a bit more of a feel for the place. And typically – what he was doing was – the first day, we interviewed him, and on the next few days, he was sizing us up!

"And later when I quizzed him about this, he said, 'Well, after all, I was looking to see where I was going to spend the next five years of my life' – which is the time of a usual surgical residency – 'And I wanted to be sure I was in the right place.'

"Well, of course, [the staff] got together and said, 'What's this wonderful guy doing here?' And it was perfectly clear he was looking us over and quite logically. But I've never before, or since, heard of an intern applicant doing that. And, of course, it's perfectly typical of the logic of Story Musgrave."

Dr Eiseman, in turn, had made a great impression on Story: "Ben Eiseman was critical for my even going there [to the University of Kentucky]. Once I had met him at dinner, that was it, my decision was made. He was a leader. He led in a charismatic kind of way – there was no question who the leader was, there was no question who was in command of the ship – it was him – he was that positive, that definitive. And so he was, more than anything else, the leader. He was more a leader than he was a surgeon or a researcher. He was simply a leader.

"I had lunch with him and other members [of the medical school], but that was the end of that game: I cancelled all other interviews. I said, 'I'm coming here' and they said, 'You're in' – again, it was the non-verbal [communication] that we are a team and this is a marriage and this fits. It was totally non-verbal, but we looked at each other in the eye and we knew – this is it, it's all done."

The move to Lexington, from New York City, was a popular one with Story's family as well. Patricia Musgrave recalled, "I went first, with Story's Mom, to find a house. We found an old farm house with acreage on Georgetown Pike Road and it was on the north side – that was where all the horse farms were. And when Story saw the house, he was overwhelmed; I mean it was just beautiful! We had a horse farm across the street and we had cows for neighbors. We had this long drive coming up to the house with trees on either side. The house, itself, which we rented, was an old farm house, all brick, with a screened-in porch three-quarters of the way around. It had a fireplace in every room and wooden floors and if someone would have taken the time to restore it, it would have been a beautiful home. And we had peonies, which grow naturally there, and Story cultivated a little garden with things like fresh corn and carrots. We had fun doing that."

The Musgraves also purchased two Great Danes to run around their newly acquired acreage. According to Patricia, "We bought two Great Dane puppies. My Dad bought us a VW van and my mother joined me – and she and myself and the three children drove down from New York to Kentucky. Then Story came down in a little VW bug with the two Great Danes."

The year of Story's internship from mid-1964 to mid-1965, was memorable, to say the least. It was a tough year in terms of the working hours required of young interns in those days and in the lack of time Story was able to spend with his family; it was the year NASA announced potential opportunities for scientists to join the astronaut corps; and it was also a year of personal tragedy when his younger brother Tom committed suicide.

Story recalled his life as an intern during that first year in Lexington. "It's thirty-six hours on and twelve off – but it's worse than that! It ended up like being thirty-eight or forty hours on and eight off for a solid year, without a break, without a single day off. You never got a day off – I mean you tried to get out of there on your day off – you tried to get a Saturday or Sunday. Even though you were supposed to be able to get out of there after what we call rounds or grand rounds – you're supposed to maybe get out of there at 11am – but you had to go back and get the patients stable for hand-off. And so it droned on until 3 or 4 or 5 or 6pm; it didn't matter. And so this thing rolled on for a year. You never got to sleep – you slept only some, every other night; that is simply the way life was. That was not right, it should never have been that way, the laws don't permit that now, but back then, it's the way it was.

"You lose a lot of the day in surgery and then you have patients in recovery who are sicker than normal, and your new patients have already come in during the day and are waiting for you. So you finish surgery and take care of these patients at the same time as you admit the new patients. And you never get done. And so you wake up the new patients at 2am to get a physical exam; they understand. The new patients come in the hospital the day before and you wake them up at 2am to get started on them. It's an unbelievable life but, of course, I was tough – I was incredibly hardy."

Story was considered a remarkable student in the surgical program. Dr Eiseman recalled, "He was charming, witty, amusing, delightful, a good listener, with a wry sense of humor – which, of course, I've seen over the years. He was totally goal-oriented – and we get an awful lot of goal-oriented, bright young people now and then – but Story had that in spades. He is so logical, has such a practical mind and a practical bent to his personality. It was clear that he wanted to achieve, not openly aggressively, but that that was what he was expecting of himself. It stuck out then, as it has ever since."

Story's family saw very little of him during that year. His brother Tom followed the family to Kentucky and lived with them for some time. Tom was restless and lacking direction, but Story was not around enough to really perceive the depth of his unhappiness and problems. His death, by suicide, was huge shock for Story. The feelings of loss and the regrets of not being able to save Tom from self-destruction would always remain with him. Barely six years had passed since the death of Story's oldest brother, Percy, in a Naval accident, and he mourned the loss of yet another link with his past, with his childhood.

Professionally, Story was about to reach another significant crossroad in his life. He read that the National Academy of Science and NASA were talking of a joint initiative to select astronauts who had a formal scientific education. That single piece of information was pivotal in deciding Story's future trajectory: at once, he knew that he wanted to join the space program and he wanted to be ready when the opportunity to apply arose.

Story recalled, "That is basically when I leaped off, but it was somewhat both a push and a pull. I sensed a little bit of discomfort in where I was, some discomfort in my trajectory in medicine. If I had somehow stayed on a pure brain research path, things might have been different, but I knew I needed to go somewhere else, and then there was the pull towards space.

"It's like most things that I've done – they have been intuitive, they have been listening to my body. I don't have the analytical answer but I can feel my physiology respond: 'Is this a perfect fit for me?' And so [medicine] was not a perfect fit at the time. It was not like when people say that 'this was a really tough decision' or 'I'm torn.' I was not torn. I was not torn between saying 'I'm going to leap off, I'm a space person' or staying on the current trajectory. It was very clear that I had to leap off – everything was positive [with regard] to leaping off. So maybe the trajectory in medicine had become a little unclear. I was not strictly in the brain anymore, maybe I was heading toward neurosurgery as well as neurophysiology, but that neurosurgery and surgery training itself was so overwhelming, that you're not studying the brain. That's why you made this leap, but you're not doing why you made the leap. I am in a clinical path and the trajectory is to make me a surgeon, not a neurosurgeon. You have to become a surgeon first, then a neurosurgeon. And so I am in a clinical surgery path. And so it's all these kind of things – I don't have a harder answer than that – other than that I was totally immersed in pure clinical surgery and maybe I had lost the way a little bit. So it was a little bit of push away from medicine, but mostly a pull towards space flight."

Story received the full support of Dr Eiseman in his new trajectory. Forty years later, Story recalled how he had broken the news to his boss that he was leaving the surgical program after only one year, and how he received an incredibly encouraging reply from Dr Eiseman – simply, "How can I help?"

Story remembered, "It was a startling reaction, but he understood – he's a mountain climber and he worked with the military services on how you deploy

medical services, how you do full surgery out in the field. And so for some reason…
he had that kind of enthusiasm."

Dr Eiseman also recalled the discussion of that day. "I can remember, Story said,
'Boss, I'd like to speak to you for a few minutes.' And I can remember that when Story
said that, I dropped what I had to do and closed the door. That's when he said to me
he wanted to be an astronaut. And I said 'What? One of those guys who's gonna go to
the moon?' – which was long, long before the moon affair. And he said, 'No, it'll be
after that – after they've gone to the moon.'

"And I knew Story well enough by that time to know that when he said this, it
wasn't something he said lightly. He talked about that, and then I can remember I said,
'All right Story, what are the chances? What kind of guys are they taking there?' And
I can still remember he said, 'Well, I figured, it's about 1 in 1500'. Typical Story! But
that's the way his mind works – an analytical approach and a numeric analytic
approach to whatever he does. Story doesn't jam it down your throat if you, yourself,
don't think that way, but that's the way he thinks. I mean any big or little decision,
that's just the way he works.

"Now the thing which differentiates Story from just a very bright engineer – and
obviously I've given a lot of thought to this man over the years – but he has, number
one, a perspective that the horizon is much further along. It is much deeper than it is
for most people and, certainly, much more than it is to most engineering type minds.
A mind like his and a personality like his could get lost in detail, but he is never that.
Story – to torture the analogy a little bit – his mind doesn't even stop at the ordinary
horizon; it goes off into space, like an artist or a poet. To me, he has that unique mixture
of engineering or basic analytic abilities and an intellectual pragmatic approach to a
problem, plus the artistry and vision. I've never known such a mixture in anybody."

Dr Eiseman reflected on the naturalness of space flight for someone like Story.
"Well, what is the greatest challenge when Story was deciding what he was going to
do next? It was to go into space and to make contributions there. And, of course, that's
what Story was going to do – that's the greatest challenge there was and it's perfectly
natural he was going to do that. He was going to train himself for as long as it took, he
was going to learn all of the things he had to learn to do it and he was going to become
pre-eminent in that. Once he'd decided that, of course he did it!"

To make himself more attractive as a candidate for space flight, Story
commenced post-doctoral Fellowships in order to study the physiology of the body in
space. He also continued as a student, completing a Master of Science degree in
physiology and biophysics in 1966 and, in addition, taught at the University.

Story explained the new direction: "They didn't have scientist astronauts at that
time, but I had some view of space flight and I thought, I'm not going to be doing

surgery in space; you don't do surgery in space. But I'm thinking they're gonna want research: what is space flight about? How does it affect the body? What is the physiology? And so I thought *physiology* – it's a study of function and it's environment physiology – as you go from earth to space, how does your physiology change? And it turns out most studies done on the human are physiological studies as opposed to other scientific disciplines, so I was right there. But physiology appeared to be that scientific discipline which would prepare me best. Plus, number one, I liked physiology the best. Whether I was to do anatomy or biochemistry or the other kinds of scientific medical sciences, physiology appealed to me the most: it was process-oriented, it was the journey – it's more a journey kind of thing – it's more synthetic in terms of looking at overall things. So, number one, I liked physiology the best, it appealed to me, but I perceived that in terms of being a researcher in space, that would be the best. And so I leaped off and I did space flight physiology; that's exactly what I studied. I studied orthostatic stuff – what are the differences between standing up and lying down, cardiovascular physiology, lower body sub-atmospheric physiology."

Story joined the University of Kentucky's Department of Physiology and Biophysics and was able to carry out his research through funding from two different sources.

He said, "I applied for specific Fellowships and I got approved. The first year, which was 1965-66, was with the Air Force, and the second year, 1966-67, was with the National Heart Institute.

"The kind of research I was doing involved blood pressures and that kind of thing; the cardiovascular system. Mostly the veinous side of the system. So for the National Heart Institute, I am doing studies on the capillary and the veinous side, which doesn't usually get the attention that the arterial side does and so that interested people."

By the time Story Applied to the National Academy of Sciences as an astronaut candidate, he had completed his Master of Science Degree and worked towards a PhD. He explained, "I did all but a dissertation towards a PhD actually – finished my comprehensive exams, language and all that as well, so I was in the coursework process there. I also took other courses including biophysics courses, pharmacology courses and did a minor in aeronautical engineering – that didn't bother anyone – I already had an MD and all that education. So I had many more courses and much more education than most physiology students would have, so I went over and took a minor in aeronautical engineering – I got exposed to that world as well, so that was nice. That kind of combined my interest in flying – which, of course, I was doing very heavily at the same time. And then I got my own airplane in 1964, and so I'm flying at the local airport and I continued my parachuting that I had begun in medical school. But to study, to take courses in aerodynamics, was very nice in terms of the flying that

I was doing and my parachuting and, looking into the future, the space program. That all worked very nicely, but, first of all, it was fun – I am a pilot, I'm flying now, and I'm a parachutist jumping out of airplanes, so, let's formally study what is going on. And so I usually do that, one way or another, when I get into something – I do it for fun, but then I pursue it academically."

In fact, Story's parachuting became the class project. He explained, "I ended up doing purely aerodynamic studies of parachuting – the aerodynamics of the human body. Lexington is where I made the experimental jumps. I was in a class about basic aerodynamics. Well, the professor of the class and the class itself thought it would be a great idea if the class did actual research in an actual project. And so my parachuting became the class project. And it was perfect. And so I owned my airplane, I owned my parachute, so I'd jump out of the airplane and in the class we'd come up with a protocol. And so we came up with an experimental protocol to look at aerodynamics of the human body – the human body as a flying machine.

"Together we came up with the instrumentation and all the recording things and we had 2 recording telescopes, 6000 feet apart; they would track me on the way down, and they would take a frame, a photograph every 20th of a second and the telescopes would have the azimuth and the elevation and the angle. Basically we got a position in space as I fell every one 20th of a second. And so that data went on an IBM card, so we had a card of data every 20th of a second in my freefall. It was cards in those days, that's the way you input to the system. And we used Fortran and we built a little program, and given that you know a position every 20th of a second, you now get the velocity, and the range of velocity is very straightforward. I also carried some onboard instrumentation, some barographs that would tell me my altitude with respect to time, and so you reconstruct things. We also used a balloon that we sent up, and so you take a balloon up and you record it with the telescopes and you can cancel out the wind effects. So if you have very strong wind effects, it may be the wind that's moving you, not your aerodynamics. So we subtracted the wind effects by sending a balloon up and getting IBM cards for the balloon and subtracting out things. Those are the details.

"It was incredibly educational for the class to have to get hardware together, to do real stuff in the laboratory, to build the hardware and to go out in the field and record things. And so, my fun, my enjoyment of freefall, ended up being a class project, and so I applied aerodynamics to what I was doing. It is that kind of synergy which I've really kind of been working on all my life."

Story was selected by NASA for the astronaut class of 1967, however, a year or two into his new career, he began to think seriously about opportunities for continuing with his medical interests and proficiency.

He explained, "It was the initial concept of the National Academy of Science – it was an absolute must – you must maintain your proficiency in science."

Once the astronauts were on board, NASA was less interested in this concept, preferring them to focus on their current duties. Story, however, felt it was important to follow through with the principle. Once again, it was to Dr Eiseman, his mentor from the University of Kentucky, that he turned. Dr Eiseman had, in the interim, moved to Colorado and was able to create an opportunity for Story at Denver General Hospital.

According to Story, "I followed him there for two or three days a month. He understood what I needed and it didn't seem strange to him. He had become Chief of Surgery at the hospital, which was a major trauma center and his kind of action! And so it was natural for me, in terms of maintaining my proficiency, to go there."

Dr Eiseman remembered, "Story, as you know, had come a long way and was down in Houston. He said, 'I'd like to come up boss and join in and keep my surgical skills up.' And I said, 'Geez, that'll be wonderful Story. I'll make arrangements just to work you right in with the surgical residents down at Denver General. You tell me when you're coming and you can just trail the surgical residents and students.'

"So here comes Story – he got in one of those fast NASA things[20] – and came out here! He would come down to the Denver General Hospital in his blue jumper suit,[21] usually some time in the afternoon. He'd store his work clothes and, of course, then he would just get into regular resident greens. It was usually on a weekend, and he would just stay up all night operating and assisting the residents at the time. And, of course, it absolutely blew the minds of all the students and residents that here was this astronaut! He was typical Story, staying toe to toe with all the residents and was terrific in the intensive care unit and with the gadgetry that went on there. His impact on the students and the residents and the staff was absolutely fantastic by what he did. We profited enormously from it, but it was typical Story. He wasn't trying to become a Fellow of the College, although I had him give a very prestigious lecture at the American College of Surgeons. The entire American College of Surgeons identified with this guy and this was very important to the College; it's part of the image that this guy was not just another astronaut."

Story loved his time at Denver General Hospital – a refreshing variant from his regular NASA duties. He said, "It lasted over twenty years. It was a teaching hospital where you have students, interns, residents, staff – and I would float within the cases and do something that was reasonable. I would pick tasks that were reasonable for my current level of proficiency. I didn't just do surgery – I delivered babies, I pulled teeth

20. The NASA T-38 jet.
21. The NASA flight suit.

in the dental clinic – I worked wherever I wanted, just to try to stay proficient with the practice of medicine. People knew me and so I could float around and stay in touch with medicine.

"It's simply working as one of the teams. I just tried to bring in my kind of checklist and systemization from the NASA and flying worlds – I tried to join the two worlds. And so I may have been some help in that regard, in terms of how you handle trauma and the emergency rooms, and what your approach is to a patient that comes in and is that desperately ill. And so I think if I contributed anything, maybe I contributed something in that area.

"But mostly I was in the receiving mode, because I was the learner and I was not proficient. In the long run it didn't end up anywhere but it was a fun thing to do, and it was a part of my spirit. I appreciated medicine far more then than I had ever appreciated it before. I couldn't wait to get there and get to work. I had Dr Eiseman's enthusiasm and support, and the support of all the team. My proficiency just stayed at internship level and I never went beyond that 'cause you can't in that time. But I enjoyed doing it and I loved going up there. I'd work all night, operate all night long on trauma patients, not sleep, do the rounds Saturday morning, jump in the airplane and go home."

As a doctor, Story's relationship with patients was not unlike his approach to nature. It involved the ability to listen, to have empathy for the situation and to communicate within that environment.

He explained, "The patient was key. My empathy for the patient was number one here and so, again, it gets down to listening. And I hadn't thought of this before, but it gets down to surrendering control – that you are not just looking at how you are going to control the patient in this situation. It's to listen to the patient and get an empathy where you can get into their body and their mind and see things from their viewpoint. What are they going through? What are their fears? What are their concerns? What are they feeling? You have to guide the situation. You have the technology, you are the physician, but, at times, you've got to be quiet so you can listen to the situation.

"Communication gets down to empathy again and it gets down to listening and it gets down to feedback. It gets down to body, mind and soul and it's how sensitive you are."

As an MD, Story was able to use his knowledge to assist with various medical projects within NASA's developmental programs. He said, "I never flew a medical mission but I helped develop the medical support system on the Space Shuttle – the two cubic feet that we were allowed! So I was very much immersed in Shuttle in-flight medical support systems. I helped design the Skylab sub-atmospheric pressure; I made lots of inputs to Skylab medical and physiological studies. The research for STS-44 – we had an extension to that mission, longer than it was supposed to be, so that we could do lower body negative pressure and that kind of thing up there. The lower body sub-atmospheric pressure – I had done that back in Kentucky."

In addition, Story was the designated doctor on each of his missions should any of the crew members require medical assistance.

The people who developed and tested the space shuttle spacesuit and its built-in life support systems, spoke of the usefulness of Story's medical background. As the astronaut representative on spacesuits, it was highly practical to have someone like Story who understood the physiology of the body. According to Joe McMann, who was NASA's lead engineer on EMU,[22] "I know that it gave him certainly a leap ahead of others when it came to understanding things like the nitrogenation embolism – the need to denitrogenate and what the effects were – the effects of high carbon dioxide – what are the symptoms? … It made him an extremely quick study on anything that had a physiological aspect to it."

Today, Story's interest in medical research reflects a philosophy developed through decades of reflection and working in space. Although no longer directly involved in the space program, he believes scientists should be doing cutting edge studies in space – ones which affect humanity in a big way.

He says, "It's got to be the kind of stuff that becomes a mirror for humanity. I like to get at those things that define 'what does this mean?' I like evolutionary studies, cosmic evolution, biological evolution. I've spoken of using space flight as that razor-sharp edge as 'what makes you?' – what part does genetics play and what part does environment play? [Researchers] have never been able to separate nature and nurture. Now space flight, because you don't have the gravity up there, might allow you to pursue those kind of things.

"I hope that in space flight they will get to some fundamental biology. I would hope they would get to some fundamental biology on why we are who we are as living creatures, how life was created. And so we're a little off the idea of medical research, but I'm interested in exobiology and I'm interested in the creation of life, the evolution of life in terms of biological research."

Though space became his calling, throughout his career with NASA, Story kept in contact with the medical world which helped to form him. He often returned to his former Alma Maters to give lectures and to meet the people who inspired and motivated him.

---

22. Extravehicular Mobility Unit (EMU) – the combined spacesuit and life support systems.

In 1994, in the context of his thirty-year reunion at the College of Physicians and Surgeons, Story recalled how important it still is for him to stay in touch with his past. In his journal he wrote:

> Trying to grasp reality of medical school, 30 years ago. What were your expectations, who were you, what drove you? What led to who you are and your place in the world in 1994? You are so blessed! I think it is very important to get in intimate touch with your past, your past person and the flow of life which led to here.[23]

23. Journal 15, page 29; Date: May 1994.

# 8. Flying

Story, consumed and consuming, lay on his back in a field, looking intently upward while chewing on the stem of a pink clover blossom. He watched the birth and evolution of the warming sky above. He warmed to the sun and to the appearance of little wisps of clouds which soon grew into strong billowy cumulus... As the heat of the earth and of the heavens cooked on, a sleek-winged, graceful bird launched, soared and flapped, soared and flapped, then soared, only soared – carried effortlessly into the ever increasing heights. The time had arrived for more birds, the leaves, the dust, and for Story – for anybody on the way to Heaven.

*A Story of Earth and Heaven*
*Story Musgrave, 1988*

Story soloed an airplane at sixteen. Having grown up on-farm, he was good with machinery and teaching himself how things worked. At the local airport – Great Barrington – he drove the airplanes like they were tractors. He played with the controls for months until he was adept, then simply went airborne. With all that would follow in Story's aviation experience, it was somewhat of an anti-climax.

As other great aviators before him – including Orville Wright, whose birthday he shares – Story developed a passion for flying. The real interest in airplanes came in the Marine Corps where he worked as an airplane electrician and instrument technician. He loved the power of the military airplanes and the energy and noise he could create while ground-testing them on the service ramp for the pilots.

It was not until some years later, though, during his medical studies in Kentucky, that Story finally earned his pilot's wings for real. He would go on to become an instructor, commercial pilot and aerobatic specialist, extending his passion for flying into the sailplane world.

By the time Story joined NASA, he was an extraordinarily experienced pilot. He earned top honors at Reese Air Force Base while acquiring his Air Force wings – in those days, a compulsory part of an astronaut's introduction to space flight.

But for all this, Story was never your average pilot – either in practice or approach. During some 18,000 hours of flight time, he built unique relationships between himself and the machines, appreciating new perspectives of both nature and of earth.

Ultimately, flying became one of Story's greatest loves.

*

"Airplanes became a very, very major part of my life with the amount of time that I spent in them," Story explained. "I flew airplanes across the spectrum from very slow sailplanes to supersonic jets and it didn't matter to me: one was not better than the other.

"The flying put you in a vantage point to see nature in a different way and the beauty there as well. It's like climbing a high mountain and looking down the valley. You are up in the air and you have a different viewpoint. You have the aerial view up there and the stars and the clouds, especially the clouds. You get a really nice view of the clouds. But the geography and the aerial view of the world is another view and it's nice to take your farm, the soil that you're been immersed in, and look at the whole layout from up above. It's another vantage point, the same as space flight is.

"It's the beauty of flight, it's the beauty of motion, it's the beauty of altitude, it's the beauty of looking at different vantage points and it's also the art form. It's being the best you can. It's flying the best, the most beautiful, the most kinesthetic maneuvers you can. It's all those kinds of things.

"So it gets down to, I think, the essence of the airplane world – it gets down to you and the machine becoming an organism in which a machine simply extends your capability. And so, in a way, it's just melting yourself into the machine and becoming one [with it]. That's the process that exists throughout my journey."

Story's earliest experiences in airplanes were not romantic ones. To a farm kid, a high school student and someone who loved machinery, airplanes were another form of motorized fun. He was more interested in how he might learn the mechanics, the minute workings of the machine, and was, as yet, perhaps even a little oblivious to the extraordinary sights and stirring emotions which might accompany an adventure into flight.

According to Story, "I started driving around on the big field – back in those days you had no keys and things. You either propped them by hand – you grabbed the propeller and spun the propeller to start it – or once in a while you had the privilege of a starter push button and away you'd go.

"So I just drove these things around in the field, just like any other machine. And I got going faster and I taught myself the aerodynamic controls, so if you're going thirty miles an hour, that's enough – thirty miles an hour and the controls do things! You're not airborne, but you move the stick to the left and the airplane leans to the left. It doesn't fly and it doesn't tip over but it leans. You go fast enough, you pick the tail wheel up, you put the tail wheel down. So now you exercise what's called pitch. You go up and down, up and down, up and down, and I just did the dance.

"So now I danced across the field, you know, waggle the wings up and down, tail up and down, and I'm dancing. Then I got where I'm dancing the wheels, so I've got a wheel up in the air, a wheel down there; I'm just dancing around. And then I'm high-speed dancing – if you can high-speed dance out there then you are ready to fly because a tail wheel airplane, if you can handle it on the ground, you can handle it in the air, it's nothing. You just trim it up and it flies itself once you're airborne. You just trim it up and take your hands off the controls and it's flying just beautiful, but that's not true on the ground. So, I got doing high-speed dances in which I really understood the thing. I took months and months and finally one day, I just leaped off – that was my solo."

For Story, this was nowhere near as significant an event as his first ride in a military jet in Korea or when he learnt to fly airplanes with instruction, really appreciating what it was all about.

It was during his time with the Marines that Story's passion for airplanes grew. On 12 April 1954, while stationed in Jacksonville, Florida, he wrote to his father and stepmother:

> The barracks in which I live in is right on the end of a runway, so when the planes take off or land, they clear our roof by around thirty feet at the most. As usual,

I'm in the middle of the fight, having the top rack on the top floor right next to the roof. When a jet comes over you can at first hear a shrill whistle like a bomb falling and, as it goes by, the roar vibrates the building as if a bomb had hit it. At night, when the company is trying to make use of six or less hours of sleep, a jet bomber will roar over and shake everyone half out of bed. After the plane goes by, the first thing to be heard in the room is my laughter and then a hoard of curses in usual Marine language.

Story later recalled, "I would sit and watch jets forever. And I says, my goodness, you know! So I sat as a seventeen-year-old or eighteen-year-old, watching the jets fly. They'd stun me every time. Wherever I was studying or whatever I was doing, a jet would fly over and I would stop and watch it go. I wanted to be in that thing; I wanted to be in that jet. So way, way back, I wanted to be in that airplane, I wanted to fly that airplane. Without a high school diploma there was no hope. And so a lot else transpired about wanting to fly a jet until I did in 1968."

Of his Marines Corps flying, Story said, "The flying I did with them [as a crew chief] was extraordinarily exciting – it was just like going to a ride in the amusement park. It was like a great ride at a park! I had little idea what was going on."

Story formally learnt to fly at Cynthiana Airport. That was in the mid-1960s, mainly during his post-doctoral studies at the University of Kentucky. For Story, much of the beauty of the experience was the grass runways on which he would take off and land: "I love a beautiful airport, I love grass. I'd much rather fly off grass and there are very few people that have ever flown off grass. But a gorgeous Kentucky airport where there's lush grass, alongside a river and surrounded by some nice trees – you just come in and there's none of the tires hitting the asphalt and smoking and screeching: they just slide along the grass."

During 1965, Story was issued with his student pilot rating, followed later by his private pilot rating. In that twelve month period, he flew 310.5 hours in a Cessna Skyhawk C172 – of which 249 hours were solo.

Story recalled, "I got my airplane as a [medical] intern and I started getting in an hour or two here and there. But it was, as the log books will show, at the end of my internship, which was June of '65, when I leaped into flying for serious. The internship just simply didn't permit anything – it might be an hour or two a week."

Once time permitted, however, Story very quickly acquired further airplane certificates and ratings – Instrument and Multi-Engine in August of 1966; Commercial in November of 1966; Instructor in February 1967, and Instrument Instructor in April 1967. Most of Story's time was spent in the Cessna 172, which his mother had helped him to purchase, but log books record that Story also flew a Cessna 150, Cherokee 140, Cherokee PA-32, Beechcraft Baron, Twin Commanche PA-30, Beech C45H and Piper Commanche 260.

Story explained, "I rapidly pursued the time and the ratings and all that. I got where I could sustain my flying, financially, because I became a charter pilot, taking people around the country, teaching people and teaching ground school. So flying, very rapidly, became profitable.

"I worked for myself. I instructed on my own, but I also instructed for other companies. You have what's called a fixed base operator and that's someone that runs a flying school and they have charter airplanes. I taught within those companies, but also, I'd have people come to me to teach them – independent. But most of my commercial flying, my charter flying, was for other companies.

"That was very demanding flying, 'cause twenty-four hours a day you can get sent anywhere in the country. Most airline pilots, when they show up for work, know precisely the time they're going to take off and they know where they're going: they can think ahead. In the old days, in the airline business, you had to train on that route; you didn't get sent on a route you had not trained for. So the charter flying was very demanding 'cause you could get sent anywhere. I fit that in mornings, evenings, and weekends.

"It was all different kinds of airplanes. Here, I've got a dozen airplanes that I have to master, the checklists on how to operate them and I'd have to fly anywhere in the country. I declined 'weather' of course – I don't mean any weather – you might fly in weather that was not good. But I declined all kinds of weather – 'sorry folks, I can't make it, can't do that one, can't get home' – I turned down loads of them."

"I would specialize at different times – I specialized in training private pilots, getting them their private rating. For quite a period I specialized in instrument instruction, teaching people how to fly on the instruments – that's in weather and stuff when they didn't have a good visual reference.

"I liked the charter pilot stuff 'cause, like I said, it was demanding. You didn't know what airplane you [would] be in and on a minute's notice I would get the call at home. I'd drive to the airport and take off for anywhere in the US. So that was very demanding flying as well.

"And I taught most everything – aerobatics, multi-engine too. The private flying, which was really the commercial flying and flight instructing – I think the most you can say about that is that it was hugely diverse. I taught anyone in a multiplicity of basically every type of airplane that was out there over those decades."

Story was an exceedingly experienced pilot when he was sent to Reese Air Force Base in Lubbock, Texas, as part of NASA's astronaut induction program. He joined a class of both astronauts and Air Force personnel for an intensive year of training in military jets.

Story recalled the preliminary testing and interviews which took place as part of the astronaut selection process. "The National Academy of Science had reduced thousands of us down to a final seventy people. They sent seventy to NASA so that NASA would do the final selection from that seventy to eleven. So the seventy went to Brook's Air Force Base for a week-long physical examination – every possible kind of device, all kinds of operational devices as well as medical devices, centrifuges, spin chairs and all these other kinds of things to get some baseline data, as well as to certify for medical reasons. And from there we went to NASA Houston – that was a separate event in the selection process. The National Academy of Science was selecting candidates based on scientific credentials. They might have had a little eye on operational considerations, but they were concentrating on pure research ideas and qualifications for research. But once it got turned over to NASA, we had one week in San Antonio to go to Brooks Air Force Base for screening and then we had a separate few days when we went to Houston Texas for principally interviews with the selection committee and a T-38 flight.

"The T-38 flight was there to show you the world you were getting into. It was a very brutal ride actually – just rough and hard. But it's brutal if you have people who are non-pilots and they're not that physically tough. And so, even today, even after all the experience I have had in a T-38, if I was to go and do that ride, it would be a very aggressive ride in terms of the things we did. And I felt an empathy for the people who were non-pilots, who had not been through that much physical hardship in their lives; it would have been a fantastically rough ride on them. In my own thinking, you might have discouraged people from entering the NASA program, thinking that they, in some way, were not qualified or able to do the job because you get thrown into that situation without conditioning or training. You might discourage people who were actually very qualified for the job: they just had no experience with airplanes."

At the time Story joined NASA, all new astronauts who had not already completed military pilot training were assigned to the Air Force for a year. The training consisted of 750 hours of lectures and laboratory work in such areas as systems, procedures, safety, navigation and communication; fifty hours in aircraft simulators; thirty flight hours in the lower performance propeller-driven T-41; ninety flight hours in the medium performance twin engine T-37 jet; and 120 flight hours in the high performance supersonic T-38 jet which was used for astronaut proficiency training.

Story thoroughly enjoyed immersing himself in the flying world for that year. As usual, he did it with gusto – applying himself with seemingly endless amounts of energy and enthusiasm: "I got the key to the building and I would fly all night in the simulator," he said. "Flying usually ends at 5pm or 6pm, but they showed me how to set up the simulators and I flew every night and every weekend; I flew every single approach in the United States. And so I lived in the simulators because you really learnt instrument flying, you really learnt the airplane – I was known for that. I did the same thing with a company called Flight Safety – it's a pipeline, just a fantastic pipeline, same as the military. You start nowhere and at the end you have your ratings and citation."

Story gained further private aircraft qualifications during this period – Basic Ground Instructor; Advanced Ground Instructor; Instrument Ground Instructor; and an Airline Transport rating. In his spare time, he coached some of the Air Force instructors to achieve civilian airplane ratings.

He explained, "In the military I was flying civilian as well; I was an instructor at the local base. I helped a lot of the Air Force personnel to gain their civilian ratings, including their airport transport rating, 'cause they were planning to go and fly for the airlines. So they taught me on-base during the day and I taught them off-base at nights and weekends.

"So I lived flying. It was a very nice, simple year. It was a great year for the family, a fabulous year for the family. We loved Lubbock – it's the plains of Texas, the best people in the world. It's cultural too and civic-oriented – just wonderful earth people, so we adored Lubbock. It was the year we lived flying; we simply lived flying.

"When you can concentrate and focus on one thing, it's a nice time in life. When you exclude all other distractions and say, 'I'm flying,' you make a very simple life for yourself. You don't do science, you don't do surgery, you don't do space. You don't do anything; you fly. And it's the simplest, most beautiful life you can have. And you're doing something you like to do."

Story's love for flying and his dedication were rewarded when he received the 1969 Reese Air Force Base Commander's Trophy as an Outstanding Graduate of the USAF Pilot Training. He received a letter from the Lieutenant General of the US Air Force with the following commendation:

> I commend you for your superior performance and exemplary professional ability which have resulted in your selection as an Outstanding Graduate of the United States Air Force Pilot Training Program.
>
> Through sustained perseverance and dedication, you excelled in flying, academic and military performance in competition with your peers. You displayed, to an outstanding degree, the ability, initiative and superior leadership qualities that form the foundation of our flying officer corps. Your exceptional performance during this important period of training is a credit to yourself, the pilot training program and the United States Air Force.

Story had broken all performance records at Reese, achieving consistently higher scores for both practical and theoretical examinations than any other person in the base's history.

Two further highlights of this period, noted in Story's log books, were visits to the Kennedy Space Center in Florida for the launches of the massive Saturn V rockets – the

Apollo 7 and Apollo 8 missions in October and December of 1968.

Story loved the world of the T-38 jet at NASA's Ellington Field base in Houston – everything from proficiency training, to instructing, to conducting functional check flights and working alongside NASA's ground crews. Above all else, Story loved the beauty of this particular jet airplane. He said, "It flies the way it looks. I've called it a classic, I've called it an eternal beauty. It's not related to an era; there's no fad about it, there's no fashion about it. A thousand years from now its beauty will not have changed; it's not in any time or place – it's eternal."

Flying the T-38 was also about testing your limits. According to Story, "This is what defines the edge. It is human performance, it is understanding the machine and the combination of your limitations. It is operated correctly or you are going to die; it is that simple. We fly week in and week out. It keeps us sharp – taking our life in our hands, operating the machine the way it should be operated – within limitations, check lists, discipline and all the rest.[1]

Over three decades, Story accumulated around 8000 hours of flying time in the T-38.

According to Kandy Warren, who scheduled the T-38 flights for NASA at Ellington field, "The man, I think, has jet fuel running through his veins! Story would rather fly than anything. He had more time in the T-38 aircraft than anyone in the world at one point; that included the military.

"The thing that I remember about Story most is he would get a T-38 on the weekend and try to do the four corners of the United States! I mean the man could put more flight time on a T-38 – I mean six legs[2] – that's unheard of. Pilots usually get tired after sitting for three legs. But I saw a flight form after he'd flown one time – I thought, oh my gosh, how could he sit in an airplane that long? He would go some place and land, go someplace else and refuel, land and refuel...

"Sometimes they will use the T-38s to go drop off a pilot somewhere to pick up another airplane or to go to training. And he would always volunteer to go if it was within his schedule. In fact I would call on him a lot because he did always like to fly.

"Just everything he did was superlative, everything he did was just to the nth degree. He was a good pilot and excellent instructor."

Carol Musgrave, who married Story during the mid-1980s, recalled his love for that world. At the time, Carol was a flight engineer on the Shuttle Training Aircraft and she shared the world of Ellington with Story. She said, "I flew back seat with him a number of times in the T-38. We flew back seat in the T-38 as flight engineers to go to and from where our assignments were.

"Something that surprised me about Story and flying – he could almost appear,

1. Story's comment on the website www.spacestory.com
2. A typical leg in a T-38 was an hour or an hour and a half.

on the one hand, like he was the wild man, but yet, really, down deep, he was very conservative in how he would fly. He would never go near clouds with any kind of potential for lightning. He would press it to the edge, but he knew exactly what he was doing and he never took chances."

Although a designated Mission Specialist, T-38 flying was part of Story's preparation for his space flights. According to Carol, "He figured out his own [training] regime and one thing was to fly these extremely acrobatic kinds of flight patterns – kind of rattle his gyros around enough where he would kind of loosen up for space! I was on one of those flights with him and I could barely even take it."

Of the 8,000 hours which Story logged in the T-38, around 3,000 hours were as an instructor – an activity he really enjoyed. He said, "I was the only NASA astronaut that was instructing – others have had the title 'instructor' – but they really didn't do it. I was the only one who really did it."

"The reason they made me an instructor was because of the instructing I had done over the years in light airplanes; I knew how to teach, I knew how to communicate, I knew what people needed. The people that came from the military – you might have a helicopter pilot that had never had any airplane time and so they were a little behind. People were not used to taking people back to the basics. The people that had trouble came right to me. Others would say, 'Go to Story if you're having difficulties, he'll fix it.' And I brought them all the way back to square one as if they weren't even a private pilot and I picked up the blocks and I went forward as fast as we could from there in the T-38; I made them a private pilot in the T-38. Whatever wasn't there, I filled in the open gaps."

One of Story's other roles was to conduct functional check flights on T-38 jets which had undergone major work. This was not part of the regular activities of astronauts and required special permission. Story loved it and found it to be highly challenging: "You're a test pilot. A functional test flight means you're doing a check flight – the airplane has been in heavy maintenance and you go out and fly it to see it's all right. So I was really a maintenance test pilot and I was part of the maintenance organization and that's the way I looked upon things. And so I was always thinking about the maintenance people. I flew like that as an astronaut as well, but I was always thinking about them. If something didn't go right, I really tried to communicate all the symptoms and signs to pinpoint the problem.

"But the functional check flight is a very demanding flight in which you've got to be sensitive to the machine. You're doing things to learn about the machine and to test the machine. You shut an engine down and you're flying on one engine. There's a lot of very exotic things you do at very high altitudes – very fast, slow, stalls, full aft stick stalls where it's falling like a leaf. You do all the exotic, all the possible things that that airplane might have to do once it gets turned loose to the fleet. That's some of the best flying I've done."

In total, Story flew about a thousand functional check flights in the T38, often four or five per day, and came to know each of the airplanes in NASA's fleet individually.

He said, "The supersonic run was one of the checks to see if the airplane did all right. And in that case, you approach it very slowly, so you just go a little faster, a little faster, a little faster, and you really do try to sense what the engines are doing. You're in a test, you know – are the engines going to get through supersonic flight? You can get into buzzes, you can get into things that vibrate – I've had buzzes supersonic and I've immediately hauled the throttles back, slowed down and brought the thing home. When you know what you're doing, then you approach it very slowly, you watch the engines and you listen by hanging on to the metal, by hanging on to the airplane itself. You listen in all the ways you can. And so you go up to mach 1.2 or 1.25, back off from there very slowly, so when you come back through, you're just looking that the airplane responds like it should. And for a while, you do have pretty significant pitch changes. When you can, you let the airplane fly itself, because if it's going to depart due to supersonic flight – if something is not right in one direction – then you want to see it, as opposed to control it."

The staff at Ellington appreciated Story's expertise and enthusiasm for the work. According to Kandy Warren, "They loved him. A great testament to his love of people is that the mechanics all loved him because he treated them with respect. After all, he's putting his life in their hands every time he climbs into one of those airplanes. And that to me says volumes. He was always good to the guys. And, of course, the pilots just loved him and respected him 'cause he did have so many hours in the T-38."

Bob "Mule" Mullins recalled Story's thoroughness. According to Bob, "Story knew the limits of the aircraft because he had been an electrician and crew chief in the Marine Corps."

David Lammon said it set Story apart from others. "If there was a problem with a plane, Story wouldn't just fill in a report, he would go and talk to the mechanic."

One of the most frequently recalled events of Story's NASA flying career was the day he saved one of Bob's airplanes which had caught on fire. It seems almost everyone at Ellington has a favorite version of that particular flight in October 1975 on the southern edge of Los Angeles, California – everything from Story's skill in maneuvering the plane to a safe landing while still on fire, through to his reluctance to eject over a local lion kingdom tourist park. It seems he acquired somewhat of a legendary status in the process.

But Story doesn't believe there was anything very exceptional about that flight. "That was by the numbers. I was darn good because I taught that procedure all the time to other people, week in and week out. And, of course, I stayed very current in what you do.

"It was at El Toro, taking off to the east. Anyway, the left engine had a compression stall and rolled back. And so there was a pretty big explosion. You're doing a compression stall – means the engine stalls; it just can't suck any air. You don't have those in commercial airliners but in these kind of airplanes you know what a compression stall is. And so I knew the left engine was stalled. Now this is right after I'd taken off. And I had just pulled the gear up and that is the point where the airplane has to have the most power – it's the most vulnerable because it's flying so slow, the drag is so high, it is just trying to get airborne, the worst possible time. But if you have a compression stall, you have to do what you have to do.

"I hit the start button to get the ignition going and pulled it to idle – that's what you do. So I have the left engine idle, I have the right engine in full afterburner – I need all I can get; I need that full afterburner. The next thing that happened is the right fire light comes on and that's not the one that's stalled, so I have a big problem. The left one's stalled but I have a fire light on the right engine. I'm in full afterburner, with a fire light on and I cannot pull this one back. When you've got a fire, you want to go to idle to shut the fire off. But I only have one engine I'm flying on – I have no choice but to leave this one in full afterburner with a fire light on, which is very bad. And then the [air traffic control] tower calls and says that I am trailing smoke and flame and asks do I have onboard indications? Yeah I do! I'm on fire and returning!

"Quickly, I noticed the left engine I had saved, the left engine's still motoring, it's running. So now, I start pushing the left engine up so I can get the right engine back that's on fire. As soon as I pushed the left throttle up the left fire light came on. So I have two fire lights. And so the check list says: if fire confirmed and you can't get it out – eject. The tower called and said you're on fire; you have two fire lights on and you can't get rid of the fire – the check list says eject. So, at that point, I just gently swung around – it's got to be gentle 'cause I don't have that much power. And there's a reason I didn't have that much power – I'd lost a lot of engine back there! I just gently did a right hand 270 degree turn and landed to the north. I came gently around and picked the nearest runway and landed. And that's it.

"The mind was not to save the airplane – the mind was not to save my butt, and the mind was not worrying about what I was going to eject over. The mind was – I have a flying machine, if it doesn't lose control, if I can keep flying, me and the machine are coming home. But you know, people asked me: 'What more were you waiting on?' Well I was probably waiting on loss of control. And the fire did come within three inches of burning out the hydraulics. The flame burnt all the way through the firewall. If I'd lost control I'd have been out of there as fast as I could without any concern for what was on the ground. I was trying to bring it home, but loss of control – I wouldn't have worried about the ground; I've got to get out.

"What happened is an afterburner fuel line had broken off. It fed all the fuel down the outside of the engine. The fuel caught fire and melted off the nozzle on the left hand engine – so that caused the compression stall. Then it burnt through the firewall all the way round to the right side, but it happened to trigger, in going through the firewall, the other firelight. And then it got to the fire sensor on the other side."

Story's return was met by airport fire trucks and the local fire chief. He recalled, "They had the fire trucks – it's amazing how fast – they met me on the roll. They pulled up alongside me on the roll. My God they were fast. They must have been out there on the runway. But I'm just rolling along there. I shut the engines down and coasted off the runway so as not to tie it up. The fire was gone – no fuel, no fire. The fire probably went out when I came out of afterburner on the engine that had the problem – the left one. The fire probably went out because of the broken fuel line – I probably extinguished the fire at that point. So I may have had the fire out airborne, but the fire senses were still hot, so they stayed on."

During Story's brief flight, unbeknown to him, pieces of molten airplane were falling to the ground. "Lots of pieces fell off; there were huge holes, huge holes! You could put your head in the rear engine and you were seeing the ground! So it melted the back ends of the engine and the fire wall.

"But anyway, I coasted to a stop, shook my head and got out. The fire guy was there – the warden I guess, the chief. And so I'm looking at the back end of the airplane, which is not nice, and he came up and said, 'Young man, are you aware of what you've done?' I'm looking at the back of the airplane – 'Ah yes, right here.' He says, 'I don't mean the airplane,' he says 'look over here.' So I turned around and there was a ring of fire! I mean southern California just doesn't like you setting California on fire! They don't appreciate that. But as soon as I had taken off on the runway, the ring of fire started there and went all the way around until I landed. And the [fire fighting] airplanes were already dumping water on it – the PBYs – that's how fast they must be; just sitting there waiting. And then it started to rain and that helped. I can't believe it started to rain! And so that was the end of that one. And they found the bad weld and they corrected that on other airplanes."

In some ways, it seems, Story often set the mood at Ellington. Bob Mullins recalled, "Story always had an air of excitement, which made a lot of us want to be here."

According to Henry Watkins, "Story is one of the easiest guys in the world to like. "He's rock solid, down to earth. For all the education and things he has done, he's always been able to differentiate between what is real and the bullshit, or 'apple butter.'"

According to Henry, "It was not unusual after a flight for Story to use the restroom, grab another coffee and go fly again – or help you get the aircraft ready so he could get in it again. He'd ask, 'What do we need to do?'"

Story would help do the refueling or change a tire. Henry recalled, "He was out here every weekend. He trusted us and you knew that. It was serious but it was fun! We went the extra mile for him – a courtesy that wasn't necessarily extended to everybody else."

Henry recalled one particular time when Story was doing his proficiency flying. Three or four touch-and-goes[3] is usual, however, one day, Story did twenty-four in a row and was just about out of fuel, pushing the airplane to the limit. "It happened on a weekend when it was quieter and you could do more. I started counting – Story just wanted to see what he could do, not to break any record."

David Lammon recalled Story's demeanor. "I remember the way he'd carry himself, looking forward to the ride; the excitement was very obvious. He is totally focused on the task in the moment – he wraps himself up in it and just enjoys life. When Story left NASA, we lost not only a great explorer, but a friend."

Joe Conway teasingly remembered Story's appearance. "You can't dress the man!" When not flying, Story would always wear white tennis shoes with the blue flight suit, rather than the standard black boots. Joe also recalled taking Story to a Country and Western bar one day. Joe explained how Story came dressed in polo shirt, corduroys and hush puppies – not exactly what you normally wear to a place like that. However, after some teasing, Joe's wife taught Story how to Two Step, which he greatly enjoyed.

Joking aside, Joe described Story as "One of the most outstanding individuals I've ever met. He can find fun in anything and never really had a sour word for anybody. Life is a joy to him."

Jack Nickel, or "Triple Nickel" as he is known at Ellington, said of Story, "He is a special person, a nice guy. It takes energy expenditure to do that, to be nice. Story gives the extra, he's so genuine. He took all of us to heart."

Jack explained how, as a research pilot, it is his role to take astronauts for check rides to test their proficiency. The research pilot also has to ask questions of the astronaut during the pre-flight briefing, known as the Protocol Brief. He remembered that the first time he took Story for a check ride, he was somewhat perplexed because he knew Story was more experienced in a T38 than himself. So, after thinking about it all for a while, Jack eventually looked across at Story and said, "You don't ask me any questions and I won't ask you any!" Story looked back at him, paused for a moment and said "Oh OK!" – while smiling and giving the thumbs up.

Roger Zwieg, a research pilot at Ellington and long-time friend of Story's, was an academic instructor at Reese Airforce Base in 1968 while Story was undergoing Air Force pilot training. He believes Story worked hard at what he did because he has a

3. A brief landing, followed by take-off.

driving force to do well, but says he was not a risk taker. Some months, Story would fly a hundred hours – twice a day, every day, in very disciplined practice. He described Story as "professional, caring, gregarious – not a classic loner, but comfortable by himself." He remembered Story as an extremely caring, thoughtful kind of individual who would down-play his accomplishments and let his actions speak instead of words.

Roger said, "Story realizes what it means to work hard to get accomplished. He could be master at many things. He would work whether under stress or in pain and was very talented at what he did. There was resentment by some people because Story was so good at what he did and yet he was not a [military] test pilot."

Story identified strongly with the mechanics at Ellington because of his background in the Marine Corps. He said, "My approach to airplanes, of course, is different to everybody except less than one percent of pilots, because my relationship to airplanes comes from the hangar; I learned them in the hangar. My knowledge of the T-38 came from working with those people in the hangar [at Ellington]. They would have all the pieces on the floor and I'd go look at the pieces. I had read about them, but the books don't tell you about all the various micro switches. The books simply don't tell you about all these things; they don't need to. You don't need to know all the pieces – the operator's manual that teaches you how to fly the T-38 has none of the guts in it; it only tells you how to operate it. So you just don't understand where things are coming from and how they work – you only know how to operate the thing. But I came into the flying world through tractors and trucks and things. I came into the military flying world as a mechanic and so that was my relationship to airplanes. I was working on things before I was operating things. So my relationship to military airplanes – it was years of working on them as a mechanic.

"I worked on the T-38 too. At times, I did more work on it than I was supposed to do. If I was caught out, if something was wrong with the airplane and I was out somewhere, I would talk to maintenance and I would go and work on it and fix it. I was not supposed to be doing these things.

"There was one day in El Paso[4] when my bosses actually came in and I'm on the ramp and there are panels all over the concrete! And I don't mess around, I do things right. I spoke to maintenance, I told them what I had, what I thought it was and they said, yes, that's what it is and here's what we need to do to fix it. I'm just working and what I'm doing is not that complex, it's just something that needs doing to make it right. It's a very simple thing once I get in, but I had to take all kinds of panels off. So I had panels all over the concrete, I've got my arms up in the airplane and a bunch of management [flew] in. And I'm there with an airplane in pieces! They just shook their heads, but they understood."

---

4. NASA pilots often used El Paso as a stopping station for the T-38s on the way to other places.

Around October 1985, NASA made some significant budget cuts and determined that, with the growing number of astronauts, only shuttle Commanders and Pilots, or those Mission Specialists who were in the military and needed to keep up their proficiency, would be allowed to fly 'front seat' in the T-38. This was a significant blow for someone like Story, a designated Mission Specialist, but also a highly accomplished pilot. In fact, the people at Ellington were more than a little reluctant to give him the news: it meant that Story was relegated to 'back seat' status and unable to fly the jet on his own again for the remainder of his NASA days.

Kandy Warren recalled, "I think Story took it graciously. He said something like, 'I lasted longer than I thought I would – I knew the bureaucracy was going to take over eventually.' And he was just happy to have the time. Of course he would still fly and get more hours than most of the Mission Specialists. I'm sure he probably did the landings, although the front seat pilot probably said they did them! They would let him just out of sheer respect and knowing that he could."

Friend and astronaut John Blaha, recalled the fun he had flying with Story during the 1980s. "We flew the T-38 around a lot during training. And Story was quite an aviator – in fact had been an instructor-pilot in the T-38 while he was at NASA and really knew the T-38 very, very well. Somewhere in the 1980s, NASA came out with a rule that only pilot-astronauts could fly in the front seat of a T-38 and so that meant that Story couldn't anymore – which was really a slap for a guy who was probably more proficient than anybody at flying that airplane. So when Story flew with me, you'd let him do many things that you wouldn't let another person do, but because he had been an instructor-pilot, that meant he had landed and taken off and done everything from the backseat and was very proficient at that. So I would let him do those kinds of things, which was kind of breaking the rules, but really wasn't 'cause he was very proficient.

"But for one mission that we flew [STS-33], we were headed out to Edwards Air Force Base to do some training. We took off from Ellington and the winds were pretty light that day at altitude. Normally we used to land at El Paso on the way, but as we were headed out – and this was typical of him – Story said, 'Let me show you something here.' He said, 'Have you ever seen a cruise climb?' I said, 'Yeah, what do you have in mind?' And he said, 'Well, let's try and go all the way to Phoenix!' Now, that is a real stretch and I said, 'You think we can make it there?' And he said, 'Sure, no problem.' I said 'OK,' but was a little skeptical. But it was Story, so I thought, well, I'll learn something by watching this. So he had that airplane in a very slow climb from about 35,000 feet to 47,000 feet as we were cruising that way. And then he was telling me what and how he was doing and so I learned from that. And he showed me how he could then cruise at 47,000 feet and then at what range to do a descent into Phoenix to maximize our capability. And we landed in Phoenix with an appropriate amount of gas – we weren't unsafe or anything, but I'd never been so far in a T-38 leg in my life! I learned something about the airplane. But that's typical of my time with Story. In other words, I learned a lot of airplane knowledge from him, which was rewarding."

Astronaut John Fabian paid tribute to Story. "I would say that there's only one Story Musgrave, but there are many Musgrave stories! He's a very, very bright guy, endless energy, great innovator, able to see through all of the minutiae to the big issues as well as anybody I've ever worked with. And he's the best pilot I ever flew with – and I'm a professional. I was an Air Force pilot, flew with a lot of people in the astronaut program and in my Air Force career, and Story is the most talented pilot I ever flew with. I think it's partly due to his enormous intellect, because he's able to take in an enormous amount of information very quickly, which is an inherent part of flying, and to react to that information in a very short period of time – maybe in milliseconds, you know; he's very good.

"I wasn't on a Space Shuttle crew with him, although I did fly in the simulator one time with Story. It was a rather interesting evening because, for some unknown reason, Story and I were asked to go over and fly the simulator. And we were Mission Specialists, we weren't Pilots and Commanders in the Space Shuttle program, so there was a big question in my mind as to why we were doing this. Were they training some new trainers and they just needed some warm bodies in the seats, or what were they doing? People would die for simulator time, for the sheer experience of it – people who weren't on crews yet. There were young pilots and would-be commanders who weren't getting any simulator time and yet Story and I were over there flying! And I didn't do very well and Story did beautifully! I found flying the Shuttle quite different to flying an airplane. It's not intuitive to fly the Shuttle like it is an airplane; at least it wasn't intuitive to me. Maybe it was for Story, because of some previous experience or whatever, but he just took right to it – and [on landing] was rock solid on the center line of the runway!"

As both a pilot and a physiologist, Story enjoyed exploring his body's ability to adapt to "g" forces or gravitational forces caused by supersonic speeds. It was not a formal study, but rather a personal experiment of sorts. He said, "There are various maneuvers you go through to increase your 'g' tolerance. There are various maneuvers you do which increase the pressure in your chest. Every amount that you increase the pressure in your chest is added onto the pressure of the heart to get blood to the brain and eyes. And so I would play with various mechanisms to see how you increased g tolerance. It was fun to fly in a way in which I could pull 'g's so that I would only get the systolic beat of the heart going to the eye. I would pull 'g's such that every time the heart beat, I would get my vision back, and then when the pressure came down, I would lose my vision. The only time the eyeball is getting blood is when the heart contracts. When it relaxes, the eyeball isn't getting any blood. And so with every heart beat, I would alternately see things, be blind, see things, be blind, and so on.

"I did inadvertently pass out doing this, but you're right on the absolute edge. And so I have passed out, but absolutely not intentionally; you don't want to do that. Mostly, you pass out when you're pulling very hard, pulling the nose up, so you lose consciousness. Then you relax, so the 'g's come off the airplane and in a second you're back. It happens dog fighting, it happens when you have to have your head up looking back over your shoulder – this is the worst possible case, but you're looking at your adversary. You're doing this and you're watching your adversary 'cause you've got to know where they're going. And so, as you're looking over your shoulder, it puts the head much further away from the heart than normal, so it's got to pump harder. You lose consciousness for a second or two and most of the time it's 'cause you've been pulling the nose up – you're not going down. So when you wake up, the airplane is soaring into the heights actually, it's soaring up into the air. But you never do that intentionally; you don't want to do that – both for operational safety, but also, it's not good for you and not good for the brain.

"The earliest times that I did that, I would wake up with some amnesia as to where I was. I mean your body's computer is rebooting, just like you have to reboot when you wake up in the morning. But after a few of those, my brain learned that when these things happened, it had to snapshot where it was before going down. After two or three of those episodes, from that point on, I never had to reboot. When I regained consciousness, I had all the details – the altitude, the airspeed, where I was, what I was doing and what I needed to do. So even though I went unconscious, I didn't have to reboot anything. The brain learns – snapshot it before you go down and stick it in permanent memory. The body is fantastically adaptive. It's like going to bed at night: you're unconsciousness when you sleep, but when you go to bed at night, and you say, well, tomorrow I've got to do this and that, or I have to wake up at a certain time, you know – you snapshot what you want to have when you get up. And when you get up you have it all. So somehow, either consciously or subconsciously, I learnt to snapshot. From that point on, I always knew precisely what I was doing and where I was."

By the time Story left the space flight world, he held the NASA record, in fact the world record, for the most number of hours flown in a T-38 jet and was probably that aircraft's most experienced pilot. According to Jack Nickel, "Eight thousand hours in a T-38 is equivalent to a thirty-year career in the Air Force – and Story isn't military!"

In the early 1990s, NASA began looking at other aircraft to maintain astronaut proficiency. Story said, "NASA was pursuing other jets, so I got a rating in a Cessna Citation. It was really nice to go off to Flight Safety – you go off for ten days to get a rating and you just live flying. You live flying sixteen hours a day, in the books and in the simulators. The Citation was a really nice experience – to get in a brand new airplane, a business jet, a really nice airplane and to do it right."

According to Story, "Logistically [the Citations] were far better than the T-38s. They could carry eight people, they were pressurized to sea level and so if you did a water run[5] at Huntsville, you did not have to worry about the bends on the way home, 'cause you were at sea level the whole trip. They had a big range and were very effective, but NASA abandoned that after only a year. But it was very nice and I did that the whole year of 1993 while training for STS-61. I was the only STS-61 Mission Specialist who was checked out in the Citation. I enjoyed the camaraderie and the spirit, the flying together – it's a little different to the helmet and the mask you have in a T-38, where you are in different cockpits. In the Citation, you're side by side with someone and then you have the center-seater: the three of you are flying the airplane."

In addition to the large number of hours in T-38 jets, Story owned a series of airplanes in which he continued to instruct others, both for general flying and aerobatics. He also became a member of the Soaring Club of Houston.

After the Cessna 172 which he had flown in Kentucky, Story purchased a Beechcraft T-34. He took his family flying a great deal in this airplane, especially daughter Holly who loved being a passenger.

According to Holly, "I just loved to fly. Literally, I was just totally on a high when I went flying. That was probably my happiest moment, being with my Dad when we were in the plane flying. It was his Beechcraft T-34. We also flew in the Cessna, but I really loved it when it was just me and my Dad in the T-34. And we would do aerobatics over the house. We'd come over and see all the kids out on the street – the neighbors and everything."

The T-34 was imbued with all sorts of memories, including one particular inspection flight. In his journal of 23 November 1974, Story wrote:

> T-34 Post Annual inspection flight with Chris Cross. Took 30 bites by fire ants on left wrist and hand during pre-flight of aircraft. Intense itching of feet, arm pits and groin – tightness in chest. Flew anyway – this was not a very smart thing to do, but again, I have to admire the way you put yourself in tough situations and make yourself perform. Chris is a pilot and could have brought us home. Acrobatic ride is adrenalin – good for the bites. Aircraft in good shape.

Story flew the T-34 for about ten years, until one day it became inoperable during take-off. The local media headlined that astronaut Story Musgrave had survived a crash of his Beechcraft T-34.

According to Story, "Immediately after pulling the landing gear up, I had a propeller failure; I had no idea why it wouldn't fly. The engine was still racing, the

5. Extra Vehicular Activity (EVA) or spacewalking training in the pool.

engine was going hard and the airplane wouldn't fly. And so I was not going to stall it. Stalling means you continue to pull back on the stick until the airplane gets so slow that it won't fly. I was not going to stall the airplane and yet I didn't understand why it wasn't flying. I just landed straight ahead and that was that. I refused to stall the airplane, 'cause to stall is bad, a stall is going to crash. A stall is going to go nose down, it's going to hit hard. So I just slid it right onto the ground and that was that. It was not nice, but it was never dangerous."

The damage to the airplane was significant enough to make it uneconomical to repair. Story said, "It's a matter of you've totally destroyed the engine, given that the engine is striking the ground."

\*

The sailplane[6] is perhaps the ultimate flying machine for Story Musgrave. "It's an extension of yourself. It allows you to become a bird. It allows you to exist in an environment in which you certainly otherwise wouldn't," he said. "The sailplane is a particular kind of airplane – it doesn't have a motor, of course. You really get to know the handling qualities and the aerodynamics, even better than you do a powered airplane, because that is what is going to let you stay up in the air, that's what's going to let you soar like a bird, that's going to let you continue to fly even when the conditions are not very strong for staying up in the air. You become one with a sailplane in an even stronger way than you do with an airplane with an engine. I really like to fly a sailplane slow, where there's very little wind and now the sailplane becomes hugely quiet – very, very quiet, just like being a bird up there. So it has that aspect to it. Humans always dream of flying themselves without a machine. The sailplane is as close as you can get to that."

Story enjoyed a special relationship with nature as a sailplane pilot. He would watch the birds soaring, observing their success in atmospheric conditions before taking to the sky himself. Sometimes he would actually soar with the birds, caught up in the same thermal currents. He described this in one of his college papers[7] for the University of Houston, Clear Lake, referring to himself in third person context:

> Approaching home he spotted a large flock of hawks circling at an immense height: even for them, a seemingly impossible height. Way beneath and slightly upwind of the hawks he started searching the air for the base of whatever funnel had thrust the birds to their present altitude. He found it, or it found him – like a whale finds a rowboat. Oh yea! Oh yea! Screaming with joy and expectation, groaning with strain and acceleration, he wrapped up tight in that funnel and hung

6. Also known as a glider.
7. The paper was titled: *A Story of Earth and Heaven*, 1988.

on. The rate of climb indicator hung on the peg at two thousand feet per minute and skyward he went, using the position of the hawks to help him remain centered. Toward its top, the funnel slowed down and deposited Story in the middle of the birds. He spotted the one which had stayed afloat the earliest in the morning, the one which, like him, had probably been up all day. Story slipped the sailplane over to within six feet of him and followed the hawk around the core of rising air. The hawk was a master, an artist: he stretched his wings to the limit, splayed each feather in his upturned wing-tips, streamlined his whole body to the vector of the wind, and pulled his feet out of sight of the air. The hawks continued to do what they do, in and around Story and in and around the sixty-foot wing-span of the sailplane. Story soared in and around the hawks asking himself and them—Why is it that here, or doing this, you accept me and/or this sailplane? How do you see me? What am I to you? Am I a sixty-foot bird – and you do have no fear? Am I a human, so close and you have no fear? Do you judge me for what I am or for what I do? Is it that, in your world, doing as you, I am one of you, and you know it? Can you tell me why you and I are soaring, soaring together? Can you tell me why you and I reach ever and ever higher, why we reach for the heavens?

Story spoke of this experience later on. "Especially with sailplanes, you go where nature takes you. It's your sensitivity – you have no control and that's why it's so nice. With sailplanes, it's the same as lying down on a raft and going down a river."

The birds were integral to Story's approach to flying sailplanes. "I'm just going up with them – but it was also practical 'cause they can find the best lift around. They're better than me, so I followed them. They have no fear – you're a huge bird. When I look at them, I don't know whether they understand I'm a human inside the machine or whether this whole apparatus is another bird. If they're territorial birds and you go into their territory in a sailplane, they attack 'cause you're a bird in their territory.

"But you've got to listen to the air, which means surrender to it, become one with it, become one with the hawks. Realize that they can do better than you can do; follow them – and I was doing that in that story; I was watching the hawks. Where can they stay up?"

Story said, "Houston was where I did most of my soaring. I did soar back in Kentucky, but again, not seriously; I didn't take it on as a discipline. I took it on for serious around 1975, got all my ratings, including my instructor ratings and I mostly taught. Most of my sailplane career I was teaching. Once in a while, toward the end of the day, I would fly some club member's sailplane. I had loads of club members who would just give me their sailplane, so I flew all kinds of sailplanes 'cause I was teaching for nothing. I was the lead instructor, the only instructor, at times, in a very large soaring club."

Soaring in Houston was filled with challenges – something which was highly appealing to Story. He referred to the geography there as the worst in the world for soaring: "But the magic of Houston *is* that it's the worst in the world! There are no hills, it's wet and the ground is wet. In order to develop a differential, you have to heat some ground hotter than others. But the first thing you've got to do to heat the ground is to cook all the water out of it. As the water evaporates it cools the ground. *Flat* is against soaring and also *water* is against soaring. So it is really the worst there is, but that made it very, very challenging. The real challenge was to stay up on a day that you should not be able to stay up. I worked [housing] developments where you have developments surrounded by greenery – they're either air conditioning or they're heating or they have their lights on in the development and the roofs are hotter than the surrounding green. I could work a development at 1200 feet and stay up all day long, or as long as I wanted to. I worked smoke stacks and I learnt how to work even wind going over a row of trees – I could stay at three or four hundred feet. And other people do too. When you live in a place like Houston, you get exceedingly good at staying up when you should not be able to. Occasionally we'd get a strong day where we could just do what we wanted to and stay up. But that was what was really magical – being a genius at staying up when you should really not be able to go soaring!"

Occasionally, in another part of the country, Story would rent a sailplane and test the local flying conditions. "I had my soaring society of America, my directory of soaring societies. I soared in Philadelphia one time because we were there, and in California. Omaha, New York: Harris Hill, the most famous site in America. It's not necessarily the best soaring but it's the birthplace of Schweitzer, of soaring in America. So in my travels, back then, I would look in the directory and see if there was a soaring site around and I would go rent a sailplane and go soaring in different parts of the country. Harris Hill was like the top of an aircraft carrier – it's just a big square hill and you land and take off on top of the hill. It's like coming down on an aircraft carrier – it's a huge amount of fun. If you miss it doesn't matter 'cause they've got a huge field down below. If you miss the hill, you've got all of Elmira Corning Airport down below. You simply go down there – it's a little embarrassing 'cause they've got to come down and tow you back up, but it doesn't matter."

In addition to his own soaring, Story became a tow plane pilot for the club in Houston. He even bought an airplane capable of doing that – the Bellanca Decathlon, which he described as a better aerobatic airplane than a tow plane: "The Decathlon was superior to the T-34 in aerobatics. It was very, very good. I originally purchased that one to tow sailplanes because the sailplane club lost the tow plane they rented – the person was no longer available [to rent it from]. So I bought a Bellanca Decathlon to tow sailplanes. It was not designed to be a tow plane, but it was adequate. But, at the same time, I taught aerobatics in the Bellanca Decathlon, so at that point I was doing serious aerobatics. I did all the outside maneuvers, which means instead of doing a loop right side up, you push all around toward the ceiling. That airplane was particularly good at that.

"Then I got into sailplane aerobatics, which is a real specialty, a real art form 'cause you don't have engine power to pull you around. And so you have to trade – you're all the time trading the airspeed of the sailplane. You see what you can do at a given airspeed and you can't fly them fast either. And so you really have the limits there from the energy you can get from the speed of the sailplane; you have no propeller to pull you around. And the sailplane rolls incredibly slowly because it has such a huge wing; it's forever getting around to roll, but you live with that. There are very few people who teach sailplane aerobatics. I did that with the Soaring Club of Houston."

Story thoroughly enjoyed the experience of being a tow plane pilot and became an expert at that as well. "Towing sailplanes was, I think, some of the most demanding and therefore rewarding flying I did in my entire career. It's just all the various places you have to give attention to. When you're towing someone behind who's learning how to soar, you're tied to someone on a two-hundred foot rope and, obviously, they're not flying that smooth – they're jerking your tail all over the sky. And where they put your tail determines where you go. The tail goes up, you go down, the tail goes left, you go right. And so all of that. And as a tow plane pilot, you are working the lift, you know; you see where the thermal is. You plan to come back around at a decent altitude and dump the sailplane off in the middle of 'lift'. So you don't just get them up there, you work the lift so that you get to understand the day. You always tow to about 2000 feet – that's where you generally drop the sailplane off. Nothing was more exasperating for me than to bring someone through an incredibly powerful lift at 1700 feet, where it just about tips the sailplane over, and they don't get off! They're just trying to get the other 300 feet. What they don't understand is if they got off where I could have left them at 1700 feet, they would be in a thousand feet per minute climb!"

As a tow plane pilot, Story also enjoyed the complexities of take-offs – the need for intense concentration with all that was happening at the local airport. "I enjoyed towing more than soaring and that's very unusual. People just want to get in the sailplane and they don't want all that incredible demand. They just want the peacefulness and the quietness of going out there soaring. The demands of the tow pilot are just huge. And the alertness, the attention that is required, is severe – all the various things, the 360 vision, and all the things that you've got to have. You're living in the mirror, of course – you've got a mirror up here and you're looking at [everything] going on back there.

"The tow pilot has to be looking at absolutely everything. You're looking for traffic that's trying to land. You're out there in a sailplane field and you're ready to tow someone and you see a sailplane appear over there – well, that sailplane has to come in; it can't wait, it's in the pattern. So you waggle your wings, pull the rope and get the heck out of there and hope the sailplane [that you are towing] saw you run away. If the sailplane and the people getting it ready have not seen this, they need to look around! There's a reason you ditched them!

"And you need to look at the sailplane configuration. The [airport] will give you a big flag; they'll give you a big 360 with the arm – that tells you you're cleared to go. But you're looking at a wing runner who's right in front of the wing and you're gonna run him over. Someone's given you the clearance to go but there's a human being that's in front of the sailplane – so you're not cleared to go!

"And then you'll see you've got the clearance to go but the spoilers are out – the drag devices used for landing. Those are deployed, so you can't go… you do the rudder and you do these things and, oh, I'm not going nowhere! And you hope they'll see it."

Rescuing sailplane pilots who had 'landed out' was something Story did frequently. At times the situation called for a little ingenuity. He explained, "Landing out means you didn't land at an airport, you landed 'out'. And that is something sailplane pilots get very good at. I have never accepted landing out lightly. For me it is close to an emergency – I just never got comfortable landing out, as good as I got at it. But it's when you've run out of lift. You're always looking at trying to make a decent field and trying to land at an airport if you can, but lift is not predictable – it depends on how hard you push. If you only want to land at airports, you can – it's just how much risk you're willing to take. You assess the day. If you have a very strong day then you can play with it, because you know that anytime you get serious about getting back up again, you can. But landing out means you ran out of lift. Some people land out routinely – they do the best they can, but if they have to land out, they do it. I never accepted that. I never planned to do it, I didn't want to do it. A lot of things happen and it's inconvenient, for one thing. But as a tow plane pilot, I ran into hugely demanding situations. People would always call. If I don't come and get them out with a tow plane, they have to get to the nearest phone and call some friend or family member to hook the trailer up and drive 300 miles to come and pick them up – and that is not nice, especially if unplanned. A lot of sailplane pilots are on the radio and they're talking to their team member on the ground and the trailer is actually following the sailplane; they do that as well. But if you've not planned it, it's fantastically inconvenient to call someone up and say, 'come and get me in the trailer.'

"So I did get a big reputation for getting people out of places. I never had anything bad happen in my attempts, but I would do lots of things. I might tow them with a tow plane to some other road; I might have to cut fences 'cause the field was too short – and tell people what you were doing; you check with people. And that whole business of how thick the grass is – two-inch grass versus four-inch grass is a huge difference in your ability to get people out. Long grass will stop you cold. I learnt this lesson – just a little bit of grass!

"And, at times, I'd tell people, 'I really don't think this is going to work.' And they'd keep talking me into it and I'd tell them, 'Well OK, here's where I'm cutting you loose; here's the place. If I don't have this altitude at this point, if I'm not off at this point, I'm cutting you loose – do you understand that? If I don't have certain performance criteria, meaning this speed and this altitude, then I'm cutting you loose.' Which means *I* pull the release – they're out of there – and I've done that to people! They'd plan what they were going to do – they'd bounce off into the next field or land straight ahead or whatever. But I had the criteria and I told them, that's it man. So I'd cut people loose if I didn't have the performance. It is a real art to haul people out of unimproved fields, to take them to some dirt road or else find them on some dirt road and get them out of there, looking for telephone lines and all the rest of that business. So that was demanding."

*

Story is such a physical person that the world of flying was a natural complement to everything else he was doing. To spend so many hours in various airplanes was not only a strive for excellence within that discipline, it was a compelling urge to explore the world from another perspective and to experience new things. When brought to the level of an art form through dedicated practice, flying provided Story with a new form of beauty – one which could be appreciated on many different levels. It became a source of inspiration for his creative writing and a retreat from other activities. Very early in his aviation career, flying also led Story to an increased awareness of the powerfulness of technology when allowed to work within a natural environment. In achieving this level of consciousness, Story found a new way to listen to the world.

"The feedback loop!" explained Story. "The beauty of the feedback loop you get into when the airplane does something and you coax it somewhere. You make some inputs to it, you perceive what it is doing, you do a little bit more and then it does its thing. The loop between what I am doing with this 'animal' and my flying comes more from horses than from machinery, although, you know, a tractor is a tractor – you learn what you do to make it turn left and right. I'm into the beauty of control systems. I like to go out with the tractor and set a good grade with the blade – that's an art form too – but it's feedback between what the blade is doing, what you're doing with the dirt and what you're doing with your hands. I always prided myself on being able to ride a horse without a bit, to ride a horse even without a halter. I got so I could simply lean and the horse would understand where I needed to go.

"So that's a key thing in the airplane. I'm always trying to let the airplane do what it wants to do. I put in a request to it – I really want the airplane to go over here – but I let it take itself over there once I've told it that; I let it fly itself over there. Trim the airplane up and let it fly itself because then you are working on the basic aerodynamic ability of the machine, that stability. You work with that as opposed to against it. You don't resist it and you don't try to control it.

"But it's very nice – the feedback loop, it's part of the aesthetics. It's how beautiful a loop is, and so of course, beauty is in absolutely everything. The control loop between what you do, what the machine or animal or whatever else you are interacting with does. In not controlling, you become one organism. It's the beauty of that loop that the two of you are in – your perception – that is beautiful stuff. A great loop is a beautiful thing. And feedback is absolutely one hundred percent everywhere in life; in human relations too. You do something and you see what happens – cause and effect – it's everywhere. But in the flying world, it's absolutely critical."

Story's approach to flying is analogous to his approach to space flight and, indeed, is central to his philosophy of life where human beings too readily try to control things as opposed to listening. Working in a spacesuit was just the same: you had to know the mechanics, the capabilities and limits of the technology, then work with it to develop optimum performance.

According to Story, "The critical part of flying airplanes is that I never held a control stick in my fist the way it's designed. If you look at the ergonomics of a stick, they're designed to be held in your fist. But I held the stick with fingertips; that lets it talk back to me. I want to listen to the airplane, I don't want to control the airplane. You can take an airplane or a horse and simply tell it what it's got to do, but you don't listen to it. If you put the airplane in your fist, you can't listen to it.

"So I can listen to the currents, listen to what the airplane wants to do and I'm not trying to control the airplane, I'm only trying to let the airplane know what I would like to do. And so it takes me there and it's far more stable, it's far more precise."

Story has often been invited to fly various aircraft – everything from the smallest airplanes to great big 747 jets. But no matter what the make or model, Story's approach has remained consistent. He said, "One time I was speaking to a huge convention in Italy and the crew knew I was on board, so they invited me to the cockpit. I talked with them all and then people always want me to fly their airplanes. But it's also a challenge: you fixed the Hubble Telescope but can you do this? You know what I mean?!

"So I jumped in the left hand seat and they put a co-pilot over there who's a little afraid of how it's going to work out – that I'm going just grab this airplane and we're going to flap around in the sky with four hundred people back there! And so, as I'm reaching to do what I'm going to do, the co-pilot's reaching at the same time – he's going to protect the stick so that it can't make any huge oscillations.

"So I reached up but didn't touch anything. I pushed the auto-pilot off and didn't touch the stick. I know damn well this airplane is trimmed. The auto-pilot's good – it trims it all out. I pushed the auto-pilot off without touching the control stick and the co-pilot was not expecting that. He expected me to get hold of the stick with a fist and then take the auto-pilot off. Then he got the message, instantly. He knew in a flash by my approach that this is going to be all right, so then he took his hands away. He knew instantly the kind of pilot I was.

"So that's it – okay, it's flying beautifully – now I'll take it flying. And then, of course, I touched it with just fingertips. I got to see how tolerant the passengers were and would be! I'm doing these rocking motions, just smooth, and the captain was enamored; he thought this was just beautiful! He knew I was an artist although I don't think the co-pilot was too enamored with doing that to all the passengers back there! I was rocking them to sleep back there – just giving them a little lullaby, just rocking the cradle! I wanted the airplane to do it, not me, so I'm doing this dance. I'm using fingertips on something that weighs four or five hundred thousand pounds. And I'm letting the airplane decide 'up here' when it wants 'down'.

"You could take a cradle and decide the frequency. You're rocking a baby but you're not hitting the natural frequency, you're controlling the cradle, right? The frequency of a pendulum depends upon the gravitational force. The higher the gravity the faster the frequency. And so you let the pendulum go – that's the natural frequency. You are not determining the frequency – your fingertips just keep the energy in that pendulum so it will keep going. An airplane will fly straight and level by itself if you leave it alone; it does not go upside down by itself. So I will put in a little perturbation but then I listen to it – when does it wish to return? What is the natural frequency of this airplane in the air? And so that is the way I'm doing the airplane.

"It's ego-less and it depends upon what level you take it, but it's letting the airplane do the flying, 'cause it'll do better than you can do. Again, it gets down to the universe and it gets down to what the natural frequencies are; your body gets into it. What are the natural frequencies, what does the airplane want to do? The laws of physics here – in the aerodynamics – what is it going to do if you leave it alone? For the people that are being rocked back there, it is a natural frequency and what is happening is so natural for them that it's the smoothest thing of all. And so the laws of physics and the laws of the universe are at work here, not you! That's what's going on, but that's delicious for the passengers – it's delicious; it's the cradle that rocks itself. It's totally in sync with the gravitational field.

"I checked with some of the passengers when I went back there. They said they noticed that we'd make a turn and then go back to the other way, but they were sipping their cocktails and were very happy about it – they thought it was a great flight."

If you ask Story what he loves about flying, it always gets back to beauty – the kinesthetics, the sounds, the mechanics, the geography, the atmospherics. Again, these are very physical attributes which can be experienced emotionally and intellectually.

"I always loved the kinesthetics of flight," he says. "I think everybody does. That's a critical part of a good air show – your classical maneuver – a fast airplane, close to the ground where you can see the speed, and then pulling up sharply and going straight up into the heavens. That is *the* maneuver at an air show; that is the one people are waiting for – there is only one real maneuver and it's that one. Being close to the ground gives you that real perception of the velocity and it is kinesthetic. Kinesthetics means a combination of aesthetics and motion and is probably considered by some to be another sense – a particular sense of motion.

"If you look at a truly beautiful airplane, even if it's static, sitting on the ramp, it has a kinesthetic to it because you envision its motion; it looks like it will fly well. In the airplane world, what looks well, flies well. You get a sense of what is slick, you get a sense of the aerodynamics and how the air is going to flow over that – you get that intuitive sense. So even in a static aesthetic, the kinesthetics is working.

"I love the beauty of nice machinery, no matter what kind of machine. And, probably, we're talking about the beauty of form. I love nice, clean lines, I love clean sweeps, clean curves, the simplicity of a line. It can be straight lines in the right place, it can be lines with little curves. I particularly love the S-shape – not wildly S-shaped, but smooth and slightly S-shaped is my most favorite line; the S-shape line is smooth. If you look at a T-38 sideways, you see it. And so that is my favorite form. My corvette does the same thing – it's got these little waves of S-shaped curves, just very slight. So that's what I like. If you look at manta rays, if you look at fish, you see it in lots of places. So the aerodynamics and the hydrodynamics are probably playing together here."

For Story, the geography and patterns of nature also play an important role in the beauty. "I do like the geography from up there. I am stuck on maps, I absolutely adore maps. I can read maps all day long like they're a book. When I go to see where I'm going on a map, I can't put the map down, I have to look at all these other places! It's disastrous to go to a map, an atlas! I love the maps of the world and I love to look at maps and be reminded of what I saw in space, 'cause I saw the real thing. I love to look at maps of the world and ring up in my head the different views I had of that geography.

"But we're talking airplanes now. It's just a different scale – how far you are up there is a different scale than space flight; you're part-way up there. So I love the layout of things and I see patterns, and this, again, gets back to formal beauty. If you're looking at a meandering river, if you're looking at field patterns, when you're looking at tree lines and all the kinds of things up there, then you see the earth become a painting. When you're down here and you're in it, well you're just in it. You see a single tree that's beautiful, but that's all you see. You don't see the big pattern of things where it becomes a painting or where formal beauty becomes part of it.

"So I love maps and I love patterns and I love geography and geometry. I see spiral eddies from the airplane and you only have to look out the window at the glint and glitter – it's there. All those things I talk about, as seen from space, they're also seen from an airplane. There were some things that were visible from an airplane all along that I never perceived, but having became a serious student of them in space flight, now I see them in an airplane."

As mentioned before, aerobatics played a special role in Story's aviation life. It was something he enjoyed, taught and appreciated, not just for the skill involved, but again, for its beauty.

According to Story, "I never fly aerobatics on instruments like some people do – they just look at the artificial horizon and fly on that. I like to watch the nose coming up when you're doing a loop, then I look over the wings to see if they're square, relative to the horizon, and I snap my head back as soon as I catch the earth behind me so that I can see what I am doing geometrically. You can fly a perfect maneuver on the gauges, you can fly a perfect loop on the eight ball – the artificial horizon. And maybe it'll fly even better on an artificial horizon and looking at the airspeed; it may be more perfect that way. I always cross check instruments, that's what they're there for, but I am trying to live in the outside world. When I'm doing aerobatics, I'm trying to live on earth because I want to see the real thing – I don't want to see the artificial horizon, I want to see the real horizon. That is what is fun to me."

Great sounding engines have always captivated Story. As with any kind of machinery, for him there is an inbuilt fascination with movement and sound. A perfect example of this occurred on a flight we shared across the United States. The dialogue between us was both amusing and pertinent. Story felt I should share it because it is so typical of his relationship to his world:

(Story) I love the sound of an airplane, I love every bit of the sound: when it starts up and as the engine runs. I love a huge piston airplane – that is fantastic sound. But also the sound is to touch the machinery and see how the machinery is going. You don't really hear with the ear, but you reach and grab hold of some aluminum or steel and you find out how it's running. That is why I spend a lot of time in the toilets of the MD-88.[8]

(Anne) Let's put this on tape – 'cause you sent me to the toilets in the back of the aircraft on the way out here. You sent me down there to listen to the engines.

8. A McDonnell Douglas airplane.

(Story) Did you hear the engines?

(Anne) Yes. It's a good sound!

(Story) It's a good sound! ... I could ride in the toilet of the MD-88s, it's gorgeous.

(Anne) It's pretty amusing sending your biographer down to the toilets to listen to the engines!

(Story) That's going to be in there right [in the book]? It is? It's perfect; it says it all! But the toilet of an MD-88 – I mean that is an engine which is humming! And it's coming right through that wall. But it's not just sound is it? It's the two engines in the rear and the fact that the toilet is right at the engine mounts. But now the engine is coming through, not just in sound, but you really – you and the engine become one at that point. I mean I could ride in the toilet the whole trip but I don't want to hog the toilet 'cause people are waiting, wondering what I'm doing in there! But I could ride there the whole trip, 'cause that now is machinery! That is really being in touch with your engine. And the respect you have for that engine and the love you have for that kind of hum – that engine's working away. That penetrates deep, that kind of sound. I find out where in the airplane cockpit I can get a hold of the structure, where I can get a hold of the aluminum or steel or whatever it is, 'cause now I feel the airplane, its vibrations. As you well know, sound is vibrations in the air getting into your ear. Well, you have the same vibrations but they're coming in your hand now. Coming in your hand through touch and pressure, and now the sound is vibrating your body. And so that gives you a good feel for how the airplane is doing. I do that with the Shuttle too; I do that with the Shuttle during launch and re-entry. So I'm always looking for how I get myself in solid contact with the machine, 'cause so many times you're on a soft seat, you know; everyone's trying to isolate you from the noise... Now I'd sleep in the toilet of the MD-88. If I could sleep there, man I would sleep as sound as you could sleep! There would be no distractions, there would be no people banging the suitcase lockers and no people talking; just the engines. So if I had a choice, I'd put a bed back there. That would really send me off to sleep!

Story also had some comments to make about the lack of synchronicity which sometimes occurs between engines on multi-engine aircraft – in other words, the vibrations in the airframe caused by engines that are running at different frequencies.

He explained, "I like the sound of a really big powerful piston-driven airplane. It's the rumble and the roar and the rawness, but it's also the rhythm. I listen for a jet's rhythm when you've got two engines. I'm listening for the hum between the two of them. Some commercial pilots don't even sync them up that well, but I like to sync them up, so I'll set the throttle on one engine and I'll play with the other. When I set the sync, I usually grab 'structure'. I listen with the ear but I grab the steel or aluminum, whatever it is – I'll grab the structure of the frame. I will set the power setting I need on one engine, grab the frame, then move the other engine up and down until I have minimized the vibration in my hand. And that is about as perfect a sync as you can get.

"I've been on airliners where I think, my goodness man! They have automatic sync control, the big airplanes, the well equipped airplanes, and I just think, my goodness, just hit the button! – or maybe the sync isn't working? But often, like the MD-88, if they get out of sync, the throb is even more powerful, 'cause now you really hear the machine running! They go in and out of sync and now you really know you've got hold of a machine!"

For Story, sailplanes provided yet another form of sound. He explained, "The sound of air in a sailplane is very important. And I love the silence, the total silence of the sailplane. The amount of noise you have is only related to the speed of the air – there's not much other sound in there. If you get into bumps, it creaks – sailplanes creak like a boat. When a boat in rough seas is being bent, it creaks; if you put a lot of pressure on an oil barrel, it creaks. Well, the sailplane's fuselage is bending – it's called oil-canning. A sailplane creaks and I like the creaks, I listen for the creaks!

"But in a sailplane I adore the sounds – being able to fly and have real silence while flying slow. As soon as you start flying a sailplane real fast, you get into wind noise. And so you can judge your speed very nicely just by the sound; you hardly need to look at the airspeed indicator. Of course, you can tell by how tight the controls are. At slower speeds, the controls are much looser. At high speeds, there's a lot more air on them, so you can tell the speed that way too.

"There's nothing more beautiful – well, maybe there's things equal – but there's nothing more beautiful than a high performance sailplane."

\*

Story loved to fly in different environments. Two circumstances were particularly important to him in terms of the beauty: flying over the desert and flying through clouds. He took hundreds of photographs of deserts and clouds while flying in the T-38.

He said, "I did a lot of my desert flying at White Sands, New Mexico and at Edwards Air Force Base in California. I have more powerful desert experiences at White Sands because it very rarely rains in California. At White Sands you can get rainbows – rainbows in the desert! You get a sunset and rainbows and all those kind of things going on.

"In the desert you have spectacular visual effects. White Sands has very special visual effects, and low angle sunrises and sunsets are very much a part of that. But there are heat mirages and you get very special kinds of clouds. The white sand itself, the rolling white sand, is spectacularly beautiful. The sand dunes add something, maybe the dryness adds something too, but it's a very special kind of air as well. You have fog up there too – fog and rainbows and cumulus clouds and sunrises and sunsets – and so, in a way, flying in the desert is [related] to the fact that the desert probably has the most powerful effect upon humans as any kind of environment does.

And that is sort of an accepted thing, despite the fact it is so barren. If you read Saint-Exupéry,[9] there's a reason he spent so much time [writing about] getting stranded in the desert, and about the desert people.

"Certain places have their thunderstorms and certain places have their special clouds, special sunsets. Florida is absolutely magnificent for its tall cumulous clouds. The clouds put me here in Florida more than anything else, believe it or not – more than the trees. The clouds tell me I'm in Florida – the Florida of my childhood, the Florida of the Marine Corps and this [present day] Florida. The clouds put me here as much as anything. Florida has absolutely fantastic tall cumulous clouds at sunset. They've been building all day, they've been doing what they do, and now they start dissipating in the sunset and you get these gorgeous walls of red."

Flying put Story in a special relationship to the clouds, which he found magical. "The sunset, of course, is a very different thing when you're flying in it. The cloud is colored red, so you're flying in red clouds, you're flying in red mist. Sometimes a color is a color only because of your vantage point, but that is not the case in sunsets.

"I spent a lot of time looking at and photographing clouds. I took a lot of pictures of clouds and with a lot of my memories of flying, in terms of nature, the clouds are very, very important. They're more important than anything else.

"The airplane immerses you in weather in very special ways. Weather is going to determine whether or not you're going to get there, whether or not you even wish to take it on, and weather also determines how it's going to go in flight. Powerful thunderstorms – my goodness – you really get face to face with them! And whether the fog is going to roll in off the ocean or not and beat you in – you don't go there. And so you have a technical need to know what the weather's doing, but it's also the nature thing – appreciation of nature, but clouds are key."

\*

There are some notable historic and contemporary figures in the flying world which have both delighted and influenced Story.

Written in the early days of flying, Antoine de Saint-Exupéry's book, *Wind, Sand and Stars* became a standard in the flying world and an all time favorite of Story's. The book is full of the adventure and passion of flying. It is essentially about early journeys – mail runs – to remote places in South America and Africa, and passages through Europe. It also takes a look at the nature of humanity as Saint-Exupéry comes into contact with both new cultures and fellow travelers. It is a mature piece, full of wonderful insights and aviation history. Story found many parallels between Saint-Exupéry's descriptions of his adventures and that of his own worlds of flying and

9. *Wind, Sand and Stars*, by Antoine de Saint-Exupéry: first published in French in 1939 under the name *Terre des Hommes*. My copy was translated by William Rees and published in London by the Penguin Group, 1995.

space flight. He also wrote in the Romantic vein, as does Story.

According to Story, Ernest K. Gann, another of his favorite authors, puts you powerfully in the cockpit – faster than anybody else. Reading *Fate is the Hunter*, you soon get sweaty palms if you're that way inclined. Gann, too, was part of the pioneering days of aviation and flew exploratory flights over the unpopulated skies of the Atlantic during the later part of World War II and into other remote areas such as Greenland and South America. Like Saint-Exupéry, his tales of aviation adventure have become legendary. Story has read both books dozens of times.

NASA provided Story and the other astronauts with access to a wide range of contemporary figures – heroes and other extraordinary individuals who were willing to share their lives with those in the world of space flight. There were many such individuals who inspired or affected Story in various ways. He explained, "The job does give you access to people that you ordinarily might not have access to – it's a privilege you have. We had people on the edge, we had explorers. And wherever you go, you get to meet whoever is there. The list is in hundreds – people who are exceedingly well-known. I have the privilege because I have something to share with them – I get to share my world."

One historical figure who came to NASA was Charles Lindbergh, the first person to fly across the Atlantic non-stop from New York to Paris in 1927, when he was just twenty-five years old. Lindbergh went on to a distinguished and diverse career which included the invention of an artificial heart; advisory services to the United States army and navy; fifty combat missions in the Pacific during the World War II; and contributions to the design of the Boeing 747 jet airplane.[10]

Story recalled, "Charles Lindbergh came and talked with us and, you know, it was history, right in front of your eyes. And, of course, it was the history of flight, so that was a huge privilege. I can't say I got to know him, but I did read his stuff, his biography.[11] He was a long term player in the aeronautical business and a student of all that. I appreciated the fact that he was a long term player. [Lindbergh's appearance at NASA] was inspiring, but it was a quiet kind of reflective discussion. It wasn't intended to be a pep talk or anything – it was just for him to say hello – but it was history, right there in front of your face."

Lindbergh died in 1974 and years later, Story found great warmth and satisfaction in visiting his grave in Hawaii.

Another inspiring guest at NASA was pilot Al Haynes, captain of the United Airlines DC-10 which crash-landed in Sioux City in 1989. The airplane lost all hydraulic capabilities after an explosion in the number two engine.

10. Source: the Charles Lindbergh website: www.charleslindbergh.com
11. Lindbergh's autobiographical book about his trans-Atlantic journey, *The Spirit of St Louis* (New York: Charles Scribner's Sons, 1953) won a Pulitzer Prize in 1954.

Story explained, "The airplane had no control systems, so they were using the engines to try to fly it; they were using engine power, back or forward, to control pitch, and left and right on the engines to control direction 'cause they had no control surfaces.

"And you have a DC-10 full of people – it was an incredible story. They landed at a small airport, but the airport was prepared for a total disaster. They had done readiness training and they had great fire rescue and part of Captain Haynes' story was to show how that community had trained for major disasters – just serendipitously. The crew almost landed the thing, but at the last minute they did not. So they crashed onto a runway."

Fatalities numbered 112, but 184 people, including four crew members in the cockpit, survived. "So that is very poignant, very applicable and very relevant. And it kind of sticks in your head," said Story.

One non-aviator who was invited to speak with the astronauts was Evil Knievel. Story remembered, "It was highly educational. He was very interesting but he was in the performance world. It doesn't matter whether it's motorcycles or spaceships, you have an attitude toward those things. You have an attitude towards performance, the ultimate performance, and towards injury and death."

Knievel's approach was vastly different to Story's own approach to the world, especially in terms of risk. "He did some things which he knew couldn't work but [due to commitments], the show would go on. He would tell us 'for this and this and this reason, I knew I couldn't make this jump; I knew what the results would be and I went and did it anyway.' And then he would show the film of the crashes. Well this was a lesson to me; I certainly didn't understand any of that. I didn't understand that, but it was a lesson in that other people think differently and other people respect their bodies differently. But he would tell us and show us X-Rays about how much steel he had in his body. And there was steel everywhere. And, of course, he kept acquiring steel along the way! The physics didn't get in anyone's way. Sometimes people know it can't work, but for some reason they keep going… but it makes you think."

Story found inspiration for the world of flight amongst his own colleagues during his career at NASA. One of the first he encountered was during his year with the Air Force, learning to fly military jets. "I knew Roger Zwieg back in the Air Force at Lubbock, at Reece Air Force Base, where I was in pilot training. For me, he defined the best in the world of flying – the reflective world of thinking about it and always doing it right – *always* doing it right, never ever a compromise. Not just right according to the book, but right at higher levels than the book, having thought and reflected upon it."

Gordon Fullerton, Story's commander on STS-51F was also an inspiration. Story said, "Gordo was your ultimate astronaut pilot. He flew every kind of airplane and he flew them incredibly well. And, of course, flying is his calling – he went back to the

Mecca of flying – flying in the desert at Edwards. He's chief pilot now at Edwards and that's the NASA side of Edwards, not the Air Force side. He rose to be the lead pilot, chief pilot at Edwards. But it's not just flying for NASA and it's not just the Air Force Test Pilot schools out there, but it's the desert. Flying in the desert is a very particular phenomenon, a very particular environment. The desert is made for flying!"

Story also appreciated the skill of the Commander and Pilot on his final space flight, STS-80 in 1996. In his journal[12] he wrote:

> STS-80 entry ... approach and landing. So proud of that team – classic flying, right on; this is a 'pilot thing' and they did it perfectly. Perfect flying, perfect team, looking at Taco and Rommel[13] suited in the front seats, doing what they do – great pilots, professionals, yet kids having fun. Mature process, mature team, analysis, STS, flight control. I did my part, put them in their suits and put them in their seats – could see the faith in their eyes that I knew how to hook them up! They could tell the knowledge was in my hands.

I asked Story if his relationship with nature influenced his decision to become a pilot. He replied, "Yes, because a pilot has a different point of view on the world. Early on, there was the farm machinery that lead to the operating of trucks, tractors, cars and all, and then I went to operating airplanes. But as soon as you get airborne then you're in a new world and you see the world from a different place. Nature is what really led me to look around and to be that kind of pilot; to appreciate space the way I do.

"It gets back to putting your body in a different place – I hadn't thought about it that way before. I'd always thought the transition to airplanes was through machinery, but you're also putting your body in different environments. I've got to put my body in it and I've got to experience my body in a bionic kind of way, not a scientific way."

Story also drew an interesting parallel of self-reliance – a thread which runs throughout his life. "If you put your body in a flight environment and you also solo airplanes, it gets down to self reliance; it's related to that. My comfort in the forest and my comfort in the ponds – knowing that I was out there alone – and, of course, there's nothing there; there's absolutely no threat there for me, but for other people it could be a threat. You see what I'm saying? Solo in the forest, solo in the airplane – you have a sense of self-reliance."

Coming home has always been an important part of Story's life journey – whether it be returning to Houston after a mission, revisiting places of his youth, such as Lexington, or settling back into his hundred acres in Florida after a month on the road. It is fitting, therefore, that he regards the final stage of flying as his favorite part

12. Journal 20, page 49; Date: 18 December 1996.
13. Ken Cockerall and Kent Rominger

of the business: "I did enjoy the physicality, I enjoyed the 'g's, I enjoyed being high, I enjoyed going fast, I enjoyed coming back to earth. My favorite part of flying was when you pull the engines back and you start that glide. I have a huge predilection – I think most pilots like take off and climb – but for me, it's coming back: it's so quiet and so gentle, I love it. That's my favorite part – pulling the engines back and starting down – that last hundred miles of maneuvering to the airport and landing."

Friend and Disney colleague, Chris Carradine summed up Story beautifully when asked if there was anything which had surprised him about Story: "He is quiet and reserved about his astonishing aviation career – he doesn't wear the fighter pilot bravado. But the flying world is a tool for Story to go someplace else. He 'wears' an airplane like a cyborg – like a mechanically enhanced human being!"

# Space

"Will we ever perceive space flight as simply evolutionary pressure... to know and to explore? Is it evolutionary pressure or is it life's longing for life?"

# 9. Space Flight

Space – a great wilderness, solitude, isolation –
a mountain to climb, an ocean, a desert, a forest
– all.

*Story Musgrave, 1989*

Story's first space flight, in April 1983, was also the Space Shuttle *Challenger's* maiden voyage. The second of the spaceships in the fleet, *Challenger* had been named after the British Naval vessel *HMS Challenger* which ventured through the Atlantic and Pacific oceans during the 1870's on a journey of scientific discovery.

When the new orbiter emerged from the Vehicle Assembly Building at the Kennedy Space Center on 30 November 1982, Story shared the historic moment by riding along the six kilometer path to Launch Pad 39A with his spaceship. For him, it was an essential part of the immersion in space flight: the spirit of preparation, the excitement of those who had participated in the development and construction of the Space Shuttles over a fourteen-year period – Story was a part of all that. But above all else, it was the ongoing drama of space exploration through which, in Story's own words, we "reach out and touch our universe". In that context, he wrote:

**Man is the bridge for life moving off earth, for life to crawl into the cosmos.**[1]

Story captured the experience by jumping on and off the slow moving crawler-transporter, taking photographs of everything – the incredible machinery as well as the overall scene of activity. The prospect of finding himself in a brand new physical and psychological environment was exhilarating.

In the midst of the high-tech hardware of the space program, Story was reliving his childhood experiences on the farm: lying in the coolness of freshly ploughed fields and wading in dark pond water. Blazing rockets would soon parallel his earliest memories of horse-power, but neither grass, nor trees, nor solid ground would exist in the new world to which he had earned the right after sixteen years of patient dedication to the space program. What Story took with him, though – a legacy from his childhood – was a Romantic view of space. He wrote:

**We are explorers forever moving outwards, or we die inwards.**[2]

*

Story was in college when the Russian Sputnik became the first artificial satellite to orbit the earth. As a child, space flight did not exist, so naturally, Story dreamt of other occupations – as a fireman, farmer or bulldozer operator. Totally uninspired by school, a teenage Story joined the Marines - a decision spiced with a sense of adventure and an interest in mechanics. Mechanics, then mathematics, the human mind, aerodynamics and medicine – the 1960s arrive and America's first decade of human space flight. With such a diverse background, the decision and subsequent

---

1. Story's handwritten note in his copy of *Transcendence:* Herbert W. Richardson and Donald R. Cutler (Editors), Boston: Beacon Press, 1969.
2. Journal 25, page 31; Date: end of 1998.

announcement by NASA[3] to employ scientist-astronauts, was Story's epiphany. It seemed that everything he had ever worked towards, his interests, skills and energy, could be combined in that role.

He said, "The epiphany which led me to becoming an astronaut – I read in some newspaper, some scientific journal where The National Academy of Science and NASA were going to explore flying people other than test pilots and they were starting those deliberations. At the moment I read that article I was a spaceperson; that's me! I only had to read the article, just like a stroke of lightning. From my aviation education to medicine, and to see in a flash that everything I've ever done in life I can apply to this new job, and that everything is there, and to see in a flash that, yeah, putting my body into ... I mean that's a new place, it's putting my body in a new environment and it's all these frontiers and stuff."

After initially applying to the National Academy of Sciences, Story was then selected by NASA in August of 1967. He and ten others, the sixth group of astronauts – or XS11[4] as they famously nicknamed themselves – were chosen from thousands of other applicants. For Story, it was to be the beginning of a colorful and distinguished career.

Being a scientist-astronaut wasn't an occupation from which Story ever considered resigning, despite the fact that he waited sixteen years to fly in space. He said, "Like a surgeon who's been waiting 16 years to operate, sooner or later, a surgeon has to operate. Sooner or later, I knew I was meant to walk in space."[5]

For Story, space was not only his occupation, it was his calling, and although space flight was his ultimate goal, his contribution to the development of the space program was by no means secondary. To him, space was very much an intellectual frontier as well as a physical one.

As a thirty-two year old with a wife and five young children – the two youngest, Christopher Todd and Jeffrey Paul, born during the family's time in Lexington – the move from the lushness of Kentucky to the heat and humidity of Texas was significant. Having completed a Doctorate in Medicine from Columbia University, as well as Post-Doctoral Fellowships and a Master of Science degree at the University of Kentucky, there were many adjustments to be made including a heavy commitment to training at NASA, which began very early in the morning and often ended late at night. For the family it meant a new neighborhood, new schools and friends, and, as was the case with all astronaut families, a dramatic decrease in the amount of time Story was able to spend with them.

3. National Aeronautics and Space Administration (NASA).
4. "Excess Eleven"
5. Quoted from an interview with American Medical News, 6 May 1983, Reprinted with permission of the American Medical Association © 1983, all rights reserved.

The Musgrave family settled briefly at El Lago, a suburb close to Space Center Houston, before renting out the house and moving again – this time to Lubbock, Texas, as Story commenced his military jet pilot training at Reece Air Force Base.

Despite the changes, Patricia Musgrave recalled a wonderful year at Lubbock with Story and the children. "Lubbock is North-West, and it's on a plateau and they have a lot of tornadoes. So when we moved in we heard the sirens going and when we moved out the sirens were going! But the people of Lubbock made up for it. We made friends right away. I had an incredible pediatrician, one of the best pediatricians I've ever had. We had a great house there, great street, great neighbors. My kids walked to elementary school. We went to the theatre – it was a very cultural town – the ballet was very strong, the theatre was very strong. People were very friendly; we made a lot of friends fast and it was a good year."

In the summer of 1969, Story completed his military jet pilot training at the top of his class, obtained his US Air Force Wings and the family returned to Houston and El Lago. By that stage, the Apollo program was making rapid progress. Within weeks, Neil Armstrong and Buzz Aldrin set foot on the moon. It was a time marked by expectation and excitement around the world and by great momentum at NASA.

Story was at Mission Control for the historic, first lunar landing. In the midst of the euphoria, he was compelled to walk outside and look at the moon. He recalled:

"I had to go outside very shortly and look at the moon; that was what was important. I was not alone – it wasn't like the whole building evacuated, but I was not the only one outside looking at the moon. Those of us that were out there knew precisely, we didn't have to ask why we did that. I looked at it and thought, 'There are humans there'. So I was bringing the space program to the standard view of the moon, but I didn't do anything other than think that there are human beings right there and they're looking back this way at this Earth, [which would look] about the size of a thumbnail… I'm inside Mission Control; I'm seeing the TV picture and I'm looking at the technology and how we're talking to them and dealing with that. I step outside just to get this picture; to look at the moon with the eyes."

During those euphoric days, it was Story's belief that the US space program would achieve a planetary landing by the end of the Twentieth Century and he fully expected to be one of the forefront explorers. A Kentucky newspaper quoted Story as saying, "Before the turn of the century, the astronaut predicts the landing of a man on Mars and thinks he'll be on that flight. He says a planetary mission is his life ambition."[6]

"I was going to Mars. I thought absolutely, certainly, I was going to make it to

6. *The Courier-Journal*, Louisville, Kentucky, 12 March 1970. Article by Beverly Fortune titled: *No Man on Moon, but… UK's* [University of Kentucky's] *astronaut says life in outer space is 'statistical certainty*. Copyright © 2002. Courier-Journal & Louisville Times Co. Reprinted with permission.

Mars when I joined NASA, because I was going to make it a calling. It was going to be a thirty, thirty-five-year career which it ended up being and, as fast as we were going to the Moon, as fast as we were developing new technologies, I was going to make Mars. We were going incredibly fast and we were incredibly good; we were urgent. We set schedules and we went fast and I was going to make Mars; that was going to be my major mission. I was going to make Mars a long-term calling and I was in a position to take care of people as a physiologist and biologist."

Apollo Astronaut Al Worden recalled that from the early days of Story's career, he was always smiling, always very business-like. He said the NASA culture was different back in the 1960s and 1970s; public support was different. There was a core of urgency, an eagerness and a freedom to do what they needed to do.

Story concurred: "It was heady, it was simply heady. We were going to the Moon and we were going incredibly fast. We were fantastic professionals, had a heck of a team and we were going to the moon. So what was it like to be in the space program in the Sixties? We're going to the moon! You can join the team or get out of the way. So that's what was going on then. We're going to the Moon and that organized the spirit; that formed a spirit. That provided urgency and that's what we were doing. We didn't care about the politics. Lots of people are making it happen. We were not in it because of the Cold War. We were in it because we're space people. I don't think the politics crept into the workers at all. We didn't give a damn about the Cold War; we were going to the Moon. So that was nice you see; that was fantastically healthy."

At a political level, though, things were a little different. Story recalled, "We [America] were not doing space for the sake of space. If you were doing space for the sake of space, you would have developed a vision of where you would be in the next decade, but we never developed any vision along those lines. You probably could not have dealt with that much infrastructure, you probably could not have spent that much money on the space program, unless you couched it in Cold War terms. You cannot spend that much money just because of the Romantic aspect of space flight, the Romantic or scientific aspects. So it probably couldn't have happened in the idealistic way: space for the sake of space. But it did cause problems with future vision. We did not have a long-term vision."

This 'fast and furious' era also bred two types of astronauts – the famed fighter jock variety, who enjoyed the prestige and the attention; and those who looked beyond the glamour and were receptive to different things, who could step back and think philosophically about what was happening. This latter group included the scientist-astronauts.

In a bid to highlight the Apollo program's potential contribution to science and, at the same time, respond to growing pressure from the scientific community for greater involvement in human space flight, NASA determined that a number of positions for astronauts would be filled from among qualified geologists, geophysicists, medical doctors and physiologists. Those applicants with flying experience would be given preference, but it was not the critical factor for acceptance, as all the astronauts would receive military pilot training in their first year.[7]

Story described the new era of space flight this way: "You've got the world of the military test pilot and you've got the world of the scientist coming together and you have to blend those two cultures – and there wasn't much there to help blend the two cultures."

It was extremely difficult for some people within the NASA organization to accept the changes in astronaut recruitment. The flying "club", which consisted of some of the best test pilots in America, had considered space flight their domain since the 1950s. The scientist-astronauts were a different breed, an unknown quantity, and as such, were often viewed and treated with suspicion and distaste. Another group of astronauts who found acceptance difficult, were those who had been transferred from the Air Force Manned Orbiting Laboratory program, which was cancelled in 1969. Incredibly, in some quarters, the rivalries and jealousies would continue for more than thirty years, often determining who would fly in space and limiting the career prospects of some very talented astronauts.

This is not something which Story likes to focus on, nor did he choose to become bitter about it. However, during his career with NASA, it did, at times, cause frustration and annoyance.

Story said, "Any people that the space program attracted were hugely competent people but [the scientist astronauts] were 'straights', they were straight kind of people, they were conservative people. They weren't just nerdy people – you may have been sort of nerd-like in your attention to detail and your focus and concentration, but they were fantastically good too – fantastically good at meeting external requirements and being adaptive to those. They were highly competent, highly motivated people."

Against this backdrop of internal politics, the American space program continued to move forward with the combined talents of each faction. Story said, "Space attracted very talented people because it was space flight – especially going to the Moon. And, of course, it was seen as a fantastically positive thing by the media. They were very interested and everybody wanted us to get there."

The Apollo program and lunar landings continued until 1972. Story had been assigned to the design and development of the Skylab program, the first US space station, which launched unmanned on 1 May 1973 and remained operational for nine months. He was backup science-pilot for the first manned Skylab mission, Skylab 2,

7. Source: NASA History Office website: http://www.hq.nasa.gov/office/pao/History/

which was launched nine days later to rendezvous with the space station, and he was a CAPCOM[8] for the successive Skylab 3 and 4 missions from July 1973 until February 1974. In addition, Story also participated in the Life Sciences Program Mission Simulation – a week long simulation for running life science experiments in the spacelab vehicle.

Frank Hughes, who later became Chief of Space Flight Training at NASA, recalled the first time he was introduced to Story. It was at the simulators in Florida where Story was undergoing his training as a backup crew member. Frank was impressed with what he saw. He recalled, "I'd have swapped him out in the crew right away. Story was so precise and honed in on what the hell was going on. It would have been a dream to get him trained and out."

For the Skylab missions, Frank worked as a flight planner in Mission Control where he was, again, witness to Story's capabilities: "Story was a CAPCOM during that period and we sat side by side on many occasions at the Control Center while the crew was in orbit. And he was a good negotiator. When they went to do spacewalks at various times, he'd be there at the Control Center and he knew a lot about what was going on."

Skylab's primary goal was to test long duration space flight and to study solar astronomy. Crews conducted solar research, carried out detailed earth observations and performed a number of EVAs[9] to install and repair the space station's equipment. The Skylab project successfully demonstrated people's ability to endure long-term space flight[10] and, at the same time, collected valuable physics, meteorological and medical data for ground-based scientists.[11]

Story captured the importance of space exploration, in the universal sense, when he told a newspaper reporter: "People once thought the earth was the center of the universe. We're not only not at the center, but we're way out in the woods."[12]

In 1971, Story took over Rusty Schweickardt's role as NASA's lead spacewalker. He said, "Why '71? It's 'cause in '71 we were mature spacewalking on the Moon and we were developing new spacewalks to do Skylab, to retrieve all the film. I was the back up on the first Skylab on Rusty's team, so I got to develop the Skylab spacewalks and that's how I fell into that. I fell into that job then because I was not necessarily

8. Capsule Communicator
9. Extravehicular Activities or spacewalks.
10. The crew of Skylab 4 remained in orbit for 84 days.
11. Skylab details were obtained from NASA/Kennedy Space Center External Relations and Business Development Directorate website http://www-pao.ksc.nasa.gov/history/history.htm
12. *The Courier-Journal, Louisville*, Kentucky, 12 March 1970. Article by Beverly Fortune titled: *No Man on Moon, but… UK's* [University of Kentucky's] *astronaut says life in outer space is 'statistical certainty.* Copyright © 2002. Courier-Journal & Louisville Times Co. Reprinted with permission.

recognized as good or the best, but because Skylab was to do the next spacewalks; those were the next ones that we had to develop."

In an interview with Nina L. Diamond, Story spoke further of his spacewalking role: "In 1971 I became the astronaut specialist in spacewalks, leading into the Skylab program. I'm also the astronaut specialist for the Shuttle suits, EVA, and others. The physiology you have in a suit is what the suit gives you – the pressure, the oxygen. It removes carbon dioxide, controls your temperature, everything. There's a lot of good anatomy in the relationship of your body to the suit: it has to work as an integrated organism. As soon as you learn that, you become more skilful in working with a space suit. You don't work against it anymore, and you don't even look at it as a friend. When I go out in this suit, I am now a new organism that has to work in certain ways."[13]

Story explained some of the challenges of testing the spacesuits: "I had to test all the spacesuits. I had to test the life support systems. I had to break them down. In the vacuum chamber, I had to put more workload into the suits than you could take out, and so you build the temperature. The physiology can't keep up with you and it becomes horrendously bad inside that suit and you wish you could tear it off. Even in a vacuum chamber it gets so bad in there. It's like trying to run a mile with a bag over your head. It is really terrible."

Astronaut Jim Voss, who flew on STS-44 with Story, spoke of Story's role in the spacewalking world. "He was acknowledged as being a real expert on the systems and how to work in a spacesuit, so for quite a few years he was the leading authority here at NASA for spacewalking, and a lot of people went to him for advice and some tips on how to work better in the suit. Story was very methodical, he had a way of doing everything and had thought about it very carefully – even the simple things of working in space – and was able to share that information with other people."

From the end of the Skylab era, Story participated in the development of the new spacesuits, life support systems, airlocks, manned maneuvering units (MMU) and launch escape systems for the Space Shuttle program. Then, from 1979 until 1982, he was assigned to the Shuttle Avionics Integration Laboratory (SAIL) as a test and verification pilot, a role which he continued for a further year after his first space flight in 1983.

Story spoke of his time in SAIL. "That was a marvelous chapter in my NASA history. It was even more important than what I did in spacewalking; it was every bit as enjoyable. I was yanked out of the spacewalking world and I didn't understand that; I thought, my goodness, I'm being taken out of that when I've put in eight years and led that effort – just at the point when things are coming to fruition... except at

13. Interview for *Omni Magazine*, by Nina L. Diamond, August 1994. Reprinted by permission of Omni Publications International Ltd.

that point it was a done deal to manufacture [the suits] – the design and testing had been done. So actually, it was a perfect thing to do. I did not accept it at the time, I didn't understand it at the time, it was against my will, but I had been specializing pretty darn heavy on the spacewalking – I have to learn the vehicle now. As soon as I got into SAIL, it was marvelous. You really learnt the software – the shuttle only operates on software. My role in SAIL was even more important than what I did in spacewalking, it turns out. It was very, very critical – I became the lead there prior to STS-1."

Of his various NASA roles, Story said: "I did a lot of other things, but if you look at what my sub-specialty was, what was my principal, I'd say spacewalking. I did the first Shuttle spacewalk; the first one that was done in the Shuttle [era], sort of by luck in some ways. It's nice when you've worked on something for a dozen years to get to be the one to test it but there was no guarantee, you know. It was luck that I got to do it. When, in the development of spacesuits, are we going to be able to do that? When is everything going to come together? Well, it all came together when it was my turn to go flying. There was some element of, since I have developed them I would do a good job testing them, but there was also some luck involved. It's one of those things that all came together. It all came together when I was going flying."

*

When Story was selected for STS-6, his first space flight after sixteen years with NASA, it seemed that justice had finally prevailed. The crew would consist of commander Paul Weitz, pilot Karol Bobko and mission specialists Don Peterson and Story Musgrave.

As far as Story was concerned, the Space Shuttle was the most dangerous human launch vehicle ever developed, in part due to the use of the two 46-metre long solid rocket boosters which were needed in addition to the external fuel tank to lift the heavyweight orbiter. The Space Shuttle was also the only space vehicle launch-tested with human occupants aboard, and having no engines for landing, there would be only one opportunity to land safely, as it would be unable to climb and fly around for a second approach to the runway.

Don Peterson recalled some early misgivings he and Story had about the safety of the Space Shuttle. "There were people who thought that vehicle was invulnerable and I don't think – I know Story and I have talked about this – and we really said, if we get to twenty-five flights without a major problem, that will be quite an achievement. Of course, we got almost exactly to twenty-five flights before we had a major problem. The vehicle is a very complicated thing, very hard to operate, very hard to keep in shape to fly, and takes a tremendous amount of work on the ground."

Following a series of Approach and Landing tests by the Space Shuttle prototype Enterprise, the Space Shuttle *Columbia* was rolled out to the launch pad and successfully completed five missions between April 1981 and November 1982. It was lauded as a major victory for the space program and a vote of confidence in the ability of all those involved in its operation.

The initial STS-6 launch date of 20 January 1983 had to be postponed after a hydrogen leak in *Challenger's* number one main engine aft compartment was detected during a 20-second Flight Readiness Firing (FRF) on 18 December 1982. As a result, all three main engines had to be removed and reinstalled on the launch pad during the repair process. Further delay was caused by contamination to the Tracking and Data Relay Satellite-1 (TDRS-1) during a severe storm.[14] Finally, a new launch date was set for April 4, this time successful. The primary payload was to be the TDRS-1. Other payloads included the Continuous Flow Electrophoresis System (CFES), Monodisperse Latex Reactor (MLR), a Radiation Monitoring Experiment (RME) and Night/Day Optical Survey of Lightning (NOSL).

Don Peterson spoke highly of the professionalism of the crew of STS-6. "I don't ever remember a cross word between people on the crew. We just got along well and did what we needed to do, and everybody worked hard and there just wasn't any friction. And that's not true of all crews. Crews are forced to be very close together for long, long hours for a long, long period of time. Story is very dedicated, he's extremely knowledgeable about what he's doing and, you know, he had a good education before he started, but some of the things he was asked to do really had very little to do with his past experience and he just learned them. He's very bright and very energetic, very capable, and he's very willing. Just give him a job and he learns it. That makes him a very valuable person to work with because, on a spacecraft, there are lots of jobs that need to be done and sometimes nobody on the crew is ideally qualified, so you have to learn something new and you have to learn it quickly and you have to do it right. And Story was very good at that. Story was never a guy who demanded a lot of personal attention or personal recognition or personal care; he just did his job. Makes him a lot easier to work with than some folks."

For Story, his first Space mission was an exciting time. He told reporter Larry Arnold that as soon as the crew was buckled into their seats and the hatch closed, he unbuckled himself and sat up to be more comfortable. "If I didn't know how I could get back in them… the Commander said we were going whether I got back in my straps or not."[15]

In addition to his children, many members of Story's extended family traveled to Florida for the launch. That included his Uncle Jack and some of his cousins, including Jack's daughter, Clover Swann. Clover recalled, "Story wasn't there with us; he was in quarantine because he was going into space. We were all really excited, and so a lot of us went down [to Florida]. NASA put us on these army buses and took us

14. Source: NASA http://science.ksc.nasa.gov/shuttle/missions/sts-6/mission-sts-6.html
15. *Lubbock Avalanche-Journal*, 5 June 1983.

around the rockets and so on, and then would take us back to the hotel. It was very strange, very interesting. I don't think we realized that we wouldn't be with Story!"

The first two days of the mission were long and strenuous, but that didn't stop Story from making the most of his spare time. Don Peterson described a little incident which occurred the first night in orbit: "We had two really long days, the first two days. The first day was like 20 hours or 21 hours and the second day was about 18 hours. And on the very first day, Story and I deployed the satellite [TDRS-1]. You couldn't hold it in the bay 'cause it didn't have enough internal power, so you had to get it out, get it's solar arrays unfurled and let it start gathering sunlight. We were worried about controlling the temperature of it and all the other things, so we were working against a clock, in a sense. We got that done but then it was very late and [Commander] Weitz says we need to knock off, we need to go to sleep 'cause we've got another long day tomorrow.

"Well, I put my hammock up on the wall of the spacecraft where my head would be near the radio because I was supposed to listen for the emergency radio. And I was going to sleep when I heard this little tinkling noise, kind of like sleigh bells, and it was Story, and he's in the airlock fooling around with the suits. He wasn't supposed to do that until the third day but he wanted to get ahead, so he's in there tinkering with the suits. And they have all kinds of little straps and buckles, and when you move them around in zero-gravity, they jingle. So he's making little tinkling noises and I would doze off and then I'd wake up. I finally dozed off and went sound to sleep and Story came over and pulled on my sleeve and woke me up, and said 'I've noticed you've had trouble sleeping, would you like a sleeping pill?' And I said 'No, what I'd like you to do is knock off all that tinkering in the airlock.' And the next day Paul Weitz, who hadn't said anything the night before, said 'Story, if you're going to play all night, you're going to have to do it outside! We're not doing that inside anymore.' But Story is the kind of guy, he got focused on a job and he would do the job, sometimes to the exclusion of other things."

Such was the excitement of that first mission, that Story rarely got to bed before 5am Houston time.

At around 4.15pm Eastern Time on the 7 April 1983, Story, wearing the new $2.5 million spacesuit, emerged from the airlock into space, followed closely by Don. It was nine years since the previous American spacewalk. One of Story's first comments to Mission Control was: "It's so bright out here. It's a little deeper pool than I'm used to working in"[16] – a reference to the swimming pool used for spacewalking training.

---

16. As quoted in *Walking to Olympus: An EVA Chronology* by David S.F. Portree and Robert C. Treviño. Monographs in Aerospace History Series #7, October 1997. Published by the NASA History Office, NASA Headquarters, Washington DC.

Don Peterson recalled: "The whole purpose of that spacewalk was to test the suit, test the airlock, work with some of the tools and just show that those systems would all work in space. And that's not as risky as it might sound. All that equipment is tested over and over on the ground and it had seen all the environments. It's not like you're going to go do something with the suit that's never been done before, so you feel pretty confident that everything's going to work. I think the people who built the suit were up-tighter than we were and that's because the suit had not worked on the flight preceding ours and caused that spacewalk to be cancelled. So they were under the gun and I think they thought that because the suits hadn't worked on the first flight, we must be scared to death to take them outside, which was not true… at least I didn't feel worried about the safety of the suit."

The first Space Shuttle spacewalk, on the third day of the mission, attraction millions of television viewers from around the world. It was noted in newspapers across the United States and elsewhere with great enthusiasm and interest. The *New York Post* printed an article on 8 April titled, *A Stunning Space: A Heavenly Stroll at 300 Miles Per Minute*. Journalist Peter Fearon captured the moment superbly with his description of the first Space Shuttle extravehicular activity: "Astronaut Story Musgrave did a joyous handstand on the rim of *Challenger*'s cargo doors last night as he and Don Peterson took the first spacewalk in nine years. In spectacular television pictures, the world watched the two Americans float, gambol, cartwheel and cavort in a stunning display of space-nastics."[17]

Story's daughter Holly recalled watching her Dad on television during that first spacewalk: "The launch was in Florida and then we flew out to California because we were going to get the landing [at Edwards Air Force Base]. We were on Huntington Beach and we knew what time the televised spacewalk was going to be and so we all ran from the beach to the hotel room, turned on the TV and Dad came on for the spacewalk. They go right up close to him, to his face, and he waves his finger. It was live, and we were like – this is so absolutely awesome that you can sit here and run off the beach to our hotel room and watch your Dad and he's doing that right now, live in space! That was really momentous for all of us kids. It was just one of those moments that is really vivid and you remember all the details of that day."

Shortly after the flight, Story gave a wonderful description of what he saw 'outside' to reporter Denis L. Breo of the Flying Physician. "It sure was a spectacular sight. I was taking in the sunrises and sunsets – you can't tell them apart from up there. Even such a simple thing as our flash evaporator was making things of beauty. It would throw out little icicles of water, and you would see a tremendous blizzard of sparklets of light of all sizes, shapes, and velocities come tumbling at you. Every hour

17. *New York Post*, 8 April 1983.

and a half, we made a complete orbit of the Earth, and it was just like getting a crash course in world geography. Seeing entire continents with the naked eye is something special. We saw oil slicks off India, oil tankers in the Persian Gulf, the swirls in the Earth's crust where Iran, Pakistan and India collided years ago and the mountains were thrust upward by the force. We saw the White Nile and the Blue Nile converge in the Sudan, the dust storms in Mexico, the thunderstorms over Africa, the tranquil beauty of the Bahamian Islands. These are all 'gee whiz' things."[18]

Don Peterson related an interesting 'aside' of their famous spacewalk: "My suit leaked! It's kind of an interesting little story, but one of the things that we did was work with tools and we had foot restraints. You had to first get the foot restraint, carry it where you were going to work and then you had to set the foot restraint up. When you were finished, of course, you had to take it all down and bring it back, and that added a lot of time to whatever you were doing. Well one of the things I was going to do was use a ratchet wrench and drive a bolt, and it was in the mechanism that launched the satellite and we were going to prove that if you needed to work with that system manually, you could do so. So I was back there and I had the ratchet wrench and I just held on with one hand and used the ratchet wrench with the other and my body floated out behind me until I was pretty much in a line. Well, when I worked my arm, my legs were reacting to the motion because there's nothing to stabilize you, so my legs were kind of flailing, almost like a swimmer, and all of a sudden I got a caution or warning alert on my suit that said I was using excessive oxygen. Now oxygen, of course, is used to pressurize the suit and if you're using too much, it either means you're breathing an awful lot – and a guy my size really can't breathe that much – or there's oxygen leaking somewhere. So I stopped what I was doing and Story stopped what he was doing and came over and, you know, the plan is, if you've really got a leak in the suit, you go back inside. You don't want to wait and see if the suit's going to leak down or the leak's going to get worse. It leaked for about 20 seconds or 25 seconds and then the alarm went off and everything seemed normal, so we just went back to work. The ground crew – we weren't in contact with the ground when that happened because in those days you didn't have the satellites in place and we didn't have a continuous [line of communication] – they didn't know what had happened. I think if they had known it had happened, they might have told us to go back inside, but since they didn't know, we went ahead and finished the EVA. And they didn't really discover that until later. Somebody was reviewing data and realized it had happened and for two years they told everybody it was because I was breathing, working hard. Working the suits is hard, it's very physically demanding and my heart rate was 193, so you are working pretty hard. But that really wasn't the cause and a

18. *Flying Physician*; article titled: *MD Astronaut Tells of Space Adventure*, by Dennis L Breo, June 1983, Vol. 26, No.2, pages 6-12.

technician found that two years later when Shannon Lucid was using her suit in a chamber on the ground. They put you in a harness 'cause the suit's very heavy. She was walking on a treadmill and her suit leaked, and it leaked just like mine did. It leaked for about 20 seconds and stopped. And this technician – and this is what amazes me, that the guy would have this kind of memory – he looked at the video tape of her and said, you know, I've seen this same leak before, I'm going to go back. And he went back to our flight and the fact is that when she was walking on the treadmill, her hips were swiveling the same way my legs were flailing and he said, 'I believe that's what's causing that'. Then they took a suit, inflated it with nobody in it and worked the legs back and forth, and they were able to reproduce it."

In a final mission highlight and contrary to standard procedure, Story stood throughout the de-orbit phase as *Challenger* re-entered the earth's atmosphere. He told Dennis L. Breo: "I was conducting my own experiment. The whole flight had been so totally exhilarating and I was on such a high that I decided to stand throughout re-entry. It's my nature to press and push, to go beyond what's expected. I had my Hasselblad camera and I was taking some photos. Also, I wanted to prove that you can stand while going from zero-gravity back into gravity. That's important if an astronaut ever has to leave the top deck and go below to throw a switch or circuit breaker. I wanted to show that the cardiovascular system doesn't have any problem going back into gravity and that you don't have to be strapped down. My standing was smooth and steady, and it shows how the STS system is maturing. We all had total confidence. Standing up throughout re-entry, instead of being strapped down, was the perfect end to a perfect trip. I was having fun, as always."[19]

Don Peterson left NASA in November of 1984, but during the fifteen years he spent in the astronaut corps, especially during the seventeen months of training for STS-6, he got to know Story very well. When asked what Story's main personal motivation was, Don offered this insight: "I guess, for one thing, Story had a fairly tough young life, didn't have much money, didn't have any status, any prestige. I think he told me once that his early objective in life was to be a caterpillar tractor operator; that was his ambition. And to a certain extent I grew up, not as tough as he did, but the same way. My family had no money and I think part of what you do is say, 'I've got an opportunity to do better than that', and you're kind of driven to take advantage of that. Obviously, in Story's case, he's succeeded far beyond what most people probably would have expected him to do based on how he grew up, but I think that's part of the drive. I think the other part of the drive is, and again I think it's something most people [in the astronaut] office share, is just that some people are inquisitive and industrious and they want to do something. You know, they wouldn't make a good

19. *Flying Physician*; article titled: *MD Astronaut Tells of Space Adventure*, by Dennis L Breo, June 1983, Vol. 26, No.2, pages 6-12.

banker or a good business owner because they're not interested in that. What they want is to go do something new and challenging and different with little bit of excitement. I think there's some of that in all the people in that office. I'm sure there are some people whose major objective is to fly a couple of flights, command a Shuttle and become a manager somewhere. I'm not knocking that; that's OK, but I think most of the people who are there, are there because they enjoy getting a feeling that they're doing something different and new and exciting and contributing to something. And I think that's part of what drove Story."

As 1985 approached, Story prepared for his second space flight, again aboard *Challenger*. It was a science mission, STS-51F/Spacelab-2, which launched on 29 July 1985. Story served as systems engineer for launch and re-entry, and as a pilot during orbit. The mission conducted experiments in astronomy, astrophysics and life-sciences and was the first mission to operate the Spacelab Instrument Pointing System (IPS), which was used to aim astronomy devices.

Commander Gordon Fullerton recalled, "Story was assigned to my crew for 51F and from day one, he's just charging like mad. In the training we'd go into simulators and I had to kind of put a restraint on him 'cause he would charge ahead and do everything himself and nobody else would get a chance to train. So he got that message and was a great help. He had the experience that the non-pilots on the crew needed to have for their kind of duties, so he was a leader 'cause everybody else was a rookie."

Gordon spoke of the continual stream of activities in Story's life. "It must be built into the genes, 'cause it's not anything that happened when he got into the astronaut program. He had like 'sixteen' degrees and he was running off doing surgery in Denver and every chance he got he'd be flying the T-38, more than anybody else. And obviously it didn't give him much chance to stay home. He didn't stay home much… He was not only in the government airplanes, but he had a Cessna 172 that I rented from him once, that he used to give lessons in, and then he had a T-34 that he gave aerobatic lessons in, and I forget what else. But once again, he didn't sleep much; he would go many hours a day and he was driven to that. I thought he ought to just cool it now and then and enjoy some of the things he had, but that wasn't Story. He was a goer."

According to Gordon, Story was a pleasure to deal with. "Actually, you know, Story's a real straightforward guy. You might imagine such a high energy guy would be talking a mile a minute and waving his arms and hard to control – not at all. He was high energy and doing stuff but he was totally reasonable and a delight to work with. He wasn't overly serious like a lot of hyperactive people, where it's the end of the world when something doesn't go well… not at all. He seemed to have a good blend of concern versus when it doesn't work out, don't fight it, move on. You'd ask him to go chase something down – he would, and yet he had lots of initiative so he figured out things that ought to be done and suggested them as well. I couldn't have had anybody better to fly in that position."

Their mission, 51F/Spacelab 2, was unique in many ways, being the first mission during which the crew worked in shifts around the clock. Gordon recalled, "Well, it had a lot of firsts. One of the firsts was just in getting ready 'cause it was the first really jam-packed timeline, science wise. We had all these telescopes on board. They wanted to maximize the use and to do that, they wanted the crew up working on them 24 hours a day – no breaks; never shut down. Every other mission, up to that point, had a sleep period where everybody went to sleep. And so we had the challenge of organizing and planning the shift operation where we had a red team and a blue team. Story was by far the other most experienced person and he was leading the other team, in effect, on all aspects of the basic housekeeping, as well as he had a lot of knowledge about operating the Shuttle in orbit.

"I remember being down [at the Kennedy Space Center] one time with Story when the Shuttle was out on the pad. The payload doors were still open and we remarked – this thing is full from stem to stern with stuff that we've got to operate. This is the gangbuster payload of the program to date!"

Unlike other Spacelab missions – where crews worked within a separate laboratory housed in the payload bay of the Space Shuttle – the payloads on this mission were operated entirely from the cockpit.

Gordon recalled the great team spirit which existed among crew members. "I remember down at the beach house – they have an old house on the launch area that families can go out to [before a launch] – and we had all the families, with the crew; quite a sizeable group. They all enjoyed each other. There weren't any real big differences in philosophy or lifestyle; it was just a very nice gang."

Before the mission could get off the ground, however, it faced some serious technical hurdles. The first launch attempt on 12 July was halted at T minus 3 seconds when a hydrogen coolant valve failed to close. By this stage, all three of the Space Shuttle's main engines had been lit and the on-board computer system had to shut them down. According to Story, the system did what it had to do and did it well, however, for the families of the astronauts and the thousands of spectators watching the launch from the four mile exclusion zone, the situation was not as clear. The words from Launch Control concerning the aborted launch attempt were followed closely by a loud explosive noise, which, in fact, was the delayed sound of the main engines' ignition. To some, it appeared to be a dangerous explosion aboard *Challenger* following the launch abort.

Astronaut John Blaha, who was acting as a family escort for the mission, recalled the difficulty of balancing his knowledge of what was probably happening, with the emotions of the families who watched anxiously from the top of the Launch Control Center building. "I remember when the families asked me if there was anything dangerous with this – and any time I was in that situation, I would lie! So I'd say, 'No, no problem, they've got it under control.'"

In *Wind, Sand and Stars* – widely recognized as the first great book about the explorations of early pilots and also one of Story's favorite books – Antoine de Saint-Exupéry wrote: "Waiting for an explosion is the longest of passage of time I know."[20] In the margin beside it, Story carefully wrote:

Launch Abort.

Story recalled the situation on board *Challenger*. "We were just hanging on, waiting for the bad thing to happen, but our crew did extraordinarily well. Everyone unstrapped and I could look down the hatch and Tony England was there, sitting at the hatch waiting. He didn't move, 'cause Launch Control didn't tell us to egress. We were waiting to get the words 'emergency egress', and so we got out of the straps and got everything else ready, but stayed on communications and stayed on oxygen hose 'cause we had not been given emergency egress. But we were ready to jump out of that thing.

"We didn't understand what all the water was for, of course. That was because of fire – they thought we had a fire underneath. And we did, I guess. They turned on all the fire hoses, so that was a little disconcerting: 'Why the fire hoses?' – 'Well, there must be something that needs water…!'

"Everyone did exactly the right thing, but you sure were thankful that it all turned out right; it was one of those cases when you were very thankful!"

According to Bob Sieck, who was launch director for the mission, Story's humor prevailed, even in the midst of the drama. "Story commented over the intercom, 'You know, all my training said that after the engines shut down, we'd be in zero-g'. And he said, 'It still feels pretty uncomfortable in here!'

Bob continued, "Story was calm, cool, collected, businesslike; absolutely unflappable. And I never saw him go berserk or anything like that; if he did, he didn't show it. I never saw his ECG when he was on EVA, but I imagine… most of [the astronauts] are pretty cool. I was a biomedical engineer in the Gemini program and we put the sensors all over them. There were a lot more sensors then than now. And then they'd get up in the space craft and we'd look at their heart rate and electro cardiogram, respiration rate and that sort of thing and, of course, blood pressure and temperature and all that kind of stuff. And they were cool; they'd kick along there –

---

20. *Wind, Sand and Stars*, by Antoine de Saint-Exupéry: first published in French in 1939 under the name *Terre des Hommes*. My copy was translated by William Rees and published in London by the Penguin Group, 1995.

70, 80 beats per minute. You'd get up to T zero [lift-off] and maybe it'd get up to 80 or 90, but that'd be it; they were cool customers. And I would expect Story's would have been the same thing. The only time I saw high heart rates of astronauts was when they were mad!"

When the crew came back for another launch attempt two weeks later, there were other difficulties. Story explained, "We got out there to go fly and the launch control team comes to one of these major milestones which are called Launch Commit Criteria (LCC). If there are any violations, you can't launch. And so periodically the launch director will ask the team for any LCC violations and you have to fess up at these points; you put it on the loop for everybody to hear. And we heard this voice come up and say, 'SRB rate gyro is hard-failed.' And that was a show stopper! I went through all my days of testing in the Shuttle Avionics Integration Lab and I looked at why it was gonna stop us. The primary computers could work it, but we would not have backup computers with that gyro down. So I said, hey, I know that one. It's 'no go'; we're not going anywhere!

"You fly on four primary computers that look at each other, but if they all fail, then you engage the backup and one computer does all the flying. So they came up with a patch for the backup computer to make it flyable with this gyro hard-failed. This takes time and so it's getting to be a really long day. Nowadays, they have 'back time' – you can only spend so much time on your back once you have strapped in; you have to launch by this time or you abort. It doesn't sound stressful to lie on your back, except all the straps are holding you in the hard points and, of course, the chairs were not designed to really support that kind of thing. But anyway, we just went on forever – hours and hours. They built the patch for the backup system, put it into the backup computer, then read the backup computer to see that the changes were there. And nothing had changed! You know what that means? It means the patch went somewhere else that you didn't plan on its going! So now we have a gyro that's dead and the backup computer is dead. But they still are going to try and fly.

"The day is wearing on. They're going to re-load the backup computer, they're going to reload the whole damn thing with the patch. They gotta go way back to square one on this whole countdown and man, that's getting rough.

"And, of course, I was sitting or standing in my seat at this point. I would stand and look at my buddies. I tried to get them out of their seats because they're really starting to hurt. And, of course, they said, 'Oh you know, we don't do that.' Eventually they caved in. And so I unstrapped Gordo[21] and I rolled him over on his side – he was facing outboard. I unstrapped Roy[22] and he faced outboard. They were lying on their

21. Space Shuttle Commander Gordon Fullerton
22. Space Shuttle Pilot Roy Bridges

sides without their straps on and they got off their pressure points and that was just hugely different; the pain went away and they're able to move now. We were convinced at this point that we're not going anywhere. A total reload and this and that – but we were just kind of hanging on.

"Time just trucked on. Then we heard that things are happening – gee whiz things are happening here! You know, we had just given up. But then we find ourselves at T minus 20 minutes and the clock is still counting. And I'm thinking, you know, they may pull this off! Under 20 minutes and no one upstairs is strapped in! And I says, 'Well, it's time!' And it's a nothing 'cause we weren't even in orange suits;[23] we were in shirt sleeves. Strapping someone in, in shirt sleeves – not parachute survival gear – it's nothing; it's no big deal. You've got shoulder straps and you've got a waist band connection. So I roll Gordo over and in two minutes he's strapped in like a bug in a rug; rolled over Roy, Karl[24] and got myself in. And we went!"

Even more seriously, *Challenger* then lost an engine during the ascent, resulting in an 'Abort to Orbit.' As described in *The Space Shuttle: Roles, Missions and Accomplishments*, after separation of the two solid rocket boosters, the center engine began to overheat and at T+350 seconds, the onboard computer shut it down.[25]

John Blaha recalled, "When the engine went down – man, the faces of that family – all the people up there were like jaws dropped and they looked at me and said, 'What does that mean?' and I said, 'No problem, it's really nothing; they'll go to orbit and nothing will be wrong.' But I knew that's not what was going on in that cockpit."

Story said, "The simulators had trained us very well. I had never had a normal launch [in a simulator]; they kill the engines every single time you fly! We knew instantly, just instantly. It was a very smooth shutdown and we looked to see the red lights, to see which one. Sure enough, the little red lights came on, on the computer. But then, almost simultaneously, we all said, 'Why are they doing it to us today? Don't they understand this is the real thing?!' We actually had a smile.

"So we trucked on and we did an 'abort to orbit' where we dumped 11,000 pounds, I think, of extra fuel through the orbital maneuvering system engines. You get more thrust when you lighten the load – and it was also very funny 'cause we did one of those in the simulator the week before. As soon as the valves opened, in the simulator, I started the stop watch, 'cause I needed to know how much fuel we dumped. So Gordo asks me and I say, 'Yeah 55 seconds'. And he says, 'Story, if that ever happens to us for real, you're not gonna get that time.' That's what he said to me in the simulator! He says if this ever happens for real, there's no way you're gonna

23. The pressurized escape suits which were introduced after the *Challenger* accident.
24. Mission Specialist Karl Henize
25. *The Space Shuttle: Roles, Missions and Accomplishments*, by David M. Harland. Published by John Wiley and Sons, in association with Praxis Publishing Ltd, Chichester, England, 1998.

time that; you're gonna be hanging on for dear life! Well, when it did happen for real, three of us timed it – Gordo, Roy and myself! It turns out that it was my job to time it, but the others also timed it! We had three of them!

"The computers – if you ever lose one engine, they will never shut another one down no matter how bad; that's in the software. And so you're not in a nice position if an engine gets some very bad problems – it's gonna run to destruction. So Jenny Howard, a wonderful gal, she is seeing good engines and things OK and she wants to activate the shutdown procedure so that if we'd gotten to a point far enough downstream and we had [additional] engine problems, rather than blow up, she wanted the computer to shut it down. So she made the call through the flight director to 'enable the limits', which means if an engine goes out of limits, you can shut it down; it allows the computer to shut the next bad engine down. So we did that, and that was fine, that was good news. But then she saw one sensor go out of specification. She's looking at a second engine now – one sensor went out, and she knew it was the sensors, cause the sensors went different directions. She saw one go off-scale limits and the other get flaky and she knows we're gonna lose a second engine; it's about to shut it down, but she's looking at the damn sensors going out again. She had to turn around right away and make the call, 'limits to inhibit' – and that will stop any more shutdowns. Well, we're trucking along thinking everything is nice and we get the call 'limits to inhibit' – and that was nasty. We know we have other problems now. We know she did that to stop another engine from going down."

When this happened, Story began to prepare for a possible landing at an emergency site across the Atlantic. He explained, "I'm the checklist reader – we're going to Spain for sure. So I go to turn the page to 'Zaragosa' and I'm gonna take us to Spain. I'm going right down this checklist – boom, boom, boom – practicing what we're gonna do. Poor Karl Henize, he didn't train for launches, he was just riding there. He didn't know anything about launches and he wasn't supposed to know. But he looks over and he sees me on a checklist that says 'Zaragosa' and I'm going down the checklist, snapping my fingers. Karl does not understand what is happening. Finally he gets up the courage and he says, 'Story, where are we going?' I says, 'Where are we going?' And so to find out where we're going, I looked at the top of the checklist and it said 'Zaragosa.' So I said 'Zaragosa, Karl!' It didn't help anybody really! 'Ah, oh, no, sorry Karl, I'm rehearsing, ah, no, Karl, I don't know where we're going! OK, we're going uphill for now!' And so it was kind of real funny. But then right after that, just seconds after that, we got into Fuel Completion Shutdown in which the tanks are out of gas. And the low level sensors that are sensing how much gas you've got left, shut the engines down. So that was that."

*Challenger* had reached a low 220km (or 136.7 mile) orbit, not ideal for the onboard astronomy experiments, however, still within acceptable limits for a continued mission.[26]

According to Gordon Fullerton, "It is the only time that's happened, other than the *Challenger* disaster, of course, which was two flights later. So that started off everything, with everybody wide-eyed! And we threw away our whole flight plan – this super-detailed, really thick book of timing that we had worked on, thrown out the window. We had to re-time everything. Most of the replanning happened on the ground but we had to take miles of teleprinter paper off the printer and rephrase everything.

"So there were lots of challenges on that. And the great thing about it is that when we got done we even got an extra day [in space]. We went eight days instead of seven.

The mission was a complete success, even with some initial difficulties with the new Instrument Pointing System. Gordon explained, "The Instrument Pointing System didn't work when we first turned it on. It took a couple days and many radio calls to get it going. It was a very high accuracy platform, built in Germany, never before flown. In the end it worked great, but in the beginning we had a lot of troubles with it. So it wasn't a ho-hum-by-the-book mission. And Story had a big part of it."

Story recalled the mission with great fondness. "51F – it's kind of dear to me. Really very dear and as challenging as the Hubble mission, and it means as much to me as that one.

"It went exceedingly well, but it was very, very demanding with that many telescopes – the cargo bay had never been that full and since that mission was never again that full. For example, they would fly a later mission with an Instrument Pointing System and only one other telescope. And so we had many more telescopes than were ever flown; we still hold the record for more telescopes and more stuff to do – the four ultra violet telescopes on the instrument pointing system, x-ray telescope, infrared telescope, cosmic ray telescope. We also had the plasma diagnostics – a plasma-studying satellite to be released. We flew precision maneuvers around it, firing jets at it and getting lined up with the magnetic field. We did burns to open up holes in the magnetosphere and radio telescopes would study that. We had to rendezvous too. We had to release the satellite, fly around it, then rendezvous and retrieve it. So it was a very demanding mission, Gordo and I and then five other people who hadn't flown before. And two of those people were scientists and not astronauts – it was one of the earliest times we did that."

Gordon recalled Story's undying enthusiasm for the mission. "When we first got on orbit on 51F, Story was out of the seat before the engines tailed down I think – just

---

26. As described in *The Space Shuttle: Roles, Missions and Accomplishments*, by David M. Harland. Published by John Wiley and Sons, in association with Praxis Publishing Ltd, Chichester, England, 1998.

helping the new guys out of their seats and showing them what to do. He was upstairs, downstairs and really getting things done – like I'd had to stop him doing in the simulators, but that was him. And he did it well. I don't remember objecting to anything he did – it was just terrific the way he got with the program and that's been sort of the way he's lived his life I think. Sometimes too much of a good thing, but certainly not too little – ever."

Gordon and Story also shared a unique relationship in the Space Shuttle cockpit. Story was the designated flight engineer, or center-seater. Story remembered, "Gordo believed in me and he had faith in me. I had a very large stick and I ran the switches in the cockpit with a stick – I could reach them. And so I worked on the communications with him; he is not trying to bend out of the harness, 'cause we worked out those kind of details. By using a broomstick, I could reach the whole cockpit, and so I was running things with a stick! Most of it is switches, but I had something that would grab a knob – so I could turn knobs or I could throw switches and I could pull circuit breakers – I had the other end of the stick and could slip something over the circuit breaker and pull the circuit breaker out. So I got a lot of responsibility on that mission that no center-seater had had before, 'cause Gordo believed in me.

"I think it set a pace; I think it opened up eyes as to what could be done when you have to do things. I think, in the past, people assumed that on launch and re-entry, even though you desperately need to do these functions, you can't get them done on launch or re-entry. And so, as desperately as you need them, I always communicated with Mission Control that there is no switch or anything in this cockpit during launch or re-entry that I can't get to. I'll get out of my seat and go get it – big deal, it's not unsafe. At mach 20 if anything goes wrong, you're all gonna get it! Everybody! Not the one who's not strapped in. If the vehicle comes apart, you got no place to go. But the launch abort – I really participated in that with the stick, helping to power down all the reaction control systems and all the rest of that stuff. I was just zipping down Launch Control's checklist!"

Story had great esteem for Gordon as the Commander: "Gordo set the tone of things and there is no better aviator, no better commander. He delegates responsibility, just like Covey.[27] He lets the 'kids' do what they got to do; the kids care, the kids have got a passion for what they're doing – let them do it!

"We worked very hard with the Marshall Space Flight Center and, at times in the past, that had been a rough relationship. But we had the smoothest possible relationship; everyone wanted to make it happen; it was totally smooth. We loved Marshall. And you know, Gordo set the tone – 'let's work together'. And so that

27. Dick Covey who commanded STS-61, the first Hubble Space Telescope Repair Mission.

couldn't have been smoother, our work with Marshall. Marshall was the payload manager and the payload trainer for that mission. And everybody had a good time. There wasn't a single irritable moment among anybody; there wasn't anything but smooth work.

"We did some outstanding earth photography; an incredible amount of great earth photography came out of that mission. I was starting to get into that on my second flight. And it was the only mission I had that took me to high latitudes; that was the only mission I did that had what is called a high inclination, so it was very important in terms of the earth viewing and photography."

*

Antoine de Saint-Exupéry – without a doubt, one of the most spirited pioneering pilots of the early Twentieth Century – wrote: "I am not talking about living dangerously. Such words are meaningless to me. The toreador does not stir me to enthusiasm. It is not danger I love. I know what I love. It is life."[28] In his copy of the book, beside these words, Story inscribed his own name!

Story said, "I was not prepared to die in the Shuttle. It disturbed me no end that the Shuttle was as risky as it was. I did not like that. I did not accept that. It should not be that risky; they should have come up with a system of less risk. They should have incorporated an escape system into the Shuttle from the very beginning. That was not just in terms of the *Challenger* disaster, but I knew, and we all knew all along, that there should have been a good escape system to handle a lot of the flight regime – the different windows in the flight environment, both for launch and re-entry. It was an institutional failure that an escape system was not included. I knew the risk and it's more risk than I wanted. It's more than I wanted and I don't accept that risk. But it's the only way I can continue to be the space person that I have identified with. I'm a space person; it's my calling, it's what I do. And so I have no choice than to put myself in that risk, but I don't accept that and I'm not prepared to die and I don't want to die and I don't like the fact that I'm exposed to that amount of risk. So I don't do what I do because it's dangerous. There is no part of going into space that I appreciate because it's dangerous. I am angry about the fact that I have to tolerate that risk, because I am not a risk taker. If I'd died on the Shuttle I would have been very much angered!

"You cannot believe how energetic I get when approaching some situation that has great risk in it, some situation in which the outcome may become in doubt if we go any further. I become hugely aversive to going further in that line 'cause I really do wish to protect my life."

28. *Wind, Sand and Stars*, by Antoine de Saint-Exupéry: first published in French in 1939 under the name *Terre des Hommes*. My copy was translated by William Rees and published in London by the Penguin Group, 1995.

Much has been written about the *Challenger* accident which occurred on January 28th, 1986 and the reasons for the disaster. Launched in temperatures fifteen degrees colder than any previous mission, the vehicle exploded approximately seventy-three seconds after lift-off. The cause was attributed to an O-ring in the field-joint of one of the solid rocket boosters which failed to seal properly in the cold conditions.[29]

Management decisions on that day had also been a factor.

Of the accident, Story said: "They didn't even have a pressurized suit; they were in shirt sleeves. It was cotton coveralls and a helmet and they had no escape system[30] of any kind. A parachute system may or may not have saved them. Even with the current escape system that we have today, it's not clear we could survive. It depends upon the motions that the cabin goes through. With the current system, you get out of your seat and walk. But if you have a tumbling cabin you can't walk, you can't make it to the hatch. Especially not with a bulky orange suit and survival gear, the parachutes, the helmets, all of that. You're wearing an eighty-pound system and you're unable to walk."

In addition, NASA added a telescoping pole to the ceiling of the Space Shuttle's mid-deck which could be extended out beyond an exploded hatch. In theory, it would guide an escaping crew member below the wing, at which time they would pull their individual parachute. However, the crew would still have to get out of their couches, to which they were tightly strapped, and hoop a harness over the pole before bailing out.

The *Challenger* tragedy, as with all who knew or had worked with those astronauts aboard STS-51L, had a devastating effect on Story. He recalled, "I was in public when that happened. Well, dealing with that day, the tears I had was when I was alone, when I was [away from the] public and I could just sit down and think about those individuals. I remembered their faces the last time I saw them. Even before the *Challenger* accident whenever a crew was going to go down and fly in space, the last moment that I would see them, I'd look in their face and I knew that this was the last time. And everyone that I sent off, I memorized without even thinking about it, the last time I saw them, in case they didn't come back. That would be the memory I had. I don't know if that's the usual thing you do or not. And I would always tell myself I'm sending 'my' crew to Florida. That's what I would kind of say: 'my' crew is off. Now for all of them, whether it was in the gymnasium, the office or flying – the last time I saw each one of them face to face, I carried that memory with me. I expected, many of those times, that those images I had would be the last time I would see them.

29. As described in *The Space Shuttle: Roles, Missions and Accomplishments*, by David M. Harland. Published by John Wiley and Sons, in association with Praxis Publishing Ltd, Chichester, England, 1998.
30. Such as a pressurized suit and parachute.

Story was watching *Challenger* launch that day from the office of the Chief Astronaut. "I was the first person in the room to call out that it was a disaster. I don't know if other people were stunned, but I was the first to call it looking at the television monitor. There were some people in the room that had been particularly close to some of the people on the crew and that's why they were in that room.

"I hate this; I hate it when it's negligence. I hate people to get 'had' out of negligence. I don't like tragedy. I don't like people to get struck down in the middle of a glorious life."

Carol Musgrave, whom Story married just months afterwards, recalled the impact of the accident. "I went through all that with him at that time. It's that whole experience of shock that goes so far beyond – it's one thing when people are watching their TVs and that kind of thing, but Story was connected so intimately with it all; we all were. It just shut down emotions; it's just hard to even describe almost the paralysis, because you can't absorb all of that kind of thing when you've been so involved. It is just a nausea that comes over you."

The result of the post disaster enquiry was that Space Shuttles were grounded for the moment. David M. Harland, in his book *The Space Shuttle: Roles Missions and Accomplishments*, gives a good account of the final accident report. "The upshot of the Rogers Commission's report was that NASA must develop a safer SRB [Solid Rocket Booster] field-joint; that it must reassess issues of landing the orbiter safely, and pay particular attention to the tire and brake failures; that it must upgrade contingency planning for aborts during the ascent phase; that it must stock sufficient spare parts not to need to cannibalize a recently-returned orbiter to enable another to launch; that it must resist the temptation to use the need to increase the flight rate to override established limits by the issuance of waivers; that it must precisely define the Shuttle program manager's authority and responsibility; that astronauts should participate in the management process; and that an independent panel should review safety issues and report directly to the program manager."[31]

Space flights resumed in September of 1988. Story's first post-*Challenger*-accident flight, STS-33, was aboard the Space Shuttle *Discovery* – a classified mission for the Department of Defense in November of 1989.

*

One thing which Story will, undoubtedly, be remembered for is his irrepressible sense of fun. Space Reporter Dan Billow, who has covered the space program since 1987, recalled his first impressions of Story – shortly before STS-33. "First thing I remember is when the astronauts arrived and got out of their planes on the runway at

31. *The Space Shuttle: Roles, Missions and Accomplishments*, by David M. Harland. Published by John Wiley and Sons, in association with Praxis Publishing Ltd, Chichester, England, 1998.

the Kennedy Space Center. We were all taking pictures – and Story was the one who popped out of the airplane with a camera, taking pictures of us taking pictures of him!

"And there seemed to be a familiarity there between Story and the press corps and he came across as a guy who was not the usual astronaut, a guy who, first of all, had fun with what he was doing all the time, even when it was just a photo opportunity, and secondly, a guy who was able to be himself. He didn't have this thing where he had to project an image. So, that was my first memory of him. He was not afraid to have fun doing this awesome job that's not supposed to be fun – at least NASA doesn't want you to think it's fun, they want you to think it's serious. But he was able to have it be serious and fun at the same time. And he never lost that – how he enjoyed doing what he does."

According to John Blaha, who was a crew member on STS-33, "My experience with Story on what was my second flight really helped me enjoy the space program for the rest of the time I stayed with NASA. I mean he sort of showed me what I'd call a path that you could really gain the full advantage of being there."

Towards the end of 1987, Story had begun studying the humanities at the University of Houston, Clear Lake. In his journal he wrote about the purpose of that study:

> We know space, scientifically, intellectually but we don't know it artistically or aesthetically. Do we have the equipment to perceive space? Are we prepared to biologically perceive space? Are we prepared to, or do we have the biological equipment to experience space? In terms of a theory of art or aesthetics, space is a good opportunity. I am in school primarily because school is fun, but I want to experience space, I don't want to miss that opportunity. I'm privileged to get to go to space and I want to have an aesthetic experience, maybe express that experience.[32]

So, as Story began preparing for STS-33, it was with an even wider view to explore the possibilities of space flight from the point of view of humanity.

A few days before launch, Story wrote in his journal about preparations for the mission:

> Last SMS training session 1-5pm. Touching and emotional – we, as a crew and as a training team, have put one hell of a lot into that effort and have gotten immensely good – are ready to fly. It was like graduation time.[33]

According to John Blaha, "An incident which I think is very representative of Story, or of anybody that's a real pro at anything – in the NBA they said that Michael

32. Journal 2, pages 31-32; Date: 29 March 1989.
33. Journal 6, page 46; Date: 19 November 1989.

Jordan made other players reach their full capability. Well Story did that a lot. During the mission, I had a task that I was doing on the dark side of the earth, so that means you have to darken the cockpit. And my task was to point at some stars and maneuver the spaceship between another star, and take marks. I was collecting star data – it was a test to evaluate if a human being could lock onto various stars to update the navigation system of the Space Shuttle. And so I was testing that and had just marked on one star and I was getting ready to maneuver to another star. And while I was doing that, the vehicle wasn't moving. I could see the sunrise coming and that's not good, 'cause it would sort of mess up the test and I'd have to go redo it somewhere else in the mission. And I didn't even know Story was watching me, but he sort of just appeared in the dark to the right of me and in my ear in a very soft voice, he said, "John, do you want the power on?" I had forgotten to turn on the power of this one controller I was using; that's why the space vehicle wasn't moving.

"He did that many, many times in training and during the mission. And when he did it for any crew member, he did it very quietly, so as not to tell anybody else, or to make it look like you forgot something. So he played a role, I think, in making any member of the crew that he flew with perform better."

For the first time, in the lead up to STS-33, Story began writing his thoughts about space flight in his journals. These journals are rich with poetic metaphors and insights into Story's feelings about the whole experience of space flight:

> The ambiance of KSC [Kennedy Space Center]. The spirit, the meaning of hardware and machinery – the communication of destiny and certainty.[34]
>
> Mind running MACH 25 through all the parts, people and procedures that must be, for me to be here. Image of the globe, parts and people... converging in Florida, coming together at KSC. Faces flying by, people who care, care on their faces.[35]
>
> Launch, SRB – like a bumpy road at 100 miles per hour.[36]
>
> Prelaunch – as if in airliner – 'you are about to be launched into space, if that is not your intended destination, you are on the wrong airplane.'[37]
>
> Launch: a horrible violent storm, shipwreck.
> Engine shutdown: passage from the storm to calm; after the storm.

34. Journal 6, page 22; Date: 13 September 1989.
35. Journal 4, page 44; Date: 21 April 1989.
36. Journal 6, page 8; Date: 20 August 1989.
37. Journal 6, page 30; Date: 26 September 1989.
38. Journal 3, page 37; Date: 2 October 1988.

On orbit: paradise island, calm, serene.[38]
Courage is admitting how frightened you are (vs Denial!).
SRBs [Solid Rocket Boosters]: thoughts of disaster and death.
Moment of truth – two minutes of it.[39]

Space: at times reality is more a fantasy than the simulations.[40]

Experience the magic, the privilege of being a "tourist" in space. A tourist in space, a safari in space.[41]

During their time at the Kennedy Space Center, prior to the launch of STS-33, Story, together with crew members John Blaha and Kathryn Thornton, paid a surprise visit one night to the launch pad, at 3am, to view their spaceship. Story wrote:

Enthusiasm of guards and the workers at seeing us there at that hour. They didn't know we had to sleep during the day if to launch at 7.30pm.[42]

A primitive, primal experience to never be forgotten – welcomed by everybody. That machine looming in the lights. Jupiter overhead ... a crescent moon on the ocean horizon. The fog moving in and out over Discovery – many photos ... Gantry lights, Discovery and us in the lights. What exuberant exhilaration! What beauty and power.[43]

John Blaha recalled, "Story was always talking about the beauty of many things he saw – he'd talk about the beauty of that night viewing – he'd say 'Look at the stars, look at the spaceship there, the way it's lit up, we're going to go to space in that vehicle.' You could be in a T-38 and you'd see a sunset from a T-38 as you're flying and he'd say, 'Isn't that beautiful?' and he'd describe it; or a sunrise, or looking at the stars as you're flying, or a moonrise. He was always doing that. To me, that was him all the time – he saw a lot of beauty in things.

"I do think his interest in looking at the beauty of the earth, as a person on the earth, he translated to space as well. So things like a night pass of the planet, or a day pass, or a sunrise, or a sunset, or an ascent – in other words, all those things. I learned a lot of things from Story on what I'm going to call the 'beauty' side of it."

Reporter Dan Billow also recalled talking with Story about the night before a launch. "He'd go out to the beach at the Kennedy Space Center where he'd see the big lights which shine on the Space Shuttle, which can be seen for miles and which go up

39. Journal 4, page 42; Date: 25 April 1989.
40. Journal 5, page 7; Date: 28 May 1989.
41. Journal 6, page 11; Comment added at a later date.
42. Journal 7, page 1; 1 December 1989.
43. Journal 6, page 48; 22 November 1989.

into the sky for what seems like forever – big search lights that illuminate. There's not much else out there – you pretty much just have the Shuttle launch pad, the big lights, and you, the astronaut, in this case, Story Musgrave, who's out there swimming in the darkness or lying on the beach looking up, and looking at satellites going overhead. And he talked about that whole experience, and then about seeing a satellite and thinking that tomorrow, he was going to be one of those satellites up there in space."

On launch day Story wrote:

> Calm, serene and contemplative this afternoon – exuberance, wild-eyed enthusiasm tempered with reflection and reality. Six hours sleep ... we will get into the charge mode here – the 'go get it done set', get the job done. Am running day one through my mind – wanting not only to do it perfect, but grand and great – to get the best and most artistic photos ever taken from space.[44]

According to John Blaha, "Story had a tremendous interest in photography. I mean both on the ground and on orbit. He could be a professional photographer."

Following the mission, Story captured some of his thoughts and experiences about the flight in his journal:

> Rocket ship – greatest carnival ride ever put together.[45]

> Opening the doors [cargo bay doors] for business; the love of mechanics, motion, mission phase.[46]

> No running water up here – missing the sound of streams, the splash and dash.[47]

> Got to leave home to find out how really good it is.[48]

> Eating over France – 'dinner in Paris.'[49]

> Crossing Pacific [in space] – less of an adventure than as a child going to the next farm. Pacific smaller in perspective than the farm.[50]

> Space – like sitting on top of the highest mountain.[51]

With each successive mission there was a more formalized questioning and exploration in Story's journals of the possibilities for enhanced experience. He hoped to

---

44. Journal 6, page 50; Date: 22 November 1989.
45. Journal 11, page 11; Date: 18 August 1991.
46. Journal 11, page 24; Date: 10 December 1991.
47. Journal 10, page 36; Date: 17 April 1991.
48. Journal 10, page 39; Date: 1 May 1991.
49. Journal 11, page 3; Date: 3 July 1991.
50. Journal 11, page 12; Date: late 1991.
51. Journal 14, page 16; Date: 28 November 1992.

communicate this to people who didn't have the opportunity that he had of working in space.

Story managed to fit a great deal into his days on the ground, typically getting to work at three-thirty or four in the morning. Friend and colleague Sharon Daley recalled that from the outside of the astronauts' office, if you knew where to look, a little desk lamp glowed in the dark and Story would be working away.

According to astronaut Rick Hieb, Story would throw himself one hundred percent into whatever he was doing – whether it was in the simulator, flying, talking to someone or working out in the NASA gymnasium: he was intense and focused.

Rick recalled a defining moment in the NASA gym. He saw Story using a weight machine – not really doing it the way you're supposed to, and Rick wasn't quite sure which muscle Story was exercising, but he was putting his whole body and everything he had into it!

Story was known for doing things his own way. For example, he would invert his bed with bricks before missions, head down and feet raised. This was to get the body used to different physiological orientations before flight. But no matter what Story was doing, Rick says he will always remember Story for his ability and love of really getting into something – "to plumb the depths, but in a fun way."

Friend Roger Zweig, a research pilot at Ellington Air Field, said that some months Story would fly a hundred hours in the T-38, sometimes twice a day every day, in very disciplined practice – a lot more than most other astronauts. He described Story as a real physical fitness person who would frequently run five to ten miles around the NASA track at lunchtime, keeping jars of raw wheat, oats and grain on his desk to eat as snacks between meals.

Joe McMann, who was NASA's lead engineer on EMU[52] for the Space Shuttle program observed, "I don't know if Story would be classed as the ultimate team player or not? To me he was so much an individual that I think maybe that would get in the way of him being a rah-rah team guy, although I'm sure he worked well with his other crew members on a particular mission. But he was still, to me, first of all, an individual; his own man.

"One day, just walking across campus, he was eating something. I looked down and he's just eating raw oats. I mean it's healthful and something that wouldn't hurt you to do, but it's not cool, it's not anything, but it's Story! ... I mean, to me, he was just always his own man, just always doing the thing that he felt that it was appropriate to do."

Astronaut Tom Akers, who participated in the first Hubble Space Telescope repair mission, said of Story, "He traveled to a different drummer than most of us – in a good way. He was very helpful to younger crew members when we were at NASA, always willing to help. Just a super-nice, easy-going, laid-back type of person, a

52. Extra-Vehicular Mobility Unit (EMU) or spacesuit.

laissez-faire in his methods, but had the big picture all the time – knew what was important and what was the trivial, or not worth worrying about. He was a good crew member, a good person to fly in space with."

Crew member and friend Jim Voss spoke of Story's approach to space flight: "Story wanted to really understand space flight and to experience it fully, so he thought about it a great deal and he put himself into space in his mind a lot and thought about the environment and the circumstances, the way human beings act and work in space, and he shared some of that with me. And usually it was the kind of thing where I would notice Story doing something that I thought was strange. Things like, when we went to the Terminal Countdown Demonstration Test in Florida, we got into the Space Shuttle and Story went over into a kind of corner and he laid down there; he just lay there for a long time. I asked him if he was sleeping, and he said, "No"; he was projecting his mind into space and was visualizing being there and was reorienting in the Space Shuttle to the way it would look to him in space. And he tried to teach me how to do that and I could not do it at that time – I later learned how to after I'd flown a few times, but I couldn't do it at the time. I had to experience it first to know what he was really talking about."

Jim recalled the enjoyment of sharing his first space flight with Story – STS-44 in November of 1991, which was also a classified mission for the Department of Defense. "It was great having someone like Story around who had such experience, because you could always go to him as a source for information. He had flown several times and really knew the Space Shuttle and the business that we were in. He was like the old guy in the shop that knew how to use all the tools and he could tell you how to do it when you needed help."

As Halloween neared, the crew enjoyed a little joke as they prepared for a launch countdown test in Florida. With rumors circulating around the Johnson Space Center that this crew liked to have fun, management stepped in and declared that the crew could not wear Halloween masks. So, instead, the obedient crew appeared before the public wearing bald caps and aviator sunglasses – in direct imitation of Story! A candid photo of the 'bald' crew subsequently appeared on the front page of *Florida Today*.[53]

Bob Sieck, who was Launch Director for the mission, recalled that day. "The van pulls up with Henricks and the rest of the crew and they're wearing their flight suits. Each one of them, rather than their own name over their pocket with astronaut wings, had a big placard that said 'Story'... And they all piled out of the van and came trundling up the stairs and all introduced themselves: 'Hi I'm Story'... 'Hi I'm Story'...

53. *Space Shuttle: The First 20 Years - The Astronauts' Experiences in Their Own Words*, Tony Reichhardt (Editor), Smithsonian Institution, Dorling Kindersley Publishing, 2002.

and then Story showed up a few minutes later and he got a kick out of that."

STS-44 was Story's second night launch. He later wrote:

> Have had two night launches in which I arrived prior to sunset, so took in the day, the sunset, the shadows on the spacecraft and of the spacecraft, then took in the night ocean and the night sky, the earth, the life and the heavens. For some unknown reason, I feel most at home going in the middle of the night, as if that is where this business belongs – it makes it even more unusual than it is already.[54]

There were a number of highlights for Story during STS-44 aboard Atlantis, one being the sight of the Russian space station MIR passing "very, very fast" at a distance of 23 nautical miles. He recorded this in his journal:

> MIR: a comet with people in it; the imagination of people in that shooting star.[55]

For the first time, Story was also able to invoke a feeling of free fall and found great delight in the experience.

> Was able to free fall and frightened myself the first few times, pulled myself back to a float, got my confidence back and went at it again. Eventually found the total isolation from objects, space and time a joy. Although in actual literal physical free fall, I felt as if I was in a disembodied freefall. The imagined freefall is more real than the actual. Perception of floating through imagination, I brought my perception to reality.[56]

Jim Voss witnessed one of Story's extracurricular activities during the mission. "One of the funny things from that particular flight – Story was always experimenting with things in space and one afternoon I went to the mid-deck of the Space Shuttle – I don't know why I went down at the time, but Story had not been upstairs for some time and when I got downstairs he had put on this belt that had some straps with some little pins. The strap was designed to hold a crew member to the wall if they were ill and you needed to work on them in some way. And so Story had put this belt on and he was just floating very slowly over towards the wall. He had one of these pins in each hand and, as I got closer, I saw that he was floating towards the holes that these pins went in and he 'docked' with the wall! It was the funniest thing to see him just very slowly drifting over there. He had launched himself from the other side of the cabin intending to 'dock'; it was really humorous."

Jim also spoke of Story's helpfulness. "When we were on orbit, Story's way was to quietly do things. He didn't impose himself on you or do anything overtly to help

54. Journal 20, pages 31-32; Date: 21 October 1996.
55. Journal 11, page 41; Date: 15 January 1992.
56. Journal 11, page 29; Date: 13 December 1991.

you, but he was always there, kind of like he was just poking around in the background, available to help you. He would ask questions at the appropriate times to maybe stimulate a question of your own. He might see that someone might need some help or may need some information when they weren't asking for it and he wasn't just going tell them what to do. But he would make himself available and would be there and do a little something – wandering over and being inquisitive himself – and that would stimulate some discussion that would allow him to help us. That was one of his techniques."

STS-44 ended prematurely. The crew came home three days early due to a failure of one of the measuring devices used for navigation. In a bit of an anti-climax, Atlantis landed at Edwards Air Force base in California without a welcoming committee because everybody was waiting for them in Florida – so the crew spent the night at a dude ranch, taking turns to ring their families on a payphone.[57]

On 24 January 1992, almost two months after the mission, the crew of STS-44 met with President George Bush. On the eve of the meeting, Story wrote:

> I meet tomorrow with President Bush: I feel so privileged, so blessed, so humble. I think of the billions of folks who are so less fortunate! I think of the suffering, pain, starvation and disease. I think of the work, the talent, timing and luck. Who gave me such intelligence, creativity, art and gave me the opportunities?![58]

The next couple of years were going to be just as fortunate for Story.

Early in 1992, NASA acknowledged with great embarrassment that its recently deployed US$2.2 billion Hubble Space Telescope[59] contained an incorrectly ground mirror. The images which were received from the telescope, although still exciting in astronomical terms, were disappointing in quality.

After a great deal of deliberation, experts determined that the best way to fix Hubble's blurred vision would be to install a series of corrective mirrors or 'lenses'. In order to do this, it would be necessary to send a Space Shuttle crew to dock with the telescope. The servicing team would have to train intensively for over a year, practicing to replace a total of thirteen major components which had failed since the telescope's deployment.

On 11 March 1992, Story wrote in his Journal with great excitement:

> Was asked if I still wanted to fly? I certainly do! I'm the Payload Commander on the Hubble Space Telescope repair mission! I will be 58+years and still in my youth, still peaking on the job. Being Capcom on HST deploy was an archetypal

---

57. *Space Shuttle: The First 20 Years - The Astronauts' Experiences in Their Own Words*, Tony Reichhardt (Editor), Smithsonian Institution, Dorling Kindersley Publishing, 2002.
58. Journal 11, page 47; Date: 23 January 1992.
59. Estimated cost at launch.

experience for me – Hubble was so phenomenal, to attempt to add to our own place in the universe… now I get to fix it. What a marvelous mission, what an opportunity – I'm back in my EVA world – the world you did so long, so hard, and so well, you will get to do a really significant and human EVA to open our eyes to the universe. You have made the urgent decisions here – go for what is great, identify, be loyal, go where angels and adventurers go.[60]

Three days later, Story could still hardly contain that excitement:

The HST is still gripping, it is big, big stuff, big as the universe. That Story, that little Linwood boy, that the St Mark's drop-out gets to do it is still a dream. I feel so deeply about HST. I felt so deeply when I was Capsule Communicator for the deploy. HST was such a romantic thing for me. I'm going back into my tank at MSFC! Getting to do MSFC one more time!"[61]

The crew assembled for this critical mission consisted of Commander Dick Covey, Pilot Ken Bowersox, five Mission Specialists – Kathryn Thornton, Jeff Hoffman, Story Musgrave and Tom Akers, who would perform a series of spacewalks to carry out the repairs – and Swiss astronaut Claude Nicollier who, according to Story, would work 'miracles' with the robotic arm.

The four designated spacewalkers spent over four hundred hours training in a neutral buoyancy environment – the giant pool at the Marshall Space Flight Center in Huntsville, Alabama. Their role involved the development of tools and procedures which would enable them to carry out the delicate repairs on the telescope.

Ron Sheffield, who was test director for the Neutral Buoyancy Simulations at the Marshall Space Flight Center, recalled, "When the crew came down for the first time, we were all there at the NBS[62] and I was doing the briefing, and Story said, 'Wait a minute, I've got something to say before we get started.' He said, 'We have no egos here. All egos are left until this mission is over. We are a team, we're gonna work as a team.' And he said that, not only to the four astronauts that were going EVA, but to all of the guys that were on the ground training him and supporting him.

"I think the attitude and the atmosphere and the execution are all critical aspects for his contribution – and I'm looking at it from purely from the point of view of the Hubble mission. But that was a real critical time."

In an interview with Nina L. Diamond,[63] Story explained the various physical training environments for the mission: "In the EVA world we do not have a single

60. Journal 12, page 40; Date: 11 March 1992.
61. Journal 12, page 41; Date: 14 March 1992. MSFC is the abbreviation for the Marshall Space Flight Center, Huntsville, Alabama.
62. Neutral Buoyancy Simulator
63. Interview for *Omni Magazine*, by Nina L. Diamond, August 1994. Reprinted by permission of Omni Publications International Ltd.

simulator, but several. We have water to give us reach, access, and visibility similar to that in a spacewalk; a clean room where you put flight tools onto the real flight instruments. We have the air-bearing floor to test how large objects will respond in zero-g; it's like being on ice, on a skateboard. We can move a 600-pound object, a phone booth like the Wide Field Planetary Camera, and it's ounces to get it moving with your fingertips. We wear EVA suits on the air-bearing floor and in the thermal vacuum chamber where you go for hours on end in real flight environments. You exercise the real suit you're going to fly, and put your tools through their paces at those temperatures. You also have altitude chamber runs where you take your flight suit to a vacuum, depressurize, and air lock just like in space. You exercise your actual suit and backpack. I brought in an imagination to pull those worlds together. No one of them is what it will be like in flight. You attack details so that nothing gets away, no stone unturned."

In addition to NASA's training environments, Story and spacewalking partner Jeff Hoffman spent hours at the Aerospace Museum in Washington, D.C., practicing the replacement of parts on an accurate replica of the Hubble Space Telescope.

Story took on the preparation phase for the mission like an Olympic athlete. In fact he studied the perfection of world class performers such as champion figure skater Dorothy Hamill – talking in detail with her and incorporating what he learnt into his own spacewalking training.

For the first time, Story introduced the now familiar terms of ballet, dance and choreography into the language of spacewalking. To him, a spacewalker was "like a ballerina on opening night." He later told reporter Robyn Suriano of Florida Today: "I choreographed every single nut and bolt, every work site, every screw, every everything – how you hold a wrench. It was basically like a ballet where I knew where every finger and every toe was to be for five days – where all 300 tools were in my head. It was a very rich experience for me. I could really see my art in that."[64]

In the midst of the crew's intensive training and the continual public scrutiny of the mission, more drama was about to unfold. Within just a few months of the scheduled launch date, Story's participation in the mission was potentially jeopardized as the result of a difficult training session in a vacuum chamber. After long hours of strenuous work in extremely cold temperatures, he suffered frostbite in the fingers of both hands.

In his journal Story wrote with concern:

> SESL [space environment simulation laboratory] – tools at minus 170F, very hard, intensive, much squeeze on tools which were stuck or sticky. On taking gloves

64. Florida Today article titled, *Story Musgrave: Astronaut and So Much More*, by Robyn Suriano, published 18 November, 1996. Reprinted with permission.

off, 7 black fingers – frozen – [I had] ignored thermal pain. Familiarity/complacency [may equate to] danger. It can happen to you. Think, think, think!! What happened? How to prevent?[65]

He said, "This simulation was 13 hours at minus 170 degrees Fahrenheit and the cold just stung. I knew it was going to hurt, but you have to love pain in this business. After 8 hours, the pain went away and I should have known better. The result was frostbitten fingers. After this, we put more insulation in the gloves and took the water coolant out of the arms."[66]

Story's second wife Carol, from whom he had separated, recalled how she received the news. "I remember getting a call from him and the depth with which he was shaken by that. Intellectually, it should have been that way. He had always protected his fingers, in a sense. They were surgeon's fingers and even flying – he would fly the T-38 just with the very tips of his thumb and forefinger. It was just the ultimate – there have been so many hurts and so many disappointments and so many assaults on him, but he just transcends them. But I think with the fingers, I think that was a very significant event."

According to Jim Thornton from the EVA office, "That was probably the low point in preparing for the mission. I was not actually there at the test, I was probably at Sunnyvale and I was traveling back. I do remember, coincidentally, that our training team was having a little dinner party that evening. At that time I had two young daughters and my wife and I had called home to check on them and the babysitter while we were at this dinner party. My daughter told me that Story Musgrave had called and had left a message and wanted me to call him back as soon as possible. And so when I called him back, he related to me what had happened in the chamber that day, that he was very upset – he had obviously sustained an injury – and he was already concerned that people perhaps would want to try to replace him for the servicing mission. He wanted us to start thinking about how we could prevent that. We all knew that Story, like several others, had a very long history with the telescope even before it was launched, so he was an extremely valuable resource and we wanted to do everything we could to keep him a part of that mission if at all possible.

"Unfortunately, some of these review committees – they used that as a situation to call into question Story's judgment. We weren't a party to that – we learned about some of the dialogue later on. People were actually questioning – is Story the right person to have a part in this mission? And there was, at least from what we understood after the fact, there was quite a bit of discussion about whether Story should be replaced because of his frostbite injury. But we used it as a rallying point to prove everybody wrong."

65. Journal 14, page 30; Date: 28 May 1993.
66. Comment by Story on the website www.spacestory.com

The accident did not prevent Story from ongoing training. "I got back in the suit the next week and continued working and developing this mission. Some people thought that was radical, but being with them for twenty-five years, they should have known I would get back in the suit."[67]

According to Ron Sheffield, Story was determined to fly the mission. "I saw the real Story come out. That was an extreme pressure on Story, 'cause he wanted to fly that mission so bad. And NASA headquarters, because of the criticality of the mission, had selected a backup astronaut, Greg Harbaugh, if one of them got sick or anything – that's how critical it was. They really didn't do backups after Skylab, they just didn't do backups of people. So I saw Story – he came out to Huntsville and he said, 'I am flying this mission'. And he couldn't get into the [water] tank, so Greg did a lot of activities in the tank. But Story went to Alaska, I think he even talked to the Russians, talked to all the experts on frostbite. He convinced all of the medical doctors at NASA, and particularly at Johnson,[68] that he could do the mission. But his guts, his stick-to-itiveness, his desire to excel, all of that came out, just the way he attacked the frostbite.

"And what he did, he didn't disappear, he came down to Huntsville to support, except when he had an appointment somewhere. He went on the trips to look at the flight hardware, came up to Goddard, we went to Boulder – we went to all kinds of places, to JPL,[69] all of the places that were building the hardware. And he never let down, but you could see the pressure on him; it was immense. First off, he had been selected 'cause they thought he was the guy that was best qualified to do it. And then he frostbites his hands and he's fighting through this and he's got all these activities. That's one of the reasons I admire Story."

According to Beth Turner, who was Story's secretary for the mission, she never ever heard Story complain about his hands. "I didn't know about it until after the fact that his hands had been hurt – at least a couple of days. I think it was another crew member that told me – Story didn't even tell me. When I saw him I said, 'Story, let me look at your hands!' He never complained."

Ten weeks after suffering the frostbite, Story expressed worry over impending tests of his hands, especially the fingers of his right hand which had suffered the worst damage. In his journal he wrote:

> Hand has been a real concern – threat to STS-61.. thermal is a concern, cold test may not look well….cold test a threat to flight status."[70]

67. Comment by Story on the website www.spacestory.com
68. Johnson Space Center (JSC), Houston
69. Jet Propulsion Laboratory (JPL), Pasadena, California
70. Journal 14, page 33; Date: 19 August 1993.

Later in the day, however, he continues with jubilation at the result:

> Cold test not a problem.... Came through cold test with flying colors! Story does what Story got to do.[71]

Story later said, "I love NASA for the courage to test. If we had not tested, this mission would have failed day one. The temperature vacuum testing resulted in adding insulation to the gloves and we found and fixed many other problems. As a result, temperature was not a problem [during the mission]."[72]

What a lot of people don't know – the extent of the damage caused by the frostbite – is that it took a full five years before Story's hands, particularly his right hand, recovered enough to even pick up a pen off the table in the usual way, which makes his determination to carry on with the mission even more poignant.

Apart from the frostbite incident, routinely working in the spacesuits was demanding and often painful. There are references in Story's journals to the ongoing pain of working in a tight fitting spacesuit. He remarked that, at times, his fingers were so sore he couldn't scratch himself. In addition, he developed blood clots under his fingernails due to the rubbing motion of the glove on the fingernails during training.

But, as you might expect, Story took a philosophical approach to it all:

> EVA – suit needs to grab me, if it doesn't grab me, I can't move it, if I can't move it, I can't move me! EVA – pressure points: pain enough to remind me that I am alive, that this is not only fantasy.[73]

According to Beth Turner, "The amount of physical endurance they put their bodies through was unbelievable. Training as much as they did in those days – they would come back from Marshall with bruises all over their hands!"

As the launch date approached, interest in the mission ballooned. NASA's reputation was on the line and the thousands of people who had helped to design and build Hubble were anxiously awaiting the outcome. Story confided in his journal:

> At times during HST preparation, the only peace that I could find was in the dental chair.[74]

However, Tom Akers recalled that, for the most part, the crew was too busy to let the pressure of it all get to them. "Most of us didn't worry. We had enough to worry about just figuring out the tasks to do, so we didn't have time to worry about that. And

71. Journal 14, page 33; Date: 19 August 1993.
72. Comment by Story on the website www.spacestory.com
73. Journal 13, page 40; Date: 23 August 1992.
74. Journal 15, page 19; Date: 11 March 1994.

that's one of the things most people do as an astronaut – you don't spend time thinking about 'If I screw this up, how many millions of dollars?' and so on. But at the back of your mind…

"Also, I heard Story say lots of times when people asked him how he felt about the mission – he would say he was scared to death. That was early on. By the time we flew, he wasn't saying that very much because the more training we got, the more comfortable we felt that yeah, we can go do this even though a lot of folks didn't think you could go do five EVAs in a row and all this complicated stuff. Story is laid back and if he ever felt any pressure, he never showed it – you know, hid it well. He was our lead EVA guy. In that respect, if he was worried very much, he never let it show."

On 2 December 1993 at 4.27am Eastern time, the Space Shuttle *Endeavour* blasted off from the Kennedy Space Center with a highly prepared crew and a 'toolbox' full of spare parts and equipment needed for the repair. It would be a difficult mission, requiring the highest level of skill and accuracy, while the eyes of the world looked on.

Story recalled, "Congress told us that if you do not fix the telescope, there is not going to be a space station. Why? Because it takes a lot of spacewalks to assemble a space station and you have to demonstrate to us that you can do what you say."[75]

Despite the high profile and importance of the mission, Story's initial concern, once in space, was directed very much towards the details. "The biggest nervousness, if there was any, was simply going out of the airlock and just moving along the bulkhead, because that is the first test – did you have in your imagination how you were going to do it? And if that doesn't work, the next five days are not going to go that well. And it wasn't even a task; it was just a move from here to there. But you see, I have that down in my imagination how that's going to go. I have that whole thing down – just moving from here to there; just moving eight feet. How are you going to move from here to there? No task involved. That had to go well or I would have been very worried."

The world is now familiar with the outcome of the mission and it is not the intention here to go into great detail about what has already been well documented in numerous publications. The crew conducted five marathon spacewalks over five days in alternating pairs – Story Musgrave with Jeff Hoffman for three of the spacewalks and Kathryn Thornton with Tom Akers for the other two.

Flight Director Milt Heflin recalled that people in Mission Control were rather "tight-jawed" at the beginning of the mission, but as each individual spacewalk was completed, people began to relax a little and to quietly triumph in what was being accomplished. He said, "We did everything we had to do and even one thing we didn't expect to be doing and we were successful."

75. Comment by Story on the website www.spacestory.com

In an interview, Story told the American Academy of Achievement: "The most difficult task is what's called solar array drive electronics replacement. You're just replacing an electronic box, but it has little connections on it, about the size of the connections on the back of your personal computer and little screws that were two or three millimeters. That had to be loosened up, and taken out to put the next box in. The screws were not captive in zero-g, they would dance their way out and go floating. These two or three millimeter screws are non-captive, and simply floated out of the container. And it took at least one screw on each connector to hold the connector in. If you see a person having extraordinary difficulty doing some job, the first thing you ask is, 'Why didn't they foresee the problems and head them off ahead of time?' I had told the program months in advance that I was unable to do that job. I had told the program, 'I am unable to do that job in space,' because of loose screws and the fact they were not captive. Because of that, we had come up with a set of clips in which you shove the connector down, and the little springs would come over and grab it. And so screws would not be required. A month before we went to go fly, we got the clips and they were the wrong size. We didn't have time to come up with new clips, so we had to go forward with a job which I had told them could not be done. I launched knowing I had to do a job which I had already told the programmers was too difficult to do. And we went forward and did it anyway. But I was pressed for hours, right at the edge of my ability, to do it. The outcome was in doubt. And with thousands of hours in a suit, that was by far the hardest work that I've ever had to do. It was just gruesome, meticulous work."

Milt Heflin, who worked closely with the crew, said it was "hands, body and communication" that he remembers most about Story, who treated his work like painting a picture – understanding how it all fitted together. Milt recalled that when those little screws got loose, Story took it like someone performing brain surgery; he didn't get flustered or lose his composure; he just took it one step at a time and got the job done.

One of the critical tasks was installing the Wide Field Planetary Camera which would correct the Hubble's vision. It was a delicate operation and Story, who was guiding the mirror into position, had to be extremely careful not to contaminate the mirror, because as he has continually reminded audiences since then, it would "not be good form" to leave your fingerprint on every single image sent back to earth by the Hubble!

The mission was not without some surprises. One of the doors on the axial-instrument compartment proved difficult to shut. Obviously the crew was not prepared for that eventuality, given the training mock-ups of the telescope with perfectly aligned doors. Ever the mechanic, Story grabbed a farm-like instrument which he had included in the 'toolbox' and was eventually able to ease the door closed.

Space reporter Dan Billow recalled watching Story's spacewalks during the mission, knowing that the Payload Commander was, in fact, operating on many levels. "Being Story Musgrave at the top of the Hubble Space Telescope – a silvery telescope with the golden solar panels and the blue earth behind, and looking back at the TV camera, kind of waving at the viewers – knowing kind of what he was feeling at the time, I knew that he would be among the few who could take it all in and be totally in command of what he was doing. The awesome responsibility of billions of dollars that were in his hands, and his alone at that moment, and yet at the same time, he has enough capacity to enjoy the moment, to get everything out of that moment that there is to get, not only in carrying out the responsibility, but in understanding what's going on, and in feeling what's going on. I remember all of that, and I remember thinking that Story Musgrave said to me one time, 'I love being in space'. And I was looking at that shot and thinking that's what Story Musgrave is thinking and saying to himself right now."

According to Jim Thornton, Story very much wanted to be the one to traverse the length of the telescope and go to the very top during one of the spacewalks. "He just kind of shared with me on a couple of occasions what it was going to be like being at the very top of the telescope and looking down. The telescope was forty-five feet tall. Looking down into the payload bay, then leaning back on the foot restraint and looking at the vastness of space – he was so looking forward to doing that task – just being on top of the proverbial mountain, so to speak, and being able to look out and look down on the Shuttle. Several times he would talk to me about how he was really looking forward to that moment. And I was proud that he got to have that moment, 'cause I think he really enjoyed it."

The mission was a blistering success and restored the Hubble Space Telescope to its original potential. The resulting images weeks later were a testament to the efforts and co-operation of an enormous amount of people: the crew, the trainers, the people who developed the techniques and tools for the repair work, Mission Control staff and the people at the Space Telescope Science Institute which operates Hubble for NASA.

There was a significant amount of ongoing publicity about the mission in the months and even years afterwards: the crew were honored for their work both at home and abroad. This included public relations appearances on both *The Tonight Show with Jay Leno* and Tim Allen's *Home Improvement Show*, in addition to a European tour.

Tom Akers recalled, "You know when you come back from a Space Shuttle mission you spend the next month or two traveling around, talking to folks that helped with the mission and we had a lot of people to go thank. For every one of us astronauts, there were thousands of scientists and engineers that had put just as much effort into it as we had. And, of course, we knew that we were the ones in the limelight and getting all the credit, so we wanted to pass that on and thank all of them for their help."

Story has often been asked if he celebrated the success of the mission in a big way. Personally, however, his reaction was low-key. In an interview in 1999, he told writer Andrew Chaikin: "I put on a smile for people. I felt humble and quiet." According to Chaikin, "Story remembered the thrill of seeing Hubble's magnificent face-on image of the spiral galaxy called M-100. Even then, Musgrave says, he didn't think about what he and his crewmates – along with dozens of flight controllers, mission planners, and engineers – had helped to accomplish." He told Chaikin: "It was transcendent. I looked at M-100 and I said, 'My God … It's just gorgeous.' And after that, then I had to think, 'Oh, it's repaired.'"[76]

Beth Turner recalled Story's demeanor in the aftermath of the mission. "I remember talking to him in his office and he was so animated and very happy. He'd say, that's a beautiful spaceship, we needed to fix it and it's a good thing we did. He would talk about the beauty of it. He was excited but not overkill. You had to ask him; he wasn't just going to walk around and say, 'Man did you see what I did?' You had to kind of pull it out of him, but once you started pulling, he was very easy to talk to."

New found fame was something Story also had to deal with after the mission. According to Beth, "He became a celebrity – not due to his own choice – but he handled it well. And anyone who watched Story do a PR got excited about space because of him; he was so sincere. I remember watching him on the *Tonight Show*. Jay Leno was asking him about the extraterrestrial question – is there anybody out there? – and Story just said something like, 'If there isn't, it's such a waste of space. Yeah I think there's somebody.' And he came off so sincere that there was no way you could ever make fun of him."

\*

In between his own missions, Story was a Capcom or Capsule Communicator for many other missions – a role which enabled him to keep up to date with the latest information and techniques of working in space.

Story had worked as Capcom since the days of the Skylab program. Milt Heflin, Chief of the Flight Director's Office, said that as Capcom, people could see Story's passion for the role and for space, and that rubbed off on others. "If he couldn't be in space, he wanted to be in Mission Control."

According to Milt, Story set some standards for how communication, both internally and externally could be done. He had great situational awareness, knew all the crews personally, which was an advantage, and was able to turn the role of Capcom into an art form.

Milt described Story as an "eloquent communicator." He could take the raw

76. *Ballet in Space: How to be a Hubble Spacewalker*, by Andrew Chaikin, Space and Science; 22 December 1999.

materials, the technical details, and paint a picture to the crew in just a few words. For example, they could be talking in Mission Control for maybe fifteen minutes about an issue or a problem and all Milt would have to do afterwards was to look at Story and nod. Story would know exactly what to do – how to communicate to the crew, concisely and clearly, what had just been discussed. He said, "As a Flight Director, if I was putting a team together for a mission, I would want to have Story Musgrave as my Capcom."

Roger Balettie, who worked as a Flight Dynamics Officer in Mission Control said Story was a lot of fun to work with. "He always seemed to have little dry quips; he was always just very easy going. We might be working a rather stressful problem, whether it was in a simulation or actually in the mission, but Story always was this calming voice… If I knew we were doing a simulation with Story as our Capcom, then I knew Story was going to be our Capcom during the flight. So not only did we get used to the way he described things to the crew, but he also got used to the way we presented information to him. It really developed a good working relationship. From a technical standpoint, Story really knew the information you were trying to tell the crew and he was so good at presenting a complex problem in such an easygoing, simple manner.

"His role or his manner in which he communicated with all his colleagues, I mean there was never a hiccup, there was never a stumble. And if there ever was a slight confusion between what we wanted the crew to do and what the crew did – whether it was our fault or whether it was the crew's fault – Story always took the blame: 'Oops guys, sorry, my fault'. He definitely engendered a lot of loyalty."

Phil Engelauf, a Flight Director who also worked closely with Story, recalled Story's wealth of knowledge on just about any topic. "In our business he was well versed in the technical aspects of everything that we did and knew not only the facts but the history that went on with the work that we did. And just the ins and outs of the space business. As we would sit on consol for hours during simulations, during the missions – sometimes quiet – he would talk about almost anything that happened to come up in conversation. He was just a very diverse individual."

This reflected well in their shared experiences in Mission Control: "Story was a much quicker study than most of the Capcoms, just because of his broad technical ability and also his ability to interface with the crews on a very human level and not just be a technical relayer of information. Each Capcom tends to have their own style. Story was a little bit less formal than some of the others and in most cases that worked to his advantage, but I don't think the accuracy or the discipline ever suffered for that. I think it was an asset in his case," said Phil.

Story explained what he was aiming to accomplish within the Capcom role. "I tried to redefine the entire way you communicate. But it's the empathy, it's the situational awareness for what is happening on board the spaceship and so it's empathy for the mission, empathy for the people, but it's being on board with them – so that is the point of view you have. It's thinking about what kind of call you would want; how life can be made easier on you.

"There is a Capcom book – there has been over the decades – called *Radio Discipline and Radio Protocol*. The call [to the Space Shuttle] is – '*Discovery*, this is Houston, over'. That is what the book says you must do and that is the call you will make when you need to get a hold of them. Well I look at that and I say, it's a total waste of time and there is no communication involved there in all of those words. You say '*Discovery*' – well, if they don't know they're *Discovery*, they have a big problem! So '*Discovery*' doesn't help anybody. Everyone at Mission Control knows what shuttle is up there and the people up there know what shuttle they are in! Nothing is accomplished!

"'*Discovery*, this is Houston'. 'This is Houston'? Who do they think is calling?! Mission control knows it's Houston; who does the shuttle think it is?! Right? Who else is calling? Nobody else *can* call! But they also know my voice; they know they're going to hear from me. You can't fool them! Even if some malicious person wanted to mess with the game, they can't do my voice. The 'over' means you've got it, but you have to come back to me and talk to me. So, in radio language, 'over' means 'talk to me.' 'Over' means you've got the ball but I need it back, so talk to me. But if I did not want them to talk to me, I would not have called them in the first place! So, '*Discovery*, this is Houston, over', has accomplished nothing!

"OK, they're in the middle of doing something, but you have called. So, a lot of times [in space] you don't have a microphone on you; you have to float over, grab a mic and talk, wherever the mic is. You may be in the middle of something. But anyway – well who should answer the mic? Who? Well, you've got seven people up there and they all go running for the mic and they all get interrupted, all of them.

"With my kind of call, I will simply do an 'aah'. I will break the silence, so they know to listen – just a little 'mmm', not even a word – just to key my microphone which is voice-activated and to let them know something's coming. And I might say – 'No need to acknowledge. In the next ten minutes, meet me at panel L1.' L1 means something; there are at least two people on the ship that can operate panel L1 – it's an environmental control system. No action required, you don't need to be interrupted, we've got loads of time, we know who's calling and we know what he wants and we know out of those of us that will be free, who would like to do L1 – not only who knows it and is good at it, but who would like to do it. And most of the time you will get a response within seconds. You'll just hear 'Go ahead Story.' I will lead them and then I will state what the switch is; they don't have to write it down.

"That is the difference between one call and another. But it's a sense of how are they doing up there? How do you manage them, how do you handle them, how do you keep their morale going? It's that kind of thing."

While working as a Capcom in Mission Control, astronaut Tom Jones remembers the lengths to which Story, as Head of Capcom, would go to ensure a happy team. "He regarded your continued ability to do a good job as the key to the mission to succeed, so a vacation schedule to him was as sacrosanct as a mission schedule – as long, as it didn't violate somebody's safety or the mission's success. If you scheduled a vacation with him and then the Shuttle schedule changed, he'd find a way to keep you on schedule yourself and get somebody else to help out. He helped me go on my raft trip down the Grand Canyon in 1995 which had been scheduled the year before. I had said, 'Story, next year I'm going down the Grand Canyon in September. I'm going to be working for you and I want you to know that I'd really like to do this, if at all possible, and I will rely on your judgment if we ever have a problem. I'll do everything I can to help you out.' Sure enough, a mission slipped two months, STS-69 from July to September and landed right on top of my vacation. And I was one of the Capcoms and he said, 'Go, go and we'll arrange backup.' So he did and I went. Then I flew with him a year later and it certainly didn't affect his estimation of me. He regarded our work together as a team as very important, so he wasn't going to undercut me."

Astronaut David Wolf recalled working with Story at Mission Control during STS-71, the historic first docking of a Space Shuttle (*Atlantis*) with the Russian Space Station MIR, in June of 1995. The mission, coincidently, represented the 100th US human space flight and, as an indication of the significance of the event, the Administrator of NASA, Dan Goldin, was in the former Soviet Union at the Russian Space Agency's Mission Control Center in Kaliningrad, Moscow. It was the first time in twenty years that the Americans and Russians had rendezvoused in space. Story, as Head of Capcom, gave David the opportunity to lead the rendezvous and docking operation which, explained Story, was a difficult task both technically and diplomatically. What was remarkable, according to David, was that Story could have carried out that historic role himself; instead, he allowed David to embrace it, which was important to David's career at that point. David would later go on to serve as the United States representative aboard MIR from September 1997 until January 1998.

During his thirty-year career with NASA, Story gained enormous satisfaction from witnessing and sharing in the successes of others. The importance of humanity continuing to work in space was of far greater significance to him than any personal achievement.

Frank Hughes spoke of Story's leadership qualities and the way he related to others: "It's a very close relationship; it's like family. You literally are dedicated as a training person to keeping them alive. When we would work on a problem, it was a big concerted effort that everybody contributed to and Story contributed a lot at various times with a procedure or a possibility. He would make a contribution and suddenly it would ease off the problem, or he would aggressively go after something to get it changed for the better. Everyone agreed to it, but you have to have a champion, someone to go forward and fight for it. And he could do that.

"Space flight is a huge distillation of all the effort of all the people. And people pour themselves into your mind, into your body to get you ready. They really do, 'cause they want to go. Vicariously, they're riding with you. The trainers – they would just love Story. They would 'go to town' and just try to do the best that they could for him and go out of their way to do extra things, just 'cause he asked for it."

When asked about Story's main contribution to the space program, Frank offered this: "Story, with all his acquisition of degrees, even when he was an accomplished astronaut, he was back among the 'proletariat' at the University, getting more masters degrees in new subject areas and so I think that one contribution [to the space program] is just that. Astronauts are not the end product of the human race. There are a lot of improvements that can still go on, a lot more knowledge. So that was one area – he was always trying to make himself new and better and faster and whatever. That somebody can be so motivated… If you look at the list of degrees, what that means is that he had to somehow motivate himself throughout those. There's an element of work that somehow you have to find a way to not sit in front of the television or not do the reading of the *Lord of the Rings* one more time or whatever the hell it is you want to do, but you go off and do this work. And he did it so much, and so many times, and so many different ways. Separately, his skills at some of those early engineering problems, in the design of the Shuttle's systems and the space suit systems and the airlocks and everything like that, he contributed greatly."

Tom Sanzone of Hamilton Sundstrand,[77] the company which developed the spacesuits for the Space Shuttle program, explained why people enjoyed doing things for Story: "I never asked Story for a favor and he didn't come through. Not one single time, even when it was unlikely that he could do it. I can't tell you how many times he said – 'I'm not sure I can be there – all I can tell you is I'll do my best' – and on every single occasion he was there. That's the way he is.

"He's an intense individual and you often hear the term, somebody 'giving it 110%'. I think that's a low number for Story! Story's 110% is most people's 200%. He's very focused and you always knew where you stood with Story and I think that's one of the things people respect about him."

Tom summed up Story's confidence and willingness to take responsibility for things, even under the enormous pressures of the first Hubble Repair Mission: "Basically the mantra [of the astronaut corps] is 'don't screw up,' or something close

77. Formerly known as *Hamilton Standard*.

to that. And there is a lot of that in sports. There are some athletes, and a relatively small number, who want the ball at the end of the game – 'give me the ball, I want the ball, I want to be the one who's going to win the game' – and the majority of the players, even pros, they don't want that responsibility at the end; they don't want the responsibility to take the shot to win the game or lose the game. But Story was a guy who wanted the ball – 'give me the ball!' – and more so on Hubble than on anything because I don't ever remember him worrying about it. I don't ever remember him saying, 'What are we going to do if this doesn't work?' And that's part of his intensity."

Story is remembered by colleagues for his ability to communicate with people at all levels – to be comfortable in a social sense and to have empathy for others, no matter who he is with. Tom Sanzone quoted from Rudyard Kipling's famous poem *If*.

> If you can talk with crowds and keep your virtue,
> Or walk with kings – nor lose the common touch.[78]

He said, "I think that was Story. He could 'walk with kings' and not 'lose the common touch' and I think that's a somewhat unique ability in today's day and age. Not too many people do that, particularly in big business.

"The NASA manager that we worked under had a saying about Story. He said, 'Story has more degrees than a thermometer!'… You know I think people liked Story because he didn't put himself above people, even though most people knew how far 'above' them he actually was. So I think that's one of the things about Story."

Story's son Todd echoed these sentiments by describing his father as "down-to-earth, having an uncanny ability to relate to all walks of life. He has a presence about him that makes people notice, simply by walking into the room. He is warm and highly energetic."

Joe Conway, an aircraft mechanic at Ellington Field who worked with Story through the years, recalled Story's widespread friendliness with people from all walks of life. "If he was in a room full of dignitaries and you walked in, he'd still holler at you!"

Colleague and astronaut Scott Parazynski said, "I think Story's one of those people that you instantly like and you never forget. I think of him as one of those guys who's the ultimate astronaut, not only in experiencing most everything you can do as an astronaut, doing the EVAs, flying the robotic arm, flying all sorts of different missions including the Hubble Repair, but just the approach to life and the mentality – he's really the quintessential astronaut. What I'll always remember first and foremost about Story is just his incredible interest in life, and his focus on life and the details, and amazement in those details. You can look at all those academic degrees and

---

78. *If*, by Rudyard Kipling, published in 1910 in *Rewards and Fairies*.

convince yourself that he really is fascinated about everything. He was the most philosophical astronaut in the office at that time, and I still think he fits that bill. He's a really unique individual and like I said, someone that you just are instantly fond of. And you always end up having an incredible conversation with the man!"

John Blaha refers to Story as the 'educator' of the space program. "I think he touched every person who was on a crew with him. He had to touch them – they had to learn something from him. And this is more than any other astronaut I flew with. In other words, he helped educate other astronauts, in flying the T-38, and in flying and preparing for a space mission. He enjoyed doing it and his crew members enjoyed it because they knew they were learning from it and were enthusiastically in the 'receive' mode."

Story loved to challenge conventions. Friend Fred Morris, who worked for Hamilton Standard,[79] recalled, "Back in the 70s, during the Apollo Soyuz project, Story went to Moscow. And the NASA contingent there – which I think was a mixture of astronauts and technologists – was kind of confined to quarters. Story doesn't put up with this – he's a maverick! So he goes out the window – he's going to get his run in today – to go take his run. And he talked about how he heard footsteps behind him – this was his [Russian] 'shadow', who was watching the Americans. Then he said he heard the footsteps getting fainter and fainter as he outran whoever was trying to keep up with him!"

Story noted in his journal:

KGB or my 'guides' followed me onto street, but could not stay with me on the run.[80]

Story's wife at the time, Patricia, believes he just wanted to explore. "He's an explorer! And then he defied them [the minders] by coming in the front door to the lobby and just kind of waving to everyone, then went up to his room… And it's like a little bit of a defiance and I think it comes from his youth, but that's what made him, though, because he is unique… It wasn't like he was trying to break the rules, but his main goal was to explore. But then, on top of it all, he wanted to enjoy the fact that he was able to do that!"

Fred Morris also recalled Story's need to be active and how he managed to fit so much into each day. "After Hamilton Standard won the EMU[81] program contract, about September 1977, we had a preliminary design review in Windsor Lochs. Lovely weather – and we had a big BBQ at one of the guy's houses – he had a big barn and a pond that was swimmable. During that BBQ, every young lady in the space

79. Now known as Hamilton Sundstrand.
80. Journal entry: 29 October 1974.
81. Extra-Vehicular Mobility Unit (EMU) or combined spacesuit and life support systems.

department at Hamilton was 'oohing' and 'aahing' about Story for a couple of reasons – one was that he looked so good with his 'Mr Clean' hair cut and the other was that he ate about six lobsters and a couple of steaks, and still ran about five miles just to be active all the time. And he was still very social with everybody. But in a given two or three-hour period, I think he was able to do all those things – eat this immense amount of really good food, run five miles and be with everybody, all at once."

*

It was becoming obvious to Story in the years after the Hubble repair mission that NASA was reluctant to fly him. Age was probably a factor, as well as the growing number of qualified people within the astronaut corps and therefore a decreasing number of available Shuttle flights. Story, however, was still in excellent physical condition and at the peak of his career in terms of his experience, his knowledge and his ability to contribute to the space program, having been with NASA well into three decades.

Story had hoped to fly the second Hubble repair mission in 1997, given all of the developmental work and experience gained from the first mission, but it wasn't to be.

Mark Lee, Payload Commander on the second Hubble repair mission paid tribute to Story. He said Story had "set the standards for training and preparation," studying until he understood everything down to the minutest detail. He saw Story as a "real pioneer in Shuttle EVAs and capability, making him the perfect person to lead that first Hubble repair mission."

According to friends, Story appeared dispirited at times during the long wait until he was assigned to another space flight. He wasn't going to force NASA to fly him, but if he wasn't going to fly another mission, he wasn't going to stay. Story was never the type to look for management positions; he wanted to fly in space. When NASA eventually appointed him to STS-80, they also said that beyond it, they did not intend to fly him again.

Space reporter Dan Billow was surprised at NASA's decision. "When Story was given the basic command and responsibility for rescuing the Hubble Space Telescope, obviously they had to go and find the guy who would be the best at doing that. 'Who is the best man we could put on the most important job we've got?' Story Musgrave was the man! But then fewer than five years later, because he was sixty-one, they kind of had a youth movement in all of NASA, and I think they looked at and even said aloud, as old as he is, he's just not going to be flying many Space Station missions in the future. We need young people because we need experience, we need them to gain the experience so that on subsequent flights they have experience. Story is not going to have subsequent flights because by then he'll be too old. And I thought that was a real lack of appreciation and lack of understanding of what kind of a man that he is.

Not only the capacity of his brain, but his physical endurance, his experience, and the fact that – look at him today – he could fly in space today, and should be flying in space. That was unfortunate; they really shot themselves in the foot by getting rid of their best guy. Fortunately, they had a lot of other good guys, but that was a bad move."

Early in 1996, Story was Capcom for STS-75. As the mission drew to a close, he wrote in his journal:

> If we don't wave off tomorrow, this will be my last shift as Capcom. Have tried to make an art of it, have given it my best. It gave a lot to me – communication and expression, thinking on my feet, currency in MCC [Mission Control Center] and STS procedures. It is another major milestone, a passage, leaving another calling for the last time.[82]

Shortly afterwards, Story made a trip to the Marshall Space Flight Center to work in the Neutral Buoyancy Simulator:

> Could be my last suited run ever, maybe last trip to MSFC – can't know. A warm spring day in Alabama – nice cumulus, bright blue, 70s, good air from the pine trees, 30 years of memories here. Triumphant suit work, artistic suit work… so alive here, doing things with real people![83]

Thinking about his last mission, due to launch at the end of that year, Story wrote:

> STS-80: need to have all those experiences, need closure, need to do those things which need doing, need to take the time to do them.[84]

The crew of STS-80 was highly compatible. It consisted of Commander Ken Cockrell, Pilot Kent Rominger, and Mission Specialists Tom Jones, Tamara Jernigan and Story Musgrave. Their primary payloads were the Wake Shield Facility, which was used to grow thin film wafers in a super vacuum for use in semiconductors, and two satellites which would study the origin and make up of stars.

As the week of the launch arrived, Story's family and friends gathered in Florida to wish him well from the Kennedy Space Center.

Patricia Musgrave, whose marriage to Story had ended in 1981, remained a great friend and was there with their children. She recalled the celebratory atmosphere: "His girlfriend bought a corsage for me and for her, and I invited our close friends. And we had a big sending-off party for them, even though they were in quarantine. And Story would call in to see how everything was and we all talked to him. It was a good party!

---

82. Journal 19, page 10; Date: early March 1996.
83. Journal 19, page 11; Date: 7 March 1996.
84. Journal 19, page 48; Date: around June 1996.

The beer was flowing, the liquor was flowing, not that everyone drank a lot, but they had karaoke and dancing and we were having a great time. It was very unique."

Story also recalled another memorable moment during the same week:

> Lane and his friend each gave me a quarter at night viewing to buy some alien ice cream!"[85]

Lane was Story's ten year old son from his second marriage.

As he had done prior to every launch, Story immersed himself in the ocean the night before:

> The endless ocean and the endless life within it. The amphibian theme of life making it out of the ocean, the soaring birds of life making it into the air and now we represent that life in an archetypal leap off the planet – the alligator and other amphibians who lie in several worlds. Face to face with nature and, at night, the cosmos.[86]

On 19 November 1996, Story launched into space on his last mission for NASA. It was his richest space experience, full of happy memories. While onboard, the crew were able to speak to their families by video phone and when Story came to the telephone he was beaming. He told his family and friends, simply: "I'm having so much fun."

During the mission, Story made the most of every opportunity, thinking of highly original ways to experience space:

> I would sleep with my compass now and then. It showed me where earth was and where the poles were! If I had had a bigger one in my pocket it would have turned me into a compass needle while I slept.[87]

Crew member Tom Jones spoke of Story's approach to his final space flight: "He flew with a different perspective on things, you know, he flew with a goal of finishing up his card, checking off all those things he hadn't had a chance to get to yet. He was very focused about that. He never said, 'Boy, I wish this wasn't my last flight'. He just said to himself, 'I'm here to get the most out of this and nothing's going to get in the way of that'."

Another delight of the mission was witnessing 'the glory' – a circular or halo-like phenomenon surrounding the shadow of an aircraft, often visible while flying above cloud. Although the shadow of the Space Shuttle wasn't visible, Story and Tom saw the rainbow-like effect on the cloud-covered earth below – stretching for hundreds of miles!

85. Journal 20, page 42; Date: November 1996.
86. Journal 20, pages 31-32; Date: 21 October 1996.
87. Journal 21, page 12; Comment added afterwards, date not specified.

The crew treated themselves to a special Thanksgiving dinner, given that the holiday occurred during their flight, but occurring as it did after the cancellation of a planned spacewalk by Tom Jones and Tamara Jernigan, the mood was less than celebratory.

Tom recalled: "It was sort of a dismal dinner because that's the day that our first spacewalk was cancelled when we couldn't get the hatch open. And we didn't know why and we didn't know if we had done anything wrong, but all we knew was, we'd just lost out on the first spacewalk and we didn't have a plan to get the second one done 'cause we didn't know how to get the door open. So we all ate a Thanksgiving dinner but we just sat around trying to cheer ourselves up. The food was OK, but everybody was down in spirits."

Story's experience and ability to make the best of a bad situation proved invaluable when the second planned spacewalk was also cancelled.

According to Tom, "I will say that having Story along and have him say to your face that 'Hey, this wasn't anything that you guys could conceivably have foreseen or planned for', and having him there to sort of buck you up and say it wasn't your fault, that we were beaten by an insidious failure that we couldn't get to, we didn't have a way of attacking it... and to hear somebody who's fixed the Hubble Telescope tell you that you did all you could – that was very instrumental in raising my spirits back up. Tammy and I were really down in the dumps because we trained for this for over a year and had been looking forward to it so much and we just had our hopes thrown away. So he was very helpful in having our spirits recover, you know, so that we could enjoy the last five or six days of the flight, take advantage of those times looking out the window and not be focused on failure but be focused on 'hey, I'm in space with some really great people and I'm sharing some special times with a guy whom you could never have dreamed of working alongside'. So he was the guy who brought me out of the dumps."

During the mission, the Space Shuttle *Columbia* and the Russian space station MIR shared a communications pass, coming within fifty miles of each other.

According to John Blaha, who was the USA's representative aboard MIR at the time, "I'd been on the MIR for two months and I knew that STS-80 was going to launch. I said, you know, it would be nice if we had a communications pass together with the STS-80 crew and so we did. During the mission we had this one pass and we came up talking on the radio to each other. The STS-80 crew, they knew that I was friends with Story, so he and I probably talked for ninety-five percent of the pass. And that was nice and made me feel good. He sort of uplifted me with that pass."

John continued, "When I was in Russia[88] I used to think that if America was

88. Training for his mission to MIR.

smart, we would have sent Story Musgrave to MIR as one of the seven. He would have wowed the Russians! So if NASA made a mistake, that's what I would say; they should have sent Story Musgrave as one of the seven. Now the other seven were all good people too – I'm not trying to be critical – but he would have left a lasting impression on the Russians. He would have been the perfect person to send there and it's a shame that they didn't – it would have made America look good. That's one thing NASA missed out on."

As a matter of fact, in February of 1993, Hoot Gibson, who was Chief of the Astronaut office at that time, proposed sending Story as backup crew member for a three month Soyuz/Salyut Mission. Story took the idea on board with his usual enthusiasm. In his journal he wrote:

> [The intention was to] go to Russia for a year, starting March 94 for a launch March 95 and to be [backup] crew [and] fly on STS-71 to dock with Salyut in June 95. It's a year and a half turn around. It's a new culture, learning, another space program... It may be they tried others and no one wanted to be a backup, Russia, language, move for a year, house, family. An incredibly rich experience – culture, Russian space... But I leaped into the abyss, I took it on, they knew that I would do it."[89]

Although Story was willing, approval by more senior management was not forthcoming. As the months dragged on and the time drew closer without any decision being made, Story brought an end to the process himself and moved on to other projects.

As STS-80 drew to a close, the mission was extended by a couple of days due to poor landing conditions in Florida. Story was thrilled at the opportunity to spend his last days in space without scheduled activities.

A final highlight of the mission was the re-entry phase during which Story once again remained standing – this time with a video camera pointed out the window. As usual, he discovered something fantastic. He recalled, "The fire and flames, the blue lightning coming back from the nose, the auroral type effects. You can visibly see the shock waves in the flame, different colors on either side during turns."

Story remains the only person to have flown on every Space Shuttle. He said:

> You can tell 'cause there are ten finger nails imbedded in the instrument panel of every one of them!"[90]

---

89. Journal 14, page 21; Date: 24 February 1993.
90. Journal 27, page 41; Comment added afterwards; date not specified.

For Story,

> The best parts of space flights are those parts between the launch and the landing![91]

In another insight into his feelings about the risks and challenges of space flight he joked, perhaps half-seriously:

> I have been a crash test dummy for 30 years.[92]

As 1997 drew on, Story knew he would be leaving NASA before the end of the year. In February, he remarked in his journal:

> Hanging up very old winter flight jacket with STS-6 patch and canvas tape 'MUSGRAVE' on it – poignant – don't expect to ever wear it in a T-38 again![93]

A lot of people couldn't believe that Story was leaving NASA, nor how he didn't fight to fly again. But Story had had his day. He mused:

> I have 25 million miles, enough frequent flyer miles for a one way trip to the sun!![94]

Scott Parazynski recalled the end of Story's career at NASA. "I certainly saw him go with remorse and I saw us losing a mentor for the office, especially at a time when we were getting ready for Space Station assembly. I really thought it would be nice to have someone with his vast experience around to help us build Space Station and also teach the rest of our office how to perform a successful spacewalk. His abilities to teach extended beyond EVA – he was a flight engineer, and robotic arm flier as well, so there were lots of areas where his mentoring and teaching would be useful even today."

Bob Sieck recalled that there was a lot of discussion down at the Cape when it was announced that Story was going to leave NASA. "There was the second guessing of, did he do something to make somebody mad? The astronaut selection of how you got on a mission – that cult that got together behind closed doors and decided who would fly and who wouldn't – you know, the speculation ran anywhere from – well, he finally made somebody that's part of that process mad at him and that did it, or let's watch this spot for developments. Maybe there's something he's going to get involved with that is really going to be highly visible and great. And he's found that and we'll see or hear a lot more of him.

91. Journal 28, page 1; Date: 3 September 1999.
92. Journal 28, page 12; Date: 27 September 1999.
93. Journal 21, Page 18; Date: 18 February 1997.
94. Journal 31 Page 13; Date: 29 March 2001.

"There weren't many astronauts that people identified with as much as Story. There were some that had higher visibility names and there were others who were incredibly good leaders and commanders for their missions. But Story was like the pied piper, you'd see other people come and go, but when Story left, it was hang around the water cooler talk: 'Well I wonder why he left?' With the others we didn't get into the second guessing scenario, but there was more of it with Story 'cause, quite frankly, he was more popular. He may not have had the name that some of the others did, but he was more popular with the processing team.

According to Bob, "This is a person that was born to go into space. This person had so much zeal and passion for what he did. I think his legacy will be the space program."

Daughter Holly Musgrave said, "He just knew that that era was done… that's just it; he's time efficient. It's done: why am I going to wait around or sit around? It's time to move on to the next."

On 2 September 1997, "having lived the vision of 1967 for 30 years,"[95] Story Musgrave left NASA.

The official statement issued by NASA included a quote from the director of Flight Crew Operations, David C. Leestma. "Throughout the Shuttle program, from its earliest stages to the present, Story has been instrumental in developing the techniques crew members use to perform spacewalks. His knowledge, expertise and friendship will be sorely missed."

In his journal, Story wrote of his thirty year career in space flight:

> You come with anticipation and joy; you depart with a sense of meaning and hope, but also with a little melancholy. You watch this landfall, this garden fade into the western horizon. You see into your past when you were there, and turning away with some real melancholy, look toward the east, to your future.[96]

*

The world of space flight is a complex business requiring many thousands of people to make it all work successfully.

Tom Sanzone put it well when he said that the routine of space flight makes it appear easy: "The thing that amazes me is not that we occasionally have a launch delay or a launch abort; it is that we can ever get all this stuff to work together to ever get into space. But that's the part that you lose with the general public, 'cause they

95. Journal 22, page 41; Date: 13 June 1997.
96. Journal 29, page 30; Date: 10 February 2000.

don't understand how complex it is. It's not getting in your car, putting the key in the ignition and turning it."

In his journals and at public appearances, Story always mentions the people who made things possible for him – the trainers, the technicians, the engineers of all the different facets of Space Shuttle operations, and other crew support staff. They were the people who were responsible for his safety and comfort on a daily basis. Story recalled that in the suit-up room before a launch, in momentary consideration of life and death, he felt an overwhelming sense of appreciation for those who were the last to lay hands on him. In his journal he wrote:

> She moved with the ultimate care and the ultimate attention to detail. At this point she had done all that she could, affected my destiny in whatever way she might and with that, she let go and let the tears flow."[97]

Ever realistic about the risks of the business, Story was known to refer to the suits as "body bags".

Later on the launch pad as the crew escape team left and closed the hatch, thoughts of destiny and death would momentarily take hold.

> Chief suit tech – the folks who send you off to your destiny, to your death, your relationship to them, they leave and close hatch – looking for that last expression, that gesture of goodbye, of separation.[98]

In a note to the mission trainers just before STS-80, he wrote:

> Thanks for your passion and dedication. What I go forward with is what you all have given to me. I still play the entire WSF FDF[99] on my piano every day but am ready for opening night and whatever surprises may come with it.

Sharon Daley, who was Story's suit technician for STS-61, the Hubble repair mission, said he "wasn't all work" and that he loved to have a good time. On the day of one of the launch attempts, he had turned up extra early to get dressed and was in good spirits. As the astronauts rode to the launch pad in the traditional van, the escape crew followed behind in another vehicle. Driving along, Sharon and her colleagues became aware of someone waving at them through the dark tinted window at the rear of the van. It was Story! He was supposed to be sitting down in the van but instead was standing up, enjoying the moment.

97. Journal 25, page 44; Date: around March 1999.
98. Journal 18, page 11; Date: 2 October 1995.
99. The Wakeshield Satellite checklist.

When the historic mission ended on 13 December 1993 at 26 minutes after midnight, Eastern time, Sharon and her colleagues waited beside the Space Shuttle as the crew members prepared to disembark. Upon opening the hatch, they discovered Story at the door on his hands and knees, having unbuckled himself and unburdened himself of his parachute.

One further thing worth mentioning: the crew of STS-61 flew back to Houston that same day. Story went straight to the office and did a full day's work instead of going home to rest.

Story's secretary Beth Turner recalled, "He wasn't supposed to drive yet! You're not supposed to drive for two days after you get back [from space]. I wasn't there; I was working the landing. They waived off a day or two and it was a midnight landing, so I would work all day and have to be up for the guests. And somebody asked me, 'How come you're not at work and Story is?' I said, 'What! I'm not coming in, I'm tired!'"

The people who worked closely with Story thought highly of him – none more so than the divers at the Neutral Buoyancy Simulators. When Story was in the training pool, it was a pleasant dive for them: he would get in, do the work and get out again. He was focused, professional and a good communicator.

According to Bernard 'B.J.' Mundine at NASA's Neutral Buoyancy Laboratory, who worked with Story on the Hubble repair mission training, Story just wanted to get down to business. He didn't let anybody else do it for him or cater to him. And he always made the best of it – of the hard work on his hands and body required by the training. He recalled, "Even the frostbite didn't slow him down."

Diver Mark Liles who also worked with Story in the training pool said that Story was always the first person in the building. He would come in hours before to prepare for the dive and to work with the tools. During training, Story would stay in the pool, often for four to six hours at a time – "a tough assignment."

Some people thought Story's methods were too far out, while others did pay attention to how he did things. At the WETF, the old training pool at the Johnson Space Center, Sharon Daley – who became one of the first female divers in the Neutral Buoyancy Simulator – would notice other astronauts doing things the way that Story had done them in the pool.

Story was the acknowledged expert whom others would seek out to learn about or discuss spacewalking. He enjoyed sharing his knowledge despite the seemingly endless queue of people that dropped by to chat about it. If Story had the opportunity to share his knowledge and experiences with others, he would do it, and with passion.

Tom Jones recalled: "He came up with all kinds of practical advice for people that really helped them do a better job in space. I mean he would tell the rookiest, the greenest rookie those things and he would tell people who had flown three times before – things that would help them out. He always helped. You know I can remember him telling us about spacewalks; I remember him telling us about propping up the end of your bed in the crew quarters during quarantine so that you could get adapted to space more quickly. I didn't think that was advice I needed to follow, but it was great to hear it and to weigh it against the other practical considerations that go on during quarantine. It's great to have his perspective on it – you listened to all of that, you know, and used what you wanted to use. So he was not regarded as anything but your 'thinking outside the box' kind of person."

Story really appreciated the team of people he worked with over the years. Milt Helfin recalled how Story, at the end of his NASA career, hired an auditorium at the Johnson Space Center, Houston, and invited as many people as he could fit into the room, just so that he would have the opportunity to get up on stage thank them all and say goodbye. Milt recalled, "He's the only astronaut, to my knowledge, that's ever done that."

Roger Balettie recalled that day. "He was amazing. He meant just to stand up there and talk, just for a couple of minutes and say 'bye, it's been great' and that's it. And that's all we were expecting. But he talked for an hour and it was wonderful. He said 'When I was young, I was fascinated by things that were big and made a lot of noise. So I was on the farm and I worked on the tractor 'cause it was big and it made a lot of noise.' And everyone laughed!"

Similarly, Richard Rapson, a NASA employee at the Kennedy Space Center, Florida, recalled how Story got everyone together and thanked them "for the good ride."

Astronaut David Brown, who was selected by NASA in 1996, recalled meeting Story on one of his first visits to the Johnson Space Center. He said, "What I remember that day is, that as an applicant to this place, I was a bit scared of everything and everybody. I had stayed up late to watch Story's EVAs on the first Hubble repair, so knew more about him than most of the astronauts. I don't remember the content of our conversation, but I remember quite clearly sitting before his desk and having his full attention. Here was someone I'd admired and I was a bit intimidated when Laurel Clark and I stumbled upon him in his office, very much unannounced. Not only did he invite us to share his time but spoke to Laurel and I as though we were the only other people in the world. I certainly think about my encounter with Story when I talk to new astronaut applicants here in Houston."

Story Musgrave's approach to space flight will be remembered for a long time to come. Beth Turner spoke of Story's contribution: "I think Story added life to the space program – the knowledge, the energy and the excitement."

Ron Sheffield put it in these terms: "I think the space program, to Story, was a challenge that he figured the whole nation needed to do!"

# 10. The Richness of Space Experience

Think of childhood Story, and be that Story in space,
as in fact you were – fun and adventure.

*Story Musgrave, circa 1988*

It is one thing to fly in space, but it is quite another to really experience it for what it is – a whole new physical and psychological environment. But in a way, that was a very easy thing for Story to do. He took to the new environment like a child would – with a sense of awe and wonder. Because his own childhood had been so rich with self-driven experience, the space environment became a natural extension of that.

Two things stand out about Story's approach to space flight.

The first was his awareness of our earth-adapted constitution. Through this, Story could explore the space environment in a way more fitting to zero-gravity. This meant having no expectations about where things ought to be in relation to your body, or about looking for the realities in the midst of new psychological and sensory perceptions. For Story, it was also about *creating* opportunities to do things differently: not doing things in a particular way because you *should* do them that way.

Secondly, Story submerged himself totally in the space experience. Just as the child loved to dive into pond water or sleep in the pine forests, in space Story was going to find out as much as he could about the new environment. He was going to *be there*, to enjoy it one hundred percent of the time. Story had always been good at living in the moment.

Story's approach to space flight had far reaching consequences. He thought about what it would be like when people left the earth for long periods of time, or permanently, to make a home elsewhere. The images of a future life in space, as painted by science fiction films and television programs, are still largely of a 'one g' environment. But unless we are able to build spacecraft which can generate a gravitational force, life will be somewhat different. Story was interested in how the human body would adapt in those circumstances. He wrote:

> I was often observing myself from the point of view of a detached but interested observer![1]

*

From his earliest days with NASA, Story was aware of the potential of space flight. With each subsequent mission, the experience became more intense, more focused and more important to him.

In a 1996 interview with Robyn Suriano of *Florida Today*, Story said: "The experience gets richer all the time. The first time you go, your eyes are so big you can hardly get them in your head, you just take it all in, but each time you go, you know more of what to look for."[2]

---

1. Story's handwritten note in his copy of *The Modern Psychological Novel* by Leon Edel: New York, Grosset & Dunlap, 1964.
2. *Florida Today* article titled: *NASA's Oldest Astronaut Finishes*, by Robyn Suriano, 1996. Reprinted with permission.

Story took a creative approach into a world of science and technology. He began studying literature, psychology, history, philosophy and sociology. He learned to write poetry and to transport himself into space in his imagination. Friend and colleague Fred Morris described Story's fascination with space as "an epiphany" and "an emotional attraction."

In his journal Story wrote:

> What are the aesthetics of space? What are the important questions? What are the sensibilities and perceptions which could be made? What sensations, what senses or combination of senses need to be used? I want to perceive aesthetically.[3]

During missions, Story would conduct his own personal experiments or activities to explore the possibilities of the new environment. For him, space was fun, exciting and filled with unique physical and spiritual experiences.

According to space reporter Dan Billow, "Being there, and feeling what you feel when you are in space – he seems to be a guy who's made for that, perfect for that. That was what he was kind of born to do and he did it, probably better than anyone else and it's too bad that they got rid of him. Having joined NASA in 1967, Story stayed around long enough to where he should have reasonably had a shot at going to Mars, but it's not the way we went. It's too bad that he was not one of the ones to go on a long duration space flight, because there again, there's the guy who you would want to have doing that. He would really hit it out of the park if that was assigned to him."

Jim Voss, crew member on STS-44, appreciated Story's approach to space flight: "I think it was an opportunity for him to experience something that most people don't get to experience, that most of us would not learn from going to space. We would go there and learn some technical things or other data, but Story would learn more things in your *mind* about space."

Story wrote in his journal:

> There is an opportunity for new experience, for an aesthetic experience, for the perception of new relationships between self – nature – spirituality – humanity.[4]

He also acknowledged the self-discipline which was required for such an approach:

> Space flight is a logistical nightmare. Only imagination can transcend its current experience. The flight plan captures and destroys any opportunity for experience. [It's] exceedingly difficult to transcend.[5]

3. Journal 2, pages 31–32; Date: 29 March 1989.
4. Journal 2, pages 31–32; Date: 29 March 1989.
5. Journal 12, page 24; Date: 10 February 1992.

"One thing that has been missing is the heart and the soul [of the space program]. I do not think we have given to people what the inner experience is, what is going on in the heart, in the head, what you're feeling, what you're thinking... That's what human space flight is about," he told Marcia Dunn.[6]

Story was critical of the lack of experiential writing and communication about space. He felt that one of the reasons for the lack of public support for and interest in the space program throughout much of the eighties and nineties was due to a failure to make it relevant and accessible in a cultural and artistic sense. He wrote:

> I'm converting space experiences into art forms. The biggest challenge is to be creative enough to make it an art form. If you don't move things into art, they're going to die. If you don't move space flight into art, it's going to become boring. It's communicative. It tells me what it's all about.[7]

＊

The privilege of viewing a Space Shuttle launch, or indeed any space launch, is something to be treasured for a lifetime. And 'privilege' is the right word to use, because one has a sense of being part of a great, almost super-human event. The countdown ends with ignition of the Space Shuttle's three main engines, followed quickly by the firing of the solid rocket boosters. The flash of light as this occurs is reminiscent of old televised nuclear test explosions. The intensity of the light mesmerizes you until you experience the colossal roar as the sound of what you have just witnessed reaches your ears from four miles away.

One of the more curious sights at a Space Shuttle launch is the erratic flight of the birds which had, just moments before, been sitting on or near the launch pad. You wonder whether their flight is a natural response to the noise or whether they have been pummeled into the air by the force of the rockets. The thousands upon thousands of birds, flying outward in every direction, are a physical manifestation of the noise and vibrations which invariably reach the spectators. Standing on the grass, powerful shock waves sweep beneath your feet as a mass of smoke and water envelops the launch pad and vehicle. Mated to the enormous external fuel tank, the Space Shuttle noses upwards out of the visual chaos, trailed by a solid tail of fire, hundreds of feet long.

It is sheer exhilaration and awe to be standing at the Kennedy Space Center, watching the reflection of the fire in the water as this monstrous artificial bird rises from the earth. The shouts and screams of "Go! Go! Go!" add greatly to the reality of the danger. You think about the mind-blowing energy and technology, the thousands

6. *Breaking the Age Barrier: 61-Year-Old To Become Oldest Person in Space*, Associated Press 1996. Article by Marcia Dunn. Reprinted with permission of The Associated Press.
7. Story's comment on www.spacestory.com

of people required to get a Space Shuttle into orbit, and the courageous astronaut crew now laying their lives in those hands.

For Story, the time spent at the launch pad, immediately prior to a launch, was full of rich images for reflection. The gantry – that tall, complex structure to which the assembled launch vehicle is docked, provided a view of both technology and human endeavor. One particular journal entry dwelt on this in some detail:[8]

> Climbing to the top ≈ always on the edge, climbing the highest mountain.

> Gantry elevator ≈ launch; spacecraft the ultimate elevator.

> Gantry: fire extinguishers, fire hoses, masks, paddles, slide wire – reminders of what your business is all about. Axes, extraction devices.

> Gantry: view of massive number of spectators, cars, buses – validation that like a bowl, rock concert, sport event, this is a major human drama.

The final moments before the Space Shuttle hatch is closed, just before the 'white room' is retracted[9] were, for Story, like losing contact with humanity, with earth:

> Movement of white room away from spacecraft – disappearance of an escape route, removal of another contact with earth; like sawing off the limb on which one sits.[10]

Launch was also a time when Story reflected on his own mortality and fragility. This is reflected in journal notes:

> Launch – a heightened sense of body awareness because it is the body which is going to get destroyed![11]

> Launch is like a train wreck, big explosion, yes, but it keeps happening and you wonder what the end will be?![12]

> When the solids light, you are going somewhere, hopefully to orbit.[13]

8. Journal 11, page 37; Date: 6 Jan 1992.
9. The place where astronauts prepare to board the vehicle.
10. Journal 11, page 37; Date: 6 Jan 1992.
11. Journal 9, page 34; Date: 14 October 1990.
12. Journal 21, page 28; Date: around March 1997.
13. Journal 25, page 31; Date: around the end of 1998.

*Top:* Linwood, Story's childhood home in Stockbridge, Massachusetts. *Bottom (left to right):* Story's mother, Marguerite Swann Musgrave; Story at age three; with his polo pony at age twelve.

*Above (from left to right):* A young Story in the US Marine Corp; Graduation from Syracuse University, NY; Official NASA portrait for Skylab. *Below (left and right):* Spacesuit design and testing.

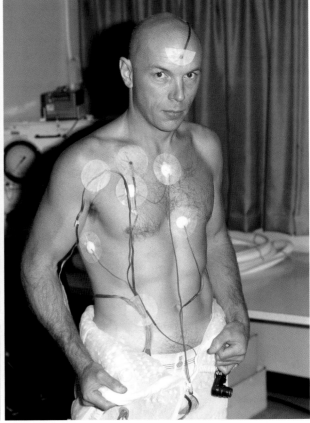

*Above:* Story and Patricia Musgrave with their five children (from left) Lorelei Lisa, Christopher Todd, Jeffrey Paul, Holly Kay and Bradley Scott.

*Far right:* With youngest son Lane Linwood Musgrave.

*Right:* Suiting up for spaceflight STS-80.

*Above:* By the time Story left NASA, he had more hours in the T-38 supersonic jet than any other human.
*Below:* Story, enjoying a moment in a T-38 before take-off.

*Above:* Ready to embark on his second spaceflight, STS-51, Story is pictured with Commander Gordon Fullerton (at left), whom he described as one of the world's greatest pilots. *Below:* In his spare time, Story flew a variety of airplanes, but especially loved the unpowered sailplanes.

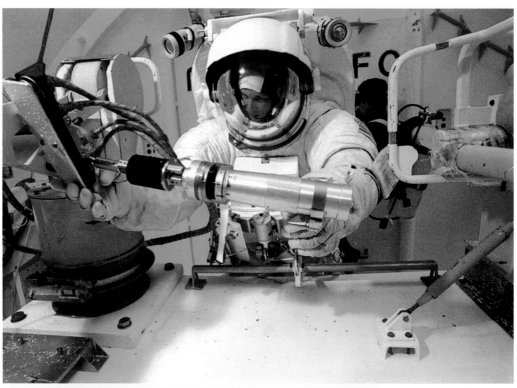

*Above:* Training for STS-61, the first Hubble Space Telescope Repair Mission, in the Neutral Buoyancy Simulator at the Marshall Space Flight Center.

*Near left:* Photography is a passion, particularly in space. Story is pictured here with twin Hassleblad cameras.

*Far left:* Taking a 'ride' on a centrifuge: the Space Shuttle reorients itself and Story remains stationary.

*Right:* Story performs a spacewalk during STS-61. He often refers to spacewalks as choreographed dance or ballet.

At home in Florida, Story *(above)* befriends a white swan, whom he affectionately named 'Goose'; and *(below left)* watering palms which he has grown from seed. *(Below right)* Story in the performance arena, this time in Sydney, Australia, February 2004. Story travels all over the world sharing his experiences with audiences.

Jim Voss recalled the days prior to the launch of STS-44. "[Story] always had interesting things going on, either in his mind or things that he was doing, something he was studying or he was trying something different. He was always reading very interesting things. One of the things I remember most about our flight was that the book that he was reading while we were getting ready to go launch on the Space Shuttle was called *The Denial of Death*.[14] I thought that was an interesting book to read before you go ride a rocket!"

Launch was an essential and unavoidable part of the space experience – it got you to where you needed to go – but Story never hesitated to acknowledge his terror of the ride. In the interview with Nina L. Diamond,[15] he described the eight and a half minute journey in some detail: "If Scottie could beam me up there, I'd be beamed up. When the solids [fuels] light, it's an explosion. The solids knock you upstream. The seats shake. Feeling the vibrations and sound pressure of 137 decibels, you're worrying about structural integrity, all the pieces holding in there, when you'd rather just enjoy the ride. It's not a steady push but a pound, and it hits you. There's turbulence when you pass through the point of highest wind shear, around 35,000-37,000 feet. But it's not painful, not physically punishing – it's shake, rattle, and roll. But for me it's fear: I worry about all the pieces holding in there. You slowly build to three g's, so the force between you and your seat is three times your weight. It feels like you're being shoved back into your seat. Everything's heavy. Then when the engines shut off – you go from three g's to nothing. But it's no weirder than being on an elevator when it takes off and how light you are when the elevator stops."

The experience of space and of the earth from space was immensely powerful for Story. Space travel was capable of giving back to us the 'nature' experience which we had, at times, almost annihilated on earth with the technology focus of our work and leisure activities, our densely populated cities and our often blatant disregard and destruction of the natural environment. Story felt the irony of the fact that technology had gotten us into space, yet in doing so, was returning us to nature:

Space is a great place to get away from technology![16]

Space – a great wilderness, solitude, isolation – a mountain to climb, an ocean, a desert, a forest – all. But it is done through and with high tech humanity. It is technology which has taken nature away in earth and gives it to you again.[17]

14. *The Denial of Death* by Ernest Becker: New York, Free Press, 1973.
15. Interview for *Omni Magazine*, by Nina L. Diamond, August 1994. Reprinted by permission of Omni Publications International Ltd.
16. Journal 8, page 3; Date: 26 March 1990.
17. Journal 6, page 22; Date: 13 September 1989.

Humanity was virtually hidden by the distance until the intensity of city lights became visible at night. Story wrote about this in a college paper:[18]

> The earth as seen from space in the day is an earth of nature, at night an earth of humanity. Except for moon-glow and some star-glow, at night, all you see is humanity. No image that I can think of would more powerfully express the interconnectedness of earth than a night photo of city lights and highways; it looks like a microscopic image of the nervous system!
>
> … clusters of lights, lines of lights, and little isolated pinpoints of light. In third world countries it is usually the pink glow of camp fires or the bright orange earth burning.

At night time you could see the continental coastline or recognize cities such as Las Vegas. Story wrote:

> South American coastline at night – city lights define coast line, black ocean.[19]
>
> Las Vegas is outrageously bright.[20]

By contrast, a view of South America by day was –

> Great clouds, deserts, high mountains, high plains and a descent into the low lands and meandering rivers.[21]

"I love space, for all kinds of reasons. For myself, and I'm being personal, it's a new relationship to nature and the universe," Story told Ted Koppel in an interview for *Nightline* during STS-61, the Hubble Repair Mission. "To look at Earth from this perspective, to look at the contrast of colors, to look at our home, to look at a place where, unless you use a telephoto lens or high-powered binoculars, you really don't see national boundaries. You get a new perspective from your home from a distance, it's against that deep dark background, and you say, 'Wow, that really is a beautiful place.'"[22]

18. Paper was titled: *Images of Man, The Global Mind, and Humanity in Space*, 1 May 1990.
19. Journal 17, page 36; Date: around June 1995.
20. Journal 14, page 50; Date: 4 January 1994.
21. Journal 17 page 37; Date: around July 1995.
22. Ted Koppel interview on ABC's *Nightline* 8 December 1993. Reprinted with permission.

Seeing the earth from space had an enormous effect on Story. "The earth is the most powerful part of my space experience and so my relationship to earth and the heavens and all, of course, continued right into space," said Story. "Clearly the love of earth is part of it and so space flight is getting the mission done in Zero-g, it's what you see out the window...it's just looking at the universe unfold before your eyes."

The window of the Space Shuttle was to become an integral part of Story's space experience. He wrote:

> Forever cleaning windows 'cause I crawl all over them. Put my forehead, nose, mouth on them, walk my fingers over them − it is worth it, the window is a window to the world and to the heavens.[23]

The window was the frame for earthly landscapes and the night sky and, at times, a mirror in which to notice his own reflection while observing the earth. In his journal Story wrote about the wonderful vantage point of the Space Shuttle, noting in a smiling tone that it would "take a tall building to cut off this view."[24]

Taking time to look out the window was like a child on the beach, exploring its universe. It is no coincidence that Story has always begun and ended his public performances of the space experience with that image of a child. He would also remain true to the Story Musgrave of 30s and 40s in Massachusetts. Of future missions he wrote:

> Think of childhood Story and be that Story in space, as in fact you were − fun and adventure. [25]

Story wrote of the earth as a garden and made reference to his garden out the Space Shuttle window. The garden was a particularly sweet sight upon waking:

> Each morning − going to the window to get the 'news' − 'good morning earth, good morning universe' − except it is dark still.[26]

Part of that news was the weather on earth:

> A snow covered landscape, white volcanoes, glaciers, running into ocean, sea ice − when the whites turn pink I am submerged in a cold winter evening... I feel the chill, the tenor, mood ambiance of pink ice and deep dark cold water.[27]

23. Journal 29, page 37; Date: 17 February 2000.
24.  Journal 4, page 44; Date: 21 April 1989.
25. Journal 2, page 20; Date: not specified; between September 1987 and April 1989.
26. Journal 6, page 16; Date: 2 September 1989.
27. Journal 25, page 29; Date: 12 October 1998.

The experiences of earth night and earth day were very different from space. Story loved to explore the contrasts as it affected him:

> Why is a night pass powerful? Daylight drowns out the subtle, the sublime, the nightly ghosts, the mysterious, the fragile. It scares away the nightly ghosts, the wisps, mists, auroras, fog, vapors, sublime/subtle – all of those words that relate to what is seen in the dark!![28]

> Ambiance of stars, city lights, aurora, moonlit waters; my body sinks into night – that I am in the middle of a work day does not take away from it – that is another, more abstract, intellectual cycle.[29]

> You feel differently about the darkness [of space] in day or night. Night time – it is a dark void, a space to hold the stars, like an earth-based experience! But! In the sunlight, it takes on a character, an identity, as if one needs light to look at the dark![30]

Story wrote vivid poetry about the view from that window. The sensual imagery of his journal notes is often very strong:

> Earth as a sexual being, warm, curved, beautiful, voluptuous, sensuous. Earth – like snuggling up to a warm body. Night – may not see a lot of earth, but can feel her warmth! But like any other body – can feel her naked warmth.[31]

A cloud-covered mountain is described in terms of a desirable lover:

> This mysterious being veiled in ever-changing clouds, this time she did not let go, teased me the whole pass but never gave me enough to synthesize a solitary image. As she passed on toward the West horizon, I smiled with anticipation of our next meeting. Down deep, I really hoped never to possess her, to let her live in my imagination.[32]

28. Journal 4, page 52; Date unknown: comment added later.
29. Journal 25, page 29; Date: 12 October 1998.
30. Journal 26, page 5; Date: 23 March 2000.
31. Journal 4, page 42; Date unknown, comment added later.
32. Journal 29, pages 12-13; Date: around end of January 2000.

The Northern and Southern Aurora held particular fascination for Story as a phenomena, and in terms of the science and the beauty. He loved to watch auroras, to photograph them and to write about them:

> Aurora is flowing color, pure color without a medium, it moves like a wave through water, but is not the water – like sound in air, through air, but is not air. Like painting the air![33]

> Like a silken scarf, a hundred or a thousand miles, a curtain flown in the solar wind.[34]

> Swinging out of the south Pacific, we head northeast and higher latitudes. Earth becomes darker and darker and then, the aurora rises, like a ghost in the atmosphere.[35]

> Cosmic winds, ions and atoms, magnetic ghosts.[36]

> 1000 mile aurora over Northern Canada. A silken cap on the earth, a pink and green glow that flows into earth's blue limb.[37]

> Aurora – like breath on a still, cold morning…Aurora – like a flock of birds or a school of fish.[38]

> Naked earth now adorned in pink and green translucent silk.[39]

> Aurora – sky dips into earth.[40]

33. Journal 27, page 29; Date unknown, comment added later.
34. Story's poetry on www.spacestory.com
35. Story's poetry on www.spacestory.com
36. Story's poetry on www.spacestory.com
37. Journal 14, page 40; Date: 30 December 1993.
38. Story's handwritten note in his copy of *Arctic Dreams* by Barry Lopez: Published by Charles Scribner's Sons, New York, 1986.
39. Journal 2, page 9; Date unknown, comment added later.
40. Journal 3, page 5; Date: early 1988.

The curvature of the earth and the geographical curves of nature were great reminders for Story of the differences between humanity and nature. It was a theme which he played with quite a lot:

> Seeing nature curve the beaches of the Mediterranean, nations carve the sharp straight striking lines in the desert.[41]

> Curves beautiful, curves of nations – cosmic curves, curves of time and space – why is humanity so straight or is it?[42]

> Nature only draws curves. Man draws lines.[43]

The earth's horizon, viewed from the distance of space with its thin blue layer of atmosphere, revealed the earth's fragility. Story wrote in his journals:

> Earth wrapped in a very thin shell of life, like a package.[44]

> It is the horizon, the curvature that lets you see the film of water, the film of air, and the film of life that covers this sphere.[45]

> Biosphere – a very, very thin rim of life on very large mineral sphere $\approx$ like a thin coating of green algae on a monolithic boulder.[46]

The play of colors was important in terms of the aesthetics of earth. Story loved the beauty of the colors, especially shades of blue – arguably his favorite color:

> Bahamas – a colored contour map of the ocean.[47]

> Bahamas – blues swirling together and blending on the mature palate.[48]

41. Story's poem: *Freewheeling on Space*, 1988.
42. Journal 5, page 20; Date: 5 July 1989.
43. Journal 3, page 41; Date: 26 October 1988.
44. Journal 7 page 49; Date: 25 April 1990.
45. Journal 30, page 23; Date: 2 July 2000.
46. Journal 7, page 40; Date: 2 April 1990.
47. Journal 6, page 15; Date: 2 September 1989.
48. Journal 5, page 25; Date: 9 July 1989.

Coral – a major contributor of aesthetics and another great blue – Red Sea coral like copper sulfate crystals.[49]

Crossing the Pacific, blues of Heaven reflected in the water.[50]

The earth is such a clean, peaceful place – blues merging and mixing with blues.[51]

Sometimes it was the uniqueness or familiarity of the geography Story witnessed which inspired a comment:

Narrowness of Panama – ocean to ocean.[52]

Looking at continents fitting together.[53]

Fault lines – viewing a cracking earth like an egg shell.[54]

Perception is affected by past experience – you know Italy because you have seen it on a map.[55]

Himalayas as sculpture – the perception is marble, only the intellect [knows it] is snow.[56]

Pure white spires of the Himalayas are like churches.[57]

Deserts were particularly powerful imagery. Story loved to fly airplanes in the desert, loved the dry heat of the desert. From space, he sought to capture the patterns of sand dunes, the art created by the wind:

If you look at the creativity of the sand and the wind, it is just poetic ... takes your breath away. The wind is actually painting.[58]

49. Journal 8, page 37; Date: 26 January 1990.
50. Journal 3, page 25; Date: 19 September 1988.
51. Journal 3, pages 33-34; Date: 24 September 1988.
52. Journal 11, page 26; Date: 10 December 1991.
53. Story's comments written while studying Basic Texts of Western Tradition, University of Houston, Clear Lake.
54. Journal 3, page19; Date: 10 September 1988.
55. Journal 2, page 34; Date: 31 March 1989.
56. Journal 2, page 41; Date: 11 April 1989.
57. Story's handwritten note in his copy of Arctic Dreams by Barry Lopez: Published by Charles Scribner's Sons, New York, 1986.
58. Story's poetry on www.spacestory.com

The poetic rhythms of wind and sand flowing across my window; dunes, and dunes upon dunes.[59]

Namibia – desert dunes and deep blue ocean. Sharp lines between the dark blue and the bright light sand. But the colors play, dance in the mind – dark blue and light brown. The wind swept waves of blue water – the wind swept waves of light brown sand. Curved lines separating sea and sand.[60]

Sahara – a very large place with very large dunes which, at some view, appear random points which organize themselves into linear dunes as the view changes.[61]

The desert is like an oasis of beauty.[62]

Patterns weren't just of the land, but also of the ocean. Some of Story's favorite photographs from space are the ones he refers to as "black and white water". Although photographed with color film, they appear to be studies in monochrome. Of cloud patterns over the ocean, Story wrote:

The face of the oceans, the currents, eddies,… the waves, the tapestry of the water.[63]

Getting to know the earth through oceans and ocean cloud patterns as well as recognizable land masses.[64]

There was, at times, a playfulness in Story's observations about the apparent scale of things. He rarely looked at things only as they were in reality: he mind was searching for the analogies, the metaphors, the poetics.

Namibia ≈ sand box. What would kids do there?[65]

Do the Himalayas look like a sculpture of mountains two inches tall on the floor?[66]

59. Story's poetry on www.spacestory.com
60. Journal 6 page 16; Date: 2 September 1989.
61. Journal 12, page 23; Date: 10 February 1992.
62. Story's handwritten note in his copy of *Arctic Dreams* by Barry Lopez: Published by Charles Scribner's Sons, New York, 1986.
63. Journal 1, page 9; Date unknown, probably late 1987.
64. Journal 7, page 3; Date unknown, probably late 1989.
65. Journal 11, page 45; Date 23 January 1992.
66. Journal 6, page 9; Date: 20 August 1989.

A tropical storm could create an interesting illusion when viewed out the Space Shuttle window with the eye. With a powerful camera lens, the effect was even more dramatic.

> Seeing a hurricane and looking into the eye – impression of falling into it.[67]

> One is affected by massive 3D thunderstorms or total cloud cover, or aesthetics of clouds.[68]

Story photographed the Egyptian pyramids from space. He questioned whether you could actually see the pyramids, because it was their shadows which stood out from the background:

> Do you see them, or a different shade of sand?[69]

> Pyramid shadows – sometimes you come to an understanding of things from what they are not, or from what is missing.[70]

For Story, the pyramids were much more than one of the great wonders of the world. They were intertwined with ancient history, with humanity; they made him think about thousands and thousands of years of civilization.

> The highest moment, the deepest feeling – seeing the shadows of the pyramids and the Sphinx, thinking of what they had seen and were seeing: a spaceship streaking overhead with a nose flattened on its window.[71]

> Privilege to see the Sphinx, but I would trade for all that the Sphinx and the pyramids have seen.[72]

Reflecting upon the transitory nature of all human creations, Story wrote:

> Pyramids, also, will pass into sand dunes in the desert.[73]

The view of earth from the Space Shuttle was largely a study of the details, however, the complete view of the planet invoked thoughts relating to the galactic and universal nature of things. Story wrote:

---

67. Journal 6, page 16; Date: 2 September 1989.
68. Story's handwritten note in his copy of *Arctic Dreams* by Barry Lopez: Published by Charles Scribner's Sons, New York, 1986.
69. Journal 5, page 1; Date 3 April 1989.
70. Journal 1, page 1; Date unknown, probably around June 1987.
71. Story's poem *Freewheeling on Space*, 1988.
72. Journal 1, page 1; Date unknown, probably around June 1987.
73. Journal 3, page 40; Date: October 1988.

When I have separated from earth, it appears much larger, imposing, mysterious – a planet – more a planet than my home. I float in the stars along an unknown mysterious heavenly body. Is this what approaching Mars at night will be like?[74]

As a foreign object, its immensity is frightening… How would one feel approaching another planet – relate to it as earth?[75]

Earth as a link between living and dead, present and the past.[76]

The earth is a massive cemetery – years and years and tombstones flying by.[77]

Looking at earth from space. Space beautiful by presence of earth.[78]

Magnificence of earth – magnificence of maker.[79]

Can you imagine a dead earth? Imagine a forming, fiery earth.[80]

Earth as the womb of life.[81]

Space is not a blank, it is a pause in the music of the heavens, it punctuates and individualizes the elements of the universe. It is the medium of the cosmos – the backdrop of the greatest art, the color of the canvas of the cosmos. [82]

In literary terms, the earth reminded Story of a living work of art:

Earth view - a living painting, changing angle of view, changing shadows, colors, reflections and refractions as sun angle changes (with respect to you) and a little change in sun position.[83]

74. Journal 28, page 50; Date: 23 January 2000.
75. Journal 3, page 7; Date: Early 1988.
76. Journal 3, page 24; Date: 19 September 1988.
77. Journal 5, page 19; Date: 4 July 1989.
78. Journal 3 page 10; Date: early 1988.
79. Journal 3 page 44; 2 November 1988.
80. Journal 12, page 24; Date: 10 February 1992.
81. Story's handwritten note in *Arctic Dreams* by Barry Lopez: Published by Charles Scribner's Sons, New York, 1986.
82. Journal 6, page 25; Date: 19 September 1989.
83. Journal 6, page 16; Date: 2 September 1989.

Views of stars were something which Story treasured on his missions. In order to see them clearly, he needed the consensus of the crew to turn the Space Shuttle lights out, so that his eyes could dark-adapt, creating a magical experience. He wrote:

> Stars – the streetlights in the heavens.
> Sun or stars as candles in the sky.[84]

> Stars, at times, appear to arise out of the city lights, as if the city lights were leaping off the earth![85]

So rich were his memories of the experience, captured in photographs and in journals, that Story could go back into space in his mind at any time:

> Marvel of space is that it leaves its trace on my soul.[86]

In 1999, *National Geographic Traveler* invited Story to contribute to their October issue which featured "50 Places of a Lifetime".[87] For that edition, Story recreated his visual experiences of the earth from space in the poetic prose *My Pockets Filled with a Picnic Lunch.*

84. Journal 6, page 21; Date: 9 September 1989.
85. Journal 29, page 8; Date unknown, comment added later.
86. Story's handwritten note in *Wind, Sand and Stars*, by Antoine de Saint-Exupéry: London, Penguin Group, 1995.
87. The unedited version of the original published piece is reprinted here with permission.

## My Pockets Filled With A Picnic Lunch

My pockets filled with a picnic lunch, I float into view of the spacecraft's windows; they are filled with earth, heavenly earth. She beckons and I follow.

High above the Florida shoreline, I abandon myself to the beach, abandon myself to earth and lift my soul toward her visceral blue Bahamas. Oh my Bahamas: floating in an ocean of space, you float me in your oceans of deep dark water, bathe me in your lagoons of shallow liquid light. Splashed with Iris, sprayed with Blue Heaven, touched by tides of turquoise, my free-falling body sinks into your sapphire sea. Now, a beam of pure white sunlight, now, earthly eyes reflected in the window pane, earthly blue eyes mirrored in your clean blue water; it is really earth, who looks into the looking glass.

And to the distant north, Bermuda, like earth – volcanic ash adorned with living coral colors, like earth – floating in a sea of space, remote, from every body and every place. And to the distant south, the Caribbean gently loops her strings of gold rimmed living Emeralds along the curving blue horizon.

Racing round this open road, invisible tracks in the visible void, I sail across the Atlantic waters – sun glint and sun glitter, gliding on the waves. Now, Namibia, desert streaming into ocean, waves of bright sand diving into dunes of dark water – visible rhythms of blue and brown, sea and sand dance upon my strings. Soaring above the African heartland: large human-like forms etched by the Kalahari, fractals sketched by criss-crossing fault lines, pink algae painted on green waters, and the snows of Kilimanjaro. Over the Mozambique Channel, on to Madagascar, and into the biological Betsiboka. On its path to the ocean the river runs from the highlands in small reddish brown arterioles, branches into myriad bluish brown capillaries and finally coalesces into a single blue vein at the shoreline.

Sailing to the south of the Seychelles my window comes to rest on the magnificent Maldives. Atolls, remnants of long gone volcanic islands, narrow focused outlines sketched in coral, sand and palm – sea after sea of pearl necklace floating in royal aqua.

More atolls, more islands, the sun and I, streaking through the sky, set down upon Australia. The shadows grow, the clouds turn pink, the water red – night comes down to earth below. The multi-layered horizon dances reds, oranges, and yellows till it rests for the night in blue. City lights and stars, at play together; I float and fly under the earth, enchanted by the pink lightning streaking above, the blazing orange trails of meteoroids shooting like rockets up into the air, the Southern Cross drifting through the luminous blue horizon, and the undulating ebb and flow of pink and green auroral mist.

All to soon, this serene silent fall through the night has moved the sun to the eastern horizon; sunrise, another day, another journey, begin. The Earth beckons and I follow.

For Story, the human being's experience of space flight and zero gravity was every bit as rich as the earth view. It was something he thought about a great deal and it became an essential part of each of his missions.

> Space allows you to live the fantasy, to be Superman, to fly and float. Space allows you to live the "pleasure principle" if you will take a few moments to do that.[88]

> Just plain living is an adventure – eat, sleep, bathroom, dress.[89]

In his journal, Story related one of his first fun experiments in weightlessness:

> On first getting to orbit and testing to touch nose with finger – finger knew prior to reach that it did not know where nose was until it had groped for it and found it (eyes closed of course). Once found, the limb seemed to remember where nose was – second try on the mark. All subsequent times, sensed that would get [it right]; knew ahead navigation was OK.[90]

Story was fascinated with how the human body perceives, reacts to, and adapts to the space environment. It was something he encouraged others to discover for themselves. He said, "It's wonder and curiosity but it's putting the body in a different situation and listening to the body's response."

Before his first space flight, Scott Parazynski remembered speaking with Story. "All my classmates had known that Story was a real philosopher, that he had a lot of great ideas, so I sat down with him for a couple of hours – myself and another rookie on the flight – and we just talked about the experiences that we shouldn't miss on our first flight. And one of the neat ones is the way that you're able to convince yourself of new reference frames in zero-gravity. You find yourself up on orbit being able to flip inverted in the mid-deck — the lower portion of the Shuttle — and then the ceiling of the orbiter becomes the floor, so you get this entirely new universe around you. It's an incredible transformation that just snaps; it looks like an entirely different world. And then you can float up to the flight deck feet-first and look down through the overhead windows and that becomes a glass-bottomed boat. And you can almost convince yourself that you're walking on earth; you can move your feet and it looks like you're walking on earth at 18,000 miles an hour from that huge altitude. It's an incredible

88. Journal 9, page 12; Date: 12 September 1990.
89. Journal 5, page 21; Date: 5 July 1989.
90. Journal 21, pages 10-11; Date: around end of January 1997.

mind transformation that you can make. And Story had a whole list of observations that he shared with us that I continue to take with me on my flights."

For each of his missions, Story carried a small notebook with a list of things to do or observe in space – sometimes more than a hundred things – which he had been thinking about for months or even years beforehand. One of the most exciting psychological and physiological experiments was always trying to evoke a sense of freefall, as opposed to floating. He wrote:

Freefall – like sliding down an infinite fireman's pole.[91]

According to Story, "It's very rare to experience freefall even though you are in freefall, because the eyes take over and the eyes are stronger than the other senses. The eyes have you floating in a stable environment. So what you perceive is that you are floating. Hypothetically, if you were to get inside an elevator in an infinitely tall building, and if someone were to cut the cables, you and the elevator would fall together and you'd be floating inside that elevator but you'd have no sensation of freefall. You would simply perceive yourself as floating inside the elevator when in fact, you really are in freefall.

"Until you invoke it you don't know that you've missed it. How I invoked it was to 'step off' a very familiar cliff that I know in Colorado, up on the mountain. I closed my eyes and I am floating in the dark and I imagined that I stepped off into the valley. It was that kind of thing which then triggered the neurophysiological phenomena which is represented by freefall.

"The moment you leave a trampoline you're in freefall. When you step off the platform of a high dive you're in freefall. On a roller coaster, after pulling the g's and heading upward with your arms floating above you, that's freefall. But floating in the dark in a spaceship with the eyes closed, everything – cardiovascular system, proprioceptive system: which is your joints and your muscles, your inner ear – everything, is indicating to you, is telling you, you are in freefall, because in fact you are in freefall. But from the moment you enter space, the eyes, having taken over, [tell] your perceptual system that you are floating in a stable environment. They suppress the input from other senses which are telling you you're in freefall and I think that it is the conflict between these senses which is probably primarily responsible for sickness in space – the space adaptation syndrome.

"So I was able to invoke freefall by stepping off this cliff and it was scary, very scary at first. I snapped my head and talked myself out of that and went back to floating and then I said, get the courage up, you can do it, so I went back and did it again.

91. Journal 8, page 31; Date: 20 June 1990.

"Falling through the dark is as delicious an experience as you can ever have; for me it's just marvelous. But having been a freefall parachutist and having really enjoyed this freefall through the dark, I wanted to fall towards something; I wanted to perceive velocity. So I tried to fall towards the earth and I could not. I could not fall anywhere. I wished to see my velocity but I couldn't do that no matter how hard I tried. A lot of people look upon these things as mind games. They are mind games but the funny thing about these mind games is you're playing mind games to invoke the reality. In fact you are in a freefall. Then I got good at this and then I could invoke the freefall whenever I wanted to. It takes a certain key to unlock that door, the perception of freefall, and if you get enough sensations coming to you then you say, oh I'm in freefall and it's the same as any other perceptual experience. I was able to invoke it also with my eyes open, after I became so good with my eyes shut, but it was still directionless freefall.

"Before getting into the freefall you have to know the direction of gravity. Here on earth, gravity is always toward the surface of the earth and that's how we've been created and evolved: that lets you perceive your three-dimensional environment; it's absolutely essential. If you don't know where gravity is, you're going to fall over instantly; it is an absolutely essential part of our orientation. In space flight it is not there. At least the real gravitational vector is not there. But just because after eight-and-a-half minutes of rocket propulsion you find yourself in zero-gravity, that does not eliminate the millions of years of creation and evolution that make you who you are. So up there you must know the gravitational direction. The fact that it's not there is irrelevant. You put the gravitational vector where you need it at the time. Most spaceships, either fortunately or unfortunately, depending upon what you're trying to accomplish, have gravitational architecture. They are designed for one 'g', with a floor that looks like a floor and a ceiling that looks like a ceiling. All the lights are on the ceiling and the floor is made for walking, so you have strong gravitational orientation.

"When you get good, you can do whatever you want. You put the gravitation where you want and you get a new spaceship. It's a whole new perception. All the three-dimensional perception of where the windows, the controls and displays are is based upon where you put that gravitational vector. So that's another very important consideration in space adaptation and, of course, about fifty per cent of astronauts get ill for the first two to three days [in space] and it's due, I think, to the sensory conflicts, these things not adding up."

Story wrote in his journal:

> With experience, falling forever through the night became as exhilarating, even more so, than a free falling parachute at night. Eventually, I achieved it as simply as flicking a switch – the freefall switch. I added objects and fell by them at incredible speed. I put the earth out there, frightening at first, and that interfered.

I felt the tension between free falling towards the earth and not closing the distance.[92]

Amazing what happens when you are out of your element! Opened my eyes to the stars – the fall went its way, stars at infinity, I now fell through the heavens, amidst the lightflashes.[93]

Tom Jones, who flew as a mission specialist on STS-80, spoke of the moments he and Story spent playing with earth-body orientations. On that flight, the crew found themselves with a considerable amount of free time due to the cancellation of the two spacewalks, and Tom and Story would often spend that time together. According to Tom, "We would say, OK, I'm riding in the Space Shuttle, sitting in the cockpit at the window and I'm flying above it like I am in an airplane – so the earth is down below me. And then you would mentally flip without moving your body – OK lets pretend now that we are upside down in the Space Shuttle with our head towards the earth and now the earth is above us. Do we feel like we're riding underneath the planet and it's looming up over our heads? You would either do this when the Shuttle's attitude changed or you would do it by turning your body over 180 degrees and lying at the window, floating at the window with your face, almost your nose to the glass, shoulder to shoulder, and just sharing that space. And sometimes we would have a camera and sometimes we didn't. Sometimes we had binoculars and sometimes we didn't. We just tried to experience the view out the window and the mental orientation of our place in space as many ways as we could and say, hey try this, think of it this way, orient yourself in the window frame here, and it was just nice to explore that in a leisurely way that very few people ever get to do."

Story continued to find new perspectives at the window:

I roll around the window like a seal, in part just to roll, in part to alter my perception of down, or to dissolve in it, in part to place the stars, city lights, in a different place. Back off just to see the window frame, but not enough to see inside of the spacecraft.[94]

It is fascinating that by doing nothing but reorienting one's expectations of the gravity vector that a very familiar surrounding becomes strange.[95]

Among the many experiences Story had in space, sleeping was one of the most creative. He spent roughly sixty different sleep periods in space and, therefore, tried to

---

92.  Journal 12, page 47; Date: 5 April 1992.
93. Journal 23, page 17; Date unknown, comment added later. The lightflashes Story experienced were caused by cosmic particles in the magnetosphere.
94. Journal 27, page 41; Date unknown, comment added later.
95. Journal 8, page 2; Date unknown, comment added later.

sleep in a different way each time.

He said, "I slept a different way every single sleep period just to find out what sleeping is about. Now the standard way is to take a sleeping bag and to put it on the floor because on earth you have the bed on the floor – you don't have the bed on the ceiling – you have an earth-based environment and everything is very straight like it ought to be. [In space] you can start out by hanging the sleeping bag from the ceiling as opposed to the floor and that's a huge amount of fun, but now it's finding out how the body adapts to space flying and how it is to sleep in a different orientation. For myself, the sleeping bag was an incredibly powerful orienter. If I put a sleeping bag on the ceiling, the ceiling became down, the ceiling instantly became the floor of my bedroom, I could never change that. Well, I didn't work on it that hard. Wherever I hung the sleeping bag, that direction was down, even on the side walls, 'cause after all when you get in bed, gravity is very important.

"I put the sleeping bag all the ways that I could and I started sleeping head first down in the bag, then crossways in the bag and then finally I did away with the bag altogether and simply floated in space. You just drop yourself out there and off you go to sleep 'cause every joint is totally relaxed. The extension and the flexion across every joint reaches the neutral point and so you sleep floating. After a while, of course, you don't know where the spaceship is. You certainly don't know where you are above earth; you don't know where the earth is either, which is fun. Basically you don't know anything. For myself, that was another absolutely delicious kind of experience – the fact that I was totally separated orientation-wise from earth – floating or freefalling, but in this case, floating. Out there in space, the body takes whatever attitude, whatever position it wants to, but the limbs are simply out there floating, so you have no sense of tension anywhere and you have no contact with anything. And so you're trying to find out where your limbs are. You don't know where they are because there's no contact and there's no tension to tell you where they are. And so you don't know whether you are over the earth, you don't know where the earth is, you don't know where the spaceship is around you and you're starting to lose a sense of where your body is with respect to itself, and this, of course, becomes the most delicious kind of experience – the loss of absolutely everything. And then, when you've lost absolutely everything, you go into freefall."

Story would sometimes sleep with the spacesuits in the airlock:

> Like four mummies, I wrap myself up in their arms and legs, dance with them all night. Like a square dance in the dark, end up with new partners all night. Square dance with mummies.[96]

96. Journal 15, page 16; Date: 25 February 1994.

Tom Jones recalled some of Story's sleep activities on STS-80. "We had four sleep bunks and obviously five people, and he liked to experience different ways of sleeping. So he said I'll let you guys have the bunks and I'll try various things around the cabin. So he would set up his sleeping bag in the airlock, sleep in there with the spacesuits, the dirty laundry and the spare gear, and then that got too crowded and smelly, so he would tuck himself in with his head sticking out in the fresh air and his body wedged in that way. And then he did try drifting around and he said he fell asleep OK. He would drift around the cabin asleep and he wasn't being disturbed by just gently drifting into the ceiling by the air currents and all, but what he would do occasionally was drift in front of one of the cold air outlets that was blasting cold air in the cabin and when it hit him in the face it would wake him up. So he said that just proved to be impractical for a long night's sleep because he kept being awakened by that. So he gave up on that and sort of fixed himself in the airlock again and just sort of wedged himself over there and let his upper body hang into the middle of the mid-deck where he would just drift and not bump into anything, but his feet were wedged in there, into the airlock. So he tried all of those things."

Commenting about the fun and the ironies of sleeping in space, Story wrote:

> Sleeping on one's feet – sleepwalking. No head-nods to wake one up.[97]

> Going off to sleep, your head does not nod, and nothing falls. I 'fell off' once with the camera in my hands – it was still there when I woke up.[98]

Story has spoken to numerous audiences about the fun of eating in zero-gravity – such things as 3D spaghetti and the enjoyment of teasing it out strand by strand, or eating soup with a spoon where the liquid collects in a line from the bowl to the spoon. Without a doubt, though, one of the more interesting experiments Story did was with a can of Coca Cola. After removing the top of the can with a can-opener, Story lifted the can off the liquid and watched it form a perfect little sphere.

> Looking at the Coca Cola I see the wonderful curvature of earth. Any object in space that was ever liquid is now a sphere. I made a blob of Coke in front of my face, and I watched it fizz. The fizz does not float to the top, it does expand though. I tried different places to catch it. I either got flat Coke or bubbles up my nose until I decided to spin it as a centrifuge. The spinning leaves the fizzing in the middle so you can now choose with a straw how much fizz you want and drink it as it floats.[99]

97. Journal 5, page 31; Date: 17 July 1989.
98. Journal 29, page 8; Date: 30 January 2000.
99. Story's comment on www.spacestory.com

How you positioned your body to eat in space could make for interesting perceptual experiences too. In his journal, Story wrote:

> Remember eating upside down relative to others and not knowing which side of the tray to put the food on, or how to orient the tray – you did have the urge to orient the tray with respect to the down.[100]

Taking it one step further, Story wrote imaginatively of new ways to make food and beverages in zero-gravity.

> Running a blob of cream, a blob of coffee and a sugar lump together.[101]

> A tea bag in contact with a hot blob of floating water.[102]

> Cookbook – think of all the ways the different things could be done. Making Jello in space – dissolve it by shaking in a bag, then squeeze it out into a sphere…. Spaghetti – slurping on two foot noodles. [103]

Story didn't spend a lot of time 'sitting down' to meals during his missions, preferring to fill his pockets with snacks and explore other phenomena both inside the Space Shuttle and out the window. With the sun rising and setting approximately every forty-five minutes, however, scheduled activities, such as mealtimes, did provide some structure to space flights in terms of time:

> The flight plan says that it is night – therefore it is night? Night is when we sleep. Morning is when we get up. Noon is lunch. Evening is dinner. One's activities determine time. [104]

The effect of crying in space was something Story was keen to find out about. After failing to find a volunteer to 'cry' on STS-61, he began putting water in Jeff Hoffman's eye with a water gun. The same experiment was repeated with Kent Rominger on STS-80. Story wrote of the resulting effect:

> Big blob – not very romantic.[105]

There were many earthly things which Story thought about in relation to gravity and orientation. The continual stream of ideas reveals not only the extent of his creativity

---

100. Journal 8, page 3; Date: 26 March 1990.
101. Journal 11, page 35; Date: around December 1991.
102. Journal 10, page 5; Date: 9 November 1990.
103. Journal 11, page 35; Date: around December 1991.
104. Journal 6, page 25; Date: 19 September 1989.
105. Journal 20, page 47; Date: 16 December 1996.

and sense of fun, but the fact that he continuously lived his space 'calling'. He said:

> Freedom from earth-based orientation leads to freedom of consciousness and imagination.[106]

Not all of Story's ideas were tested during his missions. The concepts, which are peppered throughout his journals, are wide in their scope – some possible, others poetic:

> Hang out laundry in zero-g, what would a line of stuff look like?[107]

> A cape in zero-g.[108]

> An hourglass in space – where does the sand end up?[109]

> A superball in space flight – a very light touch and it will bounce forever![110]

> Skip-rope in space, how can you miss?[111]

> Take a shell into space – hear the sea.[112]

> Dropping a stone from space into the Pacific Ocean and watching the ripples across the earth.[113]

> A waterfall from space – imagine seeing a waterfall 200 miles high falling towards earth.[114]

> Floating a candle slowly in space will keep it lit.[115]

Story's small in-flight notebook of actual things to do in space includes such diverse ideas as exploring and perfecting the process of dropping objects in zero-gravity; juggling macadamia nuts; communicating with aliens/talking to other consciousnesses; 'standing' and 'walking' on earth; personifying the earth; imagining flying like Superman; perceiving the earth as art; looking for the aviator's 'glory'; looking for rainbows; studying space debris; floating among the stars; flying under the earth; dreaming; observing the lighting effects of re-entry; and following the ocean crossings of early explorers.

---

106. Journal 9, page 31; Date: 10 October 1990.
107. Journal 13, page 19; Date: around June 1992.
108. Journal 13, page 19; Date: around June 1992.
109. Journal 9, page 1; Date: 1 September 1990.
110. Journal 3, page 49; Date unknown, comment added later.
111. Journal 5, page 31; Date: 17 July 1989.
112. Journal 12, page 50; Date: 8 April 1992.
113. Journal 9, page 9; Date: 8 September 1990.
114. Journal 9, page 9; Date: 8 September 1990.
115. Journal 9, page 53; Date: 4 November 1990.

Story also took part in routine crew antics. Tom Jones recalled some of the fun on STS-80. "We would shoot salt tablets across the cabin with a jet of water and try to pop them into his mouth from eight feet away by spraying them with water. And you know, we did some crew stunts where we tried to cram all five of us into one bunk and he went right along with that at age sixty-one, like he was a twenty-year-old, a college frat guy! And then I can remember another case where he told my astronaut candidate class in 1991, 'When you go to space, don't forget to try to go to the bathroom upside down, standing on your head. Just try it that way.' So you know, you do, because you can. And why miss an experience that somebody else found intriguing?"

Story was widely interested in zero-gravity from the point of view of other creatures as well human beings. To this end he created an imaginary dog which he called Darwin – an appropriate name given the evolutionary connotations of space flight. Story's journals during the 1990s are flavored with references to Darwin and his imagined reactions to and experiences of the zero-gravity environment:

> EVA – going out for some fresh air. Take Darwin out for a walk in a transparent ball [or] a PRS. Imagine Darwin floating inside a PRS.[116]

Story considered what it would be like for Darwin to eat, drink, take a bath, shake off bath water or drink from a bowl in space. And so alongside Story's cumulative ideas for his own creative experiences of space, he applied his ideas or theories to Darwin and other types of animals as well:

> Floating in a forest – a forest in zero-g. Imagine being a squirrel and spacewalking up and down the tree – pushing off from one tree to another.[117]

> A snake in space – how would it try to move, would it swim, thinking it is in water, or would it turn as if on the ground? What would be the natural position?[118]

> Crouching down on earth to gesture. Friendship to animals – how do you crouch in space to gesture to a dog to come? Dog's ears, hair, tail floating.[119]

Taking animals into space was something Story would have loved to do. Not only would it be fun, but it would give us alternative data and perspectives on space

---

116. Journal 5; page 47; Date: 7 August 1989. A PRS was, in concept, a Personal Rescue Sphere to transfer people between vehicles if they do not have a spacesuit. According to Story, "NASA had the idea but never went through with it. The PRS was to be used to transfer folks to a rescue ship. Normally there [would be] only two Personal Rescue Spheres on board – they had been designed to have windows, so I was going to take Darwin for a 'walk'".
117. Journal 8, page 10; Date: 6 June 1990.
118. Journal 8, page 20; Date: 12 June 1990.
119. Journal 10, page 3; Date: 6 November 1990.

adaptation. However, the only animals Story ever flew with in space were rats and, unfortunately, he couldn't get the cage door open to give them a free-spirited adventure!

Perhaps one of Story's more interesting sensory experiences related to the music he heard in space. Tom Jones, to whom Story had confided about it, referred to it this way: "He was talking about the symphony or concert or, you know, the music that would play in the spaceship, just the living, breathing aspects of the spaceship that would express themselves in sound. So there were fans running, pumps thumping. In particular, up on the flight deck, you hear the noise of the air circulation fans but that's a sort of a low white noise kind of thing. But the thing that he would pick up on, *Columbia* at that time did not have the glass cockpit displays, all the new computer screens. It had a lot of old airplane-style gauges that all ran on little electro-mechanical displays that have high frequency magnets that move the needles around various positions. So they all have little motors running in them and they put out a high pitch, almost insect-like, kind of whine that has various tones. Those tones all combine to create this surround-sound effect of this very high-pitch but low-volume serenade almost going on. And he would comment on that more than once during the flight. 'Jones, do you hear the music of space?' And so we talked about that a little bit too. You know, if you close your eyes or you look out at the dark side of the earth and you get serenaded by that, it's very conducive to relaxing and reflecting. You don't need a CD player to do that."

Story wrote in his journals:

> Music – cannot explain it: synthesis of fans, yet real individual instruments were there.[120]

> I am 'hearing' again, strongly, the music that I 'heard' on STS-80. STS-80 was a marvelous synergy with the space flight experience.[121]

At other times there was the silence and gentle motion of space to enjoy:

> The velocity, the travel so quiet, so smooth. As a very young boy I used to lie on my back in my canoe and let the river take me where it would, the motion of branches and leaves overhead would 'point the way'. Occasionally, a little eddy near the shore would turn me a couple of times before letting me go.[122]

---

120. Journal 20, page 44; Date: 15 December 1996.
121. Journal 28 page 7; Date: 13 September 1999.
122. Journal 29, page 9; Date: 30 January 2000.

Visual phenomena which Story enjoyed included small pieces of debris[123] which would travel alongside the Space Shuttle, moving gracefully in their own way:

Debris – like different leaves in the same wind.[124]

The debris – writing its own poetry. All I do is to copy it down, or take dictation![125]

On his last mission, STS-80, Story used a video camera to capture the view out of the window during the re-entry phase as *Columbia* returned to earth. Tom Jones, who had asked Story if he would be prepared to assist with the recording recalled, "Well he was filming the plasma, the plasma tube trailing behind the orbiter like a comet as we came back into the atmosphere; you can see it looking out the top windows as you streak back in. So you're inside the fireball looking down the trail of it and at Mach 20, Story's supposed to go downstairs and strap in by entry interface – and he never left, he stayed up on the flight deck. He had no cooling to keep his body cool – he was disconnected from that. He wasn't plugged into the intercom, so he was just experiencing this ride back down to earth, sort of 'Story Musgrave returning astronaut' and he didn't have any duties to do so he was not hurting anybody in the slightest. He stayed upstairs and stood up – wow, after eighteen days in space – where you experienced 1.7 'g's for five or ten minutes at a crack. For a sixty-one year old guy to stand up and do that, you know, was just flabbergasting. I just laughed at him every time I looked over there and he was still there. I couldn't believe he was going to have this grand finale of staying up there. So he stood up all the way through the landing. He certainly, he went out the way he wanted to. I guess that kind of attitude of, 'I'm going to experience this to the fullest and take every last drop of this experience and wring it out', *is* Story Musgrave."

Despite all that Story has recorded about his experiences in space, he has said that with regard to one's memory of space flight, there is an incredible amnesia; recall is not good – that's why he takes so many photos and writes things down. He said, "There's definitely something going on."

Space flight provided many opportunities to shed one's earth-based perceptions or definitions of things. Story found yet another angle of fun in constantly highlighting the ironies and ambiguities of our gravity-based language in space. He referred to it as "multi-contextual thinking":

123. Small pieces of debris from the Space Shuttle, probably due to the violence of the launch, would float away from the spacecraft and form their own earth orbits when the engines shut down.
124. Story's handwritten note in his copy of *The Spell of New Mexico*, edited by Tony Hillerman, Albuquerque: University of New Mexico Press, 1976.
125. As above.

[On exiting the airlock]: Going out for some fresh air.[126]

Open the window and smell the breeze (this is one window you don't want to open!)[127]

Sailing along in the solar wind – no contact with the boat.[128]

'Kneeling down' to pray.[129]

Touch a vacuum – how does 'nothing' have a temperature?[130]

Four corners of the earth.[131]

This house (spacecraft) is airtight. The winter storms don't enter here.[132]

EVA – walk to clear my head.[133]

Spacecraft is like a small cabin in the wilderness – EVA: take a walk in the wild.[134]

Pacing the floor. Going to go lie down awhile.[135]

It's nice to feel the ground.[136]

My life is up in the air.[137]

Space as the ultimate country outing.[138]

Spacewalk – can't skin your knee out here.[139]

Spacecraft – oil change every million miles?[140]

Pulling a tooth in space – tie string to wall and push off.[141]

126. Journal 3, page 36; Date: 1 October 1988.
127. Journal 4, page 42; Date: 25 April 1989; the bracketed comment was added at a later date.
128. Journal 4, page 43; Date: 25 April 1989.
129. Journal 5, page 54; Date: 12 August 1989.
130. Journal 6, page 18; Date: 3 September 1989.
131. Journal 6, page 18; Date: 3 September 1989.
132. Journal 6, page 23; Date: 15 September 1989.
133. Journal 7, page 18; Date: 1 March 1990.
134. Story's handwritten note in his copy of Arctic Dreams by Barry Lopez: Published by Charles Scribner's Sons, New York, 1986.
135. Journal 7, page 31; Date: 27 May 1990.
136. Journal 8, page 19; Date: 12 June 1990.
137. Journal 8, page 19; Date: 12 June 1990.
138. Journal 8, page 39; Date: 29 June 1990.
139. Journal 9, page 18; Date: 20 September 1990.
140. Journal 8, Page 3; Date: 26 March 1990.
141. Journal 10, page 43; Date: 4 June 1991.

Space is field work.[142]

Space – the ultimate 'high ground'.[143]

Looking at my life from a great height.[144]

Opening the hatch opens the world.[145]

Story approached space from just about every conceivable angle. For him it was a physical world, an intellectual world and, as we will discover further, a philosophical and spiritual world. It was about exploration, the quest for knowledge, being open to new ideas, surrendering to the environment, listening to the universe and, just as importantly, having fun. Each day was full of surprises and new challenges.

According to space reporter Dan Billow, "Story has a special talent to bring the experience of space flight home to people and he's done that very well. He delivers talks and lectures, always has, and has done interviews. He is the most wonderful interview subject there is at NASA and his enthusiasm for that is limitless.

"His great contribution would be, I think, allowing people, regular folks, to understand, and appreciate and know the importance of flying in space, of exploring space, going out to the final frontier."

Tom Jones shared his perspective of Story: "It was a gift to him to live in another environment so different that he could really look from the outside in and sort of see what a human's reaction to a totally strange environment was. It gave him a laboratory in which to measure human reactions, sentiments and emotions in a way free from all the earthly interferences that we usually have to deal with. It just gave him a way to examine your performance, your mental acuity, your talents and measure yourself against this new environment, but also to look at the spiritual side and emotional side and say, how does a human being's consciousness react when you get to space? So it was a clinic for him – every time he got to go he actually expanded the boundaries of the experiments that he was doing. I'm sure it wasn't that way on his first mission but, you know, he evolved in his six flights to a point where he could get beyond the routine of just doing good work in space, which he found out he could do pretty easily. And then he could sort of look at the other side of human performance and emotion and consciousness. So that was a real gift for him to get all of those opportunities and combine that with a particular person who had the curiosity to do that."

142. Journal 11, page 3; Date: 3 July 1991.
143. Journal 11, page 38; Date: 8 January 1991.
144. Journal 12, page 24; Date: 10 February 1992.
145. Journal 14, page 11; Date: 2 November 1992.

Story thoroughly enjoyed being able to share his experiences with Tom on his last flight. He recalled, "Tom Jones was, first of all, a great space flier. But he not only knew the earth, he had the same kind of feelings for earth that I have. He was a fantastic navigator – out the window navigator – which I've always taken pride in. He was someone that not only wanted to do space, but to experience space flight. So Tom and I had some of the greatest experiences, particularly the night passes. We got more night passes on STS-80 than on my other five flights put together. But he was really into what the experience of space flight was. He was a Romantic person, he was a spiritual person, but he knew earth as a planet and I admired that."

Tom Jones spoke in a broader context of the legacy which Story left to the astronaut corps: "I think he was a person who, in his work as an astronaut, always made people think about getting the most out of the experience and out of themselves. So he was a person who wanted you to wring out the last bit of performance from yourself but also wring out the last bit of enjoyment from the experience – not to let this privilege go by without taking every advantage of what you were being offered.

"He was the person who always reminded you of your responsibility to take full advantage of the experience on every plane. I think that's his main contribution – to widen people's perceptions and appreciation for what they were doing. And when we finally do have a colony on Mars, then he will be a guy who's looked back on probably by then as someone who ranks up there with the early rocket pioneers. He's a guy who has thought a lot more about the mind-expanding opportunities of living in space. When people finally realize that and experience it in a wide and frequent way, he'll be the one that they think of as opening you up to the possibility of doing that. He's a philosopher of the space program."

# 11. A Philosophy of Space

Flying through space with mighty wings.
No light, but darkness visible,
a velvet home for earth.
How unlikely the place from which they fell,
how unlikely the place to which they fall.
With him I flew, and underneath beheld
The Earth outstretcht immense, a prospect wide
And various: wond'ring at my flight and change
To this high exaltation.
Which into hollow Engines long and round Thick ramm'd,
at th'other bore with touch of fire
Dilated and infuriate shall send forth
From far with thund'ring noise.
Into the Heav'n of Heav'ns I have presum'd,
An earthly Guest, and drawn Empyreal Air,
Return me to my native element.
Both when first Ev'ning was, and when first Morn.
Ev'ning was and Mor`ning was before the earth was born!

*Milton and Space and Me*
*Story Musgrave, 1988*

Space was something which Story thought about all the time: what does it mean to be a human in space? The evidence can be found in newspaper articles and interviews dated as far back as the late 1960s when Story was first selected for the space program. It was his ability to see things in a wider social and evolutionary context, and to approach things from a longer-term perspective, which fostered his ideas about what space means and why we should be doing it.

> What is the impact of space? Why does space get to kids? Why does it really catch people?[1]

While Story's views may not always have been appreciated or understood to the same degree by others, he was well respected for the broadness of his thinking, not to mention his great technical and intellectual abilities which he shared with the space program for thirty years.

The media sometimes depicted Story, particularly in his last decade at NASA, as somewhat of a loner for his often bold statements and 'radical' views about the nature of life and the universe. Typically, Story would say, "Life out there? Yeah it's a certainty. I mean, you take one picture: there's a hundred trillion stars. A hundred trillion. What's a hundred trillion stars? That's one hell of a picture. Life's not there?"

However, for Story, the reality of life within the space family was one of enthusiastic acceptance. He was often called upon to share his vision and his views, both within the NASA community and externally. People responded to Story's warmth, his ability to communicate and his leadership.

Many others share Story's view that the space program needs a greater vision to explore the last great frontier, however, not everyone has the ability to communicate that. Story does and can. For him, space exploration is more than a journey in itself; it is a metaphor for the journey of life and self-discovery. He wrote:

> Space flight has great potential to create original perceptions and new images of man because humanity has a new view of the earth, the universe and a new relationship with both... It could be the archetypal Romantic adventure.[2]

*

"Visionary" is a word which friends, colleagues and even complete strangers at his performances often use to describe Story Musgrave.

NASA Administrator Sean O'Keefe paid tribute to Story in his inaugural address, which was given at Syracuse University. He said, "Dr. Musgrave, a product

---

1. Journal 5, page 23; Date: 5 July 1989.
2. *Images of Man, The Global Mind, and Humanity in Space*: a college paper submitted by Story Musgrave on 1st May 1990.

of this university, is indeed an American space icon and a person who continues to share his unique, cross-discipline view of the human experience in space with audiences across the world."[3]

Tom Jones explained Story's uniqueness. "Out of the astronaut office there are very few people who are big-picture oriented and that's not a bad thing, that's just people who are focused on getting their work done with precision and, you know, getting the next challenge out of the way – usually it lies in the next two or three years. He was one of the few people who would think way down the line and one of the few people who would think, not just the problems of getting people into space and having them stay there and work there, but what does it mean for society and civilization? Most of us don't think in such big terms. There are dozens of people there who think about getting to Mars, taking long voyages in space, about how to keep people productive and happy on the Space Station for six months at a time. Many of us think about those kinds of issues which have to do with the practical matter of moving into space and staying there. Story would think more about it from an intelligence side, a consciousness side – what it means for the human experience and what it means for the way we contemplate our own place in the big scheme of things in the universe, where we came from and so on. And so he was a very unique thinker in that regard in the astronaut office."

In a college paper titled *Images of Man, The Global Mind, and Humanity in Space,* submitted in 1990, Story wrote:

> Will we ever perceive space flight as simply evolutionary pressure…to know and to explore? Is it evolutionary pressure or is it life's longing for life?

Story's journals filled rapidly with entries on his philosophy of space, which have a strong evolutionary basis.

> Story – blood and clay sent off into space… part of this living push to spread and grow throughout the universe.[4]

Nowhere is the evolutionary metaphor of space flight more evident than at the launch pad. According to Story, "When I'm out there in the gantry getting ready to go, that's a magical moment, that's a key, that's a critical moment. It's the hour I have to myself before getting in the Shuttle and so it's that time. I have expressed this many times about being an amphibian. You know we're leaping off with this thing; it's life that's departing [the earth]; it's not just me. It's other human beings going but it's also

---

3. NASA Administrator Sean O'Keefe chose Syracuse University for his opening address on 12 April 2002. Mr O'Keefe, like Story, is also a graduate of Syracuse.
4. Journal 7, page 30; Date: 27 March 1990.

life leaping off... You look at humans who move into space; you wonder what is the motivation. Is that life pushing into the solar system? You see, you wonder what part of you – are you life, are you making that decision? And what are the roots, what are the roots down here?

"Now we are life and we're shoving off into the solar system. Well, is life trying to keep going, is life saying well, we've gotten earth let's get the next one and when we go and terraform another planet it may not be humans terraforming the planet. Terraform means to go to a planet where there is no life and you introduce life, and then 'life' forms the gases and interacts with the soils and it forms a reasonable place to live. It's what happened on earth too. Earth wasn't born with an atmosphere. Earth wasn't born with plants, it was molten lava. It did not have a nice temperate environment; it did not have oxygen. The earth was not given that stuff, life made it."

Just weeks before his last space flight Story wrote in his journal:

> Gantry – a pause in the flow to reflect on what is going on and why, what is the purpose of this. A high crow's nest point of view, vantage point like space. Gantry structure is symbolic of the complexity of the enterprise, the spacecraft, rockets and the tank, face to face with the massive forces, the power of a launch, it brings the danger of it all face to face. Your possible destinies are forced upon you. There is no denying the possibilities. The ocean, at one time in your roots, the oceans were an infinity, they were the space of that time – the biggest distances, the deepest depths, the deepest mystery, the furthest horizon. Face to face with maybe the real reason that we do all this – the quest to find meaning through exploration of this and other universes.[5]

It was the 'removal' from earth, the physical detachment, which fuelled many of Story's ideas about our place in the universe:

> Space – that moment of consciousness when you know you are from one world and are now in another. Innocent perception of a new world – the magic of psychological discovery.[6]

> At times I feel that earth is a welcome stranger out there – we are on approach to a mysterious oasis.[7]

> Is space more open space than prairies? Prairies – you move the horizon to infinity. Do you do that in space? Is infinity of space – infinite vastness – haunting, or is it simply there? Is looking at the heavens different in space than from earth?[8]

5. Journal 20, pages 31-32; Date: 21 October 1996.
6. Story's comments written during a poetics course at the University of Houston, Clear Lake.
7. Journal 28, page 41; Date: 16 January 2000.
8. Journal 5, Page 22; Date: 5 July 1989.

Human space flight is a unique and magnificent way to perceive and interact with nature. It is fresh because it is the first opportunity for humans to see their reality from this vantage point; there is the fresh experience which has not yet been apprehended by science, language and the arts.[9]

What is the meaning of history now? What does antiquity mean when viewed in the space age – the pyramids and the sphinx view – and framed in a spacecraft window? How is our sense of history changed when Alexandria, Athens and Rome are framed together in a spacecraft window?[10]

How has the world view affected the relationships of individuals, societies, cultures, nations and peoples of different races and beliefs? Is there a sense of sharing a common home and a common destiny?[11]

The image of Earth as seen from space has become a cultural icon, an omniscient and powerful symbol....A spiritual symbol of our whole space program. [12]

Story is a firm believer in life in other parts of the universe and one of the few people within the space program to publicly say so. For him, it is both a physical certainty and a spiritual intuition – something he knows with both his body and his mind:

Say a 'prayer' to life out there, the call of the wild. When you let go of all your cultural baggage, you can almost hear them![13]

He said, "If you look at the power of life to take over every cubic millimeter of earth – those things 30,000 feet down and the things that are flying tens of thousands of feet up – you know, there's life on every single square millimeter. If you took culture medium and cultured this table, you'd grow endless bugs; it doesn't matter where, there's bugs everywhere, there's life everywhere and you just walk out here in the woods and you look at the endless species – we have hundreds of thousands if not millions of species. Every single cubic millimeter of earth has a species in it. So life is hugely powerful and it will push into any area. It will push, it will redefine itself, it will mutate. It will do what it has to do to survive everywhere; it's amazingly powerful. Life arose here or it came here from Mars and then it flourished, or it came here from somewhere else, you know, on a meteorite, or it arose here, but the power of life is absolutely amazing."

9. From a college paper submitted by Story at the University of Houston, Clear Lake: *Potential Contributions of the Psychology of Consciousness toward The Perception, Experience, Understanding, and Expression of Natural Environments Including Human Space Flight*, 1990.
10. From a college paper submitted by Story while studying *World Futures* at the University of Houston, Clear Lake: *Images of Man, The Global Mind, and Humanity in Space*, 1990.
11. As above.
12. As above.
13. Journal 20, page 2; Date: June 1996.

On the subject of life beyond our earth, Story wrote:

> Aliens are no longer aliens when we take up a universal perspective. As with all humans and all creatures, being part of the planetary life force, we and aliens are posed in a universal life force – carbon to carbon, dust to dust.[14]

> We need extraterrestrials to define ourselves.[15]

> Extraterrestrials – we are not yet mature enough to meet others![16]

Story was known for attempting to communicate with other life forms during his space flights. In an article in *Florida Today*, which appeared before Story's last mission STS-80, he was quoted as saying he would "look for signs of alien life. Musgrave says he does this by simply 'being aware' that other living things are out there. While he puts his chances of making contact at less than one in a trillion, he'll keep his mind open. Others may think this strange, Musgrave says, but soon they will come around, just as people once adjusted to a round earth."[17]

He wrote, "It's humanity's destiny to explore the universe. When we start thinking and working on that cosmic level, we will transcend our parochial differences and tribal natures and become global creatures, solar system creatures. Then we'll figure out where we fit in. Living creatures, far more developed as civilizations – they've been around for a hundred million years, and we can't even conceive how advanced they are and the kinds of things they're doing. That's why I make an effort to communicate, and might be considered eccentric because I do, because I know the probabilities are close to zero. But I do tell them to come down and get me."[18]

Space reporter Dan Billow said that Story's willingness to discuss such things differentiates him from other astronauts. "It's very much a Story Musgrave thing and he's the only one who would talk about things like that. He was the only one who would talk about being in space and trying to keep his mind open while he was in space to whatever other intelligence or beings or anything else like that, that might be out there. And again, that's absolutely unique. The other astronauts are not going to talk about UFOs, not going to talk about aliens, not going to talk about that 'silly nonsense' that sounds like astrology and superstition! But Story Musgrave's not superstitious and silly; he's open to the possibility that with all the stars and all the galaxies and everything that's out there, that maybe we're not the only intelligent life in the whole universe. And he's not afraid to talk about it. And he's also not afraid to

14. Journal 14, page 41; Date: 30 December 1993.
15. Journal 12, page 37; Date: 8 March 1992.
16. Story's handwritten note in his copy of *The Spell of New Mexico*, edited by Tony Hillerman, Albuquerque: University of New Mexico Press, 1976.
17. *Florida Today* article titled, *Story Musgrave: Astronaut and So Much More*, by Robyn Suriano, 18 November, 1996. Reprinted with permission.
18. Story's comment on www.spacestory.com

try and set aside some time while he's in space to try to understand that, to try to think about that, and I think that's what he did – he would sit there and he would think about that possibility. And that's probably not absolutely unique that he thought about it, but it's absolutely unique that he would plan on doing that, set aside some time to do it, and then not be afraid to discuss it afterwards…The way he communicates is totally open and unafraid, and not worried about what you think of him."

Story told aerospace writer Marcia Dunn about "life forms out there that are millions, hundreds of millions of years older than us that are incredibly tuned to things… While I'm circling around out there, I try whatever ways I can to get them to come down here and get me. You know I'm a realist. The probabilities are incredibly slim. But what is the greatest thing that could possibly happen to me? In my wildest dreams, the greatest thing that I could do is to have something come down from out there and go take a space ride with them."[19]

Story believes that there is no hard evidence that extraterrestrial life has visited us on Earth yet.

A Space Shuttle landing provided Story with opportunities to think of the earth as some other planet. He wrote of the return of the STS-42 crew:

> View of the 'welcoming committees' approaching post-landing – are they friend or foe? In ways they look alien. Strange to look at earthlings for the first time and think of them as aliens. You are a spaceman and earthman looks like an aberration.[20]

According to Flight Director chief Milt Heflin, Story had a vision for whatever the task at hand was, as well as for what humans ought to be doing in space. He says NASA sometimes lacked vision, but that Story had that vision, whether it was to go back to the moon, or how to go to Mars, or how better to use the Space Station.

The public, more than any sector, is interested in a vision for space. One of the more popular questions Story received from visitors to the Kennedy Space Center, Florida, was "What should we be doing in space?" Visitor Scott Fenske, who listened to one of Story's presentations, remarked, "It's refreshing to hear someone outright and honest about where the space program should go."

"What should we do with space?" Story says. "Exploration! It will mean nothing unless we do exploration. Exploration is reaching far enough out there that space can become a mirror for who? For humanity and who you are! So you find out what kind of universe you've got, what your place is in it. We've spent a hundred billion dollars on a space station. One hundred billion dollars and we're not sure why we're there…we don't know why we're there. We will not be doing any real cutting edge research that helps to define what it means to be to be a human being, like the study

19. Interview by Marcia Dunn, 20 November 1993. Reprinted with permission of The Associated Press.
20. Journal 12, page 6; Date: 30 January 1992.

of what part of your constitution is genetics and what part is due to your environment – like gravity or non-gravity, that kind of thing.

"Exploration looks at the planets, the moons of the planets, the solar system; it looks way out there – bridges cosmology and theology, philosophy and astronomy. It makes those bridges. It creates those kind of Copernican shifts. Copernicus, Kepler, Darwin, Freud, Einstein, Hinesburg – all of those people came up with an idea or a scientific finding in which humanity had to make a major leap in its growth to redefine itself. The idea of evolution – it was a whole new thing. We looked at ourselves differently when we understood that we came from that process. And so that's exploration. It's going far enough out and finding out enough things about 'out there' that we go through a transformation. We grow and we change due to that fact, due to that discovery. It's not an enlightenment, it's not a reformation, it's a transformation. We, as a species, change due to that."

For Story, the Hubble Space Telescope is a symbol for humanity's quest. "The critical thing is there's no exploration unless we do very defining research where it becomes a mirror glass for what it means to be a human being. The public has told the space program for decades what they want. They want discovery and exploration and they want discovery of themselves. NASA doesn't know this part – that the Hubble pictures are a miracle. That's what people are after: power. Unless it becomes a mirror for you, it's not powerful enough."

Story frequently reflected on the value of the telescope:

> The grass roots interest is not only science, it's humanity, it's philosophy – what is our place in the universe? The search, the quest for meaning – a human quest for human reasons.[21]

> Majesty and magnificence of Hubble as a starship, a spaceship. To work on something so beautiful, to give it life again, to restore it to its heritage, to its conceived power. The work was worth it – significant. The passion was in the work, the passion was in the potentiality of Hubble Space Telescope. [22]

> HST – looking into the past, looking into the future.[23]

> More than any STS flight ever, STS-61 touches folks. It touches folks and was a magnificent success. HST, more than any other, links science and philosophy, cosmology and theology.[24]

In Story's view, the space program should be open to all kinds of people. Mia

---

21. Journal 12, page 48; Date: early April 1992.
22. Journal 14, page 46; Date: 30 December 1993.
23. Story's comment written during a course on *World Futures* at the University of Houston, Clear Lake.
24. Journal 15, page 6; Date: 5 February 1994.

Liebowitz, who worked with Story at the Kennedy Space Center's Astronaut Encounter program remembered: "He gets very passionate when he talks about the kinds of people that should go into space. He gets the space tourism questions. He gets very passionate about answering that question 'cause he truly believes that money should not determine who goes into space because otherwise, people like artists and poets and teachers and journalists would never get a chance to do it. And he would really like for NASA to re-institute the civilian in space program. Story also says that we should fly people with disabilities, older people, children and animals… he says all of this would greatly enhance space flight."

*

Story has always openly communicated his vision for space exploration, whether it be to NASA management, the press, the public or to Congress. Story's visits to Congress often became sticky issues for NASA management, who knew that he would always say what he believed, not necessarily promote the views of NASA. He said, "I don't go to Congress and give them anything else than what I believe, I'm simply not going to. I'm a simple farmer that believes in space flight."

A Congressional invitation was a privilege which was personally extended to Story several times during his career with NASA and was not something which could necessarily be repealed by nervous management. According to Story, attempts to deny the visit would be met with a "What do you mean he's not coming? Deliver the man." Story recalled, "The last time that happened, you know, I got a call at 5.30am in the morning from NASA to say, go to the airport. Don't ask questions, leave now for the airport!"

So what, in fact, did Story tell Congress? He said, "It was on the Space Station; it was on the differences between the sixties and now; it was on not being loyal to space for the sake of space; and [about] all the secondary things – using space for other people's purposes and not having a 'low cost reliable access to space' imperative; let's reduce the cost of space flight. It was things like – the rockets we use today were flying in the fifties. Access to space is now done by rockets that were flying in the fifties. Is that a space program? It's not, by definition…. I told the Congress that the number one priority at NASA [should be] to come up with a new rocket – best technology available at a certain date and launch and hand it to the world, hand it to the commercial people after you've done all the development, hand it to them; now we'll privatize space. NASA has not developed a [new] way to get into space in over forty years and it's not my perspective, that's a fact…. So it's going right down the line and saying here's the way it is. And the Congress were loving it – they hate bullshit. It's open and honest, but it's authentic, for better or for worse."

Frank Hughes, who became head of astronaut training, recalled the effects of Story's 'outspokenness': "When we lost *Challenger,* I think he really proved his metal and took stands against what was stupidity. At the end, his intelligence and his seeking gave him a little bit of a quirky nature I think, 'cause by then the average NASA manager was probably a little more conservative than he wished they were and that meant the gap between them and Story grew larger... his interest in the paranormal things. And by doing that he kind of separated himself, but that was the last few years before he left."

Story was very aware of where he stood in relation to the bureaucrats. In his journal he remarked on the realities:

> The usual emotional struggle between being a hero outside of NASA and a low level employee to whom NASA shows hostility and jealousy... Ambassador to the world for NASA but no space to park your car and the lowest paid MD...The potential resolution for this problem is there: do your own thing, hold your head high, aloof, super performance from afar.[25]

Whilst reading Ernest K. Gann's *Fate is the Hunter*, one of Story's favorite books, I was reminded of this. While flying the unpopulated skies over the Atlantic during the latter part of World War II, Gann wrote:

> The visionaries, as always, found they must be their own strength, for the hairs of pomposity prickled upon the skins of the incumbent authorities, warning them to smother this new attack upon the impossible. Fertile imaginations were ridiculed and occasionally thwarted, which was only a repetition of history; yet, likewise, they mainly triumphed in the end.[26]

Story commented, "Once in a while you get bureaucrats who are threatened by creativity, who are threatened by the people who walk on the edge, as opposed to looking at them as assets. You know, that is true of every institution. In every institution, people on the edge are a threat. It's people who are, in fact, being very effective because they're on the edge. But in my case I perceive that really, in general, [most of the people at NASA] were a very loving and very tolerant and appreciative group.

"I was not as far out on day one or in the early days as I became, because I had, you know, to put my foot in the water. I had to get into it and find out where the edge was. I had to find out how to work in that world and that world was very hierarchical. I had to find out what that world was about, and so in terms of where is that edge between the inside and the outside, I pushed it further and further, year after year because I had a record of effectiveness; I had a record of getting things done. I had a record of high performance and so you're able to push the edge further then, because people know you're way the heck out but they also know the job you're going to do

---

25. An early journal entry, 15 Nov 1974.
26. *Fate is the Hunter* by Ernest K. Gann (1961), First Touchstone Edition, Simon & Schuster, Inc. New York, 1986, page 175.

and they also know why you're going to get the job done that way."

Friend and colleague Fred Morris said of Story, "He may have been respected more by the scientific community, by the media and by the public than he was by NASA management because he was a maverick and he was willing to go to the edge and push things in the interests of common sense or just plain old space."

Joe McMann, who was lead engineer for NASA on EMU, says that Story was a risk-taker – in the sense of exploration. "It wasn't reckless risk taking, but he definitely was a risk taker. My personal view now is that we [NASA] are definitely away from risk-taking. We want to know exactly what the outcome is going to be cost-wise, schedule-wise, performance-wise, before we do it. People don't realize that we're still in the experimental business; that the Space Station is an experiment, it's not something that's been done a hundred times and we're doing it for the 101st time – it hasn't ever been done before. The Russians did not have a space station like this, Skylab was not like this. But still we don't want to take any risk, yet risk is inherent. And I think that's one of the things that probably put him out of step with the way NASA was going."

At the time Story joined NASA, he had hopes for a journey to Mars, but beyond the success of the moon landings, NASA did not have the necessary momentum, nor the support, for that to become a reality in the next thirty years.

According to Story, "There never was a Mars program, never ever. There is not today…you see a robotic thing every year or two… there is no 'human to Mars' program; never was. So people perceive that maybe there was, NASA perceived that maybe there was, but there wasn't… They work with some technologies and they think they're going there, but you know, if it is not in the phone book there is no program. It has to be in the phone book. If it's not above some door, if it isn't in the phone book, then it doesn't exist. Some people would argue with me and say, 'There is a Mars program, I saw it today'. I just say, 'Show me in the phone book. If it's not in the phone book, there's no program'. That means an organizational hierarchy dedicates three people to the job and gives them a title…. They should identify all the technologies you need and then start working on acquiring those technologies."

Story told the *Houston Chronicle*, "Space is not about jobs, it's not about technical spin-offs. It's a search for meaning. You reach beyond yourself. It's trying to find out who we are and the meaning of life. That is why it touches folks."[27]

Story thought we should take our cue from the enthusiasm of children. He wrote:

> Children are wild about space. They are innocent, don't load space with a lot of
> political or nationalistic or other non-intrinsic garbage. Even if we don't know the

27. *Houston Chronicle*, article titled: *Bittersweet Journey*, by Mark Carreau, 12 November 1996.

real reasons for space flight or can't acknowledge them, the children know them, and feel them.[28]

A longer term view of space was necessary. Story wrote:

> Space flight encourages the long term view – geological time, cosmic time, the illusion of time, relative time, poetics of time, historic/future, time prior to the human species and the time after.[29]

Tom Jones drew a comparison between Story's long term vision for the space program and that of Wernher von Braun, the legendary German rocket scientist employed by NASA in the early days of the space program. "Von Braun had a sense of destiny out there. I think that [Story and von Braun] shared that in terms of they both had the big picture view of space travel and the human destiny and adventure in space. And they knew it was the long haul that we should be thinking about, always focusing on what this would mean for us in a hundred years rather than just are we going to get the Hubble Telescope fixed next year, that kind of thing."

Story has fond memories of von Braun. The two men spent hours discussing the meaning of space, the future of space. They understood one another. Story said, "He was your ultimate technician. It starts with being a dreamer, of course, and he had imagination. So he was a dreamer and he had a huge imagination, but he was also an engineer. He was also just a supreme technologist, very charismatic, very colorful, an incredible communicator – you knew precisely what he was saying. What he did for space and how he lived space – he was complete. He was a dreamer and also the ultimate engineer and he cared about space flight with a passion. He was also an artist, he was a futurist, so he was everything. He was a real inspiration. He was as inspiring as anybody in the space program. He was as complete a space person as I have ever met and so he enjoyed my Romantic view as well."

Although Story doesn't believe renowned thinker Carl Sagan had a Romantic view of the universe, he says that he was able to communicate science, he was able to communicate a cosmos. "He was not a Romantic. He was a scientist, he was a realist. A scientist can be a Romantic too, but he was more on the realistic side. A Romantic has to be a realist, but a Romantic adds the human element. A Romantic always drops a human in the equation and portrays the human feelings and emotions to this environment. So I would say he was a little stronger on the realist side – he didn't add quite as much romance to it.

28. College paper titled *The Beginnings of a Philosophical History of Space Flight*, 12 December 1989. This was for a history course on aerospace perspectives at the University of Houston, Clear Lake.
29. Story's handwritten note in his copy of *The Unforseen Wilderness: Kentucky's Red River Gorge*, by Wendell Berry, with photographs by Ralph Eugene Meatyard, University Press of Kentucky, 1971.

"Carl was able to dedicate his life to being a communicator. That's what he did, he communicated. And so it's a kind of privilege to be able to dedicate your life to being a communicator and not have to be immersed in the details of technology or the details of science or other details. If you can simply be a communicator, you can do books and you can do television programs and you can be a popularizer and a communicator of astronomy and the universe, or the cosmos. He was not a cosmologist but he did communicate the cosmos."

Story and Carl developed a special rapport. Story explained, "We just knew we were souls from the same soup. We'd cross paths here and there – we just knew that space was the same thing for both of us. We felt the same way about it, we had the same frustrations about it when we saw exploration go down the drain."

Sagan had had close ties to NASA for many years. As expressed on the Planetary Society's website, "He was a consultant and adviser to NASA beginning in the 1950s, briefed the Apollo astronauts before their flights to the Moon, and was an experimenter on the Mariner, Viking, Voyager, and Galileo expeditions to the planets."[30]

In a journal note just two months before Sagan's death, Story wrote:

Call from Carl Sagan today – vision, calling, exploration – fellow spirit.[31]

Story recalled, "One time there was going to be some kind of big symposium. NASA had sanctioned my participation in it, but what [the organizers] wanted to debate was human space flight versus non-human space flight. Whoever was getting this together had Carl on the other side representing non-human space flight for the exploration of the solar system and I was supposed to represent human space flight, and we were supposed to have a debate. But when the leader of the panel, the moderator, wanted to set the stage here and see how to get things going, he found out that Carl and I believed in the same things right across the board and there wasn't going to be a debate. It was just going to be 'yes Carl' and 'yes Story' and we were just going to talk to each other like singing to the choir! – so they cancelled it. They went to find someone else to be on the other side of Carl and, of course, they couldn't find anybody and so that was the end of that. It was even to the point where it had been announced, but they couldn't go forward with it 'cause we were the same!"

Carl Sagan died at the end of 1996 – an incredibly sad loss for Story. "His death was right in the vicinity of STS-80, but I did talk with him a few times, just weeks before STS-80. He had had several bone marrow [transplants] fail. I used to talk to him in his car, he would call when he was in his car. He would call me from Washington State – that's where his cancer center was, where he was being treated.

---

30. Tribute to Dr Carl Sagan on The Planetary Society website www.planetary.org
31. Journal 20, page 30; Date: around September 1996.

"By that December, I was doing appearances for him, even though it was only very shortly after landing. I was picking up appearances for him like the National Science Teachers Association, things like that. So people perceived us as thinking in the same kind of ways and having the same feelings, seeing space in the same way. The difference is that he had the freedom to be a communicator his entire life, while I had to be immersed in nuts and bolts. I had to be immersed in tools and flying airplanes, and flying on Space Shuttles and all the kinds of details that you have to live in the physical world."

Story believes that the way in which we approach the whole space experience is critical. He wrote:

> There is an immense pressure and temptation to 'conquer' space, to appropriate it into our earth-based paradigm and celebrate that 'victory' among many such other 'victories' over nature. If that is the course which is succumbed to, we will never know the difference and never know what, or that anything, was missed. With humanity's technological, even evolutionary move into space, a much wider view of nature, earth and universe becomes possible, but it demands an open consciousness which is not fixed in earth-based assumptions, and eyes which are not limited to earth-based vision.[32]

Story constantly refers to an image of a child on a beach which he photographed more than thirty years ago. It depicts the essence of discovery and exploration – the child is crouching forward, feet and hands in the sand, totally immersed in the experience. It is the simplicity, yet the intensity of the child which captivates Story:

> You look at the posture of that child, he is reaching for our universe! Look at those eyes and ears as close as possible to the universe. The further we reach, the more we move inwards, as shown by the reflection of that child [in the water].[33]

For a college paper on human consciousness, Story again pointed to the need for innocence in our approach to space flight, the need for detachment from our earthly ways:

> While a true perception and experience of space flight requires a new consciousness and vision, it simultaneously provides a unique environment which may be used to facilitate enriched states of mind. Floating in the dark, drifting off to sleep, without knowing where one is over the earth, or where the earth is, or even the position of the enclosing spacecraft about you, without touching any object, without any orienting anchor, is a magical, magnificent condition in which to achieve the totally serene silent mind. In a physiological sense, the body relates

32. College paper titled, *Potential Contributions of the Psychology of Consciousness toward the Perception, Experience, Understanding, and Expression of Natural Environments Including Human Space Flight*, 15 December 1990. This paper was prepared for a course on human consciousness, University of Houston, Clear Lake.
33. Story's comment on www.spacestory.com

only to itself, it is not standing in a line, not sitting at a desk, not lying on a beach of sand, it is just there, it just is. If our actions in the free-fall, zero-gravity of space are forced to be earth-like (because not to be earth-like is a threat to stability), we will never grasp the reality of space flight. We need to be conscious of ourselves as creatures of space as well as of the earth if we are to be natural and comfortable doing things in zero-gravity, in a way fitting to zero-gravity, not to ambulation [walking] on earth.[34]

Greater care for the environment is something which Story hoped would be increased by the view of the earth from space:

Has our ecological awareness been increased? Has our concern for the earth that we will leave for others been nurtured? Do we now view earth as a lifeboat with limited resources, limited ability to absorb wastes and an ever growing population? Are we moved just a little from exploitation to care?[35]

The earth is changing on its own and changing due to the effects of life, in particular, those of [humanity]. [Humanity] is exploiting the earth at ever increasing rates... is realizing that it can overwhelm earth and that it must manage earth. If it is to manage earth, it must, through Mission to Planet Earth, understand earth.[36]

Earth will go on with or without us. We may create an environment which we cannot survive in and we will die. Without us, Gaia will return to another equilibrium with those living organisms which have a desire to live and the harmony to accomplish life.[37]

The supreme irony of evolution is that intelligence may not be a good survival factor or technique. Even when humans see the problem, they deny it and don't deal with it.[38]

In an interview with Rinker Buck of *The Berkshire Eagle* three decades ago, Story was quoted as saying that "he views America as a nation whose technology has always been several leaps ahead of its social progress. Until technological and social planning are brought 'in phase' and conceived as one, [he] foresees only exasperating results for America."[39]

Story believes that cultural re-evaluation is necessary in order to restore the

34. College paper titled, *Potential Contributions of the Psychology of Consciousness toward the Perception, Experience, Understanding, and Expression of Natural Environments Including Human Space Flight*, 15 December 1990.
35. College paper titled, *Images of Man, The Global Mind, and Humanity in Space*, 1 May 1990. This paper was prepared for a course on world futures at the University of Houston, Clear Lake.
36. Paper written 18 December 1989 for the course *Our Future in Space*, at the University of Houston, Clear Lake.
37. Journal 8, page 42; Date: 16 July 1990.
38. Conversation with Anne Lenehan.
39. *The Berkshire Eagle*, 28 December 1973: *Astronaut Points Out Ironies of Space-Age Energy Crisis* by Rinker Buck.

balance between technology and nature. On a 777 flight from Puerto Rico to Orlando, the current technology focus was abundantly clear to him. While flying over the spectacular blues of the Bahamas, no one was looking out the window. With the latest in-flight entertainment systems, people were just too absorbed to think of looking out the window. He said, "What other data do you need? Who is studying something for personal improvement on the airplane? Who is looking out the window?"

Of himself, Story wrote:

> You are counter culture in your view of nature and your opposition to the couch potato approach to life.[40]

> Productivity technology is not the only answer, the human element is critical – creativity and care. [41]

At times an element of despondency, or perhaps even anger, crept into Story's journals:

> Our world is a chaotic swirl of business – people doing too much, too busy – lack of reflection, contemplation, meditation.[42]

> What has the view of earth achieved? More money and materialism than ever, less concern for long term and non-sustainability. Less interest in earth and nature than ever before! Earth view might have [changed that] but it didn't.[43]

The ultimate wisdom of nature needs to be respected. Story cited the matter of bone loss in human space flight:

> Bone loss should be viewed as the ultimate wisdom of nature, the biology of the body is redesigning itself to new requirements – i.e. zero-gravity. With return to earth, it comes back to the old earth-based design. Too many people, including NASA, tend to think upon bone-loss and other changes as detrimental, when in fact they are the wisdom of adaptation, the right thing to be doing.[44]

As far as Story is concerned, if we follow the current path, extinction of our species is a real possibility:

> We are to our bodies as humanity is to Earth. We want to ignore it, reject it, do our own economic wealth exploitation, do our homes, SUVs,[45] do our money thing and expect somehow that Earth will always be there [for us] – it won't. It will go on without us. As a species we move along the suicide path, as individuals we don't care – it is not our future. That it is the future for our children, we don't care.[46]

---

40. Journal 6, page 26; Date: 19 September 1989.
41. Journal 6, page 27; Date: 25 September 1989.
42. Journal 7, page 17; Date: 1 March 1990.
43. Journal 5, page 33; Date unknown, comment added later.
44. Story's comment on www.spacestory.com
45. Sports Utility Vans (SUVs).
46. Journal 26, page 10; Date: 2 April 2000.

Extinction of most or all of humanity – may be the most creative of all universal solutions! … Culture, like an individual, is radically egocentric – all else is ignored! Humanity has an ego problem.[47]

Nature still overshadows us – despite our attempts to conquer her.[48]

Story had strong ideas about how we could improve our relationship with our earthly home. In his journal and college papers he wrote:

We can change things, science does. We are not passive victims of history. World is created by our observations of it. The fire of dreams.[49]

It requires leadership – identify problems, develop plans, create solutions, then take action.. It takes courage and the hope of success to address and resolve global issues.[50]

In reference to sustainable behaviors, I strongly agree that conceptualization and communication are the instruments for change... Knowledge which is *intellectual* does not change human behavior, knowledge which is *felt* changes human behavior... Lecturing to people in abstract terms *has* not and *will* not change behavior... A global sense of community at the 'emergent' level, which looks at earth and its relationship to earth through unbiased eyes, will go a long way to correct the tragedy of the commons toward which we now run.[51]

Story has worked hard to try to increase people's understanding of the earth through public communication – particularly through interviews, television programs and performances. He has accumulated thousands of emotive images of the earth which he uses to highlight both the magnificence and the fragility of the environment. Story's aim is to transform people through exploration – to give us a sense of our home planet – of oceans and geography, of different civilizations and cultures, of our history and our future. He also encourages us to look at the possibilities of life through universal care, co-operation and discovery.

In a relatively remote part of Central Florida, Story is creating a personal paradise in which to live by restoring the environment to its fullest potential. He has spent several years beautifying a hundred or so acres while creating a haven for native animals. In his home, he has no public or commercial television connection, nor does he listen to the radio, but divides his time between strenuous physical labor and a

---

47. Story's handwritten notes in *The Dream of the Earth*, by Thomas Berry, San Francisco, Sierra Club Books, 1988.
48. Journal 3, page 26; Date: 19 September 1988.
49. Journal 6, page 33; Date: 15 October 1989.
50. College paper titled, *Humanity, Nature and Spirituality in the Year 2000*, submitted 3 December 1988, for a course on global geography, University of Houston, Clear Lake.
51. Story's written comments during the course, *Visionary Futures*, 1990, University of Houston, Clear Lake.

rigorous program of ongoing self-education. He leads a simple lifestyle with a strong work ethic, contributing what he can to the betterment of society through education and the communication of his own philosophies.

Regardless of the issue or the topic, Story enjoys exploring the wider implications as well as the details. He is comfortable with both the longer-term view of things, as well as the intricacies of the current moment. Nowhere is this more apparent than in his thinking about our universal origins. His approach encompasses such things as biology, physics, evolution and spirituality – the power of life to inhabit the universe, the cultural constraints of our discoveries, and the divine nature of creation.

Of the Big Bang Theory, Story disagrees "that it all came from nothing". He says that people can accept the concept of God as "always was and always will be", yet we cannot accept the idea that the universe always was. He said, "If there was a 'big bang', why not describe it as a transitory state, rather than the beginning?" In his journals Story often explained his ideas:

> Maybe the universe did not begin, maybe it has always been.... If we presume that the universe is reducible to our scientific methods and it is not, we have no hope of knowing it! Wrong hypothesis.[52]

> My hypothesis, my belief, is that the universe had no beginning and it will have no end. To think of beginnings and ends is to impose the perception, or our individual lives, on the cosmos. If one looks at the history of science, one can see the endless errors based on imposing one's egocentric or anthrocentric views on this universe. [53]

> Copernican revolution, the history of human thinking – [rejection of the theory] that the universe circles around us and we are the only living creatures, we are the only galaxy. Take this thinking to 'we are the only universe'. It's illogical to think we are the only universe or that this one had a beginning or will have an end. Assumption should be that there is no beginning or end to anything and that there is no beginning or end to space or time or the number of universes or the extent of universes![54]

Story writes of the cosmos as inseparable from God.

> A unified, coherent, intelligent work of art, principled and revealing of the maker![55]

> Cosmic wind, cosmic breath $\approx$ soul, life, breath of God – ethereal.[56]

---

52. Journal 14, page 42; Date: 30 December 1993.
53. Journal 17, page 50; Date: 14 May 1995.
54. Journal 17, page 32; Date: around June 1995.
55. Journal 5, page 33; Date unknown, comment added later.
56. Journal 10, page 38; Date: 26 April 1991.

> We are part of this universe, this cosmos. Should we not participate fully? As a species, should we not give it our best? Should we not pursue God? All is God.[57]

Story celebrates the unknown mysteries of the universe. This is perhaps the most important part of his own personal belief system:

> Faith in the unknown versus construction of preconceived picture to control and determine the unknown. Accept, yield, surrender. The yield is like that of water! The journey, the quest. Surrender; expect surprises, surrender to the creation, to one's own body. Creation is similar to evolution – the creator and the creation are not dead, they have always been and will always be, never beginning and never ending. Creation is a continuous process.[58]

*

What is space flight all about? What have we learnt about humanity and the universe? For Story, it has given him the widest view he has ever had of nature and humanity. It has certainly raised more questions than it has answered, created new challenges and new experiences. It has given him a deeper understanding of the fragility of earthly life and a greater appreciation for the possibilities of life elsewhere in the universe. In his journal he wrote:

> We cannot maintain space flight on a utilitarian basis; it must be grandeur, mystique and the quest! Quest for meaning – purpose of life. You can pursue the quest or accept the answers of others![59]

Despite the potentiality of our discoveries and our evolutionary exploration, Story firmly believes that the same fundamental things can be learnt on earth as in space – but that space flight gives us the opportunity to look at them from a fresh point of view:

> Just as there is an outer reality and an inner experience, there is earth experience and space experience. Space gives appreciation and mystery to the ordinary experience on earth.[60]

Then, just as you would expect from a well-grounded, practical person like Story, he wrote:

> My feet are fine, right here, on earth![61]

57. Journal 15, page 15; Date: end of February 1994.
58. Story's handwritten notes in his copy of *The Unforseen Wilderness: Kentucky's Red River Gorge* by Wendell Berry, with photographs by Ralph Eugene Meatyard, University Press of Kentucky, 1971.
59. Story's handwritten notes in *The Dream of the Earth* by Thomas Berry, San Francisco: Sierra Club Books, 1988.
60. Journal 6, page 14; Date: August 1989.
61. Story's handwritten note in his copy of *The Unforseen Wilderness: Kentucky's Red River Gorge* by Wendell Berry, with photographs by Ralph Eugene Meatyard, University Press of Kentucky, 1971.

# Death and Life

"If in the current moment you're looking out towards a future which you love and which is inspiring, if you just can't wait until tomorrow comes along, then, philosophically, you really can't regret all the things that were important to getting you to where you are."

# 12. Death in Life

If you don't deal with death, you haven't dealt with life.
Every story must deal with death.

*Story Musgrave, 3 October 1990*

Few people you meet demonstrate a greater love for life than Story Musgrave. He is someone who lives with passion, both professionally and personally. According to his friends, family and colleagues, he is warm and gregarious, with a great sense of fun and spirit which almost defies the depth of the tragedies that have, in their time, impacted on his life.

Story has never hidden the fact that untimely death, suicide, mental illness and alcoholism have dealt strongly with his family. In addition to the personal tragedies, there were those he encountered professionally – as a doctor, pilot and astronaut.

Suicide was something which existed on both sides of Story's family and was present for generations. It led to the deaths of a great grandfather, grandfather, uncles, aunts. There were multiple deaths in each generation due to suicide but it was not something his family ever talked about. Remarkably, Story does not deny death nor avoid the discussion of it. The tragedies of his past, the risks to his own life, he accepts as part of his life journey. He said, "You can never fully experience life unless you accept death."

Of the more personal encounters with death, Story said, "The tragedies that I was witness to – they just immersed me in life."

*

Story's older brother Percy had scraped through high school and later Harvard University with passing grades. Like Story, he had struggled emotionally with the family break-up, but unlike Story, was sympathetic to their father and became a pawn in their father's strategy to win sole custody of his three sons. While still at school, a teenage Percy was encouraged by his father to report on the activities and attitudes of his younger brother Story – who attended the same private boarding school – and of their mother, whom he saw only occasionally. Young Percy went along with all of this.

When Story's parents separated for the second and final time, Percy had elected to stay at the family home, Linwood, with his father. Thereafter, on principle, he never spent a night in his mother's house and would mostly see her when she visited his school. His relationship with her was at best cordial, if not distant.

Percy was the only son to retain favor with their father. As a child, he had largely escaped the ill temper and abuse of his father – with most of it being directed towards Story and his mother. He was the only son to gain his high school diploma, the only son who, to his father's satisfaction, attended Harvard University, and therefore the only son to be financially supported through college because of his enrolment there. Story's choice of Syracuse University was based largely on the fact that without a high school diploma, his choices were rather limited. Syracuse was prepared to give him a chance.

Importantly, as he moved into his college years and his youngest brother Tom fell out with his father, young Percy became the sole benefactor of his father's will. In letters to young Percy, their father made his intentions very clear: some cash could be given to Tom and Story, but only according to his "own needs and financial ability."

After graduation from college in 1956, Percy became an officer in the US Navy. Very little has been documented about his life at sea, however, he was assigned to the carrier USS Wasp in January of 1959 as part of the Atlantic Fleet, Navel Air Force, Carrier Airborne Early Warning Squadron Twelve. It was a short-lived career. Abruptly on 14 March 1959, at the age of just twenty-five, tragedy struck. In maneuvers off the Atlantic coast of Norfolk, Virginia, the plane in which Percy was a passenger crashed on take-off. He and the pilot were killed instantly while another passenger survived. Percy's remains were never recovered.

Percy's death was reported in *The Berkshire Eagle*. The article stated: "Percy Musgrave III, Son of Percy Musgrave Junior of Stockbridge and Mrs Marguerite Swann Musgrave of 17 Churchill Road, Pittsfield... Percy was born in Boston Sept 5, 1933, attended local schools and St Mark's School Southborough... Graduated from Harvard University in 1956 and entered the Navy. He is survived by his two brothers – F. Story Musgrave and T. Bateson Musgrave (Tom)."[1]

Story's father and stepmother received numerous letters from well-wishers including one from the Commanding Officer of the Naval Air Force Helicopter Anti-Submarine Squadron 11, which stated: "Perhaps it would be of some small comfort for you to know that we all considered Percy to be a very valuable member of our team in Task Group Bravo. Our squadron was most appreciative of his competence and his fine performance, in that a part of his assignment was to watch over and guard our helicopter crews as we proceeded long distances from the carrier. It always gave us a feeling of added security to know that he was along on flights with us. Consequently, his loss has been a very real and personal thing to all of us."[2]

Understandably, their father was devastated by the death of his oldest son and heir. In a letter to Story he wrote that Percy's death "will always leave a scar which can't be healed. I felt he was a part of me." Percy was the only son he ever fully accepted – because he continued to abide by his father's wishes.

According to cousin Clover Swann, daughter of Story's Uncle Jack, "My father had a dislike of pomp and ostentation. When Percy III died, Story's father bought this massive stone and put it up in the cemetery. My father thought it was the most outrageous thing. The cemetery has a lot of prestigious people in it, like the Sedgewicks, the most famous family in the history of Stockbridge. But the Musgraves are not in the old part of the cemetery – not old blood."

For Story, his brother's death was a shock, but the two had never had a close

1. *The Berkshire Eagle*, 16 March 1959. Reprinted with permission.
2. The letter was dated 18 March 1959.

relationship. As young adults, they would meet up occasionally and enjoyed racing their cars along country roads, however, neither appreciated the other's position with respect to their parents. Consequently, there was a lack of mutual sympathy and understanding between them. In occasional letters to each other, they would talk mostly of sports cars and girls – maintaining a steady rivalry in these areas.

In a letter to his father and stepmother shortly after his older brother's death, Story wrote that he missed his older brother and that he would "see his face in every silver Porsche."

*

The succeeding years were the ones in which Story began his studies in the fields of chemistry and medicine. At the time of his older brother's death, he was in California, completing his masters degree in operations analysis and computer programming, but in the summer of 1959, he returned to Syracuse for some summer courses. Following this, he moved to Ohio where he attended Marietta College, completing a degree in chemistry within twelve months, in order to enter medical school in New York City in the fall of 1960.

Story, Patricia and their growing family remained in New York City for four years. Towards the end of their stay, Story's younger brother Tom came to live with them.

According to Patricia, Tom Musgrave was a very likeable person. "Tom was a great guy; he was wonderful – down to earth, very sweet, very passionate, very loving – but he was lost. He was like a little puppy dog lost in the wilderness. He didn't know what he wanted to do. He was very intelligent, extremely intelligent. He ended up working on a freight line and then went to Africa. He came back and stayed with us a couple of months before we moved to Kentucky – three children, Story, myself and Tom for three months in a two room apartment. But there was so much joy and love and peace in that place that it didn't matter."

Unlike his older brothers, Tom had attended Loomis School at Windsor, Connecticut. He was a very sensitive person who had been completely disoriented by his parents' divorce. At the time of their final separation, his wish to return to his father's home and to the farm – a decision not over-ruled by his mother – had far reaching consequences.

Like his two brothers, Tom struggled with school life and the hostility between the parents. Eventually he dropped out of high school in 1965 to become a paratrooper in the US Marines, but not before he had challenged his father, Percy. After years of intolerable dealings, one day Tom knocked his father to the ground with a decisive blow. Percy promptly had Tom arrested for assault and brought before Lee Court where the judge, in a manner of speaking, read him the riot act. Percy blamed Tom's mother, Marguerite, her attitude and her drunken behavior, for his son's downfall –

declaring in a letter that she had "poisoned his mind."

Story says that episode was a defining moment in the family's history. Shortly afterwards, Tom left his father's home.

After joining the Marines in November of 1956, Tom remained in the service for a few years, then, like Story, enrolled at Syracuse University, where he graduated with Honors in 1962.

Tom didn't get on well with either of his parents. He was in a kind of limbo as far as parental influence and affection went.

Clover Swann, Story and Tom's cousin, knew him a little. She said, "Tom was a real wacky kid; he was terrifying to me. My mother was watching what was happening to Tom in the situation and she thought, 'I'm going to really help'. She got him to go with her and my brother Mark to Bermuda one winter vacation when the rest of us went on a skiing trip up to Vermont. Mark and Tom were about fourteen or fifteen at the time. And Mom kept trying to reach out to Tom in a motherly way, and sort of be there for him, and she was in way over her head. It was probably too late.

"Tom was probably twenty the last time I spent a bit of time with him. I was fourteen and he showed up on a motorcycle and looked around for likely suspects – and I was it. Well, I rode on the back of the motorcycle – this was before helmet safety or anything like that – and it was dark. We started on this motorcycle ride and Tom, of course, was going for every twist and turn on this roller coaster road, and I was just amazed; I was sort of frozen on the back. He brought me back about twenty minutes later. I was, as one of the younger members of a large family with a lot of boys, pretty tough, so I did not scream or cry. I was brought up not to react to anything, but it was really something."

After completing his medical degree at Columbia University, Story moved his young family to Lexington, where he would undertake his internship at the University of Kentucky. It was to be a tremendously challenging year for him.

Patricia Musgrave explained, "Tom followed us to Kentucky and he got a really good job[3] – he was very well received, very well accepted and the owner of the company thought he was brilliant. He stayed with us in the house for a few months and then he was forced to leave because he started drinking and he had bought a gun. He just never really had that feeling of stability in his life, never got married. And I think he got so hopeless that he was depressed, but he wasn't treated for his depression. And he got more and more despondent, and the world was against him, and nothing was going right, even though he had a job.

"We didn't know how despondent Tom was. Story was interning at that time – he would come home and crash on the sofa and the kids would romp with him on his

3. Tom worked as an estimator for the E.H. Straus Co.

back and then finally go to bed… That one year was a very rough year for Story. He had no time and he didn't perceive that Tom was going through so much, therefore he really could not give him a helping hand."

At 12.15am on 21 December 1965, Tom's roommate found him lying on his bed with a pistol in his hand – bleeding from a self-inflicted shotgun wound to the head. He was taken to the Central Baptist Hospital in Lexington but died at 9.40am that morning. Story, who had always had a close relationship with Tom, was devastated.

He said, "I guess in a way my brother's death was the most tragic for me. He was leading a tragic life – he was a tragic person... a sense of hopelessness, the desperation. But he was a fantastic person, a great letter writer. He was, in ways, a more complete human at that time; maybe that's what got him… but you do always wonder how it could have been different."

Clover Swann recalled that when the news of Tom's death reached her parents, it totally caught them by surprise. "My father was amazing. They were at a dinner party at the Sedgewick house in town [Stockbridge]. Mom was trying not to cry, 'cause it's New England and you don't cry; you don't cry at funerals and you don't cry at anything. So Mom is starting to weep and at the same time, trying not to weep. And Dad started telling his favorite wacky stories of Tom at different stages of his life – so people were laughing at Dad's stories, and Mom's trying not to cry."

Story has carried the intense pain of that loss for around forty years. In his journal of 28 May 1989, he wrote:

> Tom would have been 50 years today! Oh what I have lost. Oh the brotherhood and fun I might have with him today. Oh how I need him to share the life of my childhood – there is no one, no one left to share and talk my childhood with – what devastating loneliness.[4]

Story continued to correspond with his father after the deaths of his two brothers but rarely saw him after joining NASA. In 1967, Story moved his young family to Houston. His father and stepmother never visited them there.

Patricia Musgrave recalled, "Some people – they don't see their folks, they don't talk to their folks, they don't have any relationship. And Story always had a relationship with his father. It may have been a bad relationship, but it existed. And I think it was because Story, inwardly speaking, was trying to reach his Dad."

At one point, Story thought he might make the long car trip to Massachusetts from Houston, but it never eventuated. He recalled, "Every summer, we went thousands of miles – one of the most marvelous things we ever did; thousands of miles with the kids every summer. The kids were absolutely perfect travelers in a VW bus

4. Journal 5, page 7; Date 28 May 1989.

without air conditioning – year after year, there was never a single complaint. They'd be rubbing the back of my neck and my head as I drove and they would tolerate hundreds of miles a day. That was a grand adventure and we just looked forward to stopping for lunch or stopping somewhere for the night with a big swimming pool. And so we went somewhere every single summer, on a nice long two week trip. I was thinking that maybe on one of these trips we would make it to Massachusetts. We did not make it that far – that is one very, very long trip from Houston."

Flying the family of seven to Massachusetts was also out of the question. Story explained, "I can't get to Linwood with the family – I have no money; none."

The last time Patricia and the children saw Percy was during their first year in Lexington. Story recalled, "Tom died in December of '64 and Todd[5] was born in May of '65. Dad came down to Lexington for Tom's funeral – that was probably the last time he saw the children. Two of them weren't born and the others were tiny. But he didn't come to see them – he came for a funeral."

If Percy was proud of what his only surviving son had achieved when he was selected for the astronaut corps in 1967, he never communicated it. Percy and his second wife Josephine received numerous letters from friends and well-wishers, including congressmen, congratulating them on Story's new career. Story, however, only recovered these letters, or rather discovered their existence, some time after his father's death.

The correspondence between father and son continued intermittently. In October of 1972, Story visited Linwood for one of the last times during his father's life. In his log book he wrote:

> Multiple conversations with Dad. He has gone way down hill since last visit. He is simultaneously addicted to alcohol, morphine and derivatives, and barbiturates and also taking large doses of tranquillizers and Benadryl. Mind is miraculously still a little with it, but greatly subdued and losing recent memory. He is much more deaf and apparently refuses hearing aid. Without more data, I feel that if he were taken off all drugs and put on a proper diet he could be a healthy, useful citizen.... Despite above, we met on better terms than since 1945.[6]

One day in 1973, Story received a phone call to say that his father had died. He recalled his reaction. "I don't think I had a second of grief that that history, that that element of my life, had come to an end. For me it was a fact of life – that's all there was to it. My father's life, for me, was nothing but tragedy, pain and fear – the entire life. And for me, in a way, it was a relief that this history had now come to an end."

Story's memories of his father never wavered. "That's the way he was from the

---

5. Story's second youngest child from his first marriage to Patricia.
6. Activity log book, 22 Oct 1972, page 96.

earliest moment I can remember, age three. He was so overpowering, so malicious that he established what the family was and he established the ambience. He just pervaded the whole thing with fear and evil – not a perverse kind of evil – just a plain old evil; it was straightforward evil."

Filmmaker Dana Ranga questioned Story about his father during an interview for a film.[7] She remembered, "I think he's still very, very angry towards his father. And I think that there is such a big thing still going on emotionally. It's very, very, very strong. It really blew me over, and it blew over my DOP[8]; he didn't know what to do – to keep filming or not? Story was suddenly very emotional – he was like a storm, he was like nature; suddenly it wasn't like this soft rain anymore, suddenly it was like this real downpour!… I wanted to know how he dealt with the pain, how did he live with it?… Because in the end, all the strength that he's getting – he's saying it's coming from nature, but it's also coming from himself."

No mention had been made to Story of the means of his father's death, but upon returning to Linwood, he set out to uncover the truth for himself. He said, "There was a sense of adventure in me. I was after the answer."

The door to his father's room was locked when Story arrived – inaccessible, he was told, because it was full of personal belongings. Unconvinced, Story, with the aid of some ropes, climbed down over the roof of the building and let himself into the room through a window. Everything appeared to be in order – that is, until something caught Story's peripheral vision. Glancing upwards, he saw a hole in the ceiling with some scattered blood and tissue surrounding it, indicating a gunshot wound to the head. Story later confirmed this with one of the servants. Apparently, Percy had held a gun to his head, called Story's stepmother Josephine into the room, then pulled the trigger.

Story said, "As with many of the suicides within my family, people would not talk about it as a suicide. I did not appreciate that and, in my father's case, I was the only remaining son. It *did* matter to me whether it was a suicide. It made a difference because I never had any indication that the man knew right from wrong; I never had any indication that he suffered for having been the person that he was; I never had any indication that he knew what he had done to other people in the world.

"His suicide – you can interpret that lots of ways. Maybe he couldn't stand himself any longer; I'm not sure, I don't have the answer and I really don't know. I know the life he was leading at the time: he was an alcoholic – had been for years – and addicted to three families of drugs. I knew that, he didn't hide that – all the bushels of bottles and the warm alcohol in the morning – so I guess that was a sign of

7. The film is titled *Story*; created and directed by Dana Ranga; released 2003.
8. Director of Photography (DOP)

unhappiness. Maybe suicide, in his case, was that 'I just can't stand myself any more.' Or maybe, eventually, his guilt had caught up to him. I was always a little curious as to whether he had a conscious, whether he had any idea what he did to people around him. Now I could go forward."

Suicide and associated mental illness had, arguably, been a genetic factor in Story's family. He said, "If you look at the genetic, if you look at the fact it hasn't missed a generation – concentrated more on Dad's side, but on Mom's side too: brother took rat poison; sister drowned in the bathtub.

"You tend to think, 'Well am I part of that plan?' You have to think that way when it's in your genetics. You have to look at yourself and say 'How protected am I from that? How safe am I from that? Do I have any predisposition in that direction?' And I never have. I'm safer than any human on earth from that because I absolutely adore every darn minute."

Cousin Rosaly Bass shared this perspective of Story as an adult. "I watched Story; he just could do anything he wanted to do. He's just an amazing guy. And I think that's one of the reasons why he wasn't a depressed person; I never felt that he was. Story would just decide what he was going to do and then he'd do it. And he had a very marvelous sense of humor. Of course, there was that strain in my family – my father[9] was totally that way – I don't think he ever spent a depressed moment in his life; everything was funny. I got my father's upbeat nature too and I think Story got it."

Story was keen to understand his father's lifelong behavior; to put it in some context which made sense. He explained, "I've gone through [Dad's] old letters; I don't know how you get that way. I don't know what the problem was. He'd have to have been a hugely frustrated man. I don't know whether he wanted to be a farmer. He was a farmer but I don't know, maybe he didn't want to be a farmer. He didn't come from that kind of background... he had no farming in his blood.

"But I wondered – what is the problem? Is it just him? Is he frustrated? He may have thought he's going to manage this estate which is a gorgeous place – a thousand acres of just marvelous land in western Massachusetts, New England, with the rivers, the maples, the pines, the rolling hills, the harsh winter but gorgeous spring, fantastic fall. Maybe he thought he was just going to manage that – kind of like an estate keeper, in a way. But we were a farm, we were no gentleman's farm."

The death of his father was the final chapter in that painful part of Story's life. He said, "There's an important lesson as to how people transcend these things and just kind of push out. I had the answer at the age of three. I might have had the answers at age two but I can only remember back to the age of three. I said, 'Man, I've come into

9. Story's Uncle Jack.

one screwed up world but it's not me. I'm going to survive this world, I'm going forward; it's not getting on me. I may swim in it, but it's not getting on me. It's not me!' And so I stuck to that."

Story's stepmother Josephine remained at Linwood for some years until she became ill. His father's final will bestowed the country home and estate, together with all its antique possessions, on Josephine. Upon her death, it would be passed to her own relatives. A considerable sum of money was also donated to support St Mark's School graduates at Harvard University – both institutions for which Percy had endless regard. Story was effectively disinherited.

It is worth noting that while reading through the tremendous amount of family correspondence which still exists, it is obvious that Story acted with duty towards his father, despite the mutual distaste which they felt for one another. If Story was in Massachusetts visiting his mother during one of his breaks from college, he would often stop by Linwood. He joined his father on shooting parties and regularly wrote to him of his adventures in the marines and later at college. Percy, for his part, never disclosed in his letters to Story just how much he resented his son; neither did he ever really show his satisfaction at his son's remarkable achievements as an adult, or in the rapidly growing young family which Story and Patricia had created.

Story explained that his father was an incredibly legalistic person. He believes that he would have ensured, to the day of his death, that there was no tangible piece of evidence which could be held against him – hence the rather obvious disparity between the letters and the reality of Percy's feelings and behavior towards Story.

Patricia Musgrave recalled the behavior of Story's father on her first visit to Linwood. "I didn't really see Story's Dad much that day, but that evening, he was having his usual drink with melba toast and he was reading his paper and he had the classical music playing. I wandered into the room and my presence was not known. I sat down and I left, you know, because he never acknowledged my presence. Then we went to dinner and [the men] had to wear a jacket and tie – you had to be appropriately dressed. We sat down, and everything was served in a very formal way.

"And Story and his father had gotten into conversation. So anyway, his father was very argumentative and he controlled everything in the conversation – he loved a good argument. I was very intimidated and I didn't say two words. After dessert, I abruptly left and went up to my room and I cried. I just cried 'cause my family was so different. My family was very loving, very self-supporting – my Dad would die for me. I had never been in a family where there was division – his Mom and Dad were divorced, of course – and I had never been in a family that argued during dinner. I just couldn't believe it. I mean, you'd have to experience it – and I had never experienced it till that day. I just left and I cried. I never had a good conversation with his Dad ever. Never sat down and talked with him ever."

Untimely death continued to weave its tragic path through the Musgrave family when, almost a decade later, Story's beloved mother took action to end her life. This time, however, Story knew it was coming.

Story recalled, "My Mom, she said that she was always going to do that – not just out of suicide, but she was going to control when the end of her life was. And so in her case, it was a little different – it was not out of depression or hopelessness.

"For her, it wasn't really suicide. For her it was a decision when life should end. I disagreed that the time had come. I thought she had a lot of life left, but she was living with me and it didn't help somehow that I couldn't turn it around.

"I knew what she was thinking. When she was unable to live alone – unable to wash the dishes, to cope with what is to go in the trash and what is to be saved – I moved her [to Houston] and sold her house. But from that point on, she made the decision. Once I moved her, that was the end. I don't know if she felt she was holding me back or what. She was doing all right; she did not have a mental illness or a dementia."

Rosaly Bass, Story's cousin, recalled how difficult a time that was for Story. "Story loved her; he totally loved her. He was concerned about her his whole life. And finally, when she started not eating, he put her in the hospital and had her force fed. And she just looked him in the eye one day and she said, 'As soon as I get out I'm not going to eat.' And he finally just realized that she was a grown person and it was senseless to force her to do something that wasn't going to do any good. So he said, 'OK', and let her out."

And so Story's mother, his last remaining link with the immediate family's past, gradually starved herself to death: she simply wouldn't eat. She died on 25 March 1982 – her death certificate stating the cause of death as "influenza/malnutrition."

Story buried her in the beautiful grounds of Lexington Cemetery, alongside his younger brother Tom.

*

By the 1980s, Story and Patricia's five children were growing into young adults, but after almost twenty years of marriage, Story and Patricia separated in 1979.

Patricia spoke of the demands of an astronaut's life on the family. "It took its toll; we just grew apart. My life was my children, even though Story always came first. And in the beginning he would always call – 'I'll be home for dinner at such and such a time.' We went out to dinner every Friday night; we continued what we did in Kentucky. But as he got busier and busier…"

Patricia made a decision not to have any more children. "Originally, when we got married, we were going to have eight children and adopt two; that was our plan. But I decided I would not get much help from Story once he became an astronaut and five children was enough responsibility. That may have been a separation, the beginning of the separation between Story and myself because he didn't agree with it."

Story and Patricia finally divorced in 1981. The children continued to spend time with both parents – Patricia remaining in the family home at El Lago, while Story moved into an apartment block close by.

It was an unsettling period for the whole family, especially for the couple's youngest son Jeffrey, who was born in 1967.

According to Patricia, "Jeff went through depression after depression and it was a very difficult time; he was the youngest. He was just going into puberty, so the instability of it all just crushed him and he didn't know how to cope. He was also the most sensitive of all my kids."

Patricia witnessed the second of Story's Space Shuttle launches in 1985, but after years of living within Houston's space family, it was not in the happy capacity of an astronaut's wife. Instead, she went to Florida out of concern for their son. She explained, "Jeffrey had suicidal tendencies and I felt I had to go down to the flight – I had to watch over Jeff."

Jeffrey was well-liked by his peers and was great at sports such as football and baseball. One of the things he and Story enjoyed doing together was canoeing along a local river in Clear Lake. However, by his late teens, Jeffrey was having difficulties at school and eventually dropped out. He obtained employment, but moved fairly regularly from job to job.

Story believed Jeffrey had developed a form of mental illness. "I would say he had an adolescent onset of schizophrenia; there's no question he had it in him. He had that in him for years – visions of suicide and violence." Jeffrey had been receiving treatment but Story says his medication was not under control, adding to his emotional difficulties.

One day an acquaintance observed Jeffrey as he purchased a gun from a local store. He then headed to the familiar woods where he played as a child. Story recalled, "He disappeared and we found him six weeks later. He had shot himself in the woods – so he was just gone for six weeks."

A month after Jeffrey was found, Story wrote in his journal of his pain:

> Want Jeff home. Are you so far down that nothing can move you – is that it? I carry on, but that doesn't mean I'm OK! I've always faked sanity, even when over the edge, and who but I could tell? I'm so lonely, so separated, so alone, but don't know, really, how bad off I am. Home is desolate.[10]

Jeffrey was buried in Lexington Cemetery in March 1989, alongside Story's mother and brother Tom. It is a place Story visits whenever he can. During a visit there in 1994, he wrote emotionally in his journal:

10. Journal 1, pages 38-39; Date: 16 March 1989.

Cemeteries – beautiful, historic. Poetic epitaphs from the heart. Permanent, stable, unmovable – the only place that will not be turned into condos or malls! Lexington cemetery will be here – what else? … Voices of billions, past, present and future! The hopes, the dreams, search for meaning… I hate to leave, as if I'm saying goodbye to them, never to see them again. I feel as if I'm deserting the three of them. I thought of joining them. I feel as if they are joined, having a party and I am leaving them – as I somehow feel that I always did – desert them and leave a destroyed life behind that I might have nurtured. Three suicides in one place … I carry such a load, how long to bear it?! I think of lying down on Jeffrey's grave and dying. Three of my most beloved there … how rarely I get to see them and how short the visit… Were they talking to me, beckoning me? Is that where it is?[11]

The impact of these three suicides was enormous. Story said, "A suicide is not just death – it's not just that someone died of old age or disease or auto accident or something, but you wish you could have done something different. You wish you could have changed that history in some way, created a different life for those people so that they would not have taken their own life.

"All three of those people were living with me around that time and the cumulative effect – one after the other – eventually what comes to you is that everyone that lives with you commits suicide … And so you think that you just can't keep anybody alive and you can't somehow create a life or ambience for them that makes it worthwhile for them to stay living.

"Suicides, you know, they're tragedies for me, but I also get anger. I have an element of anger every time I see it because those people, as hopeless as they were, they did not think of the tragedy. They did not think of the string of tragedy that they were going to leave behind which other people were going to bear forever. They were not thinking that way… I guess they couldn't. The fact that I'm thinking about that probably shows that I'm not one of them; I think that's part of it. And you've just got to show your anger on the way out, I guess; it is an aggressive act."

Story dealt with the pain and hurt of death by moving forward. "It didn't matter how much pain, I had to keep going. I'd have a major tragedy and I'd go back to work and, of course, some people didn't understand going back to work, but I think it was going forward. It was that survival mode that I got into at the age of three and it carried me this far forward… I was a survivor and I'm the same person I was at the age of three. I have an incredible determination to go forward, so in a way I am just spectacularly hard."

Dealing with a loss in this way, however, doesn't mean that the pain goes away.

11. Journal 15, pages 49; Date: 10 July 1994.

According to Story, "You bear the pain the rest of your life – it is unremitting. There is no appeal to the loss, hopelessness and desperation for some contact, some communication, but it won't happen. You celebrate what you have, not what you don't have. Does this not apply to death analogically? If you had nothing, you would have no pain, and no life either. The pain is in proportion to how good you have had it."

Story wrote of the importance which Lexington Cemetery – for him, one of the most beautiful places in the world – continues to have in his life.

> The cemetery is, of course, my base. Childhood yearnings and the cemetery – that is the synthesis, the tie, the knot. My childhood experiences of beauty, land and social grace would eventually lead to Lexington becoming a burial ground for all my beloved, and myself: Tom, Sweety[12] and Jeff – there it is! And they are all here.[13]

\*

Doctors deal with death on a regular basis and the work that Story had chosen over the years, which included medical research and trauma surgery, had its fair share of tragedy. He did not often carry the mantel of emotional detachment with those whom he treated.

He said, "I dealt with grief. I simply had grief then too and it's not that it's non-emotional and that death doesn't hurt you – it's essential.

"Death and kids was very, very difficult. Death in children was very difficult and my practice of medicine with children was always based on emotion. They were my kids and so when things did not go well for kids, it was a terrible tragedy. I will never forget any of those kids that I lost. It was terrible and the suffering of those children is the same suffering as one of mine."

In all, Story 'lost' some thirty children with whom he shared a close bond. One extraordinary episode involved a sixteen-year-old girl with Hodgkins Disease. Story nursed her through the final months of her illness, befriending her and lending her emotional support during her last days. He admired her "because of her youth, her beauty and her courage to hit this damn thing head on and never to complain or fear the inevitable."

Story was in love with her and she died in his arms at the hospital. After her death, an autopsy was carried out on her body, then, in preparation for the return to her family, and for her burial, Story enlisted the help of one of his female colleagues. While he carefully sewed the girl's body back together, his colleague washed the hair and used make-up to bring color back into the lifeless face. It was an unusual step and

12. Story's mother Marguerite Swann Musgrave. He called her 'Sweety'.
13. Journal 15, pages 47; Date: 10 July 1994.

something normally reserved for undertakers, but as the girl's family were poor and were coming to collect her themselves, Story did what he could.

Some time later, Story wrote an autobiographical narrative[14] of his care for this young woman. It is an incredibly moving account, full of compassion and the pain of loss. It also highlights the beauty that he found in the face of death and the intense nature of life, and of love, in that context.

While undertaking an early anatomy class in medical school, Story is also brought face to face with questions of his own mortality. During an initial brush with the art of dissection, he learns to look for the individual in the process and feels empathy, rather than coolness, towards the bodies before him. One particular subject catches his attention – a deceased with metastatic cancer. Upon making the discovery with the strike of his scalpel, he thinks: "I hope you didn't suffer too much, claim or no claim, I hope in life you had someone to see you through this. How many battles will I lose to metastatic cancer? How many people will I lose? … Which one of these ends is destined for me?" Again, his thoughts on this were captured in the narrative form.[15]

In his journal Story wrote:

> I was an immensely empathetic, caring doctor – concerned, sensitive, caring, communicative. As an intern, I read about the concept of scientist-astronaut … Space was my calling, it was always my calling, my destiny – still is. Space pulled me, but the cruelty, the lack of empathy, the lack of instruction and guidance pushed me away from surgery; the egos versus teamwork and compatibility. The "I am" pulled me into it, but even that was not enough to keep me at it. Freedom and independence were also very important factors. A patient possesses you almost 'till death do us part'. I would have made a marvelous pediatrician among the poor – another calling."[16]

*

Story's transition from medicine into space flight brought with it a high degree of personal risk. The Apollo 1 fire in which Gus Grissom, Ed White and Roger Chaffee lost their lives, occurred at the beginning of 1967 – the year Story joined the astronaut corps. It did not have any affect on Story's decision to proceed with his application, but it did bring home the potential consequences of his career choice.

Story said, "It was a big reality check for the family because, at that time, no astronaut had been lost and I convinced them that what I was doing was safe. And so I could not convince them after that."

Story did not get his first space flight until after the Apollo and Skylab programs.

14. The 1988 narrative was titled simply, *Joy*.
15. The narrative was titled *Max*.
16. Journal 15, page 47; Date: 10 July 1994.

Instead, he was to become, to many people, the embodiment of the Space Shuttle era.

As discussed in the chapter on space flight, Story always believed that the Space Shuttle was the most dangerous space vehicle ever flown, due largely to the use of two solid rocket boosters on take-off, which, once ignited, couldn't be switched off.

Before his third space flight, STS-33, which was after the *Challenger* disaster, Story noted in his journal:

> I am clearly frightened, shell-shocked by launching a Shuttle. I have had to live with this nightmare since the concept was fired up in 1972. Death is stalking everywhere – but Story, as you say, it's part of life, you buy into it when you accept life – but do we have a choice of life? We are now number 3 in line to go August 10. America wants a risk free life – if something goes wrong, somebody is responsible and somebody has to pay.[17]

On the day of the actual launch, delayed until 22 November 1989, Story wrote a moving description of his feelings before the flight, farewelling his loved ones in case he didn't survive. By now, his family had grown to include his second wife Carol and their young son Lane.

> I, in such exhilaration, such success and such great plans. And where in hell is Jeffrey in all this? Damn I miss him! Why, oh why, didn't I pick up on his depression and act on it? I will miss him so! Life is grand and painful. Pain in the midst of glory. I think of Lane and Carol and kids and death. I do things, I plan and prepare as if this was the end and I behave as if this was the end! But I go on, I accept it, it's my business, it's who I have been and who I am... All the risk and machinery as a child – did the same things... What a bitch to write in my journal and end up writing a death note! That's life. Kiddies, I love you all, could have done more and could have been with you more at times, but we all had a hell of a good life and great times. I'm soaring around up there – looking on you. Don't worry, don't be sad, just get on with it, do what's fun, take me along so I can enjoy it![18]

Some people have perceived Story as a risk-taker, given all that he has done in his life. However, this is not how he perceives himself. "I soloed an airplane when I was a teenager and I did eighteen thousand hours of flying, which is a huge, huge number. Six hundred [private] parachute jumps and all the other machines within NASA for thirty years; all the different vacuum chambers and all the different kinds of machines in which there is an inherent danger, as well as six space flights. I have had as much cumulative risk, probably, as any human who ever lived. And I am always looking at how I can minimize that risk. That is one of the reasons I'm so attentive to

17. Journal 1, page 36; Date: 13 March 1989.
18. Journal 6, page 48; Date: 22 November 1989.

detail and things in the airplane, why I'm unbelievably compulsive of doing things right around the airplane.

"I think there are people who are thrill-seeking. I think they're into what they do physically, seeking thrill, and I certainly do not seek thrill from flying and from space flight and those other things I've done. It's more an aesthetic kind of thing. It's more getting into space and the art and craft of the business – the zero-g, the view of earth. It's not about danger and so that's why launches are dead scary – I just really want to get through them."

During his career with NASA, Story dealt with the loss of colleagues in various accidents. Among them, of course, were the seven crew members aboard STS-51L, the space shuttle *Challenger's* final mission in 1986 and, more recently, those colleagues who died aboard *Columbia* in 2003.

In 1991, Sonny Carter, one of Story's colleagues on STS-33, was killed during a commercial flight which crashed near New Brunswick, Georgia. At the time, he was traveling on NASA business.

Story's reaction to the news of Sonny's death is something which was recalled by some of the people in Mission Control. It occurred during STS-37 and, according to Phil Engelauf, who was a flight controller at the time, somebody needed to inform the crew.

Phil remembered, "I was told about the accident and asked to go retrieve Story from the support room and bring him out to the control room where he was going to then be told that Sonny had been killed in an accident and be asked to formulate a message to send up to the crew. And I remember going and getting Story, but I wasn't in a position to tell him what was about to happen and what he was about to be told. And as I brought him out to the front room, he stood and he talked with a couple of the managers and I just saw all the color go out of his face. He sat down on a step in the control center and put his face in his hands. He sat there for several minutes and didn't speak. And the emotion of that moment has kind of stayed with me ever since. It really punctuates the idea of what a humanist Story really is. We work in a business that has its dangers, and people in the military who fly get a little bit inured to that kind of risk, and we lose an astronaut every few years in some kind of a flying accident or other. Obviously it affects people, but it's almost accepted as part of the business or part of the profession. But I was really struck with how it affected Story at that time, and the fact that Story was the individual that people looked to, to convey that to the crew. That's really representative of the way the crews viewed Story and the kind of man that he is."

Flight Director Milt Heflin, who also witnessed the scene and whose role it was to break the news to Story and ask him to formulate the message for the crew, concurred. He said it just showed the compassion that Story had for others.

In his journal Story wrote of Sonny:

> He was a complete person – artistic sensitivities and technical – he saw the archetypal elements in things. He came by one day and asked me to look into the future – see where he was going, what he was going to do and be – and that he would get back to me. I should have gotten back with him. I see his face and I remember the last contact.[19]

Karl Henize was another colleague who died prematurely. Selected for the sixth group of astronauts in 1967 along with Story, his specialty was astronomy. Eventually Karl and Story would fly together as mission specialists on STS-51F – Spacelab 2 in 1985. Consequently, the two became great friends.

One of Karl's interests was mountain climbing, so when he was offered the opportunity to climb Mt Everest in 1993, he accepted. The plan was to climb to the summit without oxygen – a method which had been successfully tried before, but naturally carried increased dangers for the climbers. Tragically, though, after reaching advanced base camp at 22,000 feet, Karl developed symptoms of extreme high altitude sickness and later died of a pulmonary oedema. Story was immensely saddened by the news and later addressed mourners at the memorial service for his friend.

\*

Story became a well-recognized American identity after STS-61 – the first Hubble Space Telescope repair mission. While in space, he was interviewed for *Nightline* with Ted Koppel and afterwards made appearances on *The Tonight Show with Jay Leno* and with other crew members on Tim Allen's *Home Improvement*. Apart from this, Story was interviewed by a variety of newspapers across the USA and was highly sought after by filmmakers hoping to document the historic mission.

One person who was fascinated by Story was a woman by the name of Margaret Ray. She had previously been arrested for stalking David Letterman and now believed herself to be wildly in love with Story.

Story's first face to face encounter with Margaret was when she posed as a journalist at the Johnson Space Center. Security had not wanted Story to speak with her, but he decided to go ahead with the interview anyway. Immediately, however, he suspected that something was awry. Margaret arrived for her appointment with no tape recorder or notebook and just wanted to 'chat'. As the conversation became unfocused, Story terminated the interview and suggested that Margaret send him a draft of the article – at which point he would give her further input.

19. Journal 10, page 33; Date: 5 April 1991.

Prior to the interview, Story had, over a period of time, received a series of anonymous letters in a format like hieroglyphics. Although unable to interpret the letters, he was fascinated with their obvious genius. Shortly after the interview, however, Story received further correspondence in exactly the same format – and this time Margaret signed her name. He knew, then, that she was the author of those earlier letters.

The next time Story encountered Margaret was in Florida when she arrived at his home one night, unannounced. Instead of knocking on the door, she initiated the watering systems in his yard. Story, wondering what was going on, let himself outside and crept around the exterior of the house. In the dim light, he saw a figure with a hose turned upon themselves, but was unable to identify who it was. Not knowing if the person was armed, he let out a blood-curdling banshee cry – causing the intruder to scream in terror. Immediately, Story knew the voice belonged to Margaret. It took some convincing of the local authorities that his distress call was genuine and that he really was Story Musgrave, but eventually the police came and led Margaret away. Story said she was pleased to leave at that point – her adventure not having gone according to plan.

In a tragic postscript, Margaret Ray eventually took her own life. She was crushed to death by an approaching train as she knelt down on a set of railway tracks. Story was deeply saddened and upset by the news of her death. He recognized her genius and understood the form of mental illness from which she suffered – schizophrenia – which had touched his own family. Margaret Ray was the mother of five children.

*

By the mid 1990s, Story had accumulated enough personal experience of death to be profoundly affected by it. He said, "I'm about as much into death as you can get into it without doing it!"

Nevertheless, Story continues to move forward with his life and with the same enthusiasm for living. He said, "I immerse myself in nature and life, and I simply push on. I push through all the tragedies. But when that happens I do get a sense of myself at three, and when the really bad things happen, I go back to that, and the kid I was back then just carries me on. Some people confuse that with non-feeling. It's not a matter of non-feeling – it's a matter of being able to bear the pain and keep going."

# 13. A Philosophy of Death and Life

Pine cone – life's longing for life, wind winding,
coning down the ground,
life's love for life.

Waves of waving purples and yellows,
singing chimes upon my eyes,
yellow purple symbiotic spectra.

Blue bells flowing, the sounds of growing.

Fragrant fertility flowering my imagination,
vines and vineyards – life clinging to life.

Canopies of greens, painted on a blue canvas.
Fallen trees – fertile ground, rotting life to living death.

Clouds appearing through the green,
disappearing through the green.
The power of cumulonimbus,
the permanence of high cirrus.

Birds and songs, birdsongs,
life calling to life.

Honeysuckle, honey bee, sensuous sucking stingers,
sweet sugar of life.

Spider's web, life catching life,
death preserving life.

Wood winds, leaves talking in the winds,
symphonies of green,
kinesthetic kaleidoscopes.

Dead leaves, live leaves, death passing into life.

Blossoms blooming, seeds sowing,
spring springing.

'Scitos skimming, blood to blood,
life to life.

Fields of flower, waves of color.

Birds soaring on the solar wind, seeds soaring on the solar soil,
my soul soaring to the sun.

Purple yellows on a canvas green.
Bird's nest, woman's womb.
Green reeds, red reeds, green life, red life;
transformations, translations, translocations;
trans, trans, transit birth, life, and death;
transit earth, planets, sun;
galaxies and universe;
Oh immortal Soul.

Water, muddy water, blood, bloody water,
mud and blood,
in my heart.

Fire of sun, fire of ants, fire my soul, heart shaped leaves
fed by vesseled vines,
canopies of life fed by floors of death,
sun of life, shades of death.
Explosions of spring, springing to my mind.

Spanish mosses motioning Chinese chimes, swinging in my life,
rhythms of the universe,
beating to my soul.

The wasps love dead wood, the wasps eat dead wood.

Mud loving tracks, life loving mud.

*Nature Walk*
*Story Musgrave, 1990*

Story Musgrave accepts death and celebrates life. He said, "Death is very powerful, it's very evocative, very painful, but if you look at death, it is one of the most powerful occasions of life. And so there's hardly anything to experience that's more powerful in a life than the transition from life to death."

Story has spent decades looking philosophically and pragmatically at death. It is interwoven strongly into the fabric of his own life and is universally evident in the natural world around him. In a sense, the whole question of death fascinates Story and is integral to his own personal, spiritual journey.

The incredible poetry and genius of *Nature Walk*, which focuses on the cycles of life and death in nature, was one of the most creative results of Story's studies at the University of Houston. After taking a short walk around the beautiful environs of the campus, he composed the piece in just ten minutes.

According to Story, "Everywhere you look, every forest you go into, you have the dead trees out there dissolving into the soil to support the living trees. You have the cycle of life and death absolutely everywhere and it is manifest in beauty. A lot of times I think it's beautiful because it reflects the cycle of life. Some of the most beautiful things, like autumn leaves, are not just beautiful, but they're like the seasons of a person's life, as the metaphor goes. That's another reason the Fall is so powerful, because the leaves are going to fall and it's almost like life stops in winter. I always think of all those cycles: the cycles of life and death, the cycles of the seasons – I think there's a relationship there."

Story's studies in Houston also brought him into contact with Ernest Becker's *The Denial of Death* – a book which reflects Story's own approach to the subject. Despite the great tragedies in Story's life and his many personal encounters with death, he was very forthright about the discussion of death and it's meaning. He wants others to reflect upon death, to come to a personal acceptance of death and, ultimately, to appreciate the great beauty of life.

According to Story, "No matter that they were personal tragedies or death, they had to happen to get you here, so you have to accept all that past. One little simple fork in the road can be an accident which disables you. One little fork in the road can send you off into a different career and different avocation. One little fork in the road can significantly alter the future that comes to you. So if you like what you have now, if you wouldn't trade it for anything, then you really, logically, have to appreciate what went before. If in the current moment you're looking out towards a future which you love and which is inspiring, if you just can't wait until tomorrow comes along, then, philosophically, you really can't regret all the things that were important to getting you to where you are. So it is a way of making short-term tragedies into long-term victories."

*

When it comes to death in human terms, Story gets right down to basics. He says, "Death is born when sperm meets egg. It doesn't come to spoil the party – it is the party! I don't look on that as a way to reconcile death; it is not just an okay way to temper a bad thing or to make it feel okay. I think that it is a factual consideration of death, that life and death are equated, that they are the same process. You cannot have death unless something is created. And you cannot have life without death because all of life dies. Everything dies."

This principle also applies to Story's perception of the universe. "Even stars are born. At the very same time a star is created, it's death is created; that's when it happens. It also happens at galactic levels, in the entire universe. If you look at an oscillatory universe where everything is flowing *outbound*, if it finds enough mass, it's going to head back *inward* – an isolatory big bang. The whole thing, the entire structure of the universe disappears when it collapses back in and a new universe is now formed. It's interesting – it may be made of totally different materials – different atoms, different molecules, a different universe from the last time around.

"So that's my basic view of death and I think it's unfortunate to have so many people look at death as an alien thing. It's simple denial of death, [as described in] that wonderful book, *The Denial of Death*, by Ernest Becker. But for me, death is a party, just like life is."

Story read Becker's book for the first time in 1990 and has devoured it many times since. But for that first year, he says that the book and its author were his constant traveling companions: "[They] went every where with me, played in every game with me, suffered every tragedy."

In 1992, Story wrote a college paper about *The Denial of Death*[1] in which he explained the basic intent.

> The book's purpose is to harmonize and synthesize the psychological and mythico-religious worlds … the book's foundations are psychology and religion... A psychological and theological approach to existentialism... The existentialist faces up to her personal death, embraces this personal dread and tragedy, subjectively, objectively, emotionally and every other which way. There is no psychological denial.

The book raised a number of questions for Story:

> What could or should life be? What is the human essence? What does it mean to be human? What type of life should we lead? What is good, what is right? What is not only the heroic individual, but what is the 'ideal' human?

In critiquing Becker, Story said, "Becker never addressed the key philosophical issues

---

1. The paper was titled *An Essay on the Existential, Metaphysical, and Religious conclusions of The Denial of Death by Ernest Becker* (*The Denial of Death* was published by Free Press, New York, 1973). The paper was submitted for a course on metaphysics at the University of Houston, Clear Lake.

of the relations between faith and denial, creative illusion, and projection."

Story concluded the essay by expressing his own basic philosophy of death:

> Death is not just a psychological issue, it is also philosophical issue. Any treatment of it which ignores the ethics and metaphysics of death must be incomplete. In dealing with death, we must deal with life. We must have some concepts of the ideal for humanity and for particular individuals. The world that we are thrown into, in and of itself, may not be all that bad. Existence is not only our world, it is us, and our awareness of that world. There are immense possibilities and probabilities for transformations in the way that we look at our world which will change our existence and which will open up new opportunities for transcending ourselves and our world.

Beauty is something which Story expressed about the universal processes of death. "The most gorgeous images that you have in the heavens, the most spectacular images you have, are star deaths. You look at the Hubble Space Telescope images: star death is by far the most beautiful stuff out there for sure."

In terms of the human aspect of death, Story said, "Death is only beautiful in that it is life and has to be taken along with life; they cannot be separated. If you have life, it will die, even stars, and it's impossible to have anything die if it's not alive already – they're absolutely together. So I think death is beautiful in that it is a very important part of the living process."

'Sex and death' is a theme which Story refers to from time to time. It forms part of his basic evolutionary approach to existence and the way that he always looks at things in the wider universal context. In his journal, he referred to the theme of sex and death as:

> … that intersection where the creation of a new life and the prospects of death meet. In simpler terms, that passing which contains or embodies sex and death.[2]

According to Story, "I think sex and death are related. Sex creates life, which is also creating death, so they're inseparable in that kind of way. I think sex is more powerful any time that you are immersed and attentive to life and to the process, to the journey. When I'm forced into a position to take more risk than I wish to, sex is more powerful. For me, it is more powerful when there is some huge tie to a cosmic process, to a seasonal process, an oceanic process, a living process of nature, of seasons, sunrise, sunset, to day cycles. When sex becomes a participation in this process, it becomes more meaningful. It's an important part of the life process; it is life. It's the whole darn thing which is going on here – cosmic evolution, biological evolution, the cycles of nature, the cycles of the seasons and the day and what goes on in nature."

2. Journal 25, page 44; Date: around March 1999.

In his journals, Story wrote:

> Nearest death – most alive.[3]

> Risk of death and injury leads to expanded appreciation of life. Especially an awareness and sensitivity of death brings you to the greatest self-awareness.[4]

These thoughts were echoed in one of the interviews for this book. Story said, "Maybe an awareness of death, maybe an intense awareness of death is related to higher spirituality. The intense awareness of death occurs at the time where you're most attentive, when you're the most sensitive."

During 1989, Story wrote in his journal:

> When you accept birth and life, or when someone else does for you – you and they accept death. It goes with it! It's all or none folks.[5]

Story wrote these words a little more than six months after the death of his son Jeffrey from suicide – a child for whom he had accepted both life and death. He also wrote:

> Death stalks all around but it is your friend, your life, your energy.[6]

Story often refers to his personal tragedies as his 'Rocks of Gibraltar' from which he draws strength, despite the personal pain. Again, it's that great appreciation for life, for wanting to get the most out of life, which arises in moments of deep sadness or melancholy.

One does have to wonder how the presence of death and the related tragedies in Story's life affected his relationships with others.

Story reflected, "Maybe I'm a little independent; maybe I'm very careful with my commitments, long-term commitments. So that may well be a result of all that went on back then, that I've got to push on. No matter what goes on, I have to keep going. I immerse myself in nature and life and I simply push on; I push through all the tragedies. But when that happens I do get a sense of myself at three years of age. When the really bad things happen I go back to that and the kid I was back then just carries me on."

Documentary filmmaker David Grusovin, who spent quite a bit of time with Story, spoke of Story's ability to move forward with his life. "Because of the litany of tragedies, I think there are elements that have made him stronger – he doesn't want

3. Journal 3, page 5; Date: January 1988.
4. Journal 8, page 34; Date: 22 June 1990.
5. Journal 6, page 2; Date: 13 August 1989.
6. Journal 4, page 36; Date: 18 April 1989.

that to happen to him; he's always trying to move forward. There's this sense that he doesn't want to dwell in the place where these things happened – I'm not talking geographically here, but a spatial thing, an idea or thought of how these things play out in the mind – he doesn't want to spend time being there. Of course it's going to revisit itself in his mind, and I'm sure it does, day in and day out, but he wants to move forward from that. And he's trained himself incredibly well in the 'move forward' thing – or not that he's trained himself well, it's just that it's part of his fabric and that is what makes him Story – we move forward – and he practices that in every aspect of his life."

Story's continuing search for meaning extended to his writings prior to launch when he was particularly aware of his own mortality. In his journals, he wrote:

> Feeling of history and being part of history – an organism being and making history. Looking at the past – seeing it come up and swallow you up and move on into the future. What is the aura while at KSC?[7] Does all of life run through you? Is it a 'Becker' time – death making life rich – dead leaves grow life? Life is rich because of death. Who is Story at KSC, three days prior to launch, what emotions, concerns? What does it mean to come face to face with space and all that space is – death, experience, existence, perception?[8]

> Prelaunch – fear of death, yet death is what is leading you to do this – the eternal search, the quest, the journey – what is death, how does it affect me and how I should live in life?[9]

The theme appears again in later journals, this time referring to a lack of personal control over death, the inherent risks:

> Off to a good day – I woke up one more time... Launch – one of my greatest fears is that I won't get to do it again. I want to survive this one so that I can get to do another one.[10]

> Fear – launch – you are not in control of whether you die or not, you are a passenger.[11]

> Woody Allen said, 'I'm not afraid of death, I just don't want to be there when it happens.' – Launch.[12]

7. Kennedy Space Center (KSC).
8. Journal 11, page 22; Date: 9 December 1991. This was written just days prior to STS-44.
9. Journal 10, page 16; Date: 17 January 1991.
10. Journal 17, page 1; Date: 11 April 1995.
11. Journal 18, page 19; Date: 7 October 1995.
12. Journal 29, page 13; Date: around end of January 2000.

Rather poignantly, Story wrote in his copy of *The Denial of Death*:[13]

> Launch – facing launch, facing dread, annihilation.

A major airplane disaster also had Story exclaiming about the proximity of death:

> US Air had a disastrous crash at Pittsburgh, 737, all 131 people dead – fell out of the sky on a perfectly clear night. I had been in and out of there 8 times on US Air in the last 10 days – including with [son] Lane.[14]

Although Story does not follow any formal religion, he does appreciate the need for human beings to transcend death; to live without fear of death. He believes that it is critical to a full enjoyment and appreciation of life. He wrote:

> If you are fearless, you are free. Fear of death constrains your actions.[15]

While studying the humanities at the University of Houston, Clear Lake, Story submitted a paper for *Contemporary Science, Technology and Society*. In it he wrote:

> Death is death, you can face it or deny it. No matter what the hopes and likelihoods of social utopia, individual death is a tragedy and it is in part the responsibility of art and literature to provide some mechanisms of transcendence to the individual. Social hope does not eliminate or lessen the essential need for the transcendence of death.[16]

To this end, Story saw the need to include death as a theme in his own writing and communication.

> How to get death into space writing – if you don't deal with death, you haven't dealt with life. Every story must deal with death.[17]

On my first visit to Florida in the initial stages of research for this book, the topic of death was high on the agenda – not only because of Story's intense, personal experiences with death, but in trying to understand how somebody so vibrant, so in love with life, was approaching perhaps the final phase of his own earthly existence. In his copy of *The Denial of Death*, Story soliloquized, "Are you doing more now because the inevitable is closer?"[18]

---

13. Story's handwritten note in his copy of *The Denial of Death* by Ernest Becker: New York, Free Press, 1973.
14. Journal 16, page 14; Date: 5 September 1994.
15. Journal 16, page 39; Date: 29 November 1994.
16. The paper was a study of *The Two Cultures* by C.P. Snow. It was written for a course called *Science, Technology and Society Anthropology* at the University of Houston, Clear Lake.
17. Journal 9, page 28; Date: 3 October 1990.
18. Story's handwritten note in his copy of *The Denial of Death* by Ernest Becker: New York, Free Press, 1973.

Many people have commented about the great physical condition which Story continues to maintain well into his late sixties, along with his continuing thirst for knowledge. Longevity is certainly something which Story hopes for and, to that end, he keeps both his mind and body in good condition. The degree of physically intensive work which Story undertakes on his hundred or so acres in Central Florida is testimony to a body which wishes to retain its vitality for a long as possible through exercise.

Likewise, Story's mental acuity continues to astonish all those with whom he comes into contact. Story rarely takes time out from a relentless stream of activities; he rarely takes holidays because he has so much else that he wants to accomplish. Keeping pace with both his energetic and intellectually-enriching pursuits can be both mentally and physically exhausting to those not familiar with his daily routine.

One of the things which Story and I discussed revolved around the ability to improve our longevity. Story has a theory that we are each programmed to age and die – that we don't just wear out. But he believes that if we have the will and the motivation to do things in mature age, then the program can slow down, or in fact reprogram itself, to enable us to do those things. In other words, waiting around for death can certainly hasten the process.

Story communicated this concept in his journal in 1992 when he wrote:

> Does having so many things you want to get done have an effect on your longevity? Does a retired body die because it has nothing to do?[19]

Certainly, Story seems in little danger of having nothing to do. Despite this, however, he is realistic about the body's ultimate physical demise:

> Nursing home visit ... God, that is where it is. That, more than any experience you've had, shows you what life is.[20]

> Life ends with pain, suffering, medical procedures, threat of illness and death – that's what you buy into the day you are born. Such tremendous hope in early life and look at how it ends! Need to see that all the time. Visit hospital, nursing home, funerals – that is where it is.[21]

With impending eye surgery in 1995, the personal reality of physical deterioration came much closer to home for Story. He wrote:

> Left eye has become much worse – went to NASA eye doctor to get new prescription for glasses – he could not bring me in to 20/20, says I need surgery

19. Journal 11, page 39; Date: 14 January 1992.
20. Journal 4, page 5; Date: around April 1988.
21. Journal 16, page 52; Date: 27 March 1995.

now! Well, a sense of finite time, mortality, vulnerability hit me kind of hard. Cataract [equates to] old age; it is related to being old, no way around it. Right eye cataract is starting now also – none of this is great with all we've got to do.[22]

Fortunately, Story's eye operations were successful and restored his vision to a high level. In true Story-style, when the doctor asked if he would prefer new eye lenses focused for near or distant vision, Story replied, "One of each!" Not your standard consideration, but then Story Musgrave has never been conventional at any stage of his life. And so he figured that with short sight in one eye and long sight in the other, the brain would take care of the rest. Within hours of the first operation, Story had checked himself out of the hospital, removed the eye patch, and returned to his office at NASA – much to his doctor's initial surprise and bemusement.

By the time of his 60th birthday, Story was in great spirits. He wrote:

> I feel so great, so hopeful over this one. It is the beginning of the end, the last leg, but the glorious leg. You have worked terribly hard in terribly constraining and oppressive environments for 60 years – Linwood, St Mark's, Marine Corps, colleges, Medical School, Internship, colleges, NASA/UHCL. You have fought the war, and a good war. It is time to think very big and very free. It is time to do and to be what you wish. It is time for acceptance of your destiny, your work, humanity, nationalities, the world. It is time to focus on your aesthetics, your art, your pleasure. It is time to do your thing, to let go of the world, to stop trying to do the whole world. Major decisions and effort are on how to handle massive amounts of paper, ideas and electronic materials – how to not be a slave to all that, to reduce it to fun and art, or get rid of it![23]

Though a dreamer, there is no denying that Story has always been realistic about the future – particularly in relation to himself. This is reflected further in his journals:

> Death forces you to clarify your real beliefs. There is no denial or fooling yourself in the face of death! Mid-life crisis is a part of coming to terms with your mortality.[24]

> If I look to the future long enough, the time will come when I won't 'be' in that future.[25]

22. Journal 17, page 43; Date: 8 August 1995.
23. Journal 17, page 48; Date: 17 August 1995.
24. Journal 24, page 3; Date: October 1997.
25. Journal 13, page 34; Date: 13 April 1992.

Story was not without humor when dealing with the subject of death in his journals. He wrote:

When I die, I want to die with a heating pad to keep me warm.[26]

Filmmakers David and Katey Grusovin visited Massachusetts with Story during the summer of 2002. Naturally, the theme of death arose during their travels, provoked by one of Story's acute observations about the demise of life.

David recalled, "We were sitting at a restaurant and the food's come and we're eating and having wine and then Story, in the middle of eating, cocks his head. I'm watching – he hasn't even said anything. And he's looking over my shoulder and he goes, 'My God, that person's dead!' There's this guy sitting behind us who looks like his jaw has just fallen off a hinge, and he's got a knife and a fork precariously placed, and it's like someone had placed them in his two hands and he's just holding them there. And a conversation is ensuing with everyone else at his table, but he's not participating. And Story's just locked on like a laser beam to this image of a human… it's as raw as it got. He sees someone walking down the street with no life – and Story's teeming with life, teeming with all his senses."

In a way, this is Story's comment on humanity – how have we all gotten to be like this as a species?

People do grow old, but Story believes it is possible for many people to be old and active: participation in living is the important thing.

*

Make death a part of life, an adventure, a victory.[27]

According to Story, "For me it's an opportunity. We're given the opportunity to participate in the whole thing."

Story has his own views about the end of life.

He said, "My own approach to that is not to accept other people's ideas about what happens after death – not to pick up a particular book and say 'that's what happens'. You can pick up a thousand different books, different religions, different mythologies and get different ideas as to what happens to you. I don't know what happens after death but I go forward, I simply go forward. I cannot change what happens so, whatever it is, I accept it.

26. Journal 12, page 46; Date: 3 April 1992.
27. Journal 3, page 42; Date: 30 October 1988.

"My own point of view is death is life; they go together. You buy into it, you must buy into it. The day you become alive, you have to buy into it. If you don't, then don't buy into life – they go together and so, for me, I go forward with faith and with hope and I just push on forward."

Poignantly, Story wrote:

> Feet in the soil, heart in the sky, soul in the stars. Faith that there is a 'God' and the faith to pursue my God.[28]

28. Story's handwritten note in his copy of *The Denial of Death* by Ernest Becker: New York, Free Press, 1973.

# *Body, Mind, Art*

"Descarte tore the mind out of the body and we've been trying to get them together ever since."

# 14. The Body

It is so much more difficult to live with one's body than with one's soul.

*D.H. Lawrence*

Story Musgrave has explored all of his worlds with his body – whether it be flying an airplane, living in space, working on the land or giving a performance. He explained, "I'm into bodily living in the real world."[1]

Listening to the body is something Story is compelled to do. For him, it is not that the body is separate to the mind, but that by listening to the body, you can enrich your intellectual, emotional and spiritual experiences:

> Try living at a different level of awareness – a level which is aware of your awareness of the world – i.e. an existential state which transcends one's immediate or functional level of existence in the world![2]

Story can be incredibly impulsive at times because he listens to his body, to what feels 'right'. The body tells Story what he needs to do – and he's been practicing that for over sixty years. He wrote:

> Descartes tore the mind out of the body and we've been trying to get them together ever since.[3]

Looking at the physiology, the evolutionary rhythms and abilities of the body while in space meant a great deal to Story. It was about biology and evolution and adaptation to a new environment. During the course of six space flights, Story also enjoyed the beauty and the spirituality of space – that, too, he felt in his body.

This is the same as Story's relationship with nature – lying in cool, freshly ploughed fields, floating in the ocean the night before a launch, or sliding his hands into a fragrant pile of soft, fertile ash. It is the union of the physical and the spiritual through surrender to the experience. Of his approach to life Story wrote:

> Take a moment of nothing, just nothing; let experience come of itself.[4]

*

In his journals, Story frequently makes mention of his body, the physicality of things.

> You've got to be in touch with your body. Your body is your sensor to this new world and you get information from it. Cognitive – you must achieve a level of awareness and contact that will allow you to see your body's response.[5]

1. Comment made to me by Story while touring his home library with him. Story loves the writings of D.H. Lawrence and others who express their experiences of the world with their bodies and minds.
2. Journal 12, page 4; Date: 27 January 1992.
3. Story's handwritten note in his copy of *Principles of Literary Criticism* by I. A. Richards: New York, Harcourt Brace, 1925.
4. Story's handwritten note in his copy of *D.H. Lawrence and Italy*: Introduction by Anthony Burgess, Penguin USA, Published: June 1997.
5. Journal 22, page 36; Date unknown, comment added later.

> My body is an instrument; I observe it… My body is an instrument; listen to it![6]

> Musicians play with their entire body – it becomes an extension of the instrument.[7]

Of course, it gets back to surrender – something which is spoken about in relation to Story's experiences in many areas of his life. He has that particular ability to surrender himself to a situation in order to understand it and experience it.

Story explained, "You have a live creature in a certain environment and that creature is susceptible and sensible to all that's going on around – working on being touched by the environment. You cannot know an environment unless you let go, release, surrender. You've got to let go of all the previous baggage – all the cultural baggage and other baggage that you're bringing into the occasion – to try and let the occasion, the situation, the environment touch you.

"It's like when one culture meets another. If you want to know another culture, you have to let go of your culture totally. You've got to not impose your culture on the new culture that you are joining; you need to simply let go of everything and listen. So I think *listen* is a key word here too; it goes along with surrender. Unless you surrender you cannot be touched, you cannot be moved by the current situation – so that is the key throughout this thing. The only way you're going to know it, is if you just let go of everything else."

For Story, surrender becomes part of the spiritual quest. "Spirituality in surrender – now you are listening to the cosmos; you are listening to your body which is part of the cosmos. Your body has come from the cosmos and so this ability to listen to what is there increases the spirituality. You're into direct revelation of what life and death are about.

"It's a matter of quieting your mind so that you can listen to the situation; so that you can listen to how your body is responding to it. If there's noise everywhere, you simply don't have the sensibility – you can't sense it, you can't listen to the subtleties, and they are very subtle. You can't listen to the subtleties unless you quiet the mind in a quiet environment. But surrender is getting rid of all that old baggage; by being quiet and by surrendering, you can listen to the body itself; you can listen to your body and mind: what is it telling you about that environment? Your body is going to respond in some very deep kind of ways.

"Now you are able to listen to the messages of the cosmos, or to God – which in my religion is all the same. The cosmos is not only sacred, it's not only created by God, it is part of God. So in that form of spirituality and surrender, you can listen to the

6. Journal 25, page 39; Date unknown, comment added later.
7. Journal 25, page 39; Date: around March 1999.

sacredness and the divineness of the cosmos, which includes, of course, your heaven and your earth."

According to Story, human beings frequently fail to surrender to an environment before declaring it hostile. Immediately, that creates a kind of barrier to the experience: "The ocean is very powerful. At one time, it was the biggest horizon we had – the way space is. At one time, the ocean was the most expansive horizon that we had and so it's powerful in that sense as well. But also, there's a vulnerability in the ocean. Probably, life arose in the ocean. There are all kinds of themes going on, but you are vulnerable to the ocean the same way you are out in space – as environments that you're not designed to be absorbed into. But I never call space a hostile environment; I never call the ocean a hostile environment; I never call Antarctica a hostile environment. They are not hostile – they are what they are! The fact that we humans, in an evolutionary sense, are not adapted to be in space without a space suit, or to be in Antarctica without special clothes, or to be in the ocean without diving equipment, does not mean that these things are hostile. It means we are not adapted to those, but are adapted to our limited environment. To call them hostile is purely an egocentric, anthropocentric kind of view of the world. It also has a negative connotation – as if, in some way, you hate or despise those beautiful environments. And so everywhere you see 'conquering space' or space as a 'hostile' environment. These things are not hostile, they're beautiful!"

Story often describes the way he gets his body into his earthly experiences. He likes to be in contact with his environment – literally! It's something he's been doing since he was a very young child. After plowing a field on the family's farm in Massachusetts, a young Story loved to lie down in the freshly turned soil. He recalled, "Damp earth! I'd be in a tractor, plowing the fields; it was our policy to plough very deeply. So on a hot summer's day when you reach down into the earth – a foot or a foot-and-a-half – it comes up very cold. You have the delicious heat of summer, but you have a cold, damp surface. The soil is almost powdery because it is very hot and it's dry, and so the soil sort of crumbles in your hand. But to bring up rich, brown soil which is wet and cold on a hot summer's day – that was delicious. So I would get off the tractor and get into the soil! I'd reach into it with my hands and run it through my fingers; squeeze it through my fingers. I'd walk in it with bare feet, lie in it and I ended up eating it too – it seemed to taste very good."

Today, on his hundred acres in Florida, Story still loves the feel of good, clean dirt. While potting palm seedlings, he'll burrow his bare hands through mulched maple leaves and into the piles of fertile ash. The soil in the rainforest areas is almost black, built from rapidly decaying biological matter and full of strong smelling nutrients, while the desert areas are deep with soft white sand. Together, it all makes for an irresistible physical environment. Despite the opportunities and demands of the external world, Story will tell you that this is where he most wants to be.

In interviews, Story has often spoken of the night before a launch when he would lie in the ocean beside his spaceship, immersing himself in nature. He told Nina L. Diamond: "The night before a launch I lie in the ocean and watch the satellites streaking overhead, and look at a fully loaded vehicle that's running, alive... I lie in the ocean, looking over my left shoulder at the space vehicle sitting there… And there's this juncture of ocean and land. You think of transitions of living things in and out of the ocean. And you are representing life leaping off the planet. I'm not just a human going into space, you know. People who think the original expedition to space was a competition between two nations miss the ball altogether. Every square millimeter on this earth is filled with hundreds of thousands of living creatures. What is this life force doing? It's leaping off the planet for the solar system. I am only a representative of the life force. We have covered this whole globe, up, down, and everywhere, and now we're gonna populate the rest of the solar system. Give us the technology and we're gonna head out across the universe. So, I lie in the ocean and think about life and death, because that occurs in the vehicle and the ocean."[8]

Story explained his willingness to be involved in his universe: "The whole thing, of course, is an immersion in the cosmic process. Cosmic evolution, biological evolution – the whole thing is an immersion in that process. It's for the pleasure of it, for the aesthetics of it, for the bodily pleasure of it, but also as a way of listening to it, as a way of understanding."

In 1996, Story told Frank D. Roylance of the *Baltimore Sun* of his approach to space flight. "Space, he said, 'is a physical, emotional, intellectual frontier, a way to participate fully in the universe. You could do it purely intellectually as a space physiologist or astronomer. But I wanted to put my body in it.'"[9]

Story explained, "It was very important – I did want to put my body in it and one of the main motivations of space flight was not only to do an intellectual, philosophical and scientific exploration, but simply to surrender my body to a new situation and see how it responded. Then, of course, if you're going to find out what that's about, you've got to listen to it and let it affect you."

Again, Story stressed the importance of not wanting to 'conquer' space if we are to understand it. "If you think you're going to conquer space, it is going turn around and conquer you, because you will not adapt to it, you will not be fluid, you will not be flexible. So you will not become a spaceperson! The idea that I am going to conquer space means that I'm going to take my earth-based person up there, my earth-based culture up there and impose it on the space flight environment. And then that means

8. Interview for *Omni Magazine*, by Nina L. Diamond, August 1994. Reprinted by permission of Omni Publications International Ltd.
9. *Baltimore Sun*, article titled: *Right Stuff Old Stuff to Him* by Frank D. Roylance, 1996.

you do not wish to be touched; you do not wish to be moved by that environment. You want to keep yourself *as is* – and that's going to make you very, very inflexible and never really become a spaceperson. So the best way to go along in space is to become a spaceperson – to let your earth-based person go."

Story's method of working in space was to ensure that he didn't forget to look outside the window of the Space Shuttle, or take time to view the earth 'below' him and the heavens, full of stars, 'above' him during spacewalks. In his journal he wrote:

> Achieving higher state of consciousness not only through floating in dark isolation, but also by being super-sensitive, super-aware to all of earth and cosmos as seen from space.[10]

He told Roylance: "I have these little interrupts and they go off all the time. I'm doing a space-walk and the interrupts say 'Look at Earth, the sky, or inward. What are you feeling right now? Listen to your body'. It's an attempt to be a total participant and, at the same time, getting the job done."[11]

Story explained, "If you don't work on that, you can be out there a whole bunch of time and not look around. So it just means look around and listen! You're not just outside working and getting the job done mechanically, but you're experiencing the process of working and you also have a sense of the zero-gravity, a sense of where you are geographically and you're getting the big picture [of the earth and heavens] as well as the small picture. And so you do that on a continuous basis. The key thing is to be a live creature in a live environment and to think about what's happening, too, and to catch it."

For Story, it's about enriching the experience of space. It's about having an experience in space, as opposed to just being there. In ways, it's about beginning again or taking yourself back to the very basics of exploration, as a child would do.

He recalled, "That started way back, I think as far back as I can remember, after going out into the forest – just to let myself go; just to hear the wind through the trees and to smell the pine needles and the red leaves of Fall: to watch the red leaves of Fall float down. Just to go out there and experience that."

After his first space flight, Story told Dennis L. Breo of the Flying Physician, "For 16 years, I've waited for this experience. This is why I got into this business – to be on the intellectual and physical frontier. This is why I took the job, what I'm supposed to be. I can't say that I expected it, but I wanted a transcendental experience, an existential reaction to the environment. I'm not talking about an illusion, of seeing something that wasn't there. I'm talking about a magical emotional reaction to the environment, to what's there. This is what I've been after all my life, to experience and feel new sensations."[12]

10. Journal 9, page 8; Date: 7 September 1990.
11. *Baltimore Sun*, article titled: *Right Stuff Old Stuff to Him* by Frank D. Roylance, 1996.
12. *Flying Physician*: article titled *MD Astronaut Tells of Space Adventure*, by Dennis L Breo, 1983.

Space flight gave Story a very special environment in which to explore and he made some unique observations about the body in zero gravity. One particular journal entry related to breathing:

> Float – breathing in; pulling your body forward into the air that you will breathe. Exhalation – pushing body away from the air. In effect, the air stays in place – your body moves in and out of the air.[13]

In much the same way, the pulse of blood through the body became noticeable as Story observed his limbs moving. "Free floating, you can feel and see every contraction of the heart. For example, if you are floating, you will see that with every arterial pulse, your limb will move. If you're here on earth, your limb is resting on a table or something, but in zero-gravity, with every pulse your limb moves: that is flexion and extension. The big biceps cause flexion of the lower arm; the triceps on the backside of the arm cause extension. When the pulse goes out – and it's a fairly sharp boost of pressure – you are able to see the entire limb, all the way out through the elbow, the wrist and fingers, extend.

"So you see that with the eyes, but now when you close your eyes, you feel that shot of blood going out from your heart to the rest of your body – and your whole body now extends a little. You actually go somewhere – you move, of course; you move through the air. You have to move through the air because you're taking a shot of blood and shooting it down the legs; you've taken mass and you've moved a mass in a certain direction, so that has to move the body in the other direction. It's Newton's second law; it's called a ballistocardiogram, except it's a perceived ballistocardiogram. In the medical world, a ballistocardiogram is when you fix the body to a table which can move and then measure the accelerations on a movable table. We don't use it much these days with all the scanning devices, but in the old days, that is what it was called. But in space, you can float yourself out there and feel the whole body extend with each pulse! It gets down now to how sensitive you want to be about things. Every time that shot of blood comes out, your finger is getting bigger. The fingertip is getting bigger and then smaller [between beats]. If you're touching something extraordinarily lightly, you will feel every single pulse come out there. Zero-g allows you to get in touch with these kinds of rhythms."

Story enjoyed learning to work in the zero-g environment, especially doing very basic things we take for granted here on earth – like moving from one point to another. He explained: "We've talked of adaptation to space flight, we've talked about the perceptions, but I think it's worthwhile talking about you, [the space flyer], as an aerobatic creature. It's the dance of how you move in zero-gravity; how you go flying across a room and then just gently grab with the fingers or bring your legs up and then hang on to something with your ankles – just wrap them around something.

"The whole idea of moving with the wrists, as opposed to walking, becomes an incredible art form. You see huge differences in people's ability to maneuver, to navigate and to propel themselves through a spaceship and to get work done.

"That kind of mobility or stability and that ability to do what you have to do, to get all the work done in the motions of zero-gravity – it's a wholly new art form; it's a wholly new form of aerobatics – how you're going to move and how you're going to hold yourself, living and working in space flight. It is just spectacular to see someone who can really move in zero-g, really maintain control of their body position, get the work done and have fun."

After watching the 3D Imax film Space Station,[14] Story made particular mention of Russian cosmonaut Sergei Krikalev and the beauty and fluidity of his movements in zero-gravity. For Story, it was not only enjoyable but inspiring to observe Sergei's response to that environment.

In space, orbital mechanics play a large role in the body's perceptions of time, of the daily rhythms created by the sun in relation to your earthly position. It is something we largely take for granted on earth, but in space, it can be somewhat disorienting. Story explained, "You're able to perceive how the daily rhythm is created. When you're [orbiting the earth] sixteen times [in 24 hours], you see that the 'day' has now changed to a ninety minute day. You get a sense of what creates the night and day cycles down here. You see it work because you are outside of the earth.

"We lose track down here. We haven't thought about it and why it is so fantastically importantly to us. But [in space] you get to see how orbital mechanics creates a twenty-four hour day and night cycle down here, which is critical to you.

"You also get a sense of the tilt of the earth. When you look at the sun and you look at the plane the sun forms, and you look at the Earth [in relation to that], then you can actually look at the geography and almost see the tilt. Now you're starting to get an intuitive feel for why there are seasons. Down here, we don't think much about how orbital mechanics creates seasons, but when you can see the geography of orbital mechanics out there, it makes a difference.

"All of these rhythms are, of course, ingrained in us – especially the circadian rhythm, the twenty-four-hour rhythm."

Night passes were an incredibly special part of the space experience for Story. Sometimes he referred to them as dark floats. They equated to night viewings of the earth in darkness, with the cabin lights turned out to assist with dark adaptation; this also enabled him to see the stars. This was something Story enjoyed when he could

14. Produced by Toni Myers and distributed by the IMAX Corporation. Release date April 2002.

grab some spare time during a mission and when he could also get the consensus of his fellow crew members to turn out the lights in the cockpit.

In an interview for this book, Story gave a vivid account of his night passes. It is presented here in all its detail and poetry:

Sometimes I would dark adapt my eyes ahead of time and get on some red goggles so that once the sun had gone, I would be totally dark-adapted, which means that you can start seeing faint light and other things immediately. The goggles let you dark adapt so you only see red light and the red light does not spoil your dark adaptation. If you wanted to go out and see the Southern Cross very powerfully and you wanted to have a powerful star experience, faint light experience, you would wear the red goggles during dinner and you would be adapted. So adaptation makes a huge difference and total adaptation may take half an hour. You're getting it very rapidly but total adaptation may be half an hour.

But most of the time, the whole process of the sun going down is so glorious that I would accept the fact that it would take me a little longer to adapt, and so the majority of the time, I would not do the red goggles; I would experience the sunset.

You get the entire rainbow very close to the earth; it's red. Up into the atmosphere it's orange, yellow and then it's green, blue and purple, and the purple is the transition between the sunset and the blackness of the sky. But to a greater or lesser extent, you get the entire rainbow and it's very sharp; at about two hundred thousand feet is where that exists – that's about how deep the atmosphere is when you're looking out at the horizon.

The sun goes down very fast, sixteen times faster than it does here [on earth] and so it's fast! When you look at the pink glow in your cargo bay, the pink glow of the spaceship, it's like turning the lights out in a movie theatre – it simply goes out, so it's very dramatic in that way.

At sunset, you usually have some wonderful silhouettes. You have cumulous clouds because it's different than a sunrise – at sunrise, there has been quiet all night, so there aren't as many cumulus clouds, there's not as much convection and there's not so much dust in the air. A sunset is more powerful in terms of the reds; it's more powerful in terms of the silhouettes of tall cumulus storm clouds and that kind of stuff and so a sunset appears more dynamic.

But when the sun finally settles down, you're left with this blue limb. And so the horizon is this gorgeous kind of blue, this spectacular blue, and it stays there all night; and that blue surrounds you 360 degrees. Your entire horizon is this solid blue – that is a marvelous thing.

And, of course, when the sun goes down you can start to see all kinds of low light phenomena that you can't see when the sun is up. It's not an Aurora, technically, but you see this fire start creeping and crawling over the spaceship. The ions are re-combining there like an aurora does, but when you fire off a rocket engine, you now see the rocket engine – that kicks off the instability – and you see this ghost start creeping and crawling all over the spaceship. Then it's there by itself; it persists, but every time you fire a rocket off, you see more of it. You can call it whatever you will, but it is a spectacular little bit of fire and it creeps and crawls over everything; the whole spaceship may glow!

Next, the stars come out. They're far brighter; they're not yellowish. Just like the sun [as seen from space]: the sun is a very bright ball of white. The stars are more pinpoint, they're more precise, they're sharper because you're not looking at them through the air. And they're whiter, but it is sparkling. There are so many stars you can barely find your own constellations. I get through the sky by following the Milky Way, which is just like a wall of light; I find out where in the Milky Way the Scorpion is – that's looking towards the center of the universe. That's the way I navigate in space because the Milky Way is so fantastically bright in our own galaxy.

You see the stars coming up, of course; they come from the east because you're traveling east – and they come up sixteen times [in twenty-four hours]. They also, like the sun, have to make it to the other horizon, so you watch them move. It's like a planetarium show but you first see them through the air. As soon as a star is beyond the earth's physical limb, not atmospheric but physical limb, you see stars through the air; to see stars in this blue background of the limb is nice.

Now, before the sun has gone down totally, when the limb is red, orange and yellow, you see stars through that as well. So in the process of the sunset, you're seeing stars through this rainbow of colors; they're moving through it. The first time you see this, you think it's a satellite rising because you see it moving. But it's not a satellite, it's just a star – that's how fast the stars move!

Your velocity sort of creates a celestial sphere and, in general, you move east. You move towards the stars and they move towards you, but that's only in the direction of the spaceship. If you look out to the north or south, roughly everything rotates in place; it never goes down. The Southern Cross is my most powerful experience of the stars, just because I love it. Maybe it's because I don't get to see it all the time while living in the northern hemisphere, but I also think, for me, it's an extraordinarily beautiful thing. But it cones 'over there' depending upon your mission, depending upon your orbit. On the Hubble mission, I thought I was going to lose it, but as you're going around the earth, it just rotates in place. It moved down into the blue limb but it didn't go below the earth's limb. So I was able to see the Southern Cross in this blue background.

If you're very fortunate, you get into an aurora phenomena: this pink and this green mist starts moving and it comes from nowhere; it doesn't have to get transported there. It pops out of the place like fog, like a wonderful mist. It is just very high energy particles as they move through earth's magnetic field into the air. That also allows it to flow like a curtain at huge speeds, because the air is not moving: it's the phenomena and the re-combination of ions and things. It does not have to move the air, so it can occur at any speed. It shoots up and down, pink and green, changing colors based upon the ions that are re-combining. The kinesthetic of the moving Aurora is just marvelous, but it's what ions are re-combined in that particular place. And so the given motion that it causes is just extraordinary and you look at the star background. You have something like the Southern Cross, which moves in a cone through this auroral mist, which is overlaying the blue horizon. It's almost like a moving painting!

There are times that city lights sort of dance with the stars. There are times you can see the lights and they are sort of like celestial configurations, and now you notice a blue limb between them. Now they start to sort of dance with the stars and so at times it's a little confusing as to what you're looking at – that is a wonderful kind of thing as well.

One time over Australia, I had this purple-pink horizontal lightning. It was going for hundreds of miles and it was trying to find it's way. It would start out trying to go somewhere, it couldn't seem to make it through – so for a hundred miles you see the lightning trying to hunt. That's the most spectacular lightning for me – the purple-pink lightning that goes horizontal for hundreds of miles.

The other lightning, it's the kettle drum effect where a cloud bursts with lightning, which sets another off fifty miles away. Each cumulus cloud, after lightning, is rebuilding its potential to get ready for the next stroke. You look at this dance where they're setting each other off and that is a fantastic rhythm. But looking down upon a big cumulus cloud, which is simply discharging it's lightning straight down, is nowhere near the spectacular image of horizontal purple lightning – that is spectacular in color, but it's also spectacular in its kinesthetics.

And all these little scenes are cumulative. All these things are happening simultaneously in the perfect night pass; they happen all together. In the perfect night pass, you have a wealth of them.

The meteorites come in between you and earth – they're just streaking in. They're like falling stars except they're between you and earth – so they're burning up. They're like a fireball up front, like a great big fat fireball, and then the trail of ionized gas goes out behind them and it persists for quite a while. I've seen as many as five or six simultaneously, in one view.

Related to those are the light flashes that you have, especially on a mission when you're flying higher up into the magnetosphere. You have the cosmic rays piling through the eyeball making their light flashes. Every mission except Hubble, they were little white bursts of light. On the Hubble mission, they streaked. I've had as many as five or six of them simultaneously. So when you get dark adapted or when you close your eyes going off to sleep and you pass through the South Atlantic anomaly in the southern hemisphere where we pass through intense radiation, it's going through the liquid part of the eye. It's not hitting the visual cortex, not hitting the retina, it's passing through the liquid part of the eye – that makes the streaks. But the experience is like the Fourth of July; it's a fireworks show in the middle of your eye – it's free; it just happens! You hope you're not paying a severe penalty for that; you hope it's not hitting the wrong thing. I've seen them on earth; I've occasionally got them on earth as would be reasonable – just occasionally.

During a night pass, if you really have no strong light out there, you can open your eyes and still see them. So now you're taking in this total scene of purple lightning, of Aurora, of blue limb, of stars, of city lights, of meteorites and now you see the light flashes.

And then, of course, you invoke free fall. Now you are falling through this environment, but directionless. You're falling through the aurora, you're falling through the stars, but not toward it and not away from it. You don't know the directionality, so that becomes a wholly new experience.

Now you immerse yourself so that you're solidly in the window. You don't know where the spacecraft is around you – it's out there somewhere but you don't have the window frame, so you don't know. And you may not know where you are over the earth. You're mixing up the stars with the city lights and so, you're kind of separate from earth because after a while you're not flying over or under it, you're separated from earth and you're falling through this visual panorama.

And at the peak of all these things, your brother and spiritual colleague brings over Catholic communion! Then you have arrived at the highest moment possible; you are beside yourself; you are totally transcendent at this point. It just doesn't get any higher!

Story has written various comments in the margins of books and in his journals about night passes. On his final flight, STS-80, he was able to share many of these experiences with crew member Tom Jones. It was Tom, in fact, with whom he shared Catholic communion. For Story, that was perhaps the highest spiritual point of all of his sensory experiences in space:

> Jones, communion – total surrender of body, soul and being to that eternal spirit, that which has always been and always will be.[15]

> Night pass: music of the pass. Floating in the stars: Southern Cross. Communion: intoxicated with the spirit.[16]

> Jones – silent words. Complete empathy, permanent spiritual bonding in this ephemeral experience.[17]

*

Story's interest in parachuting extends back to the 1960s. He made his first jump in Lakewood, New Jersey, during 1963. He recalled, "Parachuting was a different place to put my body, mind and soul into. I love the parachute itself. I probably loved being under the canopy more than most people. I think that most people thought that the freefall was the only place it was, but I adored being under the canopy as much as the freefall. I didn't treat the canopy as that's the end of my freefall and that's the end of the experience. I had just as good and just as exciting an experience under the canopy, floating down towards earth.

"It was a new experience, the freefall, and of course if you look at parachuting it is not really freefall. The airplane is probably going sixty, seventy, eighty miles an hour, so as soon as you leave the airplane you're probably in two-thirds of a 'g'. Once you have achieved terminal velocity in a few seconds, you are back at one 'g' again; you

---

15. Story's handwritten note in his copy of *Wind, Sand and Stars*, by Antoine de Saint-Exupéry: first published in French in 1939 under the name *Terre des Hommes*. My copy was translated by William Rees and published in London by the Penguin Group, 1995.

16. Story's handwritten note in his copy of *Six Memos for the Next Millennium* by Italo Calvino, Patrick Creagh (Translator): Harvard University Press, USA, March 1988.

17. Story's handwritten note in his copy of *The Spell of New Mexico*: Tony Hillerman (Ed) Albuquerque: University of New Mexico Press, 1976.

are resting on a blanket of air instead of in a chair! You are resting on air and so it is not freefall, it's basically flying the body through air, that is what you are doing. But it is a marvelous thing. It's usually very kinesthetic."

In all, Story has done over 600 parachute jumps. He began jumping at the L.S.P.C.[18] in New Jersey and made his first 110 jumps there. He wrote in a letter to a colleague:

> I was privileged to have instructors and companions such as Don West, Bob Spatola, Lee Guilfoyle, Dan Quinn, Mac McCraw, Conny McDonough, Andy Porter, Bill Markhoff and Jacques Istel.

The next 200 jumps were mostly around Lexington and Cynthiana, Kentucky. Over a hundred of these were part of a study on the aerodynamics of the human body in which Story was the principal investigator.[19] Further to this, Story also made many exhibition jumps around the state of Kentucky and formed the Bluegrass Sport Parachuting Association. The remaining jumps, a total of about 335, were scattered around several small airports.

Story paid meticulous attention to the details of parachuting. Again, it was his aversion to risk which largely drove him.

He explained, "Parachuting was a technology, just like all of my other worlds, whether it's space flight, scuba diving, flying airplanes, soaring; all of those kinds of things. It takes the technology to allow you to be there in those other environments and the technology has to be done correctly. It has a technical foundation, there are check lists, there are limits to what you can do, there are limits in the machinery. You simply have to do it right or a disaster is going to happen. So from my earliest ages I learnt to do technology and machinery to survive in that environment – so I did parachuting very, very explicitly."

Patricia Musgrave, recalled Story's early days of parachuting. "Story would do just about anything! He actually took the training for parachuting in New Jersey. I was eight months pregnant with our daughter Holly and I went to the course; I took part in it and I watched him parachute – that was very exciting; I was very happy for him. And then Story, he just 'brainwashed' me about how safe parachuting is; nothing can happen to you. And, of course, Story was so methodical, that his backpack – it would open! He was very, very proficient in that, so he had me totally 'brainwashed' that nothing could possibly happen to him!

"He would always say, 'Flying is not that safe, but parachuting is.' And then his

18. Lakewood Sport Parachuting Center (L.S.P.C.)
19. This is discussed in the chapter *The Road to Medicine*.

Mom helped buy him an airplane! So he had to alter his way of persuasion. And, of course, Story, to me, was just a wonderful guy and he could do no wrong. I believed everything and I believed in him."

During the 1980s, Story wrote a short narrative about parachuting for a college paper at the University of Houston, Clear Lake. The paper was titled *Temptation and Preservation*.[20]

> He rolls off the side of the seat and cartwheels vertically away from the aircraft. The cartwheel continues as his vertical velocity accelerates asymptotically to a terminal velocity of about 150 mph.
>
> After a moment of appreciating the cartwheel and how it would appear as viewed from a distance, Story breaks the cart-wheeling and achieves a stable earth-facing position by arching his back and limbs rearward – in essence, making himself into an aerodynamic human shuttlecock. Dipping a shoulder, he makes a couple of turns in that direction to survey the space he will fall through and his position relative to the desired opening point.
>
> He spends the rest of his 10,000 foot fall as a dolphin in the open sea: rolling, tumbling, spinning, laughing and falling.

Story said, "You'd like to be able to see yourself, but you do see your friends that are going down with you. It's a very gymnastic kind of activity; it's dance and a lot of it is wonderful motions, incredible motions. Cart-wheeling down through space is an extraordinary thing to see someone do. But the whole idea of 'flying' the body was really neat – a real art form – and to descend under the canopy was all a very nice experience."

\*

It is undeniable that Story has lived his life on the physical, intellectual and spiritual frontiers of human existence. In some fields, such as space flight, he has even *defined* these frontiers for us.

Perhaps, for Story, it begins with imagination, because it takes an incredible amount of creative energy to envision the possibilities of a new environment. Welcoming that new world and surrendering to the experience of it is the next critical phase. It is listening and feeling with your body, mind and soul that allows you to understand what you are experiencing.

20. The paper is dated July 13, 1988.

Story has taken this approach to life into other creative areas such as spacewalking, which he turned into an art form. He has also brought it to his studies and experiences of performance, art and literature. Finally, and with great passion, he has brought it into his last calling, which he defines as 'Beauty'.[21]

21. Refer to the chapter: *Self-Reflections.*

# 15. Spacewalking Ballet

Being a jumper, one must recondition to stepping out
and floating, versus stepping out and falling!

*Story Musgrave, April 1979*

One of the main goals of creating art is to share the experience of its creation – to bring it into the culture.

William Wetmore Story was a world-renowned American sculptor who thrived on the artistic spirit. He lived among a group of talented friends in Italy – a country rich in art and culture, which ultimately became his home. He sculptured with marble – perhaps the most difficult medium for a sculptor – for if an error occurs, you must start over.

Several generations later, one of William's descendants was destined to add his stamp to a much newer art form: spacewalking. That too, was an occupation which left a narrow margin for error: the price in this case could be your life. But like any sculptor, Story Musgrave was given the raw materials and tested their capabilities. Assigned to a team of the finest engineers, physiologists and tailors, he contributed to the development of the spacesuits for NASA's Space Shuttle program.

In 1983, largely by luck, Story became the first person to emerge from the Space Shuttle's airlock wearing the new spacesuit. Within a decade, Story would develop and perfect his craft to become, arguably, the spacewalking world's most famous ballerina. In doing so, he would work to communicate the experience for the benefit of the culture.

\*

In the mid-1970s, with the dawn of the Space Shuttle era, NASA management made the decision to develop a new spacesuit for EVA.[1]

Joe McMann, who was NASA's lead engineer on the EMU[2] – the combined spacesuit and life support systems – spoke of the vision for the new suit. He recalled that his former boss, James V. Correale, who came to NASA from the Air Crew Equipment Laboratory in Philadelphia, largely drove the concept. According to Joe, "After Jim saw the astronauts fall on the lunar surface with their oxygen ventilation hoses exposed, he vowed that the next suit would have no external hoses. "If they'd have fallen and cut a hole in one of those hoses, we'd probably be naming the moon after them or some spacecraft after them! So my boss decided, no more hoses – I want a suit where the life support system joins right to the suit. And I want a hard upper torso and as many hard joints as I can. I want bins of parts, where I can fit all kinds of different astronauts by pulling on a special sized arm or a leg or whatever – he drove that. So we started coming up with this concept with the hard upper torso which had openings for the arms.

"He certainly prevailed, and the success of the Shuttle suit is testimony to his inputs, as well as those of other giants of the early days."

1. Extravehicular Activity (EVA) or spacewalks.
2. Extravehicular Mobility Unit (EMU).

Story was assigned as the astronaut representative on EMU development for the Space Shuttle. Joe explained why it was necessary to have an astronaut directly involved in the process. "You had to have a spokesperson for the crew because astronauts, being extreme individualists – I mean you hear about team players and all that – but everybody in the astronaut corps wants to put their fingerprints on whatever they're dealing with. If you listen to all the different crew people who evaluated a suit, for example, you might get as many different opinions as to its acceptability as you had evaluators. And you can't operate like that, so you have to have somebody that's the astronaut's spokesperson for each system. Story was the first one for the EMU for the Shuttle... so he had to come up with consensus positions on the various questions that we'd ask."

Fred Morris, who worked for Hamilton Standard[3] remembers encountering Story during the company's pitch for the spacesuit contract. "I was the program manager elect on the EMU in 1976 when we put in our proposal and this was, to use an American expression, the 'Gunfight at OK Coral' between Hamilton Standard and Garrett Air Research.[4] Each of us had cut the space life-support business kind of in half. Hamilton had had the previous Apollo EVA system and Air Research desperately wanted it, so it was the two of us bidding against each other. And Hamilton had the suit supplier ILC Dover on their team and Air Research had the suit supplier David Clarke Company on their team and it was a very tight competition – which we eventually won.

"Anyway, part of the competition was two days of oral examination at the Johnson Space Center and, as the program manager elect, I was the ringmaster of it and the guy who had to be the interlocutor. The second day we had the suit demonstration and we had made a prototype suit for this. I got up and did a summation speech to the seven member source board, of which Story was the astronaut representative. An old friend of mine named Walt Guy, who was running Crew Systems at the time, was the chairman of the source board. Anyway I made the speech – it was a good speech – it was about five minutes long and one of the better speeches I've ever made in my life. And at the conclusion of it, one of the guys from ILC is crying 'cause I was getting right down to gut level issues about hanging on through the depression between the Apollo program and Shuttle, that kind of stuff. But Story jumps up, big smile on his face, comes around and pumps my hand. And I'd never met him before. Our team looked at each other and figured we'd got one vote. Anyway he sure as hell impressed me that day."

Story's role in EMU development was very hands-on. Fred recalled, "After the source board and after the selection of Hamilton Standard, he remained the crew

3. Now known as Hamilton Sundstrand.
4. Garrett Air Research was purchased by Allied Signal and is now part of Honeywell.

representative to the preliminary design and then the design of the EMU, so that he was frequently at Hamilton. He was at all preliminary design and design reviews... Hamilton would present a design or a design concept and it would get constructively criticized, sometimes destructively criticized, but always by Story, constructively criticized – and always from the standpoint of making it more practical for the crew. Sometimes he drove both ourselves and the program managers at NASA to a concern level because what he was suggesting was going to be either way out of scope or way expensive. But Story would put money aside as to what something would cost and he just wanted the best darned EMU that could come off the concept or off the drawing or out of the hardware phase.

"Some of the NASA people would just be ultra negative – 'isn't this dumb' and stuff like that. Story was always from a positive standpoint and he was a guy you wanted to please because (a) he knew what he was talking about and (b) he hit the right note with the people who were conceiving and executing the hardware.

"Well we used to laugh in the contractor-land that success belongs to NASA and failure belongs to the contractor. All too frequently that was the case – but it wasn't with Story, however. That kind of set him apart.

"Certainly to the design of the EMU he was ultra-important. He was not only the only voice from the crew, but a very vocal voice from the crew – one that had the force of personality, the force of experience and the force of really caring behind it. You didn't ignore Story Musgrave. And you negotiated with the program management at NASA on things that Story really wanted and you tried to give Story what he wanted, and if you couldn't afford it you tried to come up with the right compromise.

"From a personal standpoint, from Hamilton Standard's standpoint, he was 'our' astronaut. He was the one that more people at Hamilton knew, had more influence on Hamilton, had more influence on the design, on a product that we designed twenty-five years ago. So much of that was influenced by Story. He was *the* user-important part of the design team and always constructive."

Jim McBarron, whom NASA put in charge of monitoring the ILC Dover part of the project, recalled Story's enthusiasm for the job. "He was eager, very disciplined and very thorough in his work. He was extremely conscientious with all the aspects of getting the suit and backpacks ready to fly - very particular with what he thought was the way things should be done, the configuration that was necessary to fly, and very logical in his approach to working out problems. I think he was important in terms of the amount of energy that he possessed which he applied to doing things that were necessary – an unlimited supply of energy and of intelligence – high intelligence as a general characteristic – and dedication to do what was right and what was safe as well. And he was outspoken about what he thought was correct."

Fred Greenwood who became EMU program manager for Hamilton Standard in

1979 felt Story was certainly qualified to have his input into the design. "We paid an awful lot of attention to his reactions to how the suit joints worked, the torques that it took to operate the suit, because when the suit is pressurized – if you can imagine a suit that's a balloon and you're trying to move around like the Michelin tire person – it's very hard to move, so the suit has to be designed with bearings which allow you to rotate your wrist and your arms and move your legs around. And someone like Story, who was a scientist and an observer and an MD, gave us very valuable feedback on what the problems might be, what could be improved, how the glove worked and so forth."

One of the first things the design team discovered was that Story had difficulty entering the hard upper torso. According to Joe McMann, "When he started as our designated crew representative to try and don the hard upper torso – the openings were sized for 'normal' people, which was one of our problems – he couldn't get it on. You have to put your hands in that position [arms stretched out, hands side by side with the palms facing upwards] and bring your elbows in pretty closely together. He could not do it... so we quickly made a design change, practically overnight, where we put in some gimbaled joints in that hard upper torso and then he could do that... in other words he could move that opening in the suit so he could get it on. Of course it didn't matter to a lot of people, it certainly didn't hurt donning, but it did make a tremendous design change to the suit. And it turned out if we hadn't panicked so much at the time, we could have probably made the openings in our previous hard upper torso such that he would have been able to don it and we wouldn't have had to go through all that. But we panicked. We wanted to make a dramatic design change to show people that we were really paying attention to the crew, so we made this change which we carried for years... It was a very delicate design and we finally got rid of it – and, of course, the test that allowed us to get rid of it was to have Story go don this torso without those gimbaled joints in it! And he was able to do it. So we were finally able to get rid of it after all those years!"

Fred Morris remembered how Story used to don the Hard Upper Torso. "He is physically in terrific shape, but his physiognomy was such that he entered and exited this hard torso shell... in kind of a corkscrew twisting motion, different than anybody else. I'd been in it a few times; Story, of course, has been in it a zillion times, and watched other astronauts or test subjects at Hamilton get into it. You get into it kind of straightforward. Well Story didn't – he couldn't quite fit it. His joints didn't work that way, so he really corkscrewed it. And that was just the 'Story Musgrave way' of entering into the hard upper torso."

Story's knowledge of entering the hard upper torso, together with his sense of compassion, enabled him to assist a young employee from Hamilton Standard who found himself in an embarrassing situation in front of a group from NASA.

Fred Morris recalled: "We were having a demonstration at Hamilton to a group of the NASA management including Story and we had a young test subject who was demonstrating entry and exit from the hard upper torso. Well he got into it OK, and then he was having a great deal of difficulty getting out of it. Here's our test subject and us showing off to NASA our thing and our guy can't get out of the hard upper torso! It is mounted to a rigid wall – that was one of the ways you entered it so you didn't have to carry the weight on you. It was screwed into the wall so you squatted down and you stood up through it – you stuck your arms through the arm [holes] and your head through the neck ring opening. And this kid – and I call him that 'cause he was in his early twenties – was having such a hard time. He's in front of a large crowd of people and he gets embarrassed and he starts to cry. And Story, good guy that he is, says – 'OK, everybody out of here.' So he cleared out the lab, so that it was just Story and this test subject, and Story talked him out of it. Story talked to him about how you do the 'Story cork screwing'. So about one minute later, they both emerge happy. I thought, what a neat thing. It would have been easy to just laugh at it or criticize the hell out of the fact that Hamilton couldn't come up with a test subject that didn't burst into tears when he tried to demonstrate this. Story just stepped in there and did the very compassionate and learned thing because Story knew how to get out of one of these things. So that really stuck with me."

The American spacesuit was designed to be as close-fitting as possible for added mobility. According to Fred Morris, "There were a couple of real primary rules: you made the suit just as mobile as possible and just as small as possible. Story was an exponent of that – make it really difficult to get into 'cause that's going to give me more mobility. The bigger the suit, the clumsier it was, so they [astronauts] were led by Story I think. The trade was always – I don't care how tough it is to enter and exit, as opposed to a Russian suit, for example, which is a breeze to get into and out of. But the American suit was one where ease of entry was never a criteria. … Compared to the Russian suit it's way more mobile.

"And the glove is the thing that's never good enough. I think over the twenty-five years there have been a massive number of permutations of glove design. And I'm sure if you ask the guys who are going outside [the Space Shuttle] or the Space Station, 'Is the glove good enough?' the answer is 'no', never going to be good enough. The joint within the suit which gave us the most problem, which was the most complicated, was the shoulder – it has so many ranges of motion. But the thing that got the criticism always was the glove, because finger tactility and mobility were so primary to an EVA mission."

Tom Sanzone of Hamilton Standard, as it was then known, described the spacesuit or EMU in these terms. "The EMU is not a large garment. Actually, it is a small spacecraft. When you're outside the spacecraft, all you have is the EMU and a tether; that's it. Virtually everything that a spacecraft has, the EMU has. You are out there traveling at 17,500 miles an hour with nothing but the EMU and a small tether hooking you to the Shuttle."

Story refers to the combination of astronaut and spacesuit as a whole new body with a different set of operating rules which need to be assimilated. "You move it in a different way... the suit does not have the same joints I have. I combined the suit joint with my real shoulder joint and it gave me a new arm. I have a new joint that moves in different ways and that's true of every joint you have...

"The critical thing – it is not just bulk; you have a new body... It becomes intuitive when you think, I have a new body, and it's not just a bulky spacesuit. Now you learn to work with it, now you learn to work the new body you've got and you develop all the reflexes and motions it takes to get the job done... So the way you learn that is to know that you're going to make errors, to know that you have a different arm...

"When you're first in the suit and you're getting used to the suit, you have to correct with the eye on the way to the target. It's that kind of thinking which makes the work go very well."

In a 1994 interview with Nina L. Diamond,[5] Story spoke of this new relationship. "The physiology you have in a suit is what the suit gives you – the pressure, the oxygen. It removes carbon dioxide, controls your temperature, everything. There's a lot of good anatomy in the relationship of your body to the suit: it has to work as an integrated organism. As soon as you learn that, you become more skilful in working with a space suit; you don't work against it anymore and you don't even look at it as a friend. When I go out in this suit, I am now a new organism that has to work in certain ways."

One of the names by which Story was known around NASA was Dr Details. Nowhere was this more evident that in the spacewalking arena. Fred Morris, recalled: "I had gone to Russia, and Hamilton Standard was the first contractor that really burst into Russia in life support and in spacesuits. We discovered our counterparts in Russia and we used that as an entrée into NASA headquarters... This was about the time [NASA Administrator] Dan Goldin was weighing whether to bring Russia into the Space Station in order to bolster its political future... Anyway, I had been the second American I think to get into the Russian spacesuit, pressurized up to 5 pounds per square inch. And I was, at that time, hung over, jetlagged, claustrophobic, my back hurt and a few other things, but I went through with it because I could fit in the suit. I had been through the life support company [in Russia] that made carbon dioxide reduction and oxygen equipment and urine reclination equipment and that kind of stuff, so after that, Hamilton got the rather extraordinary opportunity to make a pitch

5. Interview for *Omni Magazine*, by Nina L. Diamond, August 1994. Reprinted by permission of Omni Publications International Ltd.

to [NASA's] astronaut corp. And there were maybe seventy percent of them there. This was an hour or so pitch – and something contractors didn't do was go pitch to the astronauts! Well anyway, I make my pitch and Story starts asking me detailed questions. Well I don't know squat about them because I was so excited and so jetlagged. I was very embarrassed that I didn't have any good answers to the very appropriate questions Story was asking. And after about three questions he stopped because he wasn't going to embarrass me any more. But he's a detail guy and a guy with a great memory."

It is only fair to note that Fred Morris may have been caught shorthanded on the technical details at that meeting with the astronauts, but he is widely regarded by those in the industry as a brilliant man. He went on to become president of Hamilton Space Systems International and has had a good working relationship with Story over the years, based on a great deal of mutual respect.

*

A necessary part of EMU design and development was the testing of the spacesuits in a range of simulated environments. The testing was strenuous and, at times, dangerous, but was critical in order to evaluate the suit's capabilities as they would be in space. Story became one of the test subjects who spent countless hours in the new pressurized suit. Data was collected and analyzed so that appropriate measurements could be taken and, if necessary, changes incorporated into the suit design.

Joe McMann worked closely with Story during that time. "I joined NASA in 1961 with the Space Task Group up at Langley.[6] That was before anybody knew they were going to Houston. And I was fortunate enough to be down at Kennedy – it was Cape Canaveral then – when John Glenn lifted off. I got involved with EVA with Ed White's mission[7] and helped develop the hardware and all that, so I was kind of on EVA from the start.

"I became a test subject and in that you start to see something which I call the test subject mentality, which is an extremely competitive way of going about your job and it sometimes takes you past the bounds of reason, or where an 'ordinary' person would go. The test subject, because of the way he is, or he realizes he's in a test or whatever, he goes maybe beyond that. Now the astronauts who came after the First Seven[8] – there was not so much of that anymore. You didn't see that much, but then there are always a few that have that characteristic and Story was one of those. Story is the over-achiever's overachiever. I mean he's driven. All of us are driven to some

6. NASA's Langley Research Center is in Hampton, Virginia.
7. Gemini 4 in June 1965.
8. The Mercury Astronauts.

extent. If you could take your own impulses, your own drive and multiply that by several factors, then you start to see how Story approaches life!"

Story fondly recalled working with Joe in the suit testing days. "Joe got a lot of suit time too; he liked to work out on the suit. I remember his voice – 'Thanks for the BTUs!'[9] – that's the amount of work you can pump into the suit. It's how much heat, how much work you'll do in a suit – like a plow horse! That's not nice at all when a suit is barely supporting what you're trying to put into it – Joe knows!"

Joe recalled the competitiveness of some of the tests in which he and Story participated. "A guy named Stan Fink and two others by the names of Larry Kuznetz and D. Cook – they wanted to study the environmental effects, and mostly heat, upon your performance and how your body regulated its sweat production and all that versus the environment.[10] So Story, myself, Stan the author and a guy called Paul Chaput all were test subjects in that. Stan Fink – he was by far in the best condition of any of us and also the youngest, I think. Story was the oldest, and I'd been a runner since 1967, so I'd been running for over 10 years when we did this and Story's performance was way better than mine. Even then he was one of those people who had to be just a little bit better!

"Later on, Story set up an experimental program. In the morning you would take your core temperature [rectally], take your pulse rate, your weight and then go into work. Around noon – this was in the Houston summer! – we'd go outside, take our core temperature and our weight before we ran, then run about six miles. Immediately after you stopped running you'd take your core temperature again. Now when you stop running, you're outside! You're going to take your core temperature in full view of everyone, so you had to be pretty cool and carry a little thermometer and sort of nonchalantly insert it and, you know, just maintain a very blasé demeanor, read your core temperature and get your pulse rate and all that. We did this for a year and Story ended up writing a paper on it. That was one of the little crazy things that he had us doing!"

Joe referred to the Apollo program to illustrate the sometimes excessive nature of the test subject environment. "In the Apollo days, they decided they were going to try and timeline every activity that the crew would do on a mission to the moon. They would have to do things like waste management, changing their carbon dioxide removable canisters – all these tasks. So they had a bunch of test subjects up there [in the zero-gravity training aircraft][11] who were going to try and timeline this for the crew. Well these test subjects had two motivations to really do these things well. First

9. British Thermal Units (BTUs)
10. Fink, Kuznetz and Cook wrote a paper titled: *A Study of the Effects of the Environment Upon Thermoregulation in the Long-Distance Runner.*
11. In the NASA zero-gravity training aircraft, a modified KC-135 Stratotanker.

of all, you only had thirty seconds of zero-gravity at a time and you wanted to get as much of the task as you could done in thirty seconds. Then there was the competitive aspect of it – you might be doing this task one day and somebody else might pick it up the next day, so you wanted to make it as hard for that other person to get it as possible. So what happened – they got their timeline all right – but the test subjects got so good at it that no crew member could ever do it; they could never keep up with the test subjects! And they had to throw the timeline out! What they had hoped was not to have to do a lot of training with the crew. What they found out was that they had to do *a lot* of training with the crew – the crew never got as good as the test subjects because they couldn't spend that much time on it. The test subjects – they were just totally focused on just that one thing. So we learned a hard lesson – you've got to let the crew do what the crew's going to do."

Much of the spacesuit testing took place in special environmental chambers. Tom Sanzone explained, "We have several vacuum chambers at NASA, in large part because the heat exchanger in the life support system of the spacesuit operates only in a vacuum, as it's designed to operate in space. One of the things we do for astronaut training – and we train the people that are doing spacewalks in multiple venues – is to put the astronaut in an EMU and in a vacuum chamber to check-out the life support system thoroughly."

Joe recalled one test he did that almost became a nightmare. "I was in a test one time – it was a hot test in chamber B. I had a thermally protective over-glove and I dropped it. What do you do? You reach down and pick it up right? Well, not quite because you're hung from a suspension system because of the weight of the backpack and the suit; it doesn't allow you to bend over far enough to reach down and pick up something off the floor. So there I was in this chamber with everybody watching, data being gathered and I can feel my hand heating up. I know pretty soon I'm not going to be able to stand it. So I had a little shepherd's crook and I was able to hook that glove and bring it up and get it on my hand just before the time I was going to have to abort the run. But you know, you don't want to give up; you don't want to be the one who aborts the run. And sometimes it takes you past, I think, what a reasonable person would do."

It can be a fine line between well-being and injury during a test. Joe recalled Story's frostbite accident while training for the Hubble Repair Mission. "We had a test in Chamber B – in which you can run a hot mission, like the sun is beating down on the payload bay, and you can run cold missions where it's like the extreme cold of space. And Story was in there and he was testing some tools out, some special wrenches, in a cold environment. We typically have a lot of trouble with cold environments because lubricants get real stiff. Sometimes the tolerance changes [on metals] are not friendly because one type of metal will contract at one rate, another metal interfacing with it will chill down at a different rate and the lubricant may freeze up. We never seem to know before we go in exactly what kind of results we're going to get, so we always have to put these things through a cold test. And Story was the tester. Again, part of it was training, part of it was that he was really testing out these tools. Well these tools had been sitting in there while they brought the [temperature in the] chamber down, so the tools were really cold. So as Story was testing these tools, he had problems with them. His hands started getting cold and he didn't quit; he kept going and going and going… He wouldn't quit though. He had made remarks about the cold. People were telling him – 'Story, warm your hands up to keep on going' – and he said, 'No, I can keep on going'. And, you know, the person is the best judge, but after you lose feeling then you don't know what's happened – blood flow stops and, of course, the cold is merciless… He got severe frostbite, lost a lot of skin and a lot of people feared there would be permanent damage… It certainly sounded a wake up call to us. We needed a suit with glove heaters, which we subsequently put in.

"Story always had a lot of respect from everybody. But again, we also marveled sometimes that he would go to the lengths that he did, for example, what he did to injure himself. In fact, it made us all wonder a little bit – has he gone just too far?"

According to Story, who was ignorant of the frostbite, he kept going with the vacuum chamber test because, mindful of the already heavy training timetable, he wanted to complete the test to see how the tools would perform in that environment, hoping that they wouldn't need to be redesigned. As a result of the accident, the crew of STS-61 would angle the Space Shuttle's cargo bay into the sunlight to provide warmth during the repair work, never again subjecting them to such extreme cold.

Despite everybody's concerns for his well-being, Story went right on with training the very week after the accident. According to Tom Sanzone, "It would be impossible to hold Story down in any case. Nothing stops him from anything!"

\*

Story had great regard for Wernher von Braun, the visionary German rocket scientist who was instrumental in the early days of the American space program and eventually became director of NASA's Marshall Space Flight Center in Huntsville, Alabama. It was von Braun's vision to use water as a training environment for spacewalking.

According to Story, "He knew what we needed, what it takes to train for spacewalks. He knew we were going to have to go into the water – that's three-dimensional – and he built this huge thing[12] without justification – just his dream that that's what it was going to take. He just did it. He just flat did the darn thing and so he put us decades ahead with his imagination. And he was probably the first one in it too. He got in a spacesuit and went in it.

12. The Neutral Buoyancy Simulator (NBS).

"It's very surprising that it didn't happen sooner, but my point was that imagination put it in place, not the requirement. You can develop a requirement for something or you can be pro-active and get it ahead of time through your imagination, through your imagination seeing what that'll do. You're much more futuristic if you use your imagination, if you get there before it becomes a requirement. You do it because it's a nice analog. You do it because it's similar. You do it because it allows you three-dimensional freedom – not because it's a requirement. You do it because it's the nearest thing you have to space because scuba diving or swimming in water, for humans, is the nearest thing you can do to get that freedom. And if you go to an aquarium and you watch a seal in the water, that's a three dimensional being. So it's that kind of leap from the water to space and you see that connection. The people who would have set the requirement didn't do it. They hadn't seen the requirement yet, it hadn't come along yet, but that's a lesson as well 'cause that's the edge that I want, that's the edge that I *always* want. Part of that edge is working not on requirements which are kind of retro-active, but it's walking that edge as a futuristic kind of do-it-for-the-sake-of-doing-it."

Water became the primary training environment for spacewalkers. Together with a team of highly skilled divers, astronauts would train for hours at a time, refining their operating techniques with full-scale models of the Space Shuttle's payload bay and airlock. For more specific missions, models were made of various hardware that the astronauts would be working with in space, such as the Hubble Space Telescope and, more recently, modules of the International Space Station.

Von Braun's vision for a training pool was realized in 1968 with the completion of the Neutral Buoyancy Simulator at the Marshall Space Flight Center in Huntsville Alabama. The pool was 75 feet wide by 40 feet deep and could hold 1.3 million gallons of water. Used for nearly twenty years until construction of the larger Neutral Buoyancy Laboratory in Houston, von Braun's pool was the main weightless training venue for the first Hubble Repair Mission.

Story recalled, "We had a small swimming pool in what's called Building 5 – that's our primary simulator building, mostly electronic simulators, the little link trainers and link simulators. So you're talking about 12 feet by 12 feet by maybe 8 feet deep – it was an absolute minimum kind of thing. That was the first one that we started into in the Gemini program. Gemini spacewalks did not go at all well 'cause we really didn't train or choreograph, we just sort of went and did them. Buzz Aldrin was somewhat instrumental in getting water to be part of the curriculum and in showing the relationship between your skills in the water and skills on a spacewalk.

"From there we went to Building 268, the building right next to the gymnasium, and that had an above-the-ground metal tank kind of thing. We used that at first, not for spacewalking training, but for survival training in the capsules. So for the Apollo program, in which I trained for Skylab, instead of going out into Galveston Bay, it was much more convenient to do all the contingencies and emergencies in that tank. But then, after Apollo and after Skylab, we used that tank as our development facility to move onto the Shuttle program.

"Marshall [Space Flight Center], of course, continued. All of the Skylab training was at Marshall, all of it. Great big pool, big Skylab [mockup]; all of it there.

"The WETF was the next, which is the Weightless Environment Training Facility. I worked with the people who were developing that thing because I was the spacewalker point of contact in the astronaut office from '71 onwards. And that was an old centrifuge building; that was where the fifty-foot centrifuge was. But after Apollo, we decided that we didn't need the centrifuge anymore, that we didn't need that form of training, so we did away with the centrifuge 'cause it was very difficult to get congressional approval for another large water tank when the water tank existed at Huntsville.

"So we fought for years to get one, but if you're going to train astronauts, then to fly them to Huntsville was rough and, of course, you worry about the bends coming home. When you come out of the water tank in Huntsville, you can't go to altitude or you're gonna get the bends. You're full of nitrogen from being at high pressure under water. You have logistical problems like that. And so we'd fly at lower altitudes; we'd have to take care of that and worry about that. And if you're gonna train astronauts, you might as well have the pool where the astronauts are. And, of course, the congress had to give approval. We could not build a new building and so you had to tell them that we're gonna put it in an existing facility and there aren't many buildings you can gut to make a huge swimming pool, but the centrifuge was the one; that's how come it ended up there. We put a swimming pool in there [around the mid-1970s] that would accommodate a Space Shuttle cargo bay fifteen feet across and 60 feet long. I was testing different Shuttle designs in that tank. I did some testing in Building 268 but I was testing all the designs for the cargo bay and for the airlock in that tank."

*

Tom Jones, who joined the NASA astronaut corps in 1991, remembered how Story introduced the art of spacewalking to new astronauts. "We had a class sometime in our first year to get introduced to spacewalking and EVA and he was the guy chosen to give that lecture. And rather than just give a slide presentation or something, he didn't show any films or slides, he just sort of perched on the edge of the table, the conference table, sort of sat on the corner of the table and, you know, casually perched himself there and just started talking. And he had this very intense way of looking at everybody in the room and explaining the choreography and the ballet of spacewalking, finesse, how much of a finesse activity it is – [not] a bull in a china shop affair. He talked about development of the spacesuit and how he was involved with that, the battles he had fought trying to get various design features incorporated into it and then talked about what it's like to walk in the Shuttle bay. And one of the memorable things he said – which came back to be very useful for me later – was if you are working too hard at something during a spacewalk, if you find yourself laboring and huffing and puffing, he said you're doing it wrong – there's another way to do it that's more efficient and you're choosing the wrong way. So he says just stop and think and get your breath back and do it with less force, less exertion, find a better body position. And so that was a very useful philosophy and technique to adopt. That was always my measure of whether I was doing something right, either underwater or out in space – am I getting this done with skill and dexterity or am I charging through it by just doing it with brute force and over-controlling? So that was always what was in the back of my mind."

Spacewalker Scott Parazynski, who has been involved with the building of the International Space Station recalled, "I had my very first suited run [in the training pool] with Story and just learned an incredible amount because he's such a detail-oriented person, and also a deep-thinking philosopher. He can break down the mechanics of all the things that we do and describe them in lay terms and also very technical terms that really makes for a fantastic mentor."

According to Tom Sanzone, "One of the differences between the experienced spacewalkers and those who are inexperienced tends to be that the veteran spacewalkers are very patient and let the EVA come to them. The less experienced, particularly those who have never done an EVA before, initially tend to 'fight' the suit, but they can't win. So when Story's talking about the ballet, I think it's indicative that the more calmly an astronaut approaches the job, the more efficient he's going to be."

It was Story who introduced the concept of 'dance' to NASA and the terms 'ballet' and 'choreography'. He says rather than using an engineering approach to spacewalking, he used an artist's approach. "Craftsmanship is what it is. You're out there as an artist. You're out there as a ballerina… The craftsmanship and the athleticism – it's the heart of the work and it's getting the work done with perfection the same way an athlete would, but it all starts with athletics and the training process… The idea of thinking of it as a dance, as an athletic event in which you come up with how you are going to get that job done – you repetitively practice it until it's perfected … Only on the last reiteration did I practice the final solution, so you're jumping over the high bar. You continue to do the high bar and you perfect what method, what style is going to get you over the highest level on the high bar. So you keep experimenting, you keep jumping and you perfect how you're going to get the job done. And you've got the date of the 'Olympics' coming up. The number of repetitions, the number of times you can get at this is starting to narrow, so you're converging on a solution. But what you have to do is finally arrive at a very narrow definition of how you're going to get over the bar and then you practice that enough so you're in that group. In the Hubble practice it wasn't until the last time I would do something that I'd finally arrived at the final solution… it was the last one or two, when I only had one more repetition to do."

According to Jim Thornton of the EVA office, Story was really unique in communicating the whole world of spacewalking. "He was really the first one to think of EVA as kind of an art form, the first one to really think about EVA as a ballet. It's a choreography, it's a collection of tasks which is more of an art than a science. And he was the first to visualize this and lay out this ballet that he likes to refer to it as, and the choreography of moving from one task to the next."

Tom Akers who, with Kathryn Thornton, shared alternate spacewalks with Story and Jeff Hoffman during STS-61, recalled the reason for the carefully planned choreography of spacewalking. "For it to go smooth and look smooth to anybody else, it took a lot of practice and basically that's why we use the term choreography. You could just go out and get the job done if you had all the time in the world, but when you only have six and a half hours to go and try to get a job done, you don't want any wasted motion. That's what we did in the pool and what they still do down at NASA training is to look for every efficiency. You don't want anybody standing idle, doing nothing if there's something to do. We had it choreographed so that if we knew somebody wasn't doing something for ten minutes, they could go put a tool up or get another one we might need thirty minutes from now. Unless you have surprises, it goes like that. It looked smooth and we didn't have any significant surprises."

Jim Thornton spoke of the importance of the success of the spacewalks on STS-61. "Very early in the shuttle program, the mindset of most of the managers in the program at the time was that EVA was to be avoided if at all possible. People did not see the value in it being a very important resource that you could draw upon. And so people really didn't understand it, but they knew that it was extremely risky. With one failure, you could pretty much expose yourself to certain death. So I think that frightened a lot of people that didn't understand it. And I think looking back over time, [the spacewalks on STS-61] were very much a part of our success in building the International Space Station, which is predicated on a number of successful EVAs, one after another. I think over time, people have grown to understand it better; they understand the value of sending human beings out and letting them accomplish tasks that either would be so expensive to do robotically or the tasks themselves might be so challenging that robots could not accomplish them. So over time, we certainly have evolved. Back in the early stages of the program, it was not well understood and people were really fearful of it."

Story played a big part in changing people's attitudes towards EVA, according to Jim McBarron. "I mean spacewalking is a dangerous activity, but Story was able to help convince the higher management system that it was not as risky as it was made out to be if it was done properly. I mean there were so many things which could have gone wrong in that mission in terms of the complexity of the job to be done. That was an example of his attention to detail and his persistence, demonstrating the capabilities to do a difficult job in a difficult environment. He spent hours and hours in a suit; his dedication to training is phenomenal."

Ron Sheffield, who was test director for STS-61, was impressed by Story and the rest of the crew. He recalled, "They would come down to do Neutral Buoyancy Simulations[13] and the night before they got ready to go into the simulator, the four of them would be sitting outside in the hot tub, going over the procedures for the next day. That was really unique. It gave them an opportunity to refine the procedures. I had written the original procedures, but as they got into the program, got assigned to be on the mission, they refined the procedures for themselves.

"We tried to get the crew to visit as many places as possible so that they could see the actual flight hardware in its development and final form; all of the replacement hardware. The thing that I found, sitting and watching Story in the hot tub and these other places was, he actually had it choreographed like a ballet. He knew exactly what everybody was going to be doing and when they were going to do it. I think that was one of the things that was very important.

"His work ethic was very, very strong; his physical conditioning was very, very strong. We used to go to the gym together – there was a club at Huntsville and he would get on the treadmill and stay on there for hours. The whole crew was there, but he led the way. We would run in the NBS, then go to the gym, we'd all go eat together, then we would come back and sit in the hot tub and review and they would go over the procedures for the next day. And that, to me, I always said to the rest of the crews, this is how you get to be real good."

For Story, it was part of the quest for perfection. He said, "I ran marathons and I ran races and did the absolute best that I could and so that's the challenge where you're getting all you can from the machine – you and the machine."

Tom Sanzone spoke of the intensity of the work on STS-61. "Story and Jeff Hoffman did three spacewalks in five days – over twenty-two hours of spacewalking. And the intensity was palpable. We have a device called a Glove Box, sort of like a big fiberglass box with seals that allow us to insert two gloves. Then we evacuate some of the air from inside the box so that the pressure is 4.3 pounds per square inch lower inside the box than outside it. Basically what it does is makes the glove pressure 4.3 pounds per square inch higher than the environment that you're operating in. When

13. In the Neutral Buoyancy Simulators (NBS) at the Marshall Space Flight Center, Alabama.

we're doing a spacewalk, the spacesuit operates at that same differential pressure. The Glove Box enables us, from a glove perspective, to simulate being in a pressurized spacesuit. I have yet to bring anyone to that Glove Box, including the president of our company, who didn't put his hand in there and exclaim, "Wow!" We have tools, connectors, tether hooks etc. And when we instruct people to operate them, they get a phenomenal appreciation for how difficult it is to use those gloves during an EVA."

As part of the training process, Story came up with the idea of using the Glove Box as a fitness device to do EVA exercises at different pressures.

For Story and his contemporaries, pain was often a part of working in the spacesuits. According to Joe McMann, "I remember going into a test run one time – it was going to be a seven hour run on a treadmill – walking on a treadmill for seven hours in a suit, and you know these suits for test subjects were not a perfect fit, so you did a fit check first, and you could feel places maybe where it was going to start rubbing, like on the top of your foot, or on the back of your leg, back of your knee, so you put some moleskin on there. So in this run you'd start going through the chamber, walking on the treadmill, and maybe an hour into a seven hour run you'd realize you'd missed a place! It's going to start rubbing, so every step is painful, and you've got six hours to go… when you get through there's blood inside the suit. You've worn a hole clear through your skin and you're bloody. Then comes taking off the moleskin. Sometimes you take more skin off when you pull off the moleskin than if you'd have left it on. But I mean it's painful."

Scott Parazynski spoke of improvements in the spacesuit over time, in particular the gloves. "I don't think [the pain is] as common anymore. I think the gloves are of better pedigree now – we've learned a lot about glove technology so we'd be very concerned if someone had those kind of problems right now with our current technology. It was always sort of tongue in cheek when Story would talk about the pain, so we didn't really dwell on it… I remember one of my favorite quotes from Story was something to the effect – 'EVA is a wonderful thing, so is childbirth, but they're both very painful!'"

*

Mission Specialists Joseph P. Allen and William B. Lenoir were selected to perform the first EVA to test the new spacesuit during STS-5. If Story was disappointed in not being selected to test the spacesuits, it wasn't something he spoke about publicly.

There was certainly an element of surprise that Story had not been chosen. According to Tom Sanzone, now General Manager of Hamilton Sundstrand in Houston, "Story had worked on EMU development with us for such a long time, we all assumed that he was going to do the first EVA. We didn't even talk about it – it was just commonly assumed that he was going to get the flight."

Tom has spent his entire career with the company and worked with Story from the beginning of its association with the Space Shuttle spacesuit. He said, "We were really surprised. Nobody knew the suit like Story did and it just seemed somewhat obvious to us that he would get to fly it. It was like practicing with any kind of an athlete for five years for a particular game, then, when it comes time to play the game, the coach says, 'Well, you're not playing.'"

As fate would have it, however, the scheduled spacewalk on STS-5 had to be cancelled due to a failure in each of the suits. It was an embarrassing and distressing situation for both NASA and the companies which had developed the spacesuits – Hamilton Standard and team member ILC Dover.[14]

Fred Morris recalled: "It was gloomsville at Hamilton Standard, just awful. We had worked hard to get what we thought was a perfect product and when it got into its first use, neither of them were suited to go outside. We figured there was probably only one happy person in the universe – and that was the good Doctor Musgrave, 'cause he was flying STS-6!"

According to Tom Sanzone, "It was probably the low point of my career, I can tell you. But we were still in the learning stage. We had a fan on one suit that had a sensor that regulated the speed and the sensor failed, so the fan wouldn't operate and we couldn't get ventilation. On the other suit, our backup oxygen system had a regulator where the pressure had shifted lower and we didn't understand why, so we had to cancel the EVA. I'm sure Story was very disappointed too because he had been involved with all the development. We [Hamilton Standard] took a lot of heat, I mean a phenomenal amount of heat, from the press, and personally. NASA's a very big team effort, so we felt as if we had let the team down. We worked intensely to recover and even now, years later, I can't believe with the severity of the problems we had, that we were able to get everything fixed and working by the very next flight. To be honest, I don't think we could do that today."

Fred Greenwood, who headed up the EMU program at Hamilton Standard at the time of the first spacewalk, remembered a difficult telephone conversation as the first Space Shuttle EVA was aborted. He was in Mission Control, Houston, at the time. "The guy in charge of the NASA space program was a General Abrahamson and I remember when STS-5 didn't work – it was around 4 o'clock in the morning – I found myself speaking to General Abrahamson and trying to explain to him what was going wrong, which was very difficult to do 'cause these guys were in orbit and I was on the ground and I really didn't know much more than anybody else did. But I had to promise him that we'd get it fixed post haste and we did."

On a more personal note, Tom Sanzone recalled speaking to Story before STS-6

14. ILC Dover manufactured the soft goods for the spacesuits in Delaware.

about the sudden twist of fate and the opportunity he was going to have to test the suits after all. "I said something to Story like, 'We didn't think you were going to get to do the first EVA but you are,' and he made the comment, 'The tide goes out and the tide comes in. You have to roll with the punches and things will work out!' I don't know how many times he's used that expression but my sense was that it's his philosophy of life – it wasn't related just to that event."

Joe McMann recalled Story's calmness. "He was so cool. He was always cool under pressure. He did our first successful EVA with the suit and his pulse rate was so low, his oxygen consumption was low. Story was such an overachiever – the amount of training, the physical conditioning he put himself through. He'd be all the time strengthening his hands, walking around squeezing a ball just to strengthen his hands, just to give him that extra edge in the glove, 'cause no matter how good the glove is, you're always working against it. He always bought himself that extra edge. I guess he's just kind of the peak – he just takes himself that extra measure. Sometimes maybe it's too much, but he always goes a little bit farther and I think part of it is that competitiveness thing. If somebody else trained as hard as he was training, I think he would train harder, just so he'd be a little bit better."

Some people thought that during that first EVA on STS-6, Story virtually stole the show. Tom Sanzone stated, "Story was so much the star of the team that he tended to overshadow Don. I don't think he did it intentionally. I consider Don more reserved, especially compared to Story and his level of intensity; plus, we had worked with Story in developing the suit, so he was sort of 'our guy'".

Joe McMann remembered: "Story was in tune with the suit, in tune with EVA. It just seemed to be a perfect match."

Story and Don had a number of tasks to perform. According to Fred Greenwood: "The main thing that they wanted to do was to check out how the EMU worked in space for the first time – that was the main part of the mission and so they floated around the payload bay and they went to the forward bulkhead. …One of the things they did was to try manually to move the Space Shuttle doors just to verify that the winch would work – that if an emergency came up where the electrical operators on the doors weren't working properly, they could do this manually."

The EVA was a complete success – much to the satisfaction of both NASA and the spacesuit developers and manufacturers. The crew of STS-6 returned to a hero's welcome and a new-found degree of fame. Numerous articles appeared in newspapers and magazines around the world celebrating the first American spacewalk in nine years.

On 2 June 1983, Story paid a visit to Windsor Locks, the headquarters of Hamilton Standard, to thank employees for their part in the success of the mission. His visit was recorded in the company's monthly newsletter: *The Hamilton Standard*. The headline read: "Astronaut Musgrave: First in space with Hamilton suit and first in hearts of workers." The article went on to say, "He visited Hamilton to thank the employees for 'the outstanding contributions they have made to the nation's space program.' Story toured our factory and our laboratories and our office areas. At an award ceremony during this visit, he presented a Silver Snoopy pin and a letter from the astronauts to 55 employees... Musgrave was greeted as the hero he is but also as an old friend."

Story speaks very highly of all the people who played a role in the development of the Space Shuttle spacesuit. "They were space people; they were good people; they had a passion for what they did. And they obviously did an incredible job. I was like a bull terrier; I just wouldn't give up in terms of when I believed in some design; I wouldn't let it be compromised. But we worked fantastically well together; I certainly respected them, had great relationships with them. They were real professionals, they were space people, they have the passion that people have *because* they're space flight. And that's true very often across the board. You get much more out of people 'cause their business is space, as opposed to some other business. But the other thing you had there was the art: the engineering is far more difficult; it's hard to engineer rubber and cloth. It's very easy to engineer a steel which has certain characteristics 'cause you know exactly what the steel is going to do – the stresses and the strains – and it's very easy to engineer that. It's hard to engineer cloth and rubber in terms of repetitive wear and tear, in terms of shelf life and all those kinds of things. It's a lot more difficult to engineer soft goods and to engineer the human factors. The human factor, of course, is key really to a good mobile spacesuit with a good range of motion – something you can go out and work in. So the human factor is very different – human factors and soft goods; it's just more difficult to engineer than hard goods.

"I had a good time, but obviously it's a lot of travel to Hartford. Hartford in the winter time – the flying was incredibly demanding. You fly right through New York City airspace. And going through New York City airspace in the middle of winter, alone, in an airplane [T-38] without autopilot and without a flight director, you've got your hands full. So I would go down and work the suit part down in Delaware – all of the suit components were made by ILC in Dover although Hamilton Standard had the entire contract – and I would go between Delaware and then up to Connecticut. I'd finish my work at the end of the day and take off to go through New York City airspace and land at Hartford for the next day. That was just hugely demanding."

Story formed some great relationships with the people at Hamilton Standard. Fred Morris remembered having dinner with Story shortly after STS-6. "I said, 'Story with all the years you've waited from the 60s to the early 80s' [before his first space flight], what would make you really happy in your career?' And he said, 'One more flight'. And I was always just pleased as heck that he got five more flights."

Story and Don Peterson were honored in another way – almost two decades after that first Space Shuttle spacewalk. Tom Sanzone explained that the first time the blue and yellow EVA patch was worn was during Story's and Don's spacewalk. "It's based on DaVinci's Dimensions of Man. As with most NASA patches, it contains some symbols, key of which were three stars. One represented the first US EVA by Ed White during the Gemini program, the second the first Lunar EVA by Neil Armstrong and Buzz Aldrin during the Apollo program, and the third the saving of Skylab by an EVA done by Pete Conrad and Joe Kerwin. Recently, the patch was modified for the first time and two stars were added. They represent the first Space Shuttle program EVA by Story Musgrave and Don Peterson, and the first Space Station-based EVA from the airlock by Jim Reilly and Mike Gernhardt."

*

According to Fred Morris: "At the time of the Hubble mission,[15] I was the president of Hamilton Space Systems International, which was horribly, desperately vested in the future of the Space Station, and deciding if there wasn't a Space Station, then there wasn't an awful lot of reason for Shuttle, and that all of our business which was connected with life support and spacesuits, people in space – it was just in contention, it could have been cancelled – it came within one vote in the House of Representatives, the Space Station, of being cancelled. So there was this immense political importance of pulling off a successful Hubble repair and the media was all over that, that this was NASA's test as to whether people deserved to be long-term in space and go out and do useful tasks in space. And then it was so marvelously successful. I think there were two things that really reconfirmed the idea of a space station. One was bringing Russia into the program … and the other was the success of the Hubble repair."

Joe McMann spoke of the seemingly endless committees that were formed to monitor the preparations for the crucial mission. "I'll tell you one thing which stands out in my mind – committees! There were eighteen committees; everybody had a committee looking at some aspect of it. Then there was a nineteenth committee; their mission was to oversee the activities of the other eighteen committees! It was almost ludicrous. We were doing nothing but making presentations to these panels, who then had to generate reports, and first they had to have actions coming out of reports or else why were they a committee if they didn't come up with any action? So everybody had their own agenda. If you're put on a blue ribbon committee, you gotta put your fingerprints on it, otherwise why did they put you on the committee? So there was a lot of feeling that all we were doing was making pitches for committees and not getting anything meaningful done…. Even though I criticize it, I don't know where I could really say we could have backed off. That's always the danger – people say

15. STS-61

you're overkilling, doing too much testing – OK, tell me where I can back off? Well, you really don't know until you've backed off too far."

Tom Sanzone recalled the intensity of the training for STS-61. "Of all the things those guys did on that Hubble Mission, I was most impressed that they were working with tiny screws and other small items. To this day, I am still amazed at their skill with those gloves because I've worn those gloves. We're constantly improving them and still have a way to go, but they're much better now than when Story was performing his mission.

"It seemed that from the day Story was assigned [to STS-61], he began to carry rubber balls. We'd be in a meeting with him and he'd be squeezing these balls, constantly making his hands as strong as possible. That's where the intensity comes in. Ultimately, they complete the mission and it appears easy to the outside world. The connotation of an expert is someone who makes something difficult look easy, and I think that's the epitome of Story. That's how he approached it.

"The mission had intensely physical and mental demands. Story and Jeff Hoffman were out there for twenty-two hours, effectively doing surgery. Now that we've gone to Hubble four times, we remember it as not that difficult. I have a saying I've used at work, particularly with younger people, that the road that got you to where you are, when you look back, looks like a superhighway free of challenges. I'm here, and I got here so it couldn't have been that hard. But when you look ahead, the road is full of ruts and hills and rocks, and you've got to get around all these obstacles. That's what Story and Jeff Hoffman and the other two spacewalkers were facing."

Story was the Payload Commander for STS-61 and, as such, carried the greatest responsibility for the spacewalks. It was his role to co-ordinate the development of the spacewalking procedures which were to be used to repair the telescope and to drive the choreography. Story does, however, distance himself from the role of leader, which the press has so often given him. He said, "There was never a leader to fix the Hubble Space Telescope. There was never a director of that mission, there was not a manager, there was not a leader – everyone did it. You cannot single out who did that. We function like an organism and we work by function. Whoever has the best ideas and whoever can push it further -- that person becomes the leader. You turn to that person because they have the best ideas and because they're the most effective. They make things happen, so you give them the lead."

Against tradition, Story also designated himself as EVA II, again, to take the focus off himself as the leader.

*

Story was innovative in his approach to many things in the EVA world. One of those things was the handling of large objects in zero gravity. Jim Thornton recalled, "Story's philosophy and one of our buzz words for that mission – he frequently talked about using *fingertips* – just delicately removing an instrument out of the telescope and using fingertip pressure, just fingertips, to reinstall the new box in the cavity in the telescope. It literally is fingertip pressure and forces – you can make incredibly large masses move with very small forces in zero gravity. He had this visualization and this concept which proved to be right."

Aside from technique, it was Story's passion for the job which inspired others. According to Jim, "Story is, and always has been a very passionate person. That's what makes him so unique and enjoyable to work with and be around. You can tell that the passion runs bright and burns very big in his heart and soul, and that's what makes Story the unique person that he is."

Scott Parazynski spoke of Story in similar terms. "My first job [at NASA] was to help support Story and his crew and a few other crews that were also preparing for an EVA at the time. I followed that mission very closely – in fact I was in Mission Control when Story and Jeff were at the top of the telescope putting on the magnetometer covers, just watching in awe at all that unfold… There are lots of times when I just appreciated Story's real joy and excitement for life – for example, his descriptions of the freedom of motion during a spacewalk. I think he was most animated when talking about EVA, at least in my conversations with him."

Right before STS-61, Story described how he had prepared for the entire flight. Scott remembered, "You could just see how thrilled he was to be a part of this very exciting and challenging mission."

According to friend and astronaut John Blaha, "Story took spacewalking very seriously – of course, most astronauts that were involved with that did as well – but for someone of his age, he was in incredible physical shape, worked out significantly, especially with his hands, for many, many years and it paid off."

Joe McMann recalled Story's manner. "My impressions of him are just of the consummate professional. Just very cool, structured, wants to have everything planned out, and yet willing, like on the Hubble Mission, when the situation called for it, ready to try something different."

About Story's gritty determination during the training phase, Joe said, "He probably overdid it. He probably could have backed off a lot and still been as good, but that's just not the type of person he is. He'll never stop when people say 'stop'. He'll stop when he says 'stop'… You don't have to do all that to get by, but you do have to do it if you're Story Musgrave – so he satisfies his inner demon, whatever it is."

Scott Parazynski paid tribute to Story's experience and his willingness to assist new spacewalkers. "He spent a great deal of what I consider precious time, invaluable time, thinking in detail about the various EVA tasks. My first EVA was on a Shuttle-MIR docking flight, STS-86. Story was still in the office at the time and I very excitedly conferred with him on this and described my entire timeline of things that we would be doing. And then we spent a great deal of time going through basically tether hook by tether hook, hand over hand, the way I should really think about performing that EVA – how to strive for perfection, how to think about all of the things that possibly could go wrong and then being prepared to handle them. And that's the kind of approach that he always took and that's the kind of approach that I now take when I prepare for my EVA flights.

"EVA is an athletic event. In fact, the way I approach an EVA mission is treating it as if it was a major national athletic competition or even the Olympics. And the amount of previsualization that you have to go through – we practice this dozens of times in the pool before we go execute it, but even before you get in the pool, you previsualize exactly what you're going to be doing, thinking about how you're going to translate, how you're going to orient – how you're going to pirouette, if you will, to avoid hitting radiators and other sensitive structures. And that's the kind of mindset that I picked up from Story – not just thinking about your body's envelope going through space, but the whole volume of your spacesuit system and your backpack, your helmet, your lights, your boots that extend your body much beyond your regular normal physical size, then all the tools that you're dangling off of you. You have to keep all that in mind and also try and make it graceful and not damage any hardware when you're out there. And I think, particularly with Hubble – it's such a priceless national treasure – to go up there you really want to do no harm, that's your first job, and then you can only make it better.

"Another thing I learned from Story is that when you approach an EVA task, you have to do things efficiently, so you need to not only be thinking about the immediate job at hand, but the ripple effect – if something doesn't go exactly as planned, what does that mean to the tasks that follow? Again it's kind of the choreography, keeping that global perspective all the time while you're doing very minute technical things to the telescope or whatever."

Fred Morris described Story as self-effacing. "He doesn't in any way exude what a celebrity he is or certainly he was when he was the oldest [flown] astronaut. One time he visited Hamilton Standard in Windsor Lochs and he stood up in front of the space department, six or seven hundred people in assembly, made a speech which was great and everything, and then he had a later date in Essex, Connecticut. I drove him down there – it was a distance of maybe sixty miles. During that sixty mile drive down there, he signed about two or three hundred photographs of himself. Instead of taking it easy, he was doing his astronaut duty by personally signing, not with a stamp, but with a pen, two to three hundred photographs which I then brought back to Hamilton and passed out to people that really appreciated them."

Fred added, "He never used his position, notoriety or fame. He was just a consummate constructive inputer to a design – as an engineer, as a physiologist. Spacesuits were a mixture, I think, of engineering, physiology, and magic and art! For a long time, back in the Sixties while we were doing the Apollo suit, we didn't know whether we wanted tailors or engineers to be the designers, and after a while you had to kind of mash the skills together and I think Story recognized that and he mashed them all together – he was always just plain constructive."

Story has his own heroes of the spacewalking world. One of them is Tom Akers, fellow spacewalker and crew member on STS-61. According to Story, "I looked at Tom as the ultimate spacewalker. I watched his form and his form was just gorgeous; it was fantastic. His concentration and his body position and his handling of tools – if you gotta go out and do a walk with someone, Tom was just incredible. He was born and raised small town, which I think makes a difference. Tom was immersed in big cars, big powerful cars, and he was always working on cars in the [NASA] parking lot; he always had a car that needed to be worked on. That's the way I would pick out the spacewalkers: the ones that couldn't resist working on cars and vice versa, the ones who had a flat tire and had to come in and get help. But Tom was absolutely marvelous, so he worked on things all the time and unfortunately, I don't think NASA even understands that that is the way to look at people, that they have to have been born and raised with some contact with a garage and some contact with tools; you simply can't get it later on. It's no different than taking up the piano at fifty; you can start the piano at five, or you can start it at fifty. The final result is very, very different. Getting things early is a unique opportunity to instinctually know how to do those things. If you take it on later, it is not instinctual. And if people have been raised only on books or computers, they are a different animal than someone who's been raised in the garage or raised with equipment and tools, or fixing things. It doesn't have to be cars and trucks or equipment, it can be fixing anything. But it's that kind of imagination you use to get a physical sense of the world and a physical sense of what is broken and what it's going to take to make it work. Tom came from that kind of world but it really showed and so in a suit he was fantastically powerful – he was tall, which matters, but also he was very, very good in a suit, very strong in a suit. He had a huge sense for tools and he had a wonderful concentration and a wonderful motion; a huge economy of motion. And the other part about spacewalking is – you have to do that motion right the first time. You really have to have the concentration if you're gonna take a hook off and you're gonna put it on a tool. You need that concentration because the suit is not going to do what you planned on it doing. You cannot use the same forces that you usually do for the normal arm. You've learnt that suit, but you haven't learnt that absolutely perfectly. And so you've got to have that economy of motion – that you deliberately reach out and do what you're going to do and it works the first time; that is efficiency... If you look at the still photographs of Tom –

sometimes I'll freeze frame a video when I'm watching him – it is spectacular! It's a very different ballet than dancing. Spacewalking is its own dance, it's its own ballet and he defines it. Of course, it takes a good spacewalker to be able to see a good one – to appreciate that *there* is the ultimate form: the form that you're looking at."

Scott Parazynski remembered some good advice Story once gave him. "He said, 'The only thing expected in EVA is the unexpected.' And that has just been the gospel truth – every EVA that I've ever watched or participated in, there's something that even to the extent of the training that you've done, there's something out there that would surprise you that you never could have anticipated. It may be something very minor, it may be something that you did think about before the flight and you have a response for it immediately, but often times there are little things that come out and grab you that you never could have anticipated."

Jim Thornton says that part of Story's legacy will undoubtedly be the Hubble spacewalks and the role he played in their development and success. "I think that really brought EVA out of the closet, so to speak, and demonstrated that it was a valuable resource which the program could draw upon and use. I think that was really the beginning of the enlightenment in managers' minds about how valuable EVA could be. I think Story is largely responsible for that. If those EVAs had not been successful, I don't know where we would be today.

"Story is a wealth of knowledge and someone who had not only a huge amount of experience but inherent knowledge, someone who had pretty much been there since day one. He was very confident and very relaxed in approaching training for EVA, even on STS-6 and I think it's just because he's so familiar with the suit. I mean he had a huge part in its development. He was really in on the ground floor of all that, so he was just intimately familiar with the suit, was largely responsible for a lot of the early tools that were developed, so he had a tremendous foundation and tremendous knowledge about it – I guess one of the founding fathers of shuttle EVA. And so his comfort with it – he tried to make other people be more comfortable with it too, you know, maybe with varying degrees of success.

"I would say we're much better off, we're much further down the road than if Story had never been a part of the program and a part of EVA. I think a large part of our success is certainly directly attributed to him and his efforts. I think it would be safe to say our evolution to where we are today would have taken much longer without some of Story's contributions. He certainly caused us to advance at a much more rapid pace than we would have otherwise. I think the technique and the approach to things in general – I am very much a believer of what he was preaching in the early days about this whole spacewalk, the whole EVA being a ballet. There's a certain choreography to make it efficient and to make it worthwhile because every minute that you're EVA is extremely valuable. There are a lot of different ways to calculate that. You're constrained by consumables and you have to make every minute count. So his approach to maximizing the efficiency, not only of the time but of the human element as well – he was very much of a believer in [eliminating] any wasted motion while you're EVA, just to conserve the crew member's own energy. So he preached very much on thinking before doing. And I think a lot of those things are things we emphasize today. He was probably one of the first to bring those ideals out, to throw them out there for others to adopt."

# 16. Art and Literary Influences

You find a work of art, a poem – you go look for it in
your fundamental depths in nature which are you.

*Story Musgrave*

If you want to understand Story Musgrave, looking through his library and listening to him speak about various books is certainly a good starting point. His college papers, too, from humanities courses, provide further insights.

In an interview with Ted Koppel during STS-61 Story gave his reasons for studying the arts. "The interest in literature and the humanities is to try to put this all in perspective, to try to look on my twenty-five years as an astronaut, to try to look at the privilege. You know, there's millions of people that could be up here and doing exactly what I'm doing.

"And so my interest in [space], in terms of literature and philosophy, is to try to catch – not only to do these kinds of things, but what is the meaning of it, what is the meaning of it to humanity? How do you put it in perspective? How do you come up here and have a great experience? You know, it's like Thoreau going to the woods, it's a new experience into nature. It's like the American renaissance, the whole bunch, the Moby Dicks. You can think of Moby Dick and his quest. You can think about the mission you're on, the kind of quest you're on here today. So all of these things come together. But the principle thing is not only go do it, but to put perspective on it and to give it to other people, other people that could be here as well as you."[1]

In his journal Story wrote:

> Do we have the equipment to perceive space? Are we prepared to biologically perceive space? Are we prepared to, or do we have the biological equipment to experience space? In terms of a theory of art or aesthetics, space is a good opportunity. I am in school primarily because school is fun, but I want to experience space, I don't want to miss that opportunity. I'm privileged to get to go to space and I want to have an aesthetic experience, maybe express that experience. [2]

Beyond literature, Story also looks to human performance for creative inspiration – other people who have passion for what they do. He said, "If you haven't got passion, find something else to do, because it cannot turn out!"

*

One of the things that really strikes you about Story is the variety of his reading, which becomes apparent as soon as you step into his library in Florida. All the books are coded and most are arranged thematically, except for those which he keeps close at hand for quick reference. The books cover topics such as existence, transcendence, spirituality, consciousness, creativity, travel (including books by some of the world's

---

1. Ted Koppel interview on ABC's *Nightline*, 8 December 1993. Reprinted with permission.
2. Journal 2, pages 31–32; Date: 29 March 1989.

greatest explorers), literary criticism, space, earth sciences, humanity and nature. If you look closely at some of the books, the letters 'STD' have been written on the spine which means "a standard of ideal" – which, according to Story, is "something that takes a philosophy and expresses it well... They're people that write in the way I would like to write, that I would like to able to emulate." It may be something which serves to re-enforce one of Story's own philosophies.

Another thing to note is that when Story moved from Texas to Florida in 1997, he reduced the number of books in his library – of which there were literally thousands – by almost half. It is an ongoing process whereby Story continues to streamline his library towards just the essentials. In his journals, there is a hint as to why he does this:

Don't keep a library as a library – got to be a working, functional thing![3]

Story refers to his composition system as his "pipe organ" which is also located in the library. In the center of the system, a few computers of various vintages contain programs which assist him with his creative writing – dictionaries, thesauruses, encyclopedias of poetry and other reference material. In a semi-circle around the main desk are the books which Story wants to have in his immediate circumference while he composes.

Writing is important to Story. He has studied the technical as well as the creative side of writing: "*The Poet's Handbook*[4] is pretty close to me; I have done it innumerable times – I have multiple copies. It's about technical aspects of poetry. Everyone has to know the technical side of whatever they do. You've got two things – you've got form and you've got content. You may be the most creative person in the world, but if you have not done the details and learned the technical aspects of poetry, then you can't write poetry."

Books about creativity are high on the list of reading and revision for Story, for example, *The Creative Process*,[5] which is a collection of works by various writers. Story explained, "These artists like D.H. Lawrence, Wordsworth, Einstein – they are writing about where they think creativity comes from and so it's very, very nice. It's by the people who really did it, by the artists themselves, writing about where their particular creativity came from. And so that is one of my foundational books in the world of creativity, but I have an entire shelf on creativity."

Few people will argue about Story's memory for detail. He can relate the content of books just by glancing at the covers. Books which are important to him have been

3. Journal 31, page 2; Date: 14 August 2000.
4. *The Poet's Handbook* by Judson Jerome: Writer's Digest books, an imprint of F&W Publications Inc. Cincinatti Ohio, first paperback printing 1986.
5. *The Creative Process*: Brewster Ghiselin (ed), New York, New American library, 1952.

notated, highlighted and coded with his own meaningful reference system from page to page. Story writes his philosophies and experiences in the blank spaces between paragraphs, in the empty front and back pages, or in the margins of these books. He said, "Most of my writings along the margins of books and most of my writings in the journals are not about the subject at hand: it's the perception. I work that with my past memories and my imagination and something comes out. They are written for my use as a creative journal so they can be embodied into my art. I re-read them and I re-write them in different colored pens, so there'll be no question that each was another perception. Sometimes I'll cross out what I wrote before – you can still read it, but I crossed it out – 'Oh I got that one wrong.'"

It is not unusual for Story to own several copies of the same book because eventually he runs out of places to write his thoughts; they flow so continuously. He also likes to keep multiple copies of books in locations which are easy for him to access – his library, his living areas at home, or at his office in California. By surrounding himself with a carefully chosen collection of works, Story is able to rapidly assimilate an abundance of creativity. He said, "In your imagination, you pull that all together."

Looking through the library, you can definitely get a feel for where Story draws much of his artistic inspiration. The library is also home to Story's creative journals. He wrote in one of his college papers:

> I have and do keep a journal and use it at all times. I am noted for doing this because I am seen taking endless notes in circumstances and situations in which there couldn't possibly be any useful information....I may be in class or in a NASA meeting or at the theatre or the museum, and after taking in the information or object in the traditional sense – giving it a chance to speak to me directly in its own context and in its own agenda – I then ask it a seemingly ridiculous set of questions such as,'How does this enhance my experience of space flight?' or 'How does this contribute to the meaning of space flight for humanity?'[6]

Story accumulates books which 'speak' to him emotionally, which have a humanistic way of relating to the world. He wrote:

> You find a work of art, a poem – you go look for it in your fundamental depths in nature which are you.[7]

According to Story, "D.H. Lawrence is at the top of my list and I think the most sensual writer; the person that deals with sensations and perceptions – I think, for me,

---

6. Paper was titled: *A Personal and Scholarly Look at the Process of Creativity.* May 1990.
7. Story's handwritten note in his copy of *Wind, Sand and Stars*, by Antoine de Saint-Exupéry: first published in French in 1939 under the name *Terre des Hommes*. My copy was translated by William Rees and published in London by the Penguin Group, 1995.

the most powerful writer in history. I have huge admiration for D. H. Lawrence. I'm into sensations, I'm into perceptions, into bodily living in the real world – and that was him. But he said it, his language – the language of D.H. Lawrence and Italy. I think he deals with the way you use your body to experience things, not only your mind. It gets back to down to experience again. He deals in sensations, he deals in perceptions.

"Other inspirations – I am a Romantic; Walt Whitman was a Romantic. He was a transcendentalist but he was much more. He was so expansive. He represented the cosmos in his catalogues, in his flowing poetry that seemed to capture everything. I love Whitman. I started studying him along with the American Romantics, such as Emerson, Thoreau, Hawthorne – but I think he's an extraordinarily ecological, expansive poet. It's really very democratic, but I think his poetry is so free, so emotionally driven, so authentic, open, honest and so expansive – it's so universal. He deals with the whole universe and he deals with expansiveness of human beings to embrace the entire universe. 'Song of Myself' – that's what it's all about; that's the individual who embraces, absorbs and metabolizes the entire universe. I like his poetry, I like his catalogues, I like the flow, I like the spontaneous flow of one thing to the next – it's a marvelous flow. And it's all-embracing – it's like embracing the whole universe. And it's like my theme of 'naked in nature'. Whitman wrote:

> How is it I extract strength from the beef I eat?
> What is man, anyhow? What am I? What are you?[8]

"I wrote down my interpretation of this as 'naked in nature'. That's Whitman, that's space flight. Not bringing yourself, not projecting into the new environment your own culture, not projecting into space flight your earth-based self, not interpreting space in terms of earth-based knowledge. But it gets down to 'naked in nature'. It gets down to surrender too and making yourself sensible and sensitive to a new environment.

Story's poem *Nature Walk* takes some of its inspiration from Whitman' style of writing. He explained, "In *Nature Walk* – that's Whitman. Whitman must have been working in my head when I went through and almost catalogued events. There's almost that rhythm of death to life, life to death, death to life. That kind of rhythm certainly has to remind you of the way Whitman wrote. When I read my little jottings[9] and get reminded of how Whitman wrote, I can't help but think that my reading of Whitman influenced my writing of that little poem. I can't help but think that having read Whitman made a difference to the way I write. When I compose at the computer, Whitman will be sitting right off my left shoulder there, and I want to glance over there and I want to always be reminded of what he did.

8. *Leaves of Grass* by Walt Whitman (1891): Story's copy - edited by Sculley Bradley and Harold W. Blodgett, published in New York by W. W. Norton, 1973, page 47.
9. A reference to his handwritten notes in *Leaves of Grass* by Walt Whitman.

"I will scan a bookshelf of roughly a hundred books. When you're composing it's hard to emulate a dozen people simultaneously and you're not, but you just have a sense of the way they wrote and so you work from that."

As a group of writers, the Romantics were an important part of Story's studies. They wrote about nature but also captured the human experience of nature. He said, "The kind of poetry that's closest to my soul – emotion has to be the source of that poetry. And the higher the emotion approaching ecstasy – that is the kind of poetry which gets a hold of me also. If you read Coleridge's *Biographia Literaria* or you read Wordsworth on "emotion recollected in tranquillity,"[10] they pretty much catch it. If you're going to communicate nature to someone else, the poet goes and experiences a certain emotion and then they write poetry. Within that poetry they are absolutely not describing and telling you about their emotional response. They write poetry which immerses you in nature in such a way, through their description of nature, that they create the same emotion in you. And that is what poetic emotion is, particularly, I think, Romantic poetry. It is imagistic kind of poetry – the kind of stuff that comes from the penetration of the inner."

Religious writing also has a place in Story's library. He explained, "The kind of poetry that stirs me into spiritual ecstasy is the poetry that was written by somebody that was in spiritual ecstasy and so, of course, I mention St. Therese of Lisieux, St. Theresa of Avila, St. Augustine. Those are models which I use: the reading is absolutely propelled by religious ecstasy."

"And what I liked about them was that religious ecstasy produced an extraordinarily poetic form of writing because they let their emotions, their ecstasy do the writing. That is very much in consonance with the Romantics, how they were able to go out into nature and have a semi-spiritual experience out there which propelled their poetry. Their kind of writing is so authentic, so from the heart and just an outpouring from the depths, that their emotions and their ecstasy shaped their writing; I consider it extraordinarily beautiful."

Another style of writing which Story admires is of Eastern influence and philosophy – again, it is the relationship to nature, the aesthetics which appeal to him. He said, "The Japanese are thoroughly aesthetic; their lives are aesthetic. It's not only in their personal lives but their work. They have a sense of simplicity, a sense of elegance, a sense of peace – [the way] they look at a cherry blossom, the tea ceremony, everything, it's inseparable to them. Life, for them, is aesthetics and science. Very often someone is led to an 'elegant' solution. Einstein probably came to the theory of relativity through its extraordinary beauty. I don't think that he arrived at that by simply working the mathematics. I think he arrived it at it first from the beauty of it and then he defined it."

10. Samuel Taylor Coleridge's *Biographia Literaria* (1817); Wordsworth's preface to *Lyrical Ballads* (1802).

Story appreciates the Eastern influence in the work of the American transcendentalist Ralph Waldo Emerson.[11] He wrote a college paper about this.

> I perceive the aesthetics of Emerson to be more similar to the aesthetics of Japan, in particular to the Zen Buddhists, than to any of the other Oriental aesthetics, although it is certainly clear that he had read and was influenced as well by the Hindus, the Chinese, and the Persians... I think it is the major factor in Emerson's popularity and his immense influence on subsequent art and literature. This cross-cultural fertility brought a richness and diversity to the Western tradition, in a way, compensated for many of its consciously or unconsciously perceived deficiencies; there was an inherent need for it. Emerson and the other Transcendentalists not only perceived this need and filled it, but they felt and believed in this religion and aesthetic which resulted more than anything else from this marriage of the East and West... Emerson and the Japanese are very similar in their sensitivity to nature, responsiveness to nature, perception of reality, transcendence of natural experience, aesthetic forms and themes, and in the interpenetrations of their art, culture, and religion.[12]

Story explained the importance of people like Emerson. "Emerson began Romantic poetry or Transcendental poetry in America. He started the movement here – that was his key. Rousseau[13] was of, course, one of the earliest. He was before the English Romantics, but he was Romantic in his dealing with things. I love the way he writes. *Reveries of the Solitary Walker* is an extraordinarily nice title. The content is a little depressing – he was totally rejected by his society, by his culture, but he was ahead of his time. And so when you're ahead of your time, you pay the consequences – till the culture catches up with you. He's a marvelous writer; he is an essayistic kind of writer. I plan to use the essayistic style in my writing as well."

In an interview, Story told the American Academy of Achievement: "American transcendentalists, they went out into nature to find God. Their spirituality was in nature, even though Emerson was a preacher on the pulpit, he ended up going out into nature for direct, face-to-face communication with God – if you want to call all of this creation part of God. Thoreau, of course, did the same thing. Whitman expressed the whole universe in his poetry and in his catalogues. That attitude almost defines what we call American Romanticism, or American Transcendentalism. I feel particularly close to them, because I am now out in the universe. I'm in a position to see nature from another point of view, to be outside the earth and see the big picture, to have an absolutely clear shot at the skies and to see stars that you can't see from down here, Magellanic clouds, auroras, a new perspective of nature. You can go back a hundred

11. Ralph Waldo Emerson, 1803-1882.
12. *Similarities in the Aesthetics of Emerson and of the Japanese*, May 1990.
13. Swiss-born Jean-Jacques Rousseau (1712–1778).

years earlier to the British Romantics, the Lake Poets, Wordsworth and Colleridge, Shelley and Keats, and you see the same thing, whereby people come face to face with the universe. They are looking for direct revelation and communication from God's creation. It's clear to see why I like the English Romantics and the American transcendentalists. I like their poetry as literature but also, from a philosophical point of view, I have very close ties to them."[14]

In his courses at the University of Houston, Clear Lake, Story studied the feminist aesthetic, which he likens to the Japanese aesthetic. He wrote:

> Japanese and Western feminist aesthetics are similar in their differences from the Western tradition; in their greater sensitivity to their worlds; truer and more appropriate response to the "signals" from their worlds; more aesthetic in their experience; truer perceptions of realities which are influenced less by ideologies and other value systems; proximities in principle to matriarchal mythologies; the artlessness, objectivity, simplicity, and elegance of form; thematic communication of creation: becoming, being, change, and perishability; and in the relationships of their art to everyday life, culture, and religion.[15]

Importantly, Story believes that the feminist aesthetic can help us to express the experience of space. Story's own personification of the earth, through his poetry and performances, often exhibits that quality. In his journals, Story wrote about the role of his own feminine sensibilities:

> The sensibility of Story will show his feminine side – the feminine sensibility, the feminine ego versus the macho fighter jock… It is the mentality, the lack of sensibility of the typical military fighter jock that allows you to express space, even though we have been in space for 30 years. It is possible that space will finally be caught 30 years after we have been there.[16]

> Put feminized ideals into space and express them… Is it possible that space has not been experienced because the feminine ideal has been excluded? The Eastern tradition has also been excluded.[17]

For similar reasons, Story appreciates the poetic and prosaic forms of the Romantics or transcendentalists, because they incorporate the human element in the communication of their experiences.

When asked what he considers will bring about greater communication and appreciation of the space experience, Story says: "You have to fly a Whitman, you have

---

14. American Academy of Achievement, 22 May 1997: http://www.achievement.org (an in-depth interview, well worth reading). Reprinted with permission.
15. *The Similarities of Japanese and Western Feminist Aesthetic*, April 1990.
16. Journal 1, page 45; Date: 25 March 1989.
17. Journal 7, page 41; 3 April 1990.

to fly a Wordsworth, that's what you have to do. You have to fly someone who will surrender to the environment. It is not 'conquer' space; it is go into space with the susceptibility and sensibility and sensitivity, such that space will move you. You will have an emotional experience of space, although what comes to you has got to be embodied in emotion. If it is not embodied in emotion, it is not going anywhere! It is the Romantic viewpoint but it is in all artists; that's what drives authentic art... It's looking out that window, it's looking at the heavens, it's looking at their art and it's the kinesthetic art of pulling off a mission. You need the Romantic spirits out there that will surrender, that will give themselves over to the space experience, such that they will want to listen.

"I think there has been too much 'doing' up in space, too much business. I don't think people have said, 'I've got to go up there and have an experience – I have to turn all the lights off; I have to see the stars; I have to go out and not only fix things but I have to experience the work; I have to step outside of myself and, while I'm working, watch myself work. I have to feel that tool; I have to feel the torque coming back my way; I have to maintain a peripheral vision on the world, not just on the wrench.' And you have to work on having that experience, the same way as the Romantic poets.

"Romanticism is a realism; it starts with realism: Romanticism is not counter to realism. 'What exactly is coming into my sensations, what is my perception?' Romanticism then says, 'What does it mean to be a human being whom you've dropped in this situation?' It means not only look at the object out there as to what light it is sending you or how you sense the object, but how you perceive it and what it means to be a human being who is receiving that information. And it gets down to John Dewey's *Art as Experience*.[18] It gets down to being a live creature in a live environment and having that experience... I think that kind of idea is important to getting to space-related artistic expression. There is very, very little good space poetry that has come out of the space program."

It is possible that artists and writers feel eclipsed by the way the Western world does space. According to Story, "The problem with the whole space thing is that we dominate it with technical and scientific information to the point where the artist says, 'I can't improve upon that.' So I think in a way the artist has defaulted because there's so much technical information, so much scientific information and engineering information, that the artist says, 'There is the reality and I can't improve upon it.'

"We essentially knew space before we went there. We had communicated even before we got humans in space; we communicated the technical and the scientific. So I think the overwhelming amount of data was informational data, even from astronauts – what was done historically, what happened up there. All that information, I think, discouraged the Romantic from coming in. They said, 'Well, we have all that,

18. *Art as Experience* by John Dewey: New York: G.P. Putnam's, 1934.

so what is an artistic view going to matter?' And it does matter 'cause the other is not meaningful, it's just hard data!"

While Story studies a wide range of themes, they all relate to one another in some way and to Story's way of looking at the world – through nature, experience and spirituality. The body and the mind are also at play. Importantly, since he began formal studies of the humanities back in the late 1980s, Story found a way of relating all of these themes to space.

According to Story, "Marcel Proust, I think, is the most powerful person to penetrate the inner. Dorothy Richardson, Virginia Wolf, James Joyce, but especially Marcel Proust. The psychological novelist – usually after the turn of the [19th] century – I use them a lot. I look to them to emulate. For me, Proust was the ultimate master by far. He's in a league of his own – you know, *Swan's Way*[19]… If I wish to capture consciousness – like adaptation to space – that's what you've got to do. It's an exercise in cognitive psychology; catch what's in your mind and then being able to express it. This kind of stuff is key. I did take a course in the psychological novel. *Swann's Way* was not part of the course; I found it on my own. So like most courses I took, I would read two to three times more books outside of the course than inside it; they weren't part of the reading.

"For stream of consciousness, I have James Joyce's *Portrait of the Artist as a Young Man*[20] and *The Modern Psychological Novel*[21] by Leon Edel. They're in the realm of the psychological novelists: the people that penetrate the head. It's what's going on in consciousness and so, obviously, that is key to what I need to do to talk about space flight or some other environment: to talk about what's in the head. I frequently revisit these books. They get continually pulled on and off the shelves!"

"I am, of course, very interested in spiritual things and I crossed paths with *Varieties of Religious Experience*[22] by William James in a *Philosophy of Religion* course that I took. This book was on the reading list, but it wasn't something we covered in class. I would really have liked to have covered it because it was far more meaningful to me than the others. James' main premise is that religion is an experience; it's a human experience. It's an extension of his theories of consciousness and his theories of experience in which he expressed his psychology. He just takes his works on consciousness into the religious realm. And so he looks upon what is spirituality and what is religion and, for him, it is an experience. I agree with that. I am very much into the world of experience and existence, so I certainly harmonize with him. In fact, my theoretical understanding of and my own interest in having an experience and expressing the experience – which is expressing conscious phenomenon, cognitive

19. *Swann's Way* by Marcel Proust, translation by CK Scott Moncrieff: New York, Modern Library, 1928.
20. *A Portrait of the Artist as a Young Man* by James Joyce: New York: Penguin, 1976.
21. *The Modern Psychological Novel* by Leon Edel: Gloucester, MA: Peter Smith, 1972.
22. *Varieties of Religious Experience* by William James: New York, New American, 1958.

psychology – probably, the foundations of my thinking on that come as much from William James' studies as anyone else's. I did take some courses on the *Philosophy of Consciousness* as well. James is the foundation for all of that. My approach to orientation in space is a cognitive approach and it comes from James. That's the way he approaches religions: 'What is religion? Religion is an experience!' My approach to formal religions is very close to that of William James: I do think religions are primarily experiences."

"John Dewey does *Art as Experience*[23] just like religion as an experience. It's a different form of science, but *Art as Experience* does not deal with just beauty and fine art. Fine art is art, but nature is art as well. A well constructed brick wall, a well constructed house, a dinner, how you put a dinner on a plate, how you cook, how you prepare, or anything else – for Dewey, absolutely everything is a form of art if you make it a form of art. That is one of the points which he stresses, as do I. Make an art out of living! There are lots of books here on Dewey or related to Dewey, but *Art as Experience* is one of the key foundations for my philosophy and my approach to art and to beauty. John Dewey does not deal so much explicitly with what beauty is, he deals with art, but for him, everything is art – painting, sculpture, bricklaying, absolutely anything you want to do in life, you can turn it into art."

One of Story's key philosophical interests is the human journey or species evolution. He is interested in both the billions of years that have shaped our current existence and in the future of humanity as a species. According to Story, Loren Eiseley's *The Invisible Pyramid*[24] is important from the point of view of humanity: "He's a humanist and he's dealing in the trajectory of the human species. I'm interested in the big view of the species, trajectory for the species and ethic for the species – the sustainable behavior and all the rest of that."

Another book which closely relates to Story's view of the world in evolutionary terms is Teilhard de Chardin's *Phenomenon of Man*.[25] Teilhard was an archeologist as well as a Jesuit priest who made some significant archeological discoveries while working in China. Story said, "This is another one of my books which is in the top twelve. What he does is link cosmic evolution and spiritual evolution – that's very nice – the way the cosmos works and the way spirituality works. He links the physical with the spiritual. In terms of philosophy, I am right there with him, all the way – it's very important stuff to me; it's evolutionary. I mentioned him in the Ted Koppel interview[26] but that's my philosophy, that's the link between cosmic and spiritual evolution; they're all the same to me."

Story has often referred to himself as a pragmatist and explains it in these terms: "I am a pragmatist – that if it works, there's some truth in it. And so there's a didactic

---

23. *Art as Experience* by John Dewey: New York: G.P. Putnam's, 1934.
24. *The Invisible Pyramid*, Loren Eiseley: New York, Charles Scribner's Sons, 1970.
25. *The Phenomenon of Man* by Pier Teilhard de Chardin (1955): translated by Bernard Wall, New York, Harper & Row, Publishers, Inc. 1975.
26. Ted Koppel interview on ABC's *Nightline* 8 December 1993 during STS-61.

form of truth: if it works, if it's operational, you can learn from the way you operate things and if things function in the real world, there is some truth in them.

"C.S. Peirce was the earliest one in the foundation of Pragmatism as a philosophy. He was the earliest, so, in some ways, he was more instrumental. C.S. Peirce, John Dewey and William James – they are all pragmatists and they formed the philosophy of pragmatism. All three, put together, are an American philosophy – maybe the only philosophy that Americans founded. They've worked on all the others, but in terms of pragmatism, it was founded here. They take a pragmatic approach and that is my approach, my epistemology of 'How do you know the world?'"

As an adventurer and explorer, Story is captivated by authors who have the ability to communicate their own experiences or those of others who have reached out to discover the world and universe around them. Story is full of enthusiasm for their spirit of adventure.

One of Story's favorite adventure writers is Barry Lopez. He says, "Barry Lopez's *Arctic Dreams*[27] – the way he caught the Arctic: the way he caught the spirit of the Arctic, the nature of the Arctic – I would just love to do something like he did! He's out there in the Arctic; he's a Romantic – he's also scientific and factual – but he has a Romantic view of things. And he's an incredible nature writer – he catches the spirit of a place, the ambiance of a place. He's absolutely marvelous! As a nature writer, I guess there's no one I have more respect for. His chapter on 'Ice and Light' reminds me very much of my night pass [in space] with snow on the ground – it's ice and light; you have ice and you have these incredible light shows, sunsets and all the rest of that. But he's as dear to me as any nature writer. So, space is a different nature; it's a different place. I'd like to do with space what he did with the Arctic."

Other adventure writers and nature enthusiasts whom Story greatly admires include Rachel Carson, Wendell Berry and Henry Beston. He said, "Rachel Carson, of course, was one of the first to write about the ocean – not just ecologically, but to write about the ocean itself. She was also the first ecological writer in the world and led the ecological movement when there was none: she pioneered it. Wendell Berry and Gene Meatyard's *The Unforseen Wilderness*[28] is about wilderness in Kentucky – but out there in the forest. *The Outermost House*[29] by Henry Beston – again, it's an experience. He is in Cape Cod, Massachusetts, and undergoes the North Easters that blow in, really wintry weather and so he is out there in a little shack on the beach with the North Easters blowing in!"

The writing of mountaineers is also very interesting to Story. In his journals he likened space to climbing a mountain. Space and mountaineering both involve

27. *Arctic Dreams* by Barry Lopez: Published by Charles Scribner's Sons, New York, 1986.
28. *The Unforseen Wilderness: Kentucky's Red River Gorge*, by Wendell Berry, with photographs by Ralph Eugene Meatyard, University Press of Kentucky, 1971.
29. *The Outermost House* by Henry Beston: New York, Penguin Books, 1987.

enormous challenges and physical risk. Story said, "Jon Krakauer's *Into Thin Air*[30] is about how not to do things. I found some neat lessons there about attacking the details, doing things right, forming up a team. There are some neat lessons on the secondary agendas too – conflicts of interest and how that leads to failure… I had read lots of mountaineering books before, but I had read them more for their Romantic views of mountain climbing."

An example of the more Romantic approach is H.W. Tilman's *Mt Everest*,[31] written in 1938. According to Story, "It's the analogy between his life and the quest hero or archetypal figure – the final stage in the archetypal quest for self. When he died, he was up in his 80s and he was rowing to Antarctica or something like that!"

Story wrote in the margin of this book:

> The quest for self-definition, knowledge, understanding… The quest is also for God. Metaphysics. One gets to know oneself in the pursuit of God.

Story recalled, "There's nice stuff in there: death by impact, fire or water – well that's space flight! It's the launch out of the ocean – death and a resurrection. A physical, intellectual and spiritual search – that's what space flight is about; it is really a spiritual quest. But Tilman is trying to climb Everest in the 1930s. He was an incredible Romantic, went to war…"

Two pioneering aviators who became celebrated authors of the Twentieth Century are Antoine de Saint-Exupéry and Ernest K. Gann. They capture not only the spirit of flying and adventure, but the nature of humanity, technology and the environment. Needless to say, Story has enormous empathy for their worlds. He explained, "*Wind, Sand and Stars*[32] by Saint Exupery – I've been with that for decades. That's about the early days of flying in the 1930s from Europe to Africa, then from Europe on over to South America. It's poetic, but it's his sense of the environment and his sense of nature and his sense of the machine; he's highly dependent upon a machine. I've read *Wind Sand and Stars* ten, twenty, thirty times. I keep reading it and reading it and reading it – I can't read it enough!

"Ernest K. Gann – *Fate is the Hunter*[33] – he's as close to me as anyone. I have read this book the usual ten, twenty, thirty times. If there are a top five books in my world, or a top dozen, it's there. He puts you in the cockpit, in that situation, in that experience. Again, it always gets back to experience. He puts you in the experience deeper and faster than any writer: you sweat with him, you fear with him and you feel with him. It's a marvelous thing. And so if there's some way I can put people in space

30. *Into Thin Air: A Personal Account of the Mt. Everest Disaster* by Jon Krakauer: Anchor Books, USA, 1997.
31. *Mt Everest* is part of *The Seven Mountain Travel Books*, by H.W. Tilman: published by Mountaineers Books, 1985.
32. *Wind, Sand and Stars*, by Antoine de Saint-Exupéry: first published in French in 1939 under the name *Terre des Hommes*. My copy was translated by William Rees and published in London by the Penguin Group, 1995.
33. *Fate is the Hunter* by Ernest K. Gann (1961), First Touchstone Edition, Simon & Schuster, Inc. New York, 1986.

the way he puts people in airplanes, in that environment, it would be very nice."

On taking up a copy of Charles Lindbergh's biographical *Spirit of St. Louis*,[34] Story commented, "I knew Lindbergh a little bit. He came and talked to us [at NASA]. He was a professional aviator. He didn't just make that flight, he lived aviation. He was a pioneer but he was an engineering pioneer, a great technologist and forward thinker."

Great fiction has also played a role in expressing the spirit of adventure. Story enjoys a wide variety of fictional authors: "Olaf Stapleton was supposed to be a science fiction writer but I think he was a philosopher! I think he was beyond science fiction – he changed me, he transformed me forever in *Star Maker* and *Last and First Men*[35] – his sense of the future is so outrageous... Stapleton – he had to have been there! The imagination which is in *Last and First Men*! It is about eighteen different species of humans as they go through transformations. He goes to all the planets; he star travels. He sees the way things have happened on other planets – other intelligent creatures, other humanoid creatures and how their species evolved, how their behavior led to all kinds of scenarios – most of which were not great. His language also is star travel. I use his language, especially in the last part of my performances."

"Edgar Allan Poe's *Narrative of Arthur Gordon Pym of Nantucket*[36] – that's an extraordinary tale. It's a book as opposed to a poem. After loads of travail and adventures on the sea, they go way into the South Pole and run into a paradise down there. It's very strange that you run into a tropical paradise after going to the poles, but it's Poe! I enjoyed that book quite a bit; it's very imaginative."

Story often makes reference to *Moby-Dick*[37] in his performances as a symbol of the quest, the journey: "Moby-Dick was quite a book. It wasn't about the whale, it was about the quest: the whale was symbolic. The book is highly technical, gives it all to you in incredible detail – what it took to go to sea – like what it took to go into space!"

Literary form is something to which Story pays great attention, for example, letter writing as a form of narration. For this reason, Story enjoys Samuel Richardson's *Pamela*.[38] According to Story, "It is an epistolatory – one of the first and greatest epistolary novels in which you use the letters someone wrote to communicate the total story... I look upon letters as an instrument. I might write letters home, I might communicate space flight in terms of emails, but the epistolary – that's important to

---

34. *Spirit of St. Louis* by Charles A. Lindbergh: New York, Charles Scribner's Sons, 1953.
35. *Last and First Men and Star Marker: Two Science Fiction Novels* by Olaf Stapledon. Dover Publications, Incorporated 1972. *Last and First Men* was first published in 1930; *Star Maker* in 1937.
36. *The Narrative of Arthur Gordon Pym of Nantucket* by Edgar Allan Poe: Viking Press, USA, reprint edition, 1975.
37. *Moby-Dick* by Herman Melville (1851): Edited by Charles Child Walcutt for the Bantam Classic edition, New York, Bantam Books, 1981.
38. *Pamela: Or Virtue Rewarded* (first published 1740) by Samuel Richardson: a more recent edition was edited by Peter Sabor, Viking Press, UK, 1981.

me. I think it's a nice way to communicate things, like Van Gogh, through his letters to his brother Theo.[39] It's a nice way to communicate; it's an instrument that you add to your didactic writing."

For Story, experience can also be gained through the study of art history. Again he has related it back to getting the most out of the space experience. He said, "E.H. Gombrich is incredible: *Art and Illusion*.[40] He's a psychologist and he's an art historian. I love art history; I love reading books on art history. I learned from doing art history! You look at art history and you look at what is said in a picture – and so I learned how to look out the window of the spaceship, having read art history; you know, the interpretation of it. I get in the spaceship window and I become an art historian. I treat what's out the window as a painting, as a work of art. And so I learnt how to look; I learnt how to see things."

In a similar way, Story brought the experiences of great photographers into space. He explained, "Susan Sontag's *On Photography*[41] is a neat philosophy of photography. I learnt something from that too. When you have the camera in your hand, it influences what you see. She's a thinker on all kinds of different levels. It's concepts like: if you have a camera in your hand, you view the world differently; you look at the world as if it is a picture, something you want to take home. So you don't see the world when you have a camera in your hand. And that's why I put the camera down; even in space flight, I put the camera down and say, 'No photographs!'"

Galen Rowell was another photographer whose work and published books were powerful for Story. Tragically, Galen was killed in an airplane accident towards the end of 2002. Story said, "I knew Galen! An organization once wanted me to come out [to San Francisco] and speak, so, just as humor, I said, 'I'm not coming unless you can get Galen Rowell to come'! And they said, 'We happen to know him and he'll come!' He was a nature photographer, a mountain climber and mountain photographer – his stuff is extraordinary."

For inspiration, Story draws not only on books, but on great human performances; the performances of people who are passionate about what they do. He views these as art forms: "It's people who are the best at what they do – the Peggy Flemings and the Dorothy Hamills, the Torvilles and Deans, Olympic athletes – the people who are the best at what they do are the people whom I admire. I admire performance, risk takers, designers, that kind of stuff.

"Peggy Fleming – I don't think her grace has been equaled since her figure skating Olympics. They've gone on to triple jumps and that kind of thing, but for pure

39. *The Letters of Vincent van Gogh*: Edited and Introduced by Mark Roskill, New York: Atheneum, 1927.
40. *Art and Illusion* by E. H. Gombrich (first published in 1960): a more recent edition was published by Princeton University Press, USA, 2000.
41. *On Photography* by Susan Sontag, Anchor Books, USA, 1977.

grace, for really beautiful kinesthetics, I don't think that has been equaled. Torville and Dean, of course, that was a singular moment in figure skating history. They simply nailed it – they nailed their art, drama, grace, athleticism, they did the whole thing. Torville and Dean hit it, and I believe in life if you play one perfect note, you're immortal, whether or not anyone hears it. One perfect note is enough and so if you achieve that level just once, that's it. And, of course, I believe all humans in whatever medium or venue, whatever they do, should strive to hit that perfect note. That's part of what drives me."

Story often mentions Dorothy Hamill, whom he spoke with prior to the Hubble Repair Mission. He said, "We talked about human performance, talked about the relationship between building routines in athletics and building them in spacewalking." Story was able to incorporate some of these ideas into the way he choreographed the spacewalks for that mission.

Another female athlete from the past who inspired Story was a young Kentucky girl by the name of Gay Nutter, whom he got to know personally. From a very young age, she displayed incredible talent on the tennis court. According to Story, "She was on the edge of performance. At the age of twelve she was the number one woman in the state of Kentucky. But it was the entire drama of somebody coming from Parris, Kentucky, with incredibly regular beginnings – to come from nowhere and, at the beginning, to only have the [use of] cement city courts. Once she got good enough, she got the privilege of playing on the indoor courts, where you could practice all year round, but that came later. So to come from just a plain old regular background and to achieve her levels at the earliest of ages, on the public courts, with her father as her coach – it is that kind of drama. It's the same thing; it's how do you arrive at the best you can? She was amazingly influential; I enjoyed the drama as to how it was going to go. It's the kinesthetics and the grace and the ball – the motion of the ball, the motion of a great swing, the anatomy and the physiology of a fantastic swing. But to see a twelve-year-old who is 4 feet ten and 100 pounds overpowering people who are 6 feet 4, and two hundred pounds – to see that kind of power attained by form – she overwhelmed them in terms of the speed of the ball. It gets down to form – there's a relationship between the form and how it is going to function."

A more recent source of creative inspiration for Story is Cirque du Soleil – the Canadian-based human circus show. He has been to their shows countless times: "I can repeatedly go to whichever show and come away with the same inspiration because it's everything – it's art, it's dance, it's theatre, it's perfection for the sake of perfection, it's beauty, it's kinesthetics and it's grace. It is performing at a level which you simply cannot believe that human beings can do! And so, again, it's people on the edge, it's people who have worked and worked and worked to perfect their art."

One great non-human performer which inspired Story to immense heights was the famous racehorse, Secretariat. Story says, "I play that video tape continuously. I play a lot of Secretariat's races, but I principally play the Triple Crown. I used to go and see him, but again – it's the perfect note, it's the Torville and Dean, it's the Peggy, the Dorothy. Secretariat happened to be a horse that did that same thing – different mediums, different venues, different arts."

Story would often go and hug the horse and look it in the eye. Todd Musgrave, who shared one of these moments with his father, remembered the importance of Secretariat. "I think he believes that the performance of Secretariat on that day in the 1970s was the best ever by any athlete, animal or human. He really felt a sense of greatness in that horse and that meeting the horse 'in person' somehow allowed him to absorb the greatness."

Again Story said, "Whether it's literature, whether it's painting, some other art form, it all gets down to going for that perfect note. If you record one perfect photograph, one extraordinary thing, then that's it – you hardly need to go further."

Dedication to a calling is hugely inspiring for Story. He explained, "Those are the people that are my inspiration; those are the people who motivate me, who I continually 'play' in my life. I don't have as much admiration for people who only pass through something, where it's just a stepping stone to the next thing – they may have made a quick mark, but the people who have a calling, who have a passion, who live things, are very important to me. One of those was a fellow named Roger Bourke who was a trainer. He trained astronauts, but he trained them all the way through. And he [trained] them for decades! He trained me on the Apollo program, on the Apollo simulator, but he trained on all systems. Nowadays, you have a hundred trainers for the Space Shuttle – you have trainers for environmental control, electrical power, guidance navigation, the trajectory, launch and entry. Roger trained every system on Apollo and he trained every Apollo crew. He did the whole thing – he did it over decades – and so he kind of defined the genre of what an astronaut trainer was."

Story works hard to nurture the creative process. He draws inspiration from all of these sources and uses it to communicate his own experiences and philosophies. Of the creative process, Story wrote:

> If the passions are not in the original experience – the replay, the creative process, and the artist's experience of the creative object – then 'it' is not going to work! Passion is the energy for every step of this catabolic process; it is the fuel for this creative engine and, without fuel, it stops.[42]

---

42. A college paper at the University of Houston, Clear Lake, titled *The Enhancement of Artistic Creativity and Productivity Through the Application of Specific Visionary Procedures.* December 1990.

# 17. Communicating Through Art

Poetry is a symbolic expression of passion,
a symbolic expression of human will.
Poetry is a fountain of immense heights,
a spring from the ultimate depths.
Poetry is what we do and what we are when
we are in harmony with ourselves and with the universe.
Poetry is listening to the universe with an ear which
has never heard before.
Poetry is speaking to the universe with
the purity of the universe.
Poetry is the emotion of touching, of doing,
of creating, of being.
Poetry is physical, biological, spiritual language;
a language to be heard, to be held, and to be held by,
to be read, touched, and sensed.
Poetry plucks the strings of nature, the nature of our
strings, vibrates and resonates the harp of life.

*Story Musgrave, 1988*

Story uses art as a way of bringing the experience of space and his philosophies of life to people. He has worked for decades to develop and perfect the content of his art which he calls "the principle, the essence and the ideal":

> Experience is a total integrated whole, involving the entire organism... I wish to appeal to your bodies as well as your minds... Descarte tore the mind out of the body and we've been trying to get them together ever since.[1]

Some of the art forms which Story has used to reach audiences include poetry, spoken word performances and, more recently, the *spacestory.com* website which was the brainchild of his son Todd. But inspiring others is not enough, according to Story. The experience, in whatever form of art it takes, needs to be transformative. Story likes to focus on the broader meaning and values which are imbued in all great art:

> The final work of art catches something of the essence of what it is to be human.[2]

*

Story's ideas for developing creative performances of the space experience date back to around 1990 when he began to play with the content and format in his journals. By the time he left NASA in 1997, Story had researched and developed the concept to a degree where it could actively be pursued at both a public and corporate level. Like all good art, Story's performances have evolved and ripened over the course of more than half a decade. It has become creative theatre – incorporating such elements as photography, poetry, drama and music.

According to Billy Specht, Manager of Education for Delaware North Parks, the company which operates the Kennedy Space Center's Visitor's Complex in Florida, Story is an enigma. "The more he shares with his audiences, the more they crave. Through his presentations, he takes his audiences on a journey through the human mind. Story begins his presentations with a slide of a toddler exploring a shell on the beach and brings the audience back to that same slide to conclude his presentations, proving that it is human nature to explore our world. He inspires and enchants his audience when he shares his views of the cosmos and anecdotes about his missions on the Space Shuttle."

Story has been involved with several Kennedy Space Center related education programs. In addition to special multi-media performances for various groups who visit the Space Center, Story has been a regular guest at the Astronaut Encounter program at the Visitor's Complex – a family oriented, theatre-style, interactive show

---

1. Story's handwritten note in *Principles of Literary Criticism* by I. A. Richards: New York, Harcourt Brace, 1925.
2. A college paper for the University of Houston, Clear Lake, titled *The Enhancement of Artistic Creativity and Productivity Through the Application of Specific Visionary Procedures.* December 1990.

which enables people to meet with an astronaut every day of the year.

Tony Gannon, who worked with Story at the complex, referred to him as one of a select few who will be remembered in the history of space flight, along with the big names from the Mercury, Gemini and Apollo eras. "Story comes from the past – Apollo, Skylab, Apollo Soyuz – but he did Hubble, which looks to the future. Story is a link between the past and the future."

Mia Liebowitz, an actress who hosted the Astronaut Encounter program, remembered what it was like to share the live theatre environment with Story. "When it came to being out in front of people and communicating his message, he was very enthusiastic. Story's the kind of person who wants you to be creative, and he would challenge all of the actresses to go with it, to follow his lead. He never came out the same way – you always knew he was going to pull something to keep it fresh, which I appreciate as an entertainer. After doing the show for two years, you always have to find a way to keep the show fresh, because if you're bored, the audience is bored. And even though I would hear the same 'Story stories', like the Coke stories, and the spaghetti stories, it always felt like we were doing it for the first time 'cause it was so much fun. We really could play off of each other and he wanted to emphasize the fun to the audience, but then he really wanted to emphasize that it was so important to experience space. People would ask him, 'How do you sleep in space?' and it was always important for him to explain how he had done it several ways and tried to sleep from every angle because he just wanted to get the most out of the experience as possible. And you could tell by listening to him that space really was an experience. And the audience responded to that."

The Astronaut Encounter program caters to a wide range of ages, cultures, interests and intellectual levels. Mia explained, "You have a mix, you have the people who know nothing about space and want to 'know', and then you have the people who know something and want to know more. So you've got a fantastic mix where you get the same questions but, every now and then, you get the person with a fantastic question like, 'Do you snore in space?' And Story was so excited that someone would ask that question because that really took some thought. The questions that really challenge are the [sorts of] questions that he asks himself in space. So when someone else comes up with that, he's thrilled."

According to Mia, "Story would have his 'on' days and his 'off' days. Some days he was telling [the audience] stories that were so technical that it was completely over everyone's head, but it was his way of challenging the audience to think in a different way, to use their brains. I would say to him afterwards, 'You know, I think it was over their heads today.' Then he'd reply, 'Do you think so? I might have to adjust that, but I think some of them understood it. I think for the ones out there who needed a little bit more detail, I wanted them to have that too.'"

Mia believes Story wanted to reach as many people as possible: "It was his need to really give the experience to everybody and not to just 'dumb it down'. So every time we would go out there [on stage] to share the space experience, he would throw something in. A little kid might ask him 'What's the speed of the rocket?' or 'What makes you float [in space]?' and he would go into details. The joke at the end would always be – I'd say [to the young person who had asked the question] 'Did you get that?' And the three-year-old would reply, 'Aha!' Everybody in the audience would laugh, and Story would laugh and say, 'You know, I think they did understand it.' I think it was very important for him to be able to do that, to be able to give just enough for the people who are at the high end of the audience but also give those experiential stories that made everybody appreciate it. It made him such a neat person to work with.

"My favorite question that Story was asked – I'll never forget this question – a little kid raised his hand and said, 'When will they send normal people into space?' By this point the audience had gotten an idea of Story's character and everybody just started laughing. Story himself just kind of smiled and gave the pregnant pause, gave everybody the chance to let it just settle in. He replied, 'hmmm' and then followed up with a serious answer – that he really feels that NASA should institute a civilian in space program. But it was just great, because you got the sense that this kid, in one question, totally summed up Story's existence!"

Story would always deal politely and intelligently with questions from the audience, even those intended to shock him. Mia remembered, "We had this little kid ask a question about the diapers – 'It must feel horrible when you wet yourself in a diaper and you have to sit in it?' It was a total shock question because this kid was fourth grade and all the other kids started to laugh. A lot of the astronauts would be really put off by something like that, but Story just sees any question as an invitation for information and so he's going to turn it around to make it a positive thing as opposed to thinking 'how dare you ask the question?' So I kind of angled it... 'Did you know that Story was the reason why men started to wear diapers in space?' And so he took that angle and worked it."[3]

Mia recalled her first impressions of working with Story. "When I met Story I thought 'O my gosh, you must have been 'up there' doing pranks left and right.' And it wasn't until I put it to him in those terms that I got to see the serious side of him. He said 'Yes, but you know, that was really serious. It was fun but it was serious. You don't realize that some people up there don't even want to experience this.' And that's when I really got to know Story, got to know how important is was for him that he did all

3. Story was the first male astronaut to request a diaper to wear underneath the pressure suit and spacesuit instead of a UCD or Urinary Containment Device. Now all astronauts wear diapers while wearing those suits.

the absolutely fun, childlike things, because it was all about the experience. And for someone so intelligent to also be that childlike, it's so fantastic. And I think that's what draws people to him. After the shows, we would have people coming up and they were just enthralled. After listening to him for half an hour, the line of people waiting to meet him one-on-one was always an hour long."

Story's ability to communicate with audiences is both verbal and non-verbal. According to Mia, "He's so open, he really is. His body language – he invites people to get to know him. On stage, he opens himself to people. You know, for an actor or an actress, theatre is the study of life, and I see Story – that's how he lives his life. He wants to share his experiences, so every person that he reaches out to, it's like he's carrying out a mission. He really understands that the only way you can [reach people] is by creating relationships. It's easy to get up on stage and give a performance and have people walk away and go, 'Oh that was a great performance, what a neat guy' and tomorrow they don't remember you. But Story, understands that if he spends that minute or two with the people afterwards, giving them that individual experience, not only are they going to remember his stage performance, but they're more than likely to take away with them a sense of wanting to know more and to really bring that with them throughout life, as opposed to just that day. He makes that kind of connection with people.

"I think that's the key. I think Story, no matter what he does, needs the interaction, he thrives on something else to interact with, whether it be the slides or the person on stage or something. He needs the interaction 'cause he thrives on the energy. He loves passion and when someone is passionate about something, that brings him to another level because he's so passionate about everything he does. When he can find someone, especially in the performance arena, that's like that, it doesn't matter what media, as long as they're passionate about what they do, it makes him his best. I think it challenges the other person to be at their best too."

Mia recalled, "It was never a boring day when Story was there. I was always challenged to bring my energy to another level. It was never run of the mill. It was never – let's go out there, do the show, come back and relax. It was more like – let's go out there, do the show – God knows, he's going to try and throw me off, so I'd better be on my toes, come up with things to play around with and then see where it goes from there."

Christina Florencio, who also worked with the Astronaut Encounter program, says Story's personality shines. She described him as charismatic. "Audience numbers would grow when people saw Story at the open air stage and they would hardly ever move away; he gets their full attention. It's like he's teaching a class up on stage – he tells them how he feels. He gives the impression of loving to talk to people."

Story has also enchanted audiences at The Center for Space Education, part of the Astronauts' Memorial Foundation which honors those astronauts who lost their lives during their careers at NASA. Facilities Manager Dave Dunn says that Story is able to communicate appropriately with people from a whole spectrum of education – from children through to MBA students and university professors. He says that Story gets onto a personal level with everyone, immediately putting them at ease: "He can always get an audience to laugh."

Mary Beirman, a representative of the Australian Organisation for Quality, arranged for Story to speak at an international quality conference in Sydney, Australia, in February 2000. Mary had previously heard Story speak at a gathering in Austin, Texas, a few years earlier and remembered why the invitation to visit Sydney was extended to him: "We were planning our quality conference and it came back to me, thinking about if I wanted to get somebody to talk about the essence of quality, and to inspire people, who would that be? And immediately Story was the one who came to my mind and I didn't look for anybody else."

Mary recalled the predominant message which she carried with her from the first time she heard Story speak. "The more that I sat there and listened to what Story said, the more that I could make this linkage to what we'd been trying to do with quality systems and what we'd been trying to get people to understand about how to look at things, how to engage with things, how to approach whether it's living your life or whether it's doing a job or whatever, the certain quality of doing things that he expressed. He wasn't saying any words that were related to quality, but what he spoke of was quality and the essence of it. And that just triggered my whole thought process about what I was doing with my work. It just really made me think about what I was doing and the impact that you can actually have if you engage in something that you believe in, if you put yourself into it. And that's what he was doing, what he was telling me when I heard him talk. The message he gave me was really clear and one of the things I really liked about him was that he came from the heart. And when he was talking to that group of people, he was talking to us as human beings. He wasn't giving us a lecture; he was telling us his experience and that was interesting.

According to Mary, "He's been a soul willing on his journey to travel and look at things differently, like in the Space Shuttle when he does things that other people wouldn't do – he's out there reaching out, trying to find out what it's all about – what he can do and how it can be different, how you could enjoy things differently or experience things differently. And I think that's probably one of the things that made the biggest impression – a willingness to have an experience and not to be stuck in the conformity of what everybody else wants you to do or to be."

Frank Candy, one of Story's agents, says that the first time he saw Story speak, the audience got to their feet and gave him a standing ovation for five minutes. It was a performance for the Missile, Space and Range Pioneers – a non-profit organization of NASA and ex-NASA employees. Since then, Frank has worked with Story on many occasions and described him as "entertaining, dedicated and sincere."

According to Story, a number of elements make his form of communication successful. "I try to do a total performance. It's starts, of course, with human-to-human communication and empathy… I listen to the heartbeat of the audience, I listen to the breath go out of them. I really know what's going on out there and whether they're on board or not, or whether I'm ahead of them, behind them, above them or below them. I've got to get synced up with them … I cannot do a performance alone and I think that's probably the most important thing.

"A lot of it is to give them what you believe, so you cannot do it without emotions; you cannot do a great performance without emotions. Your emotions have got to be authentic. For me, I make it very easy: I never do or say anything that I don't believe and so for me the emotions come naturally.

"The next thing is to talk poetically. It's like poetic prose, to the extent that I will generate poetic prose … I pay attention to the metrics, I pay attention to the rhythms. I use a lot of alliteration that I generate spontaneously… I add the medium of poetry to the language, to the extent I can. I add the body communication too and so whatever posture's on the screen I try and have that posture [on stage]… I try to stay in pretty constant motion, so I try to stay dynamic with my body but I try to have my body represent the subject.

"I try to communicate with music and so it's total immersion. I like to work the theatrical world of performance, art, poetic prose, body language, lots of body language, interaction with the screen, interaction with the audience.

"The kind of messages I always want to get are serious. I want to be able to take my simple picture of nature, the same way as the Romantics do. They go out into nature but they're called Transcendentalists. The American Romantics, were called Transcendentalists, that's what I am and I aim at – transformation. Yes, I use pictures of the earth or pictures of the heavens or pictures of the technology, but that is really not my message. What I'm trying to do is to get people to think and reflect on what is going on there. I try and communicate principles – the principle of the matter. Even if it's something as purely technical as spacewalking, I'm not trying to give them what happened in that particular spacewalk, I'm trying to catch what the principles of spacewalking are and give that to them. I'm trying to teach not just a particular photograph but what geological principles, what oceanographic principles, how those kinds of things work.

"I'm also looking at things that bring the world together such as the galactic kinds of ocean currents, the galactic patterns of the weather, the galactic stars, all the rest of that business – those things that are going to reverberate in them.

"The kinds of messages of course are, at bottom, philosophical. I expect the audience to be affected. I expect them to be changed.

"I try to make everything memorable, so when I build a performance what I'm always thinking of – is it powerful, is it evocative, will it reach out and get a hold of them? I know I have to have at least a handful of powerful moments that will grab them and if they can hang onto those, the rest will come back. It's like a movie: if you have one defining moment, the whole movie will stick with you.

"Art is communication, for the artist. Art is communication on a multiple levels, so art is a particular thing which is right in front of your face – a particular item that comes in through your sensations but then, through perception and consciousness, it reverberates with a lot of other things within you.

"Your imagination takes that perceptual experience and it works it through its memories and you come out, through imagination, with a whole new message. So I think that is exactly what art is about. It is to communicate on all different kinds of levels and in different ways."

The quality and vibrancy of the photographs which Story uses in his performances have a great impact on audiences. He described this in his journal as:

> Big camera, big pictures, big slides with magnificent color, resolution, focus and enlargement capability.[4]

Story went to considerable lengths to develop his photographic techniques so that he could do great photography in space. He used both Nikon and Hasselblad brand cameras during his spacewalks. To increase his proficiency, he practiced using these cameras while traveling in T-38 jets where the conditions are somewhat similar to those of spacewalking, in that you are wearing a helmet and gloves, and are moving at a very high speed.

Spacewalks were opportunities to experience the work through nature. Even though intensely focused on the task at hand, Story would still remind himself to look at the view all around him as he worked in the vacuum of space. After STS-61, the Hubble Repair Mission, Story noted in his journal:

> The view from looking above telescope and seeing the entire continent of Australia! The elbow camera caught it.[5]

Bill Daley, who was part of the Earth Observations team that worked with astronaut crews up to a year before their missions, spoke of one of the more coveted tasks of space flight: taking photographs of the earth. The Earth Observations unit was created in 1982 as part of the astronaut training program. Scientists with expertise in

4. Journal 20, page 33; Date: 22 October 1996.
5. Journal 14, page 41; Date: 30 December 1993.

particular fields would be brought in to talk about things like oceanography, geology, meteorology and the environment. Bill's role was to assist crew members to identify various geographic positions throughout a mission which would be suitable for photographing particular features or views of the earth, taking into account such factors as day time, night time, sleep periods and work schedules. The crew would also be assisted with technical information about what camera lens to use or what angle to shoot at. Bill recalled that Story was extremely knowledgeable about geography and the use of the camera. What he remembers most about Story is that he would always shoot "beautiful things." Story was also the only person ever to photograph Lake Murray, a beautiful lake forty miles north of the Fly River in Papua New Guinea. It is practically always covered in cloud.

Part of Story's own method of training in photography was to practice changing lenses and filters on the various cameras thousands of times, so that in space it would be completely automatic – he didn't want to waste time or miss any great photo opportunities if they arose.

Despite spending many hours at the Space Shuttle windows, Story was conscious of the need for balance, both in work and art.

> Photography teaches you to view the world in a different way. Need to put the camera down in space once in a while and also to view the world for its sake, even when doing photography.[6]

Story loved to photograph all aspects of space flight – earth-based ones as well. Shortly after STS-33, he wrote of his visit to the launch pad:

> 3am night viewing of spacecraft a primitive moment … Xenon lights and gantry lights – such night beauty, focused beauty. Took photos from all angles, distances and lenses. Fog rolled in – starting at the top of lightning rod and moved down. Ethereal scene.[7]

Other memorable photographs surrounding launch time include those Story took of Challenger's rollout to the launch pad for its maiden voyage – STS-6 – which was also Story's first space flight. The photographs show the vehicle making its way to the launch pad, early in the morning in a scene, once again, bathed in fog. Story was riding the "crawler" along the causeway and jumped on and off the slow moving transporter in order to capture the scene.

In an interview, Story revealed how he selects the slides to be used in his performances. "Well, it happens to my body. I listen to it all the time. Creativity is a very, very large part. You have ten billion brain cells or more and you have all this stuff going on, you're consciousness is only a very small part. I specifically listen to the body to

6. Journal 19, page 48; Date: June 1996.
7. Journal 7, page 1; Date: 1 December 1989.

catch the essence. If I'm looking for a striking photograph that is really going to be powerful and evocative, I am – more than anything else when I bring transparencies across the light table – I am listening for a bodily response because in this funny set up that we have, the body seems to know more than the intellect about what is really evocative and powerful. And I think that gets back to beauty again. There is no such thing as beauty without an emotional and a bodily reaction, and that is key."

In 1999, Story's son Todd Musgrave came up with an idea to take the art form one step further – to be able to share the space experience with a much wider audience. Spacestory was to be a new creative vehicle for Story which would take advantage of one of the newer types of global technology – the internet. Todd said, "For Dad, life is a relationship to nature and beauty. It is also about privilege and identifying what privileges exist in one's life and how to give to others that do not have this privilege."

*

Story has also had the opportunity to share his experiences of space in a new arena – with colleagues at both Walt Disney Imagineering (WDI) and Applied Minds Inc. – two California-based companies for whom he has consulted in both a technical and creative capacity since leaving NASA.

Colleague Earle Markes recalled being present during one of the performances where Story described the lengths to which he had to go to in order to achieve some of the images – not only finding landmarks, but at the same time eliminating the velocity of the spacecraft by turning his body and the camera. Earle recalled the colorful "human-like" images of sand in the desert and referred to Story's "extraordinary technicality to achieve art and beauty."

Vanessa Godson also remembers the beauty – that is what stood out about Story's presentation to staff at Applied Minds. She says that people in the office often ask Story about space – they all want to know what it was like – and Story is always gracious. She says, "If you love what you do, you can talk about it again and again and again."

Alice Hargrove recalled that the best meeting she ever attended at Walt Disney Imagineering was the one which Story hosted – he communicated so well his unique vision and recollections of what he had seen in space. She said: "Story can completely put an audience in a spell. This guy is really an artist!"

Chris Carradine, Vice President and Executive Concept Architect at Walt Disney Imagineering, and close friend of Story's, says that perhaps Story's key motivation is making an artistic contribution to culture. He thinks Story is also motivated by the thought of being a representative of us in the universe.

According to Chris, Story has been able to merge science and art, therefore adding the element of art to exploration. "He is expert in a way that enables him to use disciplines in complementary ways. He addresses intelligent curiosity and expresses it as an artist."

Chris refers to Story as a tool-maker: "It's all about tools – the transcendence of the tools, being able to communicate the meaning without getting lost or absorbed by the tools, so that he is able to reach a higher goal."

Poignantly, Chris points to Story as a grand student of history; it is another one of his tools: "More tools means more difference that Story can make in the world."

Of Story's non-verbal communication ability, Chris explains, "He looks more deeply at you than other people do. It's his unquenchable curiosity and abiding confidence which he wears so calmly." Chris says that Story's often bold mannerism is totally non-threatening but it does somehow make you tell him very personal things about yourself, so that you get to feel close to him quickly: "It's a special quality of great leaders. Story has the measure and demeanor of a leader and is an explorer. He explores you as a form of communication."

Story was originally recruited to the world of Walt Disney Imagineering as a Disney Fellow after leaving NASA. Being a Disney Fellow was the highest creative level that you could work at within the organization. In that role, Story was able to develop and work on a whole range of creative concepts within the entertainment business from theme park ideas, to films, to television programs and other forms of media.

Al Horais, Senior Principal Production Designer, WDI, said that Walt Disney Imagineering is a haven for people who are very creative, very experienced, yet with a degree of humbleness about them, and says that Story fits in well. Al believes that to be good designer, no matter what the field, you need to be able to become a nine-year-old again, and he says Story has the ability to see things that way. "His enthusiasm, his curiosity and hunger to know things is insatiable!"

Walt Disney Imagineer, Mark Huber, describes Story as the fullest 'experiencer' he's ever met. "He is a searcher – for reality, for truth – and uses art and science to achieve that. He is constantly looking under rocks to see what's there, constantly moving through life, experiencing things."

Scott Petri, who worked closely with Story for a number of years at WDI, sees Story as a gifted intellect and scientist with a certain naiveté about him. He says Story still has the heart and wonder of a child, which is a great asset for working for an R&D corporation. He believes Story shows empathy for the entertainment world, especially that of film, because, to him, storytelling is a metaphor for life. Of Story's approach to things, Scott says: "What is life about? A state of wonder, self-actualizing your curiosity. The journey is the goal. Story has been a universal touchstone for everyone here because he has been an experiential space person."

Friend and WDI colleague, Rondi Werner, believes that it is important to Story to influence and educate children, as well as to inspire others. From that point of view, she believes Disney has been a good fit for him. However, she feels that, for Story, being part of yet another very large organization does have its down side: Story has no politics or agenda and often seems to wonder why things aren't always so simple. Anything that interferes with the process of moving forward with his creative ideas and projects can be frustrating for him; at times, the world moves too slowly: "For him, it's all about pushing the envelop and squeezing it all in, trying new adventures, seizing opportunities and inspiring others."

Clint Hope, a colleague at Applied Minds – a technology creation company – says that Story has a sensitive, emotional side which is balanced with a technical side.

One of Story's strengths, according to Clint, is that he can take complicated technologies – and all sorts of complex concepts – and communicate them clearly. He is especially good at looking at systems, taking into account the 'human in the loop' and working out what the optimum system would be. "He will stop and take a look at the process."

According to Clint, Story is strong on perspective, focus and the ability to hit a Zen-like level: "If he was Japanese, he would be a Samurai!"

For Story, the worlds of entertainment, arts and technology are a happy marriage. He is as comfortable there, if not more so, than he was within the corridors of the space program. In his new-found niche, creativity is not only acceptable, it is an imperative – and being on the edge is necessary to success.

*

It was largely as a result of his studies of the humanities that Story began writing a great deal of poetry and poetic prose to capture the essence of space and space flight. He recalled, "I was always poetic in nature but I began to write when I was doing my creative courses, my poetry writing courses, my short story fiction writing courses. I got exposed to the medium – what it was and how to do it. And, of course, the roots went way back to when I was doing storytelling [as a child].

"I'm not the first space poet, there have been many hundreds of others. Other people have written about space but we are the first people to travel into space – and write about the experience."

Why is it important to Story that the experience of space is captured in poetry or prose? In his journals he wrote:

> The subject of the art is long lost unless art is made of it. Art gives form to reality. It will not only express the humanity of space, but will also define it.[8]

> Space has been expressed as a chronological list of people and events and performance of check lists. An art or literature of space would return all the humanity of space which has been repressed by the 'performance principle.'[9]

8. Journal 1, page 17; Date unknown, comment added later.
9. Journal 9, page 21; Date: 23 September 1990.

Story told the Academy of Achievement: "I think the experience of space needs to be communicated in terms of what is in one's head and one's heart. Most of our history in space has been communicated in terms of action – what people do, a chronological list of events which have transpired – as opposed to the human experience of having done those things. It's one thing to be out working on the Hubble Telescope and doing the ballet that you do to run the tool as expertly as you can, but what's the experience of operating the tool? What's the experience of getting ready? And what's the experience of a great pass over South America? I can relate almost the entire earth to you in terms of what a South America pass is, of what a Shark's Bay, Australia, pass is. I can just roll that through my head. I think we need to capture what that experience was, and then get it into the right form. Poetry is its own medium; it's very different than writing prose. Poetry can talk in an imagistic sense, it has particular ways of catching an environment. Meter, rhyme, rhythm, alliteration, structure, all of those things are tools for bringing out the senses."[10]

Berlin-based filmmaker, Dana Ranga, spoke of Story's talent as a poet and how his experiences of space were the trigger for much of his creativity. "I think that maybe it made him find the right switch and tap into the poetic state of mind... he is very intelligent and he comes from an artistic family... I understood that artistic side and that the connection to it is much deeper – that it doesn't come just because he went into space and he's looking for means to express whatever happened in space. No, the basis was there before. And then later I was able to understand what he said about his mother, the fact that he was making theatre at home, the fact that he was open to all these things – to storytelling, to words – and that words were important. It's not that he's just one of these guys who's trying to do it, but it's haunting him, it's part of his being. This is the thing that taught him how to be creative."

There are literally hundreds of pieces of poetry scattered throughout Story's journals since the late 1980s. Like most other things which Story has done in his life, he threw himself whole-heartedly into the world of poetic expression – learning the history, the technicalities, the tools – and eventually becoming a talented poet, performer and critic. He wrote:

Writing is like programming: technical and artistic, precise and creative.[11]

Story has developed a poetic style which exhibits a high degree of sensuousness. He also animates his subjects – a technique which, in his writing, creates both energy and emotion. He mused:

It has got to flow, got to pull people along, or it will fall back into a book of details.[12]

---

10. American Academy of Achievement, 22 May 1997 http://www.achievement.org. Reprinted with permission.
11. Journal 1, page 42; Date: 18 March 1989.
12. Journal 4, page 51; Date: 14 May 1989.

The lyrical tone of Story's lines are, at times, reminiscent of the works of Coleridge, Wordsworth, Scott, Byron, Shelley and Keats – some of his favorite poets of the Romantic period in Great Britain. In consideration of those poets, together with the American Transcendentalists, Story wrote in his college papers:

> Through the imagination, the poet recreates the earth and universe, transforms the perceptions of nature into forms which have some meaning for humanity, some forms which will help humanity discover its essence and raise it to higher levels of virtue and spirituality.[13]

> Romantic poetry creates myths and images which catch human significance, the essence of what it is to be human.... These are the essentials, the consistent and internally logical expressions of the relations of aesthetic and religious experience, the relations of poetry, nature, and theology – the process of transcendence.[14]

Story's knowledge of literature is extensive. He uses it as a source of inspiration and a data point for his own writing. Of his own purpose he wrote:

> Explore creativity books not only from stand-point of creativity per se... but also to express it, catch it, express the archetypal images and emotions.[15]

Story believes that art is a tool for cultural vision:

> Poetry not only defines culture, it makes culture. Impact assessment – how will it affect individuals, societies, special groups, cultures, nations?[16]

Through writing about the experience of space, Story hopes to capture the depths of humanity:

> Space is huge, inner space is even bigger – the biggest.[17]

At the University of Houston, Clear Lake, where he studied the humanities, Story became poetry editor of the literary arts magazine *Bayousphere*. He enjoyed selecting the poetic material for the publication, something which gave him a chance to practice his skill as a literary critic.

It is worth emphasizing that Story was studying world literature and

---

13. Essay for Romantic Literature, University of Houston, Clear Lake, 8 May 1992.
14. A college paper for the University of Houston, Clear lake, titled *Conceptions, Identifications and Mechanisms of Transcendence in Romantic Poetry*, May 1992.
15. Journal 4, page 8; Date: around April 1988.
16. Journal 8, page 30; Date: 19 June 1990.
17. Journal 4, page 35; Date: 31 January 1989.

developing his style of writing through much of the late 1980s and early 1990s. He found time to do this while training for his last four missions in space. Instead of watching television or attending the theatre, Story attended night school. The pressures to complete training for missions were also parallel to the completion of assignments and preparation for university exams, but Story thrived on it all. The additional means of personal development was a more satisfying way for him to spend his leisure time. And he enjoyed the contrasts between the two very different avenues of interest:

> Just the fact of a scientist, astronaut, pilot, engineer communicating in poetic form and taking and showing a Romantic view of things is an example of factual integration of poet and science. A Romantic, educated, sophisticated, poetic pluralist makes a go of it within the NASA system![18]

During an interview with Story, I ventured to ask "Where does God fit in the process of art and creativity?" Story's reply – "Well, 'he' is the most creative process known… I look at creation and evolution. You look at star birth and star death. You look at everything out there; it reinvents itself continuously. It is born, it grows and dies and life springs anew. If you look at the entire process of the cosmos, the universe, it is spectacularly creative. Its form goes back to finite and then it blows up into this huge expansion of incredible life and incredible forms and then goes back to nothing and then it's back out there again. It's Whitman, but Whitman's creativity is a reflection of the universe… If you will surrender and let go and become part, if you will, of God's creative process, then you are ultimately creative, then anything goes. You see but that's what surrender is. Surrender is getting to the point where you are listening, when you're at one with all of this business out here and if you get rid of all of the biases and all of the rules, you are simply listening – body, mind and soul – to the creativity of the universe."

18. Journal 5, page 27; Date: 10 July 1989.

# Journey

"I surrender to this, can't know it – joy that I can't: it is the quest, the journey and a deep faith in the hope and meaning of it all – I go forward."

# 18. Lasting Impressions

If you got within eye contact distance, you were going to meet Story; it's just the way it was.

*Bob Sieck,*
*Former Launch Director,*
*Kennedy Space Center*

Story Musgrave has shared his journey with many people. Closest to him are his family, who have lived his callings for several decades. Then there are the friends and colleagues who have worked alongside him and shared his passion for all that he does.

There are so many stories about Story. Everyone has a favorite moment, a little anecdote or insight. These help to characterize just who Story is and how he got to be like that. Together they form a unique collection of lasting impressions.

*

Story's family has always been incredibly important to him. According to Patricia Musgrave, he had a good relationship with their children as they were growing up. "They didn't have that much time with him, you know, but the time they had with him was quality time; he made the time. I mean Story is all or nothing. It wasn't necessarily 'normal' –I went to all of the basketball games, baseball games, swimming team meets, I worked on the swim team meets. Jeffrey had a camping trip and it was a fathers' camping trip and I was the 'dad'. And I got an award for that. I got an award for being the dad! I slept in this tent, all men – I was the only mom; Story was not available. But when he was available, he made himself available, but it was not a normal way of bringing up kids. It really wasn't normal because he wasn't around; he just wasn't around."

Daughter Holly recalled, "I think that probably the biggest thing was that he just loved to play when we were growing up. He always liked to play games. He wasn't, you know, coming home being an orderly father; he just loved to play. So I just remember us playing an incredible amount – with five kids – him being the biggest instigator.

"When I was in the second grade he bought the motor cycle and a lot of times he would take me riding. It was a BSA1000; I would be riding behind him. You know what a BSA is? It's a big bike! So we'd go riding around at night or ride up to the store.

"We did a lot of things as a family. We belonged to the pool and would go out swimming. My dad had bought us a little Honda motor bike – it's just a tiny little kid's one – and one of us would get on the motorcycle and others of us would be on our bicycles and we would ride out to these woods called Wildwood. There was a big old ditch and we used to go in and out of that. We were real outdoorsy; it was kind of a small town atmosphere because we were forty miles outside of Houston and, back then, in the old days, there were a lot of astronaut families in the neighborhood.

"We had a very simple lifestyle. I remember the big special occasions were driving all the way out to the Galleria – they have an ice-skating rink and we'd go ice-skating. And a place called Farrells; they had hotdogs. Or getting ice-cream if there was a birthday. We'd have a big family dinner and Sunday nights we'd watch the Disney channel, the Disney movie, and the big thing was to have a bowl of ice-cream."

Story encouraged his children in whatever they chose to do. According to Holly, "He encouraged us – we were big in sport, we pursued sports and music and he was, of course, big on education. He always wanted us to see what we wanted to do; we were pretty much on our own. He never said, you should do this or you should do that.

"I remember as a little kid, vividly, he had bought these wooden desks. Well, he had all of our little desks along the wall and that was the study room and he would be sitting there at night, every night, working and playing his music and I'd come up and ask him, 'Dad, what do you do at the office?' 'cause I had no idea what an astronaut did. You fly in space, what can you possibly do in an office? And I would ask him for years, I had not a clue. And his answers, I just never seemed to get any of them. So that was like a big question mark for a number of years for me growing up."

On weekends, Story would take the children to the NASA gym and they would play while he worked out. Afterwards, he would take them all to McDonalds. Holly explained, "We had a routine, we had a simple routine, all the little favorite places we liked to go."

As his children became teenagers, Story learnt to skateboard so that he could share that activity with them. They would take it in turns to ride, towing their skateboards behind the car. He also bought a Volkswagen 'bug' for each of them – all different colors.

Holly has a favorite, treasured photo of her father. "This picture I have on my dresser of my Dad – he's got a NASA sweatshirt on and it's just blue skies. It's at the Florida beach. We're having a meal at the beach house before the Shuttle launch and the astronaut crew is together. And that picture, to me, just captures my Dad. He's got this NASA sweatshirt on and he's sitting on the beach house porch... He's got this smile on his face – kind of a confidence in a way, but I don't think that's the right word: it's life, just capturing life. At that moment he's got his family, the crew, he's got the beach there, he has his NASA sweatshirt – I love that picture."

Daughter Lorelei Musgrave praised her father. "He couldn't do a better job as a Dad." Although she recalled that he worked an awful lot, she said he was very attentive to his kids, gave them all a great deal of love and taught them to believe in themselves. She added, "He's been the same for the forty years that I've known him; the same person throughout his life."

Lorelei also spoke of her father's motivation which has enabled him to "do it all". She said he has so much drive in his body, which she refers to as his "natural car".

Todd Musgrave spoke of his father's respect for all forms of life. "I was watching TV, perhaps a football game. Dad was busy moving furniture around, looking for the cricket that was making noise, only to go silent when he got close to it. He spent about twenty minutes trying to capture the cricket and then he released the cricket outside. The cricket episode is reflective of his appreciation for life and the effort he will make for preserving the smallest of creatures."

One of Story's favorite activities is reading. Todd explained, "Dad loves literature, or the ability to further his education, not only for the sake of understanding, but also because of his views on ageing. He will forever challenge and exercise his mind in order to keep it active and young... He has read more books at a quicker pace than anyone I am aware of."

Holly described her father as gracious. "He's very gracious with people. Not even the word 'hospitality', but 'gracious'. He's very gracious because he's very non-judgmental. He may think he's judgmental 'cause he likes to joke and poke fun, and criticize, but he's actually very non-judgmental, 'cause when he meets people, he really appreciates what they have to offer. He's more interested in getting to know them than trying to say what he's accomplished to them."

Personality-wise, Holly describes her father as both an introvert and an extrovert. "The extrovert is more his performances and his charismatic side, but the introvert is where he really is in his soul – he's kind of seeking and likes to really dwell and reflect and he likes his peace. It's very much about peace, having peace and I'd say peace is a big thing. He likes the quietness, the solitude."

Though Story now lives in Florida and his children have their own lives in other parts of the country, he has remained close to them. The family gets together every Christmas in Houston at the El Lago home. Story and Patricia, his first wife, have also remained close. According to Patricia, "It's a testimony of love. I love Story for the person he is – he is the father of my children; we were married at one time. He is a dear friend; I respect him greatly. And so if he had a problem and if he needed something, I would be there by his side. I've never said that to him, but we've been through a lot together and, you know, sure there were differences, there were hurts and pains, but they're over with. We had twenty-one years of marriage. But the link is the children of course; it's great for my kids."

Patricia added, "He's an amazing person, unique in his time."

Story's youngest son Lane, who was born in 1987, did not have the opportunity to grow up around his father. The only child from Story's second marriage, his parents separated when he was only a few years old. Lane does, however, have fond memories of visiting his Dad. He recalled, "Usually he would pick me up on a Friday afternoon and then we would just go to his house and sometimes we would go to a toy store and he would buy me Lego or a super Nintendo game or something like that and we'd go home and do that for a while. And then sometimes after that we would go to the NASA gym. There usually wasn't anyone there 'cause it was late and we'd go to the racquet ball courts and stuff and play dodge ball – I think we called it monster ball 'cause he had some balls that had monsters all over them. Then there was this giant rope that was hanging down in this wide open area and I'd always grab onto it and he would push me back and forth, which was fun. Whenever we would drive to NASA, he would always let me sit on his lap and he would do the shifting but he would let me drive. Even when I was six years old, he would let me actually have full control of the steering wheel while he would do the pedals – I remember that was so much fun."

Over the years, Lane and Story have come to know each other better. Lane has made regular visits to Story's Florida home. According to Lane, "It's been hard to treat him like a dad when I didn't see him very often, but when I do see him it's nice 'cause we kind of just pick up where we left off and I can talk to him about things that I wouldn't talk to other people about. So, it's good… I just love the way it is now – we email and talk on the phone and everything, but I think we're still pretty close."

It's the everyday things which Lane enjoys doing with Story during those visits. "I remember early on we would always play Battleship while we ate. He would have these elaborate strategies and would take it so seriously – I think we're pretty competitive. We also love watching James Bond movies and we always laugh a lot about different characters in the movie."

Lane was a small child at several of Story's space launches, however, as he got a little older, he began to understand what they meant: "At two and four [years of age] I don't remember anything, but at six I understood kind of that he's going into space and he wouldn't be back for a while, but I didn't realize how dangerous it was and everything. But I think when I was about nine I really realized how dangerous it was and was just really, really worried. But it was a fun experience 'cause we got to stay in a hotel and I got to play with all the other astronauts' kids. Then we'd go to the [Launch Center] and they'd always have tons of food and a lot of fun games to play with. But then when the time came for him to lift-off, it was just pretty scary – I didn't really like it."

Like a lot of other astronauts' children, Lane was also too young to be allowed to see Story during the quarantine period before a mission. He explained, "You have to be eighteen, so I'd never get to see him before he went off. But there's a time, I think it's the day before the mission, when you go to this place right by the launch pad and the astronauts stand on one side of this ditch and we stand on the other side and you can talk across the ditch, but you can't go closer than about twenty feet."

These days Lane and Story are able to talk about Story's experiences in space and much more. Lane says his father is very unique. "He's an artist, he writes poetry and, overall, he's just really, really creative – I think that's the type of person he is. Everything he does is unique and I've never seen him do something where he'd say, 'Oh that's a nice way to do it.' He'd always try to find a better way to do it. I really think that's a great way to live."

Lane's mother Carol spoke of Story's complexity. "He's just always going to have to seek self-expression in different ways, I think. He is so difficult to try to just encapsulate because there are so many different levels to him. Looking back to some of the genetics that go way back – to Joseph Story and William Wetmore Story – what I would call their technical intensity – Story has that engineering, incredibly detail-oriented ability to grasp and master technicalities. I looked at it as the same type of genetics, just with a different expression, 'cause they took it to the extreme as well. After the Challenger [accident] happened, that's when Story decided to go back to school 'cause there was such a lag in time and training and that kind of thing. And just kind of matter-of-factly deciding that he had wanted to read the classics, he'd decided that he was going to write the most excellent of literature. What a demarcation! But I look at it as William Wetmore Story, just peeling off this incredible legal career and becoming an ex-patriot to Paris or Rome to do his sculpture."

Early on in their acquaintance, Carol asked Story what his hobby was. She recalled, "What was so appealing to me – I remember him saying, 'Oh, I'm cataloguing human knowledge.' I went, 'Wow, this is a big thinker'! Here he was, the astronaut's astronaut, the flying ace and whatnot, but he was so far from that stick and rudder mentality with the breadth of his interest even back then."

Carol believes Story has made certain sacrifices to achieve all that he has. "He epitomizes, to me, just hard work at the extreme, the self-discipline it takes to achieve excellence. So very few people will ever sacrifice what he did and does."

When asked what these sacrifices might have been, Carol offered this: "One of the things is intimate relationships. I did an awful lot of thinking and studying and going back, also trying to figure out through his childhood, and I think every event that's happened in his life has been part of a destiny – even very negative things worked together for preparing him for who he is. When I say intimacy issues, I don't mean physical intimacy but what it takes to be able to let down and soften. I think that part of that difficulty with a deeper level of intimacy comes from so many painful experiences and having to always to move on in strategic ways – and it's that moving on and that focus on productivity at all times – they almost are diametrically opposed to it I think. I just think movement is germane to who he is and I think that he always has to have that. Movement, as well as that genetic, creative drive."

Carol believes it was Story's childhood which formed him. "That was all the forming of him, along with all the abuse and whatever. That is where the whole story of transcendence, that is where all the roots were secured in the ground – his will to just survive. But I think it goes beyond that – just to transcend, and he ultimately transcended it. But that's where I think he built this self-absorption, that inwardness – that he had to anchor himself through himself, for better or for worse. I think he is an introvert as opposed to an extrovert. I draw a line between the two: what recharges you in the end? And I think some people seek out other people – it's what fills their cup, whereas Story goes inward and to his books and to his mind."

Story and Carol dated during the lead up to Story's second mission, STS-51F/Spacelab 2 in 1985. As a flight engineer on the Shuttle Training Aircraft, Carol was very much involved with the mission. "I think one of the favorite moments was when I was flight engineering. Our main courtship time, which was just a glorious time, was during 51F and I was flying an awful lot during that period of time myself. And I remember Story was in quarantine but we arranged – I snuck in and he snuck out – I had one of the government cars that we could go back and forth in. We went out and parked somewhere and I remember we just played music and talked and laughed, but it was mainly just the romance of the heavens, looking up. And somebody came up – it was a guard and the lights shone on us. And what Story said at that time was hilarious. The guard said "What are you two doing?" and Story said something like: "We're working on mission training!" It was just a very funny comeback."

Married in April 1986, Story and Carol's union lasted only a few years. Despite this, Carol remembered how Story's thoughtfulness, later on, caught her by surprise. "We were separated and he was going with another person at the time, I believe, and he was invited to the White House. And he invited me to go with him because he just thought it would be a very special thing for me to do and that I deserved to do that. And I thought that was such an intuitively thoughtful and wonderful thing to do. I went, of course, and it was an extremely memorable event."

According to Carol, another trait which characterizes Story is humbleness. "There is an over-riding humility in Story. Even though he can be unnerving to a lot of people, he has still such an appreciation, he can step back and see the privilege of the position he's had and I think that has been so critical to him being able to grow and keep that childlike desire to explore; he doesn't calcify. I think that's a very grounding thing and I remember also, along with it, the feeling of the need to 'give back', that this is a privilege and a unique one, and he would speak a lot in schools."

Friend and mentor Ben Eiseman, who knew Story during his internship at the University of Kentucky and later on at Denver General Hospital, also spoke of Story's humbleness. "One of the elements I think in Story's personality that is absolutely essential is a humbleness. He has that innate humbleness that he's not totally certain he's right. He's going to analyze it, come up with his own decision on the basis of the data he has, but he has an innate humbleness of spirit."

Tom Jones who shared Story's last space mission, STS-80, enjoyed Story's down-to-earth attitude. "Because he had this eccentric reputation, when I first met him and listened to him talk – you know here's this veteran of the space program who had the perseverance to wait sixteen years to fly in space the first time – and you're so impressed with the guy's dedication and excellence that you think of him only in terms of these sort of mythic accomplishments. And so what surprised me was how easy he was to get along with and work with on a daily basis."

Ron Sheffield, who was test director for the Neutral Buoyancy Simulations for STS-61, said, "I found that with all of his degrees that he really didn't come across as an arrogant 'me'; he was really the team player."

Roger Balettie, who worked as a Flight Dynamics Officer in Mission Control said of Story, "He was always friendly, he never ever was pretentious. Sometimes you'll get some of these former fighter pilot types who kind of have that cockiness about them but Story was always just one of the guys. It didn't matter if you ran into him at the grocery store or during a meeting, he was always the same – just extremely friendly.

Obviously he's a brilliant man. He definitely knows what he's talking about and is extremely well respected. It was always interesting too – when you were in a meeting with Story, if he started to speak, everyone was quiet, because he didn't say much, but what he said was important. He never talked just to hear himself talk.

"He always strikes me as almost born out of time. He strikes me as he would have been a Columbus, he would have been a Lewis and Clark, an explorer. He has to know something new. He doesn't want to be stagnant, he doesn't want to go to the office and be an accountant. He has that drive, that passion of wanting to expand what we know and where we've been, for the benefit of everyone. And I think everything about him really fits into that: his selflessness – I want to do this, not only for me, but for everyone.

"I really think they missed creating a role for him to be an official NASA spokesperson. Right now he's out there and he's promoting them and promoting space flight. NASA really missed a bet by not making him an official ambassador."

Darlene Cavalier, who helped to co-ordinate some of Story's post-NASA theater performances, recalled, "My first impression of Story, already realizing his astonishing academic and professional achievements, was how simply unassuming he was. He took his role seriously and truly wowed the audience during and after his performance. I heard several people comment that he provided a sense of personal inspiration. To hear this celebrity speak of the unprivileged life he had led and how determination, knowledge, persistence and the drive to excel yielded such incredible results, is, in a real sense, analogous to a fairy tale story. Yet, there stood a man, eager to share his experiences and insights with the world, young and old, successful or not. All of them walked away inspired and hopeful."

Filmmaker Katey Grusovin recalled her first encounter with Story's performance persona. "I think back to that moment when I first saw him at the Powerhouse.[1] And I think about the response of everybody in that room. Story has the most incredible ability to excite your curiosity and wonder about space and who you are. But it transcends space, it's something else. I actually think Story is a brilliant communicator. I think that's what he is, absolutely what he is superb at, with clearness and simplicity. I think it helps if you're on his wavelength, but I just go back to that – it's clean and simple, it's powerful.

"He had this absolute ability to hold the audience. I thought it was really powerful how he [used his body] in the middle of the slides, you know, where you have the universe projected onto him. It's his artistry, it's his perspective – it was the biggest mind-blowing thing… talking to friends and acquaintances afterwards who said it was just the most incredible experience they'd ever had."

Story does not fit neatly into the Western culture. Katey explained, "One of the paradoxes with Story as well, is that he is a creature of America but he's also not your typical American. In a way his story is kind of the American dream, but at the same

1. Powerhouse Museum, Sydney, Australia.

time it's not. It's the money factor – I think he genuinely detests the consumer kind of culture. That's a really interesting dimension. The space program is this incredible American enterprise which was fueled by the Russians as well. I don't think you could have had it without a cold war; it would have never gotten anywhere. Then you have this person within it who has to do this dance – who flowered within NASA, but also had to play a game as an outsider. An insider who was an outsider. And finding the edge, walking the edge, being on the edge, and knowing how to play it."

Television producer Tracy Day spoke of Story's openness and honesty in an interview situation. "I think that, you know, when you're talking about institutions, a lot of times [people] are afraid to express an opinion if they think that the opinion is not going to be popular or that the institution isn't taking that same stand. And I think Story just doesn't care. Story is, I think, someone who thinks about things quite independently and doesn't think about the internal politics of it all. That's my sense anyway. He does his own analysis, and says what he thinks.

"He's outspoken but he has so many credentials; people respect him across the board. Even if he's the only person speaking, or taking a certain position, if you will, even if everybody else disagrees with him, even if he's out there all by himself, there is still, there seems to be, based on all of the people I've spoken with, a tremendous respect for him. They don't dismiss what he has to say, even if he's the only one saying it – which I thought was very interesting."

Tracy found Story a delight to watch on-screen. "He makes his points very clearly and very colorfully, so for broadcasts I think he's a very effective speaker. He's very unique in the way he expresses himself and all of that.

"I would say that he is a truly independent thinker, with wide and deep knowledge in many areas. I think he's quite eccentric. He's someone who, you can imagine if he's on a panel of people in suits, Story, because of his language and his passion, and his presentation, he stands out.

"What's interesting – people who are more comfortable with more traditional, conservative people, people who are dressed in suits and people who speak in institution-speak – for many people, that kind of presence translates into credibility. And so they're a little taken aback by the way Story presents his ideas. And what I think is so interesting and unique about him is he has all the credentials to back up everything he says. And I think that if another person with those eccentricities, which are so charming and so delightful, particularly on TV or in person, that if he didn't have the credentials, it would be a very different kind of thing. But he has both, which makes him extremely dynamic, I think."

Ron Sheffield recalled Story's total unselfconsciousness. "I asked the guys who worked for me back East and on the West coast here, 'What do you remember about Story?' And they all came back – the funny thing they remembered about Story is that one day he had a headset on and it kept falling off. So what he did is he taped it to his bald head so it wouldn't fall off! They all remember that. Their comments ranged from – 'The thing I remember about Story is he had a perfect head for taping the head set on', to 'I remember him using the tape on the headset'!"

Ron also remembered Story's forthrightness, from which he never varied. "Story said what he thought was right – he didn't care to whom he was talking. And he could just as easily have told the President of the United States."

Story's passion for space flight has extended over four decades. According to Tom Jones, "I guess he's just so totally focused on space travel and the human reaction to it, all the time. He never steps out of that role of thinking about it, and looking at it from another angle that he hasn't tried before. And most of us engage and focus and work very intensively, get the work done, and disconnect and then do something different – let off some steam, and he's always a guy who… you have to make him come up for air, to make him talk to you about something that's not space-related 'cause that's what he's always thinking about or reflecting on. And working in the office with him day to day, he would always be sitting at his desk, doing either email or reading a document, or preparing or training, or taking notes for himself, writing in his notebooks. So he was never off-point, he was always on. So that's my impression of him, this guy who just lives, eats and sleeps space travel."

In Brian O'Leary's autobiography, *The Making of an Ex-Astronaut,* (published by Houghton Mifflin, 1970), he described what was often referred to among the astronaut office as "the Musgrave Maneuver." In effect, O'Leary was describing Story's reputation for over-achievement. According to Carol Musgrave, "It's an interesting kind of perspective. I think it was the idea that nothing would stop Story! It could be seen almost in a negative way too as just incredible ambition or promoting the self, or an internal drive that he almost couldn't even control, however, I look upon it in a higher way as Story's transcendence."

Jim Thornton from the EVA office remembered Story's thoroughness. "He was just impressive by his preparation. Whenever he would come into a training event, whether it would be a neutral buoyancy test or a classroom training session, it was obvious that he had done his homework and thought about a lot of different ways to approach things. It would be interesting to go up to his office to visit with him – he'd usually have a big stack of index cards in front of him on his desk and that was his way, I think, of drilling himself. That was his method of preparation for whatever it was that he was studying – whether it was procedures or how to do a Hubble repair task or if it was a malfunction that he was rehearsing for the suit or whatever. He would have this thick stack of index cards and he would be going through those one by one, just kind of drilling himself on what his response would be."

According to Jim, Story would try to challenge and stimulate people's thought processes during preparation for the Hubble Repair Mission. "He has ideas on virtually everything. A lot of them we adopted. There's some we just totally dismissed as being too far out there and we didn't think it was practical, and he would accept that. I think that's the kind of person that he is. He was not necessarily married to his own ideas; he would just be in brainstorm mode and think of a lot of different approaches – some were probably the right approach and others weren't going to work."

Bob Sieck, who was launch director at the Kennedy Space Center for each of Story's flights, said Story lives and breathes space. "He's just a very genuine person and he always has space on his mind. He always does. Whatever you're talking about, immediately Story will get the conversation transitioned about something to do with space... He's genuinely interested in you and your participation in the program and it obviously comes across the tremendous passion that he has for space flight.

"I think it's the psychological and the human aspect of it. Not only the effect it has on the people that fly, like himself obviously, but the effect and impact it has on the population and the people. He does a good job of tying the emotions that go along with human space flight and putting it in terms that elementary school kids or us gray beards and everyone in between can understand. He humanizes space flight. He's just so passionate about it and puts the human touch to it better than probably [anyone] – I mean there are some very articulate and outstanding astronauts out there – but I think he characterizes the best of any of them."

Roger Balettie agreed. "One of the things I remember most is that space flight was not a job, it wasn't a career, it wasn't a profession, it was a passion! It was something we all believed in. You could see it in the way people got excited about it and there was no grumbling when you got picked to work the 2am to whatever shift. You knew that you were picked 'cause you needed to do that and they needed you. Story, definitely, is the public embodiment of that passion. People can look at Story, they can see his accomplishments, they can hear it in his voice and the way he talks and presents it. It's a passion that doesn't leave you when you leave NASA.

"One of my favorite memories of working in Mission Control was when we were working on the STS-71 mission, the first docking of the Shuttle with MIR. I was on the FIDO team and Story was our Capcom. And this was a big deal, this was like the Hubble mission; this was huge, high profile; everyone was watching. After we finished the actual docking, when we were mated and people were able to breathe again, and everybody is starting to wind down during one of our break periods, Story gets up, he comes down to where we were sitting – down in the front row at Mission Control – and he was congratulating everyone on a great job. He goes, 'You know what? You guys are my heroes!' And I can't tell you how much that meant to us. The fact that Story Musgrave, this world-renowned, famous, powerful, influential astronaut comes down and says something like that."

Beth Turner, who was Story's secretary for STS-61, the Hubble Repair Mission, recalled the first time she met Story. It was in the astronaut office and they were both trying to get a cup of coffee in a confined space. According to Beth, who described herself as a pretty heavy girl at that time, "He said something kind of cute or funny or sarcastic, and I said, 'Story, if you're not careful, I'm gonna sit on you!' Well, Story's eyes got real big and he said, 'Oh really?' Immediately he had turned it around! I said, 'That is not a compliment, that is not a good thing!' And from then on we had a real great joking relationship. He was always fun to be around. You never knew what to expect."

Being organized was important to Story. According to Beth, who worked with Story on a daily basis at that time, "I remember he had these little shelf dividers you could sit on top of your desk – they were maybe three foot in length and they had three shelves – and you could put maybe a five by seven paper in each little cubby hole. He had these on his desk and it was all organized into different notes or pictures he needed to sign, research information. You'd say – Story can you find a picture? And he'd pull it out. He was just very organized."

Story's generosity impressed Beth. "He's one of the most giving people. The astronauts can fly ten items in an official flight kit and then they can fly twenty personal things. Each crew member gets to fly these things on a mission. And Story was so just uncommercial. He was in it to do a better turn for mankind – not to be magnanimous – but he was just in it for the big picture. He would give these slots away. First time flyers or second time fliers have mums, dads, aunts and uncles, and everybody wants to fly something on the Shuttle, so these little slots become very precious. Story might fly stuff for his kids, then the training team, but that was pretty much it. But then he would divvy it up among the other crew members so they could fly extra stuff for their schools or stuff like that."

According to Beth, "I always remember just joking around with him, having fun. You remember 'Story stories' with laughter usually!"

In June 2003, Story was inducted into the Astronaut Hall of Fame at the Cape. Bob Sieck listened to Story's speech as he received his medal. "When he was inducted, as it were, he made a comment to the effect that, I really work hard at making the space program successful and, 'cause I am who I am, I do it my way. And he said, sometimes I got rewarded for it, like this here – and he shows his medal – and he said, other times I get my butt kicked for it! Which of course everybody roared about, 'cause he is, you know, very outspoken."

Many people refer to Story's charismatic personality. Bob, for instance, explained that whenever Story visited the Kennedy Space Center, workers would be drawn to him. "He's like the pied piper…walking through the work area down here with his blue suit with the little nameplate that says 'Story' on it, not 'Dr Musgrave' or anything like that… I mean, as soon as he walks into the high bay where the work's going on, everybody just stops what they're doing and goes over there and says 'Hey Story, how goes it? Good to see you!' and that sort of thing. There's a crowd around him immediately.

"Everybody knew Story and he made it a point to get acquainted with you. If you got within eye contact distance, you were going to meet Story; it's just the way it was."

Friend Mort Kasdan, who has known Story for many years through family connections, describes him this way: "Story's a man's man. He is a man that other men can admire and respect... There's nothing superficial about Story. I mean what you see is there – there's no thin veneer – he's solid wood all the way through. Whether you agree with him or not about things, you know where he stands and where you stand in the relationship."

Mort also says Story is very generous with his time. "Time is the most precious thing we all have in life and Story is very generous in sharing his time with children, with anybody. And the president of the hospital staff and the projectionist at his lecture are not treated any differently. I mean everybody is always treated with respect. He is a gentleman."

Another thing which impressed Mort is Story's appreciation for all those who worked with him in the space program. "The last time I saw him lecture it was pretty much the usual space stuff, but it was devoted to the people who supported the astronauts – the people that dressed him and the people that trained him and all these sorts of things. A lot of people ignore that – ignore the people who do the tasks which are routine, but without being done properly, people can die."

Over the years, women have been especially attracted to Story. Former colleague Frank Hughes remembered, "I think with Story, there were always a lot of things about him – one is that the women just fell for him all the time. I think there's a certain quality that he has that brings out the best and the worst of all the women he ever meets. It's partly because he's so damn good at what he does, so that's an attractant. Aside from being good looking, he just has a magnetism about him. And I think there are groupies that deal with baseball players and race car drivers, but I think intelligence is a hell of a big aphrodisiac. And he's as good or better than most. He's very sincere, very impressive, so there's a lot of adventures that way. Not all necessarily bad or good; with Story, you think of women in his life."

Filmmaker Dana Ranga, who profiled Story for a film,[2] made this observation. "I think that every time he looks into the eyes of a woman he changes. He takes up... he's like a chameleon, he gets into another mood and sometimes it's melancholic and sometimes it's, you know, the full rational thing, sometimes it's the child thing... I think the other pole of the woman is very, very important."

When asked what Story was most passionate about, friend John Blaha, who flew with Story on STS-33, said, "Story loves women; his one love in life. I mean I think airplanes and space flight are right behind it, but I told you there what his real number one love was, and maybe still is."

Ron Sheffield, who spent a good deal of time with Story in the lead up to the

2. The film is titled *Story*. Created and directed by Dana Ranga; released 2003.

Hubble Servicing Mission, recalled, "Everywhere Story went he had a good looking lady on his arm! No matter where he went, if there was a good looking lady, Story was there! There's just something about him… first off, he shaved his head when other people weren't doing that; that made him stand out. But he was a smooth talker."

According to Beth Turner, "The joke around the office was Story was always dating young girls – we'd always give him a hard time about that. He had that reputation and I guess it is a little bit deserved!"

Mia Liebowitz, who worked closely with Story for a number of years at the Astronaut Encounter program at the Kennedy Space Center said, "Quite frankly, I think he just loves people. He appreciates beauty in any form. It just happens that women I think are, in general, prettier to look at than men. I think that's why there's such a fascination. I don't think for him it's necessarily about women, it's about beauty in any form. And then the passion. So if he sees someone that's passionate about something, he wants to get to know them a little bit and open up."

According to Holly Musgrave, her father really enjoys being around other people. "I think that he enjoys people because he's intrigued with how other people think and he needs that part. He really needs other people because that's life experiences, and that's the learning from other people and what they're doing. If somebody is from a totally different line of work, he is so interested to learn about that line of work and what they're doing and that's very intriguing to him. So he has to have the social side."

Ron Sheffield recalled how Story would be quite demonstrative at times. "He's one of the few men who will walk up to you and give you a big hug and say, 'I love you'. And this is 1993. I had had some organizational development training and I felt very comfortable with him doing that. But there were other people who felt uncomfortable. But to me it was an accolade!

"I last saw Story at the last HST launch.[3] He was with a bunch of German photographers and I was in the stands. I walked down and was standing back from the group. Well, he stopped and he said to them – 'Come here Ron, I love you'. And he told these guys, 'This is Ron Sheffield, he taught me everything I know about EVA'. I said, 'Wait a minute, time out Story, that's not true'. And he said, 'Yeah you did'. He remembered, knew exactly who I was."

Ron added, "I would say he was a true professional, with a heart of gold, and that's really about all; you can't say it any better than that. He had a genuine concern for those around him and he shared credit with those that worked with him."

When asked if Story has changed, Bob Sieck offered this. "He's still the same Story – you could pick him out in a crowd of a thousand. I could anyway! He hasn't mellowed a bit. Physically I'm sure he's changed a little, but he still reminds me of the same guy I saw about twenty years ago."

3. March 2002.

Joe McMann, who was NASA's lead engineer on EVA said of Story, "From my observations, he has not changed. He has that determination and that focus and it's just incredible. It's interesting when I look at how I spend my time and compare it to the way Story spends his – he doesn't waste a second of the day. In a way it's a model for how you could live your life and this is how you could turn out if you have that kind of focus, you could become another Story Musgrave! Not all of us have that determination or that mental energy which it takes to be that focused all the time."

According to Jim McBarron, who also worked for NASA on EVA development, "I don't think he's changed very much. The physical characteristics have changed, but in terms of his energy and his wit, I think it has been maintained for the whole period of time. The thing that probably surprised me the most was how he managed to get everything done that he did in his lifetime. I don't know where he got the time and energy to do all that he did."

Filmmaker Danga Ranga has this view of Story. "I think probably – when they say there is nobody else like Story Musgrave within the astronauts, it's because he has this incredible life experience and he was lucky, genetically, to be able to live through it.

"I think the wonderful thing, the special thing is, he's doing [space] both rationally and emotionally in a very balanced way. And this is where he beats everybody, because he's very balanced in that point.

"I think he knows how to formulate it on the edge so that people can say, OK, he's crazy, but, we also know it's true. So they let him be a little bit – oh Story's the crazy guy – but on the other hand they know damn well that they wouldn't have the courage to do what he did and to be open the way that he did.

"It was the fulfillment of a dream and an expectation which nobody else has lived up to or achieved until now – not the people I've talked to. I thought, this guy went through hell already and what it was that made him go into space gave him ten times more strength and insight than all the other people ... and I think that this pain that he had to bear, or these experiences, this childhood history, basically made his texture, made him attentive, opened his eyes and ears to life. It made his soul open up; it made it bloom... And I think this is why he is *the* person who went up into space, and I think he's the only one who brought the right message back."

Friend Sharon Daley was asked before STS-61 to describe Story. She came up with the metaphor of a tree. "I described him as a tree; one with age and experience. A large tree with many roots that touch those who know him – they are strong and supportive – a canopy to shade, comfort and protect... The tree reaches out to the sky and relies on the earth for support, much as Story. He really does not know how he impacts people and that he has 'roots' that touch them. In addition, it's the comfort that people get from seeing and hearing from him. Story has given so much in his life. He is not perfect, but he is real, kind and strong."

# 19. Self-Reflections

I have tried to grow up, unsuccessfully
for sixty-six years. I've given up lately.

*Story Musgrave, 28 January 2002*

"I have high hopes for the future, so where I am today, I have to love what I have today. I have incredible opportunities; I am blessed with health. Everything is fantastic as far as I'm concerned. How can I regret the fact that it took every bit of my history to get me to here? How can I regret my past when I have what I have today? That's a philosophy of life."

Story has made statements like this on numerous occasions. It is something he believes; something he lives. It always gets back to the journey, the doing.

He said, "Living the journey, not so much the destination. The destination is the future; where you came from is the past. It's the journey that matters, and so I think that's the key to living in the moment."

In his journal he wrote:

> Discover what your talents are, what [you have] passion for. You choose what is good for you, that activity in which you can be the best you can be. Must enjoy it. Look inward, find out who you are, where you fit.[1]

Where does someone like Story take his journey after all that has happened in his life over seven decades?

"The current path is a new calling. The current path is Beauty. I am making another leap off into an abyss, which I've done in the past, but this leap off into Beauty is the last leap off."

*

Story Musgrave has had a lot of risk in his lifetime and despite the fact that a great deal of it has been physical, you cannot help but focus on the intellectual risks. He has pushed the boundaries of human imagination, of science, of social acceptability, of philosophy. His outspokenness is a direct result of that; the honesty and authenticity which cannot be detached from who he is.

Story is aware that, at times, the way he is, the way he thinks, separates him from mainstream society. This he expresses with the same directness and often subtle humor that he's known for.

> I pretend to be sane often enough to get the job done, long enough to stay employed.[2]

> Living on the edge. Edge of heaven and earth, life and death. Edge of experience, technology, frontier.[3]

---

1. Journal 22, page 6; Date; 22 May 1997.
2. Story's handwritten note in his copy of *Transcendence*: Herbert W. Richardson and Donald R. Cutler (Editors), Boston: Beacon Press, 1969.
3. Journal 3, page 5; Date: around January 1988.

Identify oneself with the requirements of immediate existence, reliance or own ingenuity, not human opinion. [4]

Space – an outer, physical edge. Story also pushes to the inner edge of madness in pursuit of the unknown.[5]

I have never regretted doing anything, but I have regretted not doing some things.[6]

I have become a variable vagabond; my mind and imagination traveling, floating throughout the universe.[7]

I'm living in a dream world, but somehow I pretend not to be in a dream at NASA… I'm in a continual dream world and it surprises me how very well I can survive in the real world.[8]

You are an alien there [at NASA], an outsider. In the sense of conformity, where it is, who has it, you don't. You are a classical creative visionary, way ahead of your time, poetic alienation, artistic alienation, alternative persona.[9]

I do many an attempt to reality test – response is usually, "well, you are in touch with something, but you are not thinking like a normal human." At times like this, there is no one far enough out to check with![10]

And, perhaps the best self-description of how Story walks that edge:

Toe the line, work the edge, test the limits of all issues and philosophies. Define the boundaries, highlight the tensions, the spaces of all knowledge systems.[11]

At the same time, Story has an aversion to the social niceties. They are a distraction from the real path which he desires:

Last three days, a solid serve of meals, cocktails and talking until midnight… minimize one-on-one hours at a table when could do 1000 school kids! Reach 4 people versus 1000! Not into small talk, cocktails and 3-4 hours of dinner.[12]

Cocktail party is contactless sociability.[13]

4. Journal 3, page 23; Date 19 September 1988.
5. Journal 7, page 49; Date: 25 April 1990.
6. Journal 8, page 46; Date: 11 August 1990.
7. Journal 12, page 18; Date: 3 February 1992.
8. Journal 12, page 20; Date: 5 February 1992.
9. Journal 20, page 10; Date: 14 July 1996.
10. Journal 9, page 7; Date: unknown, comment added later.
11. Journal 4, page 10; Date: 11 July 1988.
12. Journal 15, page 13; Date: 19 February 1994.
13. Journal 15, page 44; Date 19 February 1994.

Story is the kind of person who doesn't like to waste time. He has made a point of learning continuously. When traveling, he carries several books and reads during every spare moment.

> Only purpose of life is to learn: meaning of life. People are teachers to others – by purpose. Everyone can offer you something.[14]

> What mountain are you climbing and what tools are you using to get there?[15]

Continually exercising both the body and the brain is also a means to longevity, something which Story desires.

> Longevity and health are very, very significant issues at this point, and in fact, always were. But you have delayed your own launch until the age of 62 years – if you are to do something and enjoy something beyond this point, longevity is key.[16]

> We are going to the gym each day, that is a good barometer for your spirituality. When the gym becomes important to you, you seem to have the right spirituality, attitude and life… the gym not only helps, it serves as a signal.[17]

> Longevity is a key issue – we want it, we want to live to a hundred, now get the courage to go for it! We not only want it, we need it to get done what we must. We've got a large agenda, a full plate – need time.[18]

> Here we are at 60, starting a new journal, on the eve of cataract surgery … yet we are all hope and optimism. 60th birthday perceived as the biggest, the best and most significant birthday that we have ever had!! Who knows why, but it is felt as a distinct passage, transformation, boundary crossing, milestone, wicket, stage, edge – it is perceived as a point at which I embark on a distinctively new life, a new way of business, new perspective, perception, and a new and vitalized spirit![19]

Story does not like to dwell on negative things; that is another personal philosophy. There are many things which could have been expanded upon in this biography, but in the search for who Story is, how he got to be like that, it was important to leave the reader with the impression of how he lives his life – and transcending those things which are not inspiring and transforming is a major part of that. Two journal entries, in particular, highlight this:

14. Journal 5, page 13; Date: June 1989.
15. Journal 5, page 15; Date: June 1989.
16. Journal 18, page 2; Date: 19 August 1995.
17. Journal 16, page 3; Date: 17 July 1994.
18. Journal 16, page 3; Date: 17 July 1994.
19. Journal 18, page 1; Date: 19 August 1995.

The good, the great and the grand – no one wants to hear about your frustrations, only your victories – transcend the losses, push out of mind, don't talk about them.[20]

Don't look for the fruits of your labor – just labor perfectly.[21]

Story is a survivor. There have been seemingly endless challenges, tragedies and bureaucracies which needed to either be attacked head-on or worked through to get to this current point. Through a great deal of self-analysis, Story eventually arrived at the metaphor of water, which he felt best described his character. He said, "I look upon myself [metaphorically] as 'water'. Life, therefore, for myself, is like water. I can't be beat down and I'm tough. Flexible but tough. If you hit water, it moves out of the way, but you don't hurt it due to it's flexibility."

In his journals he wrote:

Water seeks it's own level; so does Story.[22]

I am water, push me, pull me, splash me, drink me – you can't burn me![23]

Where do I leave off and where does my environment begin? I swim in water or space. I switch roles and look at myself. I become the water, I breathe, and I am now the air and enter and envelop Story.[24]

Story as water in a divergent stream – must I follow one path or can I take all? – yes!… Water is archetypal, experiential, meaning etc… All experience of life must have water – water is life.[25]

In their creation, Story never intended that his personal journals would be read by anybody else, but he decided to make them available for this biography. For this reason, the entries which appear should be viewed in that context. They do, however, give us a tremendously rich insight into just who Story is and what he believes.

Story has written a great deal about love and relationships in his journals, and therefore sensitivity is necessary in order to maintain the privacy of the individuals concerned. One particular extract, however, reveals the real romantic soul within him and the importance of love in his life:

We are in short break here – so nice not to be on the road.

---

20. Journal 19, page 27; Date: 22 April 1996.
21. Journal 23, page 24; Date: 12 August 1997.
22. Journal 7, page 55; Date: 27 May 1990.
23. Journal 9, page 8; Date unknown, comment added later.
24. Journal 9, page 46; Date: 19 October 1990.
25. Journal 9, page 50; Date: 26 October 1990.

> Love and beauty: analogically related.
> Love is not in the object, there is an object of love. Love is in us, but love of what?
> I am in love, immersed in the experience of love, but in love with what?
> Love is a relationship, interaction.[26]

Intimacy is a part of that necessity:

> Biological need for intimacy.
> Intimacy fulfils the need, the real need.
> I can control my solitude, not my intimacy.
> Easier to be solitary. Need to be intimate.[27]

One had to ask the question about relationships in Story's life and how much the early relationships, or lack thereof, impacted on later years. Story said, "It's a very good question – did this make it more difficult for me to develop relationships with other people later on? I have had friends and intimates that think it may have played a role in my faith and confidence in how much I was willing to anchor myself to other people. There's no question that I have been, in an Emersonian way, a self-reliant person. If you read a lot of his essays, that's me – self-reliance. And so my anchor was always me. And it was always in my own self-identity and developing that. And so at the earliest ages, I was responsible for my life. I said, man what kind of world is this? So I knew it had to be me and not out there. And I knew that I was not messed up, but that there were parts of the environment that were horribly messed up. But this was not me, so that was rather straight."

Story's mother has been an important figure in his life; he loved her enormously. He explained, "My Mom loved me; my Mom had unconditional love from the beginning on. I think she communicated to me that I was special – maybe that happens for all moms and children. But her relationship with me was that I was some other sort of being in this world, that I was not ordinary and I think she communicated that to me. But she had unconditional love – she accepted me for who I was. She probably was of immense influence, but she never tried to influence me – that wasn't the way she worked. She never tried to bend me, she never tried to give me her belief systems or her way of life, other than leading by example, so she just provided a medium for me to grow in – by example, very little guidance, just the lessons of who she was. And I think I came out a lot like her – my feminist side and my kind of laissez-faire approach to other people, my gentleness, sensitivities – they could have come from her 'cause I'm a lot like her in that way... My being in the space program – it was no different than the day I didn't graduate from school. And I did not sit with the graduating class,

26. Journal 31, page 25; Date: 26 June 2001.
27. Journal 5, page 16; Date: June 1989.

I sat with her. It was no different than that. And you see, that was a part of Mom that I really respected and adored – in victory or in defeat, she accepted who I was."

Story emphasized the importance that women have had in his life. "My relationships with women – part of the magic of that is my physical participation, you know, with the universe, with the earth. So that is in everything I do, it's an outlet for bodily interaction and bodily expression and bodily sensations.

"A romantic relationship – in a way, it's participation in the universe and the processes. Believe it or not, I take it to that – it's highly personal of course, but it's also a sensory bodily participation in the processes which are going on and I see that and I feel that, even at that kind of level which I do with nature. I'm always feeling the universe at play… I live it all the time. But I think it's part of the quest; the sense that, I always know that I live – from the big picture – in a very small little world. I always have a sense of the history and the trajectory and the future.

"I not only look at the particulars and the personal relationships and the details of the particular person and the particular moment, but I also feel my participation in the bigger process. I feel I bring it to a higher level and I just always have that running in my mind that this is a way of physically participating in the universe. When I go out into nature, I'm always picking up dirt – people notice that – I always pick up a handful of dirt in my hands. I go out and touch and I go out and feel the nature. And nature is hugely compelling with me but so are women. So the whole thing is, it's a physical participation in this bigger picture, this bigger process. It is not just the individual relationship. That is why it is very powerful for me.

"And so it's very neat and it's a human to human interaction. But it's bigger than that. You get into feeling reproduction, you get into feeling evolutionary forces, you get into feeling the participation in the process and you get a sense of evolution and the trajectory and propagation of the species and you do all of those kinds of things.

"So I have enjoyed the particular, I have enjoyed the personal, I have enjoyed the exploration and it's an exploration in which two people go and explore – they explore the relationship. They explore the intellectual and they explore the physical."

Relationships help to define who Story is. "The mirror is very important for self-identity – who am I? Well I don't define myself, I listen to other people. My rock is me – there is no question, my self-identity, that I am my rock. But I use other people to help define my rock. I'm an incredibly good listener; I'm an intense listener. I work on that… And so they do have a huge influence because I am sensitive and I listen and I'm always looking to remold myself and to reinvent myself and I do that through interaction with other people."

Through the years, Story has spent a great deal of time living alone. He said, "I do exceedingly well on my own. And so I guess maybe it's living in all worlds. It's that you can live with people, but at times people have thought I was a loner – I am not a loner. I've struggled with that myself – not with being a loner, but my own perception as to whether I was somewhat introvert or extrovert… I'm both – I live in both those worlds. I am very private and I can do exceedingly well in isolation; I do fantastically well in isolation. But I'm also comfortable being an extrovert. I'm comfortable with performance, which is a very personal human thing."

There is perhaps nothing more important in Story's life than his children. In time, those relationships have gotten stronger and he is in regular contact with each of them. He explained, "We've been at it forty something years! I have a good bunch of kids and you never quite know how the family dynamic is going to evolve. But this particular family dynamic – the critical thing you can say about this – is acceptance; acceptance of the other people. And so it's non-judgmental. It's sort of like my Mom: here is this sibling, here is this brother, sister, daughter, son and you simply accept them for what they are. You don't expect more and you don't expect less and you don't want more and you don't want less and you don't wish they were different; here they are. And this is my relationship to the children, but it's also the way the children look at each other. You don't look at them in terms of what things they might be or how they've failed or succeeded; you look at them through their own eyes as to how life has treated them and you hope that life will treat them well. You don't impose external standards on them. And so whatever happens to them, you're not looking at them in terms of their successes or failures, you're looking at them in terms of how life has gone for them. You want life to go well for them.

"But the kids – I was very good at letting them go when they entered teenage and adolescence. At the point at which they wanted to be on their own two feet and be their own being – well, I was letting them do that long before they got into the teenage, adolescent years. I always let them do that and so the transition in the relationship from father and child into being two adults, I was exceedingly good at that. I gave them as much guidance as they wanted and no more. And I let them grow. I let them become the adults they wanted to become and if I made any errors, it was in a lack of direction and a lack of control. I never directed them in terms of a college, in terms of occupation, in terms of being something – I never directed, I only supported them in the directions they wanted to go in. And throughout those years, I never lost contact with the kids in their teenage or adolescent years; there was never a break because I moved the relationship from father and child – I moved that relationship in a timely fashion, at the appropriate times, toward our being two adults.

"My relationship with them today is very, very solidly on [the fact that] they are adults and I'm an adult, and we're friends. You never totally get rid of the child-parent relationship, but I have, as much as you can. We didn't carry that baggage as we've gone forward. We've been able to reinvent ourselves and to redefine the relationship in terms of being two adults, two caring adults."

Despite the lack of parental intervention in their trajectories, was it possible that Story still had some expectations, even unspoken ones, for his children as adults? Being the kind of person he is, who is incredibly self-motivated and hard working, was this something he projected onto his children, even unconsciously?

According to Story, "I've tended to think that they do what they want to do, but maybe I'm not totally realistic on that. It is possible that the kind of life I've led is imposing. It may be that, in some way, it's perceived as an impossible standard. I've never thought of it as a standard, and as I've said, I have never put expectations on them; I've *never* put expectations on them. And they don't put expectations on each other; it's kind of an acceptance. On the other hand, you know, it's hard to say that's perfect.

"The hope for the children is simply that they arrive at a peace with who they are and that they arrive on some trajectory through life – occupation may or may not be important to them. Occupation is important to different people to different degrees. I hope they achieve a serenity and a calmness and a peace with the world they have."

A lot has been said about the strains of being part of an astronaut family – in particular the long hours, the dedication to career, the risks. Story doesn't accept the mainstream negative view of that. "I don't accept the idea that there's a lot more pressure on the families of astronauts. There's more risk, there's more damn danger and there's no question about that. There are dangers in the airplane, dangers in the machinery and dangers in space flight. And that is not pleasant and I have been on that roof [of the Launch Control Center where the families view the launches] on many other missions. I've been with families at launch time and that's not pleasant. They are hurting and they should be hurting; I've seen that.

"In my own case, of course, space flight – which is not true for most – was a calling. My thinking about it and my dedication and passion for it was beyond just being a professional. And so it was not just a job for me, it was a lot more than that.

"If you have someone who has a calling, then you have to share the calling. And so it's not just long hours and travel, but if you have a calling you have to share that. As a spouse, you have to share that. It's almost like a mistress – I don't know if that's the right term – but it's almost like that… You have risk and if you have a calling, that's the ultimate kind of occupation – to have an occupation which is so important it becomes what you call 'a calling'. And then you have the fact that, as a child or spouse, you are attached to a professional that is not nine-to-five. It requires, and the person wants to give much more than nine-to-five. It's not just demanded, but you have the urge to do that. And so that can become competitive as well.

"On the other hand, you have to also look at the positive side, in that you are attached to someone who is ecstatic about their work. They are not doing nine-to-five in a job that they don't like. And I know people who are in a nine-to-five job they don't like and they come home and they're miserable and they take it out on their family, 'cause they had to put up with eight hours during the day doing something they don't like.

"And so in terms of looking at relationships and the family in the space flight business, there are those aspects about long hours, a lot of travel, and the passion for the job that you have to share. But there are the positive sides – you have somebody who's doing what they want to do; you have someone who is excited about their work – they don't come home in a miserable mood; they come home and they've had a great day. They had a day doing something they were excited about, that they found meaningful. And I mean this is the simplest of terms, the simplest of ideas. If you had a great day, what kind of organism is coming home, if they had a great day at work? If they went to fly these machines and they had a great day in the simulator, or came back from a space flight? And so, you know, in looking at the downside, you have to look at the upside too. And it is fantastically rewarding to be able to have someone that has had a good day. You're gonna be different if you had a good day. You also get to share in technology, you get to share in the frontier, you get to share in this interaction of different kinds of people and travel, and you get to share in the whole thing. The family and the people that you have relationships with, they get to share in all this as well."

Lots of people have guessed at Story's motivation to do all that he has done in his life. Of himself he said, "What has driven me throughout life is a restlessness. I don't know if it's the right word, but it's the quest, the journey. You climb one mountain, you're looking for the other. You come over the hill, you're not happy – it's the next challenge. You just round the hill of this mountain and before you get to the top of that one, you're looking for the next one. It's the journey. And so restlessness might not be the right connotation – but it's the motivation, it's the quest, it's the journey, the seeking. And in a way, 'dissatisfaction' is not a word that has a good connotation either – except you're not satisfied with knowing what you know – you're not satisfied with being who you're being. It's a restlessness; you have to keep moving. It's a hunger. And so you think you're gonna be a doctor, you think you're gonna pursue the brain and the nervous system, you think you're gonna do this and that – well you don't – you're on the move. Maybe in the current life in which I cannot get comfortable with my priorities, it may be the same thing at work, which will never settle down. Maybe I'm looking for something – I'm trying to arrive at something which is a somewhat steady state that I'm happy with. But if you look at the past, when was I ever happy with anything?

"So I was wondering if what was at work today was the same thing – am I looking for the next thing? I tell myself I should be able to build a life now and that's the life – that's the final life."

Story still leads a very busy and often complex life involving lots of travel. At times, the mixture of private and public activities becomes a little overwhelming. In his journal he wrote:

Striving for simplicity in all aspects of life.[28]

Finding a balance is key. According to Story, "I'm trying to find a final life here in which there's a balance between things that I want to do – my own art, my own writing – and other things like performances, creativity with different companies and being at home."

The surprise for many people is that the "final life" which Story is developing surrounds the concept of beauty. For some, it is a concept that is difficult to grasp.

According to Story, "Beauty is the final discipline. Beauty, as a calling, is a very unusual concept. I don't know of any human being that says that their calling or their occupation is "I do Beauty." That was an epiphany. I've had an interest in beauty for as long as I can remember. I had pursued the formal study of aesthetics and I knew I was going to use beauty as a context – it would be the principal concept in which I would work within Imagineering and other innovations, that I would look at things and beauty would be the way in which I would make them compelling, unique, and something you had an experience of.

"As far back as I can remember, I was into that; I was into the stars, I was into the soil, I was into creatures, I was into the curvature and the flow, the little whirlpools. I was always strongly into kinesthetics, motion. I was always very powerful on the beauty of motion and listening to the wind through the pine trees. As far back as I can remember, I was into those things. I was into touch as a sensory system, the beauty of taking up a huge chunk of soil… I always stopped to watch the sunsets, the flight of ducks, the flow of ice down the river, the patterns, you know. I have to say that even before I knew beauty as a formality, I would look and see it just about anywhere.

"Beauty – it's a knowledge system; it's a way that we know the universe. We have evolved to appreciate beauty. It's been an evolutionary strategy that we could appreciate beauty; we live longer and we are healthier; it's part of our constitution to appreciate it."

In his journals Story wrote:

My business is beauty, beauty everywhere, nature, everyday living, and art. My topic is not art, it is beauty, beauty for the sake of beauty, in all its paths and manifestations.[29]

Is not beauty also the good, the truth? Is not beauty also moral, a sense of moral, related to the positive, uplifting?[30]

Beauty is a process, a journey – it is not a perception, emotion or an object, it is a process!![31]

28. Journal 12, page 18; Date: 3 February 1992.
29. Journal 31, page 13; Date: 29 March 2001.
30. Journal 31, page 22; Date: 7 May 2001.
31. Journal 31, Page 49; Date: around February 2002.

Again, it is the power of a New England Fall which will forever touch Story; which continually spreads its magic over his imagination.

> Beauty is Fall colors... All senses – eyes, sound of wind through trees, "rustle" of leaves on the ground, under foot, the smell of Fall... the deep inhalation reflex – physiology, holding leaves, playing in leaves, the softness of the walk, temperature... crisp air, winter coming.[32]

*

In January 2002, Story was a guest facilitator at a corporate convention. During one of the question and answer sessions, someone asked him about his failures. In his journal he wrote:

> [They] asked what failures I learnt lessons from. [I replied] "As far as I am concerned, the whole damn thing was a failure!" Well, I am surprised that I said that, but it is a better answer than if I had said it was an outrageous success.[33]

This was an unusual revelation from someone who has achieved so much in their lifetime. But what it gets back to is how Story perceives himself. Striving for perfection is the quest. He said, "The state of mind is an openness and a willingness – accepting the victories and the defeats.

"If you look at the Hubble repair, there's the journey right there. For better or for worse, I accept the outcome. But I'm going to do the best I can along the way and it's the playing field that matters. My plan showed I was going to get it all done, but I can be surprised. I knew in my own pragmatics, I knew that I could have been stopped, and I felt like I had almost stolen something; I felt like I got away with something, doing what I did. I hoped the dance would go the way it was supposed to go, but I knew before and I knew after, I could be stopped where that's the end of the game and it's over and I will not have completed it. When I got done, there was a sense of humility in that I was allowed to do it."

Story said recently, "Life is full of lots of dead-ends and a very few moments of the highest ecstasy. One would like to live on top of the mountain all the time, but the dead-ends are necessary. If one is not experiencing dead-ends, then one is not exploring enough and one is going to miss the magic because the first steps were not taken."

I asked Story if he considered himself an explorer, given that space flight is often described in that way. He replied, "A little, but not as much as you might expect. I was a personal explorer that's for sure. Space has to be done right. It's a very sterile environment; it has to be done technically correct or you get hurt. So it is a highly

---

32. Journal 31, page 24; Date: around February 2002.
33. Journal 31, page 38; Date: around Jan 2002.

technical thing and you're trying to arrive at a state where there is no danger. You're trying to arrive at a state where what you're doing is totally routine and reproducible, so that's not exploration. But it was a huge personal exploration in terms of adaptation to space and the zero-g, the introspection, the geography and all of that stuff. I was an explorer in terms of working to find Uluru, to see it with the naked eyes and the binoculars and to get a picture – that's an explorer – like a covered wagon going across some continent. I was definitely an explorer in terms of photography. But the inner experience was definitely a huge exploration – the cognitive experience and the various things you might do to bring that out, the various intricacies of experiments. That's exploration for sure. A great spacewalk is exploration, a great dance is exploration – you are in new territory. Exploration is not just climbing Everest; exploration is being on some edge."

I was also interested to know how Story generally viewed his thirty years with NASA. "It was just being the best I could at each little part, on each chapter, each day, sometimes doing very well, other times not so well. That's how I view it, just like that."

Was there a predominant emotion from that period of Story's life? He said, "It varies so much. It's the ecstasy of arriving at Florida three days before launch; the spirit of flight. It's Tom Jones serving communion – my God! It's the spirit surrounding [space] flight – which I'm much higher than most people. Most people are somehow not so much into it. But it's the mission spirit; so often it's not presented in life. Mission Control meant as much to me as my own flights; that was an incredible high. There was a lot more art to Mission Control – the art of communications and empathy; being a team member.

"The Shuttle Avionics Integration Lab – being the lead for testing the Shuttle software for the three years before it flew – a huge responsibility. We caught fatal errors in the software all the time. Technically, I had to know much more than the vehicle; I had to know what it was supposed to be doing. In that lab I was the ultimate technician.

"So the predominant emotion – I guess it's the heat of the battle. I never felt any pressure, but you're on a mission."

There has been a lot of opportunity and privilege in Story's life – much of it resulting from his dedication to the space program. Reflecting on it all, Story has found plenty to be thankful for:

> Life is so contingent – has treated you so well! Appreciate it, live your blessings, how can you ever be down? You have responsibility to make something of your blessing![34]

34. Journal 13, page 19; Date: around June 1992.

# 20. The Way of Water

What the hell is all this about?

*Story Musgrave, April 1988*

For those who love the business of space, it will be hard to forget the day of the *Columbia* accident. Like the day of the *Challenger* tragedy, people tend to remember where they were and what they were doing.

Living in the Southern Hemisphere, I found out when I awoke, several hours after the event. With a sixteen hour time difference, it was the Second of February in Sydney. My friend Rob in Florida indirectly gave me the news. In an email he had written: "So sorry about your friend" and left me his cell phone number. Initially confused about what he meant, it suddenly dawned on me that *Columbia* was due home that day. I quickly searched the online news, then, like everybody else, turned to the television for confirmation. There wasn't a lot to see – except the incredible images of the Space Shuttle as it burned up across the United States of America. And the horrible realization that no one could have survived.

During the creation of this book, the thought had sometimes passed through my mind – what if there is another accident in the space program? What will Story's reaction to that be? What will my own reaction be after so much interaction with the people that make up the space community, the wider space family?

Story had said that the odds were high that it could happen. He was realistic. This view was largely based on the danger associated with the twin solid rocket boosters and the sheer physical brutality of the launch process. The Space Shuttle was, as he often described it, "a butterfly strapped to a rocket". If another tragedy occurred, most people expected that it would be during a launch, so the shock was even greater when it occurred during re-entry – an event which, although dangerous, was considered less of a risk than launch. The fact that it came at the conclusion of a much-followed, high profile mission added to its impact. The loss of another seven human beings was almost incomprehensible.

Back in August 2001, I had the privilege of watching a Space Shuttle landing at the Kennedy Space Center. I sat on the bleachers with other visitors to the Cape and beside us, in a private area, were the families, friends and colleagues of the crew – full of excitement as they waited for them to return to earth. There were many VIPs present that day, including the NASA administrator, who was rather conspicuous in his Bronx baseball cap. Dozens of media lined up to capture the moment with their telephoto lenses. I was in awe as *Discovery* came in for its final approach and landing, with the multi-colored chute expanding behind.

I had all that in mind as I watched the news broadcast of events that day in February. And I kept visualizing the agony on the faces of those who were waiting on those same seats on the day *Columbia* didn't arrive.

Needless to say, those people who participated in interviews for this book, the ones who gladly recounted their experiences with Story throughout his thirty years with the space program, were numb. There were those who knew those seven astronauts personally, had worked closely with them and were even in Mission Control when the accident happened. I suspended further interviews for several months, allowing people to grieve and to come to terms with what had happened. Some were tied up with the investigation process.

Story and I had met David Brown in Houston in April 2002. Story knew the American astronauts aboard *Columbia*, but David was especially in our minds because he had welcomed us that Friday afternoon as we traversed the halls of the astronaut building. David leapt to his feet when Story and I came upon him in the office he shared with the crew of STS-107. The others had departed for the day, so David shared with us the details of their forthcoming space flight – a dedicated science mission, much to Story's delight. I got the sense that David and Story were very much alike as they stood face to face. Both men were pilots, doctors and astronauts; both were unassuming but with a sense of confidence in themselves and a certain 'presence' about them. In the weeks that followed, David and I corresponded: he was keen to share his thoughts about Story for the book. That was also typical of others we met in Houston. Information was largely volunteered rather than asked for. People just admired Story and wanted to contribute to this biography.

*

On the First of February 2003, at the time of *Columbia's* re-entry, Story was at his home in central Florida. He knew *Columbia* was returning that morning and, as for the conclusion of many other missions, he was listening for the sonic booms as the Space Shuttle flew overhead. Anyone indoors would hear the glass rattle in the windows, but Story typically witnessed these arrivals among nature. He wasn't wearing a watch, preferring to be surprised when his spaceship came overhead.

As time went by, Story began to feel that something had happened: either they had delayed the landing for another day – although that was unlikely because the weather was great and there had been no technical problems – or somehow he had missed them; missed the sonic booms.

It was Story's friend Patrick Whelan who drove by to give him the news. Patrick knew that, by design, Story had no television signal at his house, so together they returned to Patrick's place to watch the news as it came to hand. The images on television confirmed it all: the image of *Columbia* streaking across the sky as it broke up. Story absorbed what he could, then went home to be alone; he had to be alone.

Story recalled, "The phone was ringing by the time I got home – I could not answer it. I was not going to answer it and I was not going to get involved. It was too troublesome to me to get involved. I was not going to answer the phone; I wasn't going to do this one. It was a little strange to me; I don't know why. It's not that I'd left NASA, it's not that I didn't care – I couldn't do this one. It was very disturbing.

"It was more disturbing – painful to the point of being disturbing – and I don't know why, but it was worse than *Challenger*. I 'replayed' more on this one what happened, what happened to the crew. When *Challenger* first happened, I did not know – no one knew – that the crew was alive till they hit the water. And we didn't know that for weeks. We didn't know that until we went down and found the cabin intact and found people. I'm not sure how long it was – three weeks or a month; it was quite a long time with *Challenger*."

Story's immediate reaction to the news was to carry on in a characteristic way. "I went back to work [outside] – that's what I do – I made a decision that I'm not going to get involved. I always do that when there's something very traumatic: I'll go to the gymnasium, or go out there. When Tom died, I continued to work. It doesn't mean you don't care; it means you care too much. So I went back to the tractor."

During the course of that day, I and many others tried to reach Story by telephone. I had no idea what I was going to say when I heard his voice, but as we had shared so much in recent years in the development of this book, it seemed like the right thing to do. For nearly a week, Story's telephone rang constantly with requests for media interviews, television appearances and support from his family, friends and colleagues. He told me later that his answering service recorded over three hundred calls. One of them was mine.

Without a doubt, Story was somebody people listened to; his opinions, his thoughts mattered to the world. People knew that he would be authentic and honest. Encouraged by family and friends, Story did begin to return some of the telephone calls and to speak publicly about the immediate catastrophe. And to the NASA family and wider community, his words in later days offered hope and a vision for the future of space exploration.

The media requests were wide-ranging. According to Story, "There were all kinds of requests at all levels – the national media, whether it's ABC, NBC, CNBC, CNN – there was everything at all levels, down to Orlando, Cocoa Beach and to local stations around the country and around the world actually. I tried to be effective and look at how I can make most difference. I gave the best I had. So I'd go out and I'd do some media and then I'd go hide again. I'd go out for a while – out means do the voice mail or go out [and do interviews] – but then I'd come back and say enough's enough. I'd have to come back home again. But then, on my own, I'd get up and I'd go back out again."

Shortly after the accident, Story was scheduled to appear at the Kennedy Space Center Visitors Complex, for the Astronaut Encounter Program where he was able to share his own experiences of re-entry with the audience. He said, "I was able to give them the STS-80 experience of having looked out the overhead window, having videoed it. And so this is just very poignant; it's how you see the heat; it's a way of personally experiencing the heat. And it was very nice to be able to give that to them. If I had not done that little experiment, that I'm going to experience this entry…The experience of STS-80 – the high point was looking at the kids [fellow crew members who were much younger than Story]. It was even higher than what you saw out the window or other things. Watching the kids work and bringing me home – my life was in their skills. The maturity of them – that I could yell and scream about the aurora and flame and all that's going on and it doesn't disturb them. They know when they've got to focus on their job and they know when they can listen to me and they know when they can do both at the same time because they are mature aviators. A less mature aviator – anything you do to communicate the experience to them, it's a distraction and they're unable to do their job and so you have to cease that, but not this gang. This gang was mature, they knew how to focus, they knew how to tune me out when they had to, and so they got to experience the flying, they got to have the fun of bringing the ship home – it was *Columbia,* of course – and at the same time, they got to experience the sensory phenomena. And every video that was shown those weeks afterward is the video that I had created at the overhead window. So those kinds of experiments to try to catch what it's all about, again, are important."

Story had always enjoyed the re-entry phase of his missions. "We had gotten a little familiar with entry; entry became a friendly thing. We knew about the heat rejection system – it had held us up for a couple of years, the Shuttle's first flight. We were almost as scared of that as we were of the solid rocket boosters. And even though in the early days we were losing tiles – and if you lose the wrong one, it's the end of the day – we continued to fly which we should not have. But we survived. But we got familiar with entry and it was not something people feared. And so it's a very nice day [the day of re-entry]. You get up, you've done as much as you can the day before, and you get up six hours before you light the engines to come home. You just tidy up the cabin and get it ready to come home and do the burn and come home. As much as you like space flight and you don't want to come home – but it's in the plan to come home; come back to mother earth. You've got a nice glide back home; it's a nice experience – back to mother earth and back to family and friends and NASA. It's a very beautiful day. And you don't have fears. It's a rough ride, it chugs along, it's got some vibrations – you can hear the wind noise and can hear a little bit of mach shake. It's there, it's impressive, but it doesn't have all the signs of impending disaster the way a take-off or a launch does."

Over the coming days, the *Columbia* accident began to take its toll on Story, both physically and emotionally; he was exhausted. Some of it came from the demands of the public, but some of it from his own imagination which placed him in the cockpit with the crew. He thought about what it would be like to be there during the re-entry – he had done it for real six times before. He thought about the structure of the Space

Shuttle, what impact the fatal forces would have had on the vehicle and ultimately, what those aboard might have known as things progressed. Story remembered, "With each piece of data I would change the scenario, 'cause I now had a piece of data which would be able to let me come closer to what actually happened. All the imagery, the reliving, the empathies and the scenarios – I died a hundred times building a scenario."

And having spent many years working space flight in Mission Control, Story also imagined the last moments of STS-107 with his colleagues there: the shock, the disbelief – until there was no hope left for the crew. He said, "I know what it is to be there when there are problems. I know the empathy a controller has for the crew that's flying. And so I played that drama as to what signals do you get, what data comes to you, what visuals come to you and when do you know it's the end of the day?"

*

For Story, the *Columbia* accident brought back memories of *Challenger* and the enormous risks associated with flying aboard the Space Shuttle, which he had spoken out about three decades ago.

He explained, "The whole schizophrenia of NASA saying 1 in a 100,000 [chance of having an accident] – that you'll fly 300 days every year and not have an accident. But you knew; you built the system. And so it was a totally different thing – you knew that things were not right long before it happened to *Challenger*. And you knew the risks, you knew the risks of the solid rocket boosters – you'd been through the development. After *Challenger*, we got our stuff together... We knew about temperatures and O-rings and all the icicles on the gantry. You don't launch with icicles everywhere; the exhaust plumes are gonna blow them around like missiles.

"The shuttle is too fragile, too vulnerable, too complex – it can't be safe – it's the most dangerous vehicle we've ever flown, by far – you can't make it safe by its very constitution. But since *Challenger*, I have had huge respect and admiration for the way they've done it. A difficult machine to operate, but they've done the best they could. And I've respected the team and they've made great decisions."

Story felt very vulnerable after *Challenger*. "*Challenger* was far more effective in that regard. After *Challenger*, every single commercial airplane takeoff was incredibly disturbing to me – it's like we're doing a launch and it was really, it was almost like shell shock. I have total faith in the airlines, it's the safest way there is to travel. But after *Challenger*, every single take-off in a commercial airplane was a horrible thing. It was just like impending disaster that's gonna hit – man, it's gonna hit."

The *Columbia* accident was effective in bringing Story emotionally and visibly back into the world of space flight, six years after he left NASA. "It did root me again. It rooted me, like everyone, back in the space flight business. It hauled me back into involvement in the space business and identification of me as a space flier and understanding that I have to get into that.

"You have to ask, what does it mean to the program? What does it mean to the Shuttle program, Space Station, what's it mean in terms of space flight – is it worth it? You get into all those questions. And where do we go from here?"

As with the *Challenger* accident, there were personal connections to the crew of *Columbia*. "I knew some a little closer than others. They were all, of course, relatively recent [astronauts]. But you know, that nice talk with Dave Brown; I knew KC rather well. And Mike Anderson – he had helped send me off on STS-80.  ·

"It was a nice crew, it was a talented crew. It had a nice mix of gender, it had a nice mix of culture, it had a nice mix of different religions, different parts of the world. I also sensed that they were different. They had an esprit de corps for what they were doing. Scientific missions like that are very nice. They are far more demanding, 'cause you not only get up and get down, but you have weeks of work getting experiments done."

In the weeks that followed, as Story watched the progress of the accident investigation, particularly the public release of memos written during the mission by concerned engineers, ideas began to emerge in his mind about what could have been done to avoid the tragedy.

"I am always after answers. When someone dies unexpectedly, or someone dies and there's any question, I always want a post-mortem so that you get the genetics out and the family can genetically understand that this is part of their life history, the way a relative died. In the hospital when someone dies you get the answers. When an airplane crashes, I'm always interested in what the [investigation] board comes up with, how that happens. So I'm always interested in getting the truth to come out."

Story explained his motivation in this instance. "There were gaps. I couldn't see the flow, I couldn't see the logic. I couldn't see how things were dealt with. I hear the numbers – 500 miles an hour, three pounds, but it didn't do any damage: I can't add that up. What are we saying? Three pounds at 500 miles an hour and it doesn't do any damage? And you see all this debris go up with the impact and you say there's no damage? What are we saying?! And so I see gaps in the logic – that's not logical to make that statement. It's not – the question is simply not logical. So I don't see it dealing with the facts and dealing with the data and I don't see a continuous decision process that really comes to grips with it.

"Before the accident, and now during the investigation, it all comes down to and starts with one point – do you need to put eyes on [the probable site of the impact] or not? Are there enough indicators out there that tell me I've got to put eyes on it? There is very little downside – you lose half a day. We do spacewalks every single flight now to assemble Space Station. You had two competent, trained people and you had the equipment. Were they trained to go under the belly? They were trained to go underneath the belly and do a contingency closure of the external tank doors. A hundred percent of every crew that flies in space is certified to do that. But turns out it was most likely the leading edge of the wing that was hurt and so all it takes is taking that person's boots and moving them up and down the leading edge of the wing.

"To choreograph what it takes to get eyes there is not even interesting; it's not a challenge. But everything converges on that decision point. And the next decision is – is it OK to come home or not? If you're not OK to come home, you do a rescue mission. If you assess the damage and you can't come home, then you don't. You're forced into a rescue mission – there's no other option. You do a rescue mission and then, if you're very confident with the repair job you did on *Columbia* when you go back and revisit, then humans fly it home. But you go up there prepared to have it come home alone with a software patch if you're not that confident in your repair job."

There has been a lot of discussion and speculation since the accident about whether or not these things were viable. Story instantly dismisses such talk.

"There are personal things here. I, technically, know it's not a challenge – it isn't even interesting what it takes to get eyes out there. And so this is a personal thing. I don't like the system to look at spacewalkers and say you are so incompetent you can't crawl out there without damaging things! I don't like the world looking at spacewalkers and saying – that simple a thing, you are not capable of doing. So that's very personal because I'm a spaceperson, but I'm also a spacewalker. I built all that stuff. I built the capability to go out and close those huge payload bay doors by hand, to latch all the latches. I came up with all the contingency things, but so you look at spacewalkers and you call them incompetent! They can't even crawl out there and look? And so I don't like that. And so, it's partly involvement, but it's partly a sense of pride in the capabilities that spacewalkers have developed and that I developed all along the way.

"When they say they're not equipped, that also gets to me, 'cause it says that in a crisis, NASA has no imagination and cannot come up with a solution for something which is very simple; that NASA has no response to a crisis. With Apollo 13, the service module engine is damaged, we're dead. We can't get home, because when you loop around the moon, you use the service module rocket to get home, therefore we're dead. Let's all go home and let them die! Well no; the lunar module engine will bring us home. If you look at the endless crises that NASA has been able to pull off, when you say they have no equipment to go look at it, you're saying NASA has no imagination! And there's endless equipment, there are endless handrails. There are endless ways to get a little structure to go do that – it's a nothing, it's not even interesting. You say there's no equipment, well there *is* equipment! And so, you know, there's those kind of elements. Spacewalkers are not competent? NASA is not competent, they have no imagination and in a crisis, they have no capability of responding creatively to something they didn't expect to have to do? That is simply not true. To say we have no equipment is ignoring the history of NASA in a crisis.

"NASA has forgotten that it did practice spacewalks. NASA has done four practice spacewalks in which they had no reason to do them. They did them to get more astronauts some spacewalking experience and to exercise some Space Station tools. So NASA considers spacewalking so benign and so safe that they're willing to do practice spacewalks like the one we had [planned] on STS-80."

Story's words, which were characteristically honest and filled with more than a little frustration and even anger, were followed by actions. It took more than six weeks of telephone calls and emails by Story, but the *Columbia* Accident Investigation Board did respond to his requests to participate in the investigation process.

Before going to Houston to speak with the Board, Story went to the Kennedy Space Center to look over one of the remaining Space Shuttles to test out his ideas. While doing so, he also visited the hangar where the pieces of *Columbia* were being laid out for the investigation. As expected, it made quite an impression on Story. He recalled, "All it did was strengthen the experiences I had on the first day. I was always trying to build the story as to what happened in the cockpit, but here was the story. The story was there.

"Starting in the mid-70s, especially in the later 70s, we had worried about [heat protection] burn throughs and here it was. There's more data there on what it's like to do a re-entry from space than all the rest of the data we have forever. It's all there. Every single little piece, how it burned and what went on and the whole story was just so clear. They don't have all the pieces but they've sure got enough of them."

Story paid tribute to the people at KSC who were working in the hangar. "It was people going about their business with a passion. They knew that what they were doing was very important; it might make a difference in the future."

The visit to Houston to the Board was also memorable. "The Board knew why I was there and I presume the astronaut office did and the flight controllers. I had to go, just to communicate a perspective. I had to create some other view, other than they had a bad day at launch and that's all; that on launch, that's when they died. I had to change that view because that view was wrong. And that view I saw even on [the day of the accident]. Those kinds of things were being communicated – that you can't do a walk, there's nothing to hang onto down there, it's dangerous, you'll damage the tiles, not trained, don't have the equipment, don't have a manned maneuvering…. So I knew on the day of the accident that I would be involved; I had to do that. I couldn't let all that sit – the idea that they had a bad day on launch and that was it. Apollo 13 had a bad day when the oxygen tank blew up but that's it, so they had a bad day and it's all over. I could not let that sit. They didn't let that sit with Apollo 13. You know, 'failure is not an option'? Where did that go? Failure is an option, of course. Apollo 13 was a failure, but you pick your new battle and you succeed at that. It doesn't mean you didn't fail overall – you did – but you pick a new battle, you salvage what you can. That's what is meant by 'failure is not an option'… I didn't know where that went; there was a numbness. It gets down to coming to grips with the reality – maybe you don't want to know. Maybe no one wants to know something could have been done. Maybe they just don't want to know that. It's not nice.

"Taking a walk is the only thing that would have changed history. It's the only thing that would have given us a different outcome."

On 26 August 2003, the Chairman of the Columbia Accident Investigation Board, Admiral Harold Gehman, spoke at a press briefing as Volume 1 of the board's report was released. His words indicate that Story's efforts did, in fact, make a difference.

He said, "From my understanding, to go out and take a walk and lean over the wing to see if you had a hole in the RCC[1] is not very risky. It's well within the capability of the training of the astronauts. If they were really curious and really had a lot of engineering curiosity, they were really suspicious and if they were really concerned about pinning down everything that might be wrong with the orbiter, they would have attempted, first of all, to get some imagery. And if the imagery was inconclusive, which it may have been… you know, they may have gotten the imagery and it proved nothing. I consider that going out and taking a look at the wing to be relatively a prudent thing to do."

\*

In August 2001, I travel to Florida. Right in the middle of the wet season, I'm continually chased indoors by torrential rain. The thunderstorms are spectacular and together with the high humidity, it is all reminding me very much of home. More than nine thousand miles from Australia, I have come to define this project and to immerse myself for a while in Story's world.

Twelve months earlier, through our literary correspondence, I had questioned Story about capturing his life in words. I can still recall his matter-of-fact reply: "No one is doing it or intends on doing it." Neither did he. In relaying this and also acting on what must have been some wild intuition, he subtly suggested I pursue the idea myself. And so the proverbial seed was planted and, just over a year later, I am in Florida.

This is where my own journey begins. And so, like stepping over the puddles, I step across into the imaginative world of another.

One day, Story asks me how I will approach the biography. Totally unprepared for the question, from somewhere in the depths comes my reply: "Who are you? And how did you get to be like that?"

As time would show, those questions drove the entire biographical process.

1. Reinforced Carbon-Carbon Panel.

During one of our interviews Story said, "What does life mean? I'm not sure. For me it's an opportunity to participate in the quest and the journey. For me it's an opportunity to participate in cosmic evolution and I'm part of this great big scheme and I go forward; I play my part. I try and enrich what this process is; I try to live up to the possibility and the potentiality and opportunities that I have been given. I go forward with a smile on my face. I go forward with faith and maybe I don't know what it means and maybe I don't know where it's going, but I have faith and I have hope. I enjoy a quest."

Story wrote frequently in his journals about the journey:

> The quest – to live till eternity with the ultimate questions. I live them, breathe them and sleep in them. My life is to pursue them and to live in and for them.[2]

> What the hell is all this about? You'll never know, but maybe you can express it.[3]

> Live in the moment, the past is history, the future is a mystery, the destination is unknown.[4]

Life, for Story, has been an amazing adventure. There have been incredible highs mixed with incredible pain, but hope has always prevailed. Far beyond the space program, Story Musgrave's legacy lies in the human journey – in the ultimate pursuit of knowledge and in the infinite quest for meaning. He wrote:

> The journey: live in grace, beauty and perfection and know (faith) that the end will take care of itself![5]

2. Journal 27, page 2; Date: 2 April 1999.
3. Journal 4, page 6; Date: around April 1988.
4. Journal 28, page 1; Date: 3 September 1999.
5. Story's handwritten note in *The Dream of the Earth*, by Thomas Berry, San Francisco, Sierra Club Books, 1988.

# Acknowledgements

There are many people to thank for their generosity during the creation of this book. Story demonstrated enormous faith in me and I went forward with confidence that I could not only document his life and philosophies in a way which would capture him as an important historical figure, but also pay tribute to him for the way in which he has explored every aspect of his existence. I am grateful to Story for his support and assistance, which included traveling with me to various places of significance in his life; giving me access to some four thousand pages of handwritten journal entries and hundreds of family letters; and creating a path which enabled me to speak with so many of the people who have been integral to his journey.

My friend Mary Beirman provided the opportunity for Story and I to meet, and for that I thank her. In February 2000, she invited Story to Sydney, Australia, to speak at two events. As a result of assisting Mary with preparations for those events, I was introduced to Story. After an inspiring week of working together, which included a motivating and challenging walk to the top of the Sydney Harbour Bridge, Story and I began to correspond by email. We shared and wrote poetry, and I got to know a little more about his philosophies.

The idea for this book arose later that year, as I became interested in knowing more about Story's life. Then, in July 2001, I found myself on an airplane to Florida. The purpose of the trip was to spend some time with Story and to discuss the possibility of a biography. By the time I left the USA, the idea of capturing Story's life in a book had become a mutual reality.

During subsequent visits to the USA, I had the privilege of witnessing two Space Shuttle launches, a Space Shuttle landing and meeting literally dozens of extraordinary people. Story would say to them, "This is my biographer! Will you talk with her?" No one refused. That, in itself, says a lot about the respect and esteem with which Story is held. And people were thrilled that there was finally going to be a book about him!

With warmest regard, I mention my friend Tricia Brownlee, who shared in the creation of this book. Intelligent and widely-read, she became my sounding board for ideas and provided many thought-provoking questions along the way. She diligently read each chapter multiple times as it was compiled and gave me endless encouragement. No one was more excited for me at the completion of this book than she was! For her friendship and care, I am forever grateful.

Kristine Murgatroyd, my friend of almost thirty years, came up with what became the subtitle for the book. She took one look at its water-filled cover, asked me why I had chosen water as the visual theme – which, as you have learnt, is Story's metaphor for himself – and immediately said, "The Way of Water". It is not easy to come up with a great headline for a book, but Kris did so in a matter of seconds! Kris and her husband Geoff, who currently live in New Jersey, also provided Story and myself with much appreciated hospitality – and one of the most hilarious dinner conversations I've ever had – during our visit to the North East part of the USA.

Story's immediate family was very generous in sharing their memories of him with me. I would like to thank Patricia Musgrave, Lorelei Musgrave, Holly Musgrave, Todd Musgrave, Carol Musgrave and Lane Musgrave. In addition I would like to thank Story's cousins Clover Swann and Rosaly Bass, who gave me some wonderful insights for the book. The family also provided me with welcoming hospitality on my visits to Texas and Massachusetts.

The space family, as it is known, shared with me some great anecdotes. And like a chain reaction, one interview often lead to another. I would like to thank Story's fellow astronauts – Tom Jones, Don Peterson, Gordon Fullerton, Jim Voss, John Blaha, John Fabian, Mark Lee, Rick Hieb, Scott Parazynski, Tom Akers, David Wolf and Al Worden for speaking candidly about Story. I am also grateful to David M. Brown, who later lost his life aboard *Columbia* in February 2003. His contribution has become all the more precious.

Others to thank include the people of Mission Control who enjoyed reminiscing about Story: Milt Heflin, Phil Engelauf and Roger Balettie.

I would also like to thank Bob Sieck, who was Launch Director for each of Story's missions. I enjoyed our interview immensely.

In Houston, other colleagues and associates who gave of their time and memories include Beth Turner, Bernard J. Mundine Jr., Bill Daley, Frank Hughes, Jim Thornton, Michael Hess, Mark Liles, Ron Sheffield and Houston restaurant owner, Frankie Camera, who has served Story and others from JSC on many occasions.

I met a wide range of people at the Kennedy Space Center in Florida, including staff and visitors to the Cape: Mia Liebowitz, Billy Specht, Christina Florencio, Debbie Land, Jennifer Skaja, Jeff Soulliere, Tony Gannon, Fran Carr, Julian Cross, Kathy Davis, Marie Hopper, Michael Lazor, Richard Rapson, Dave Dunn, Scott Fenske, Betsy McKinivan and Tom Troszak. They willingly outlined their impressions of Story.

One of the highlights of my research was the world of spacewalking and the people who were involved in spacesuit design. Special thanks go to Tom Sanzone who not only gave me a great interview, but who put me in touch with others. His enthusiasm for this book was endless. Tom and his wife Brenda read the chapter *Spacewalking Ballet* and provided welcome and much appreciated feedback. Thank you to Fred Morris, Fred

Greenwood, Joe McMann and Jim McBarron II, who were also involved with spacesuit development and shared some great memories of Story's role in that world.

The flying world at Ellington Field, where the astronauts maintain their proficiency, provided some of my favorite memories. Thanks go to Roger Zwieg, Bob Mullins, David Lammon, Henry Watkins, Joe Conway, Ace Beale and Triple (Jack) Nickel. Thanks also to Kandy Warren who walked down memory lane as a flight scheduler for the NASA pilots for many years.

The NASA Astronaut Office and History Office also provided support, as did Jody Russell of the Johnson Space Center, who obtained great results searching for NASA photo IDs. Tammy West put me in touch with many people.

I would like to thank Story's friends: Rob Corum, Mort Kasdan, Doug Warner, Patrick Whelan and Frank Candy who all provided non-space-related perspectives.

In particular, I would like to mention Sharon Daley, whose hospitality and friendship during my visits to Florida has been wonderful. She has shared many years with Story as both NASA colleague and friend, and provided me with numerous insights and ideas. Our four-hour interview one evening set a record for the research!

Media representatives showed me a different point of view: thanks to Dan Billow, Bob Dows, Connie Leonard, Tracy K. Day and filmmakers Dana Ranga, Katey Grusovin, David Grusovin and to Darlene Cavalier, who has worked alongside Story at many of his speaking engagements.

Those who shared Story's days in medicine provided rarer insights into another facet of his career. I thank Doctors Ben Eiseman, Dominic Purpura and Edgar Housepian for their wonderful memories and humor.

In California, I would like to thank Story's associates and friends – Alice Hargrove, Amy van Gilder, Chris Carradine, Clint Hope, Earle Markes, Mark Huber, M.K. Haley, Rondi Werner, Scott Petri, Al Horais and Vanessa Godson. They are part of Story's current life, a very different life, since he left the space program.

I would like to thank the people at the Norman Rockwell Museum, in Stockbridge, Massachusetts, who allowed us to tour *Linwood*.

I am grateful to those who gave me input or ideas for this book, or proof-read the text: Roger Brownlee, Lance Lenehan and my parents, Bernard and Moira Moses.

Without question, this book would not have been possible without the support of my friends and family in Australia. In particular, I would like to thank my husband Lance for his unquestioning support of all that I do in my career, and my son Oliver, whose birth in the midst of all of this, was welcome and joyous.

Finally, I want to express my thanks to Story for his incredible friendship and love. Life will never be the same again.

*Anne Lenehan, Sydney, Australia, June 2004*

# *Photo Credits*

*Front Cover:* Main photo by Anne Lenehan.
Smaller photos at the bottom of the front cover (left to right): 1 & 2 courtesy of Story Musgrave; 3, 4 & 5 courtesy of NASA; 6 courtesy of Roger Brownlee.
*Back Cover:* Photo by NASA.
*Wrap Around Cover:* Inside Back Cover - photo by Lance Lenehan

*Theme pages:*
Childhood: photo courtesy of Story Musgrave
Nature: photo by Anne Lenehan
Mechanics: photo by Anne Lenehan
Space: photo by NASA
Death and Life: photo by Florida Today
Body, Mind, Art: photo by NASA
Journey: photo by NASA

*Color insert in center of biography:*
Page 1: Photos of Linwood, Marguerite Swann, and young Story Musgrave – courtesy of Story Musgrave.
Page 2: Portraits of Story: US Marine Corp and Syracuse University – courtesy of Story Musgrave; portrait of Story Musgrave for Skylab, by NASA; photos of spacesuit design and testing – by NASA.
Page 3: Family portrait – courtesy of Story Musgrave. Photo of Story Musgrave with Lane Linwood Musgrave – by NASA; suiting up for STS-80 – by NASA.
Page 4: Photo of T-38 and Story Musgrave piloting a T-38 – by NASA.
Page 5: Photo of Story Musgrave and Gordon Fullerton – source unknown. Every attempt has been made to locate the legitimate owner of this photograph. If you are the copyright owner, please contact the publisher.
Photo of Story Musgrave in his sailplane – courtesy of Story Musgrave.

# Medical Research

**Factors affecting focal discharges of epileptogenic cortex.**
F. S. Musgrave, M. Sanaman, D. P. Purpura.
The Physiolgoist 5: 187, 1962. Presented by Story Musgrave at the September 1962
meeting of the American Physiological Society, Buffalo, New York.

**Effects of dilantin on focal epileptogenic activity of cat neocortex.**
F. S. Musgrave, D.P. Purpura.
Electroenceph. clin. Neurophysiol. 15: 923, 1963. Presented by Story Musgrave at the
December 1962 meeting of the Eastern Association of Electroencephalographers, New
York, NY.

**Synaptic and non-synaptic processes in focal epileptogenic activity.**
D. P. Purpura, E. S. Goldensohn, F.S. Musgrave.
Electroenceph. clin. Neurophysiol. 15: 1051, 1963

**Intracellular potentials of cortical neurons during augmenting and recruiting
responses.**
D.P. Purpura, R. J. Shofer, F.S. Musgrave.
Federation Proc. 22: 457, 1963

**Cortical intracellular potentials during augmenting and recruiting responses.
II. Patterns of synaptic activities in pyramidal and nonpyramidal tract enruons.**
D.P. Purpura, R. J. Shofer, F.S. Musgrave.
J. Neurophysiol. 27: 133-151, 1964

**Pathophysiology and Pharmacology of Experimental Focal Epileptogenic Lesions.**
Franklin Story Musgrave, College of Physicians and Surgeons, Columbia University,
New York, New York, April 23, 1964.

**Pathophysiology and pharmacology of experimental epileptogenic lesions in cat
neocortex.**
F. S. Musgrave. Presented at the May 1964 meeting of Columbia-Presbyterian Medical
Society.

**Effect of topical tetraethylammonium ion on the initiation and course of cortical
spreading depressions in the rabbit.**
F.S. Musgrave, D.P. Purpura.

**Effects of two weeks of exercise on leg volume changes with lower body negative pressure.**
Richard C. Mains, M.S.; F. Story Musgrave, M.D. ; and Fred W. Zechman, Ph.D.
Department of Physiology and Biophysics
University of Kentucky Medical Center, Lexington, Kentucky

**Comparison of the effects of 70° tilt and several levels of lower body negative pressure on heart rate and blood pressure in man.**
F. Story Musgrave, Fred W. Zechman and Richard C. Mains
Department of Physiology and Biophysics
University of Kentucky Medical Center, Lexington, Kentucky
Published October 1971

**Changes in Total Leg Volume During Lower Body Negative Pressure.**
F. Story Musgrave, Fred W. Zechman and Richard C. Mains
Department of Physiology and Biophysics
University of Kentucky Medical Center, Lexington, Kentucky
Published June 1969

**Pulmonary Mechanics with a Simulated Postural Blood Redistribution.**
R. C. Mains, F.W. Zechman and F. S. Musgrave
Department of Physiology and Biophysics
University of Kentucky Medical Center, Lexington, Kentucky
Published 1968

**Plethysmographic Determination of Leg Volume Changes During Lower Body Negative Pressure.**
F. Story Musgrave, M.D., Fred W. Zechman, Ph.D. and Richard C. Mains, B.A.
Department of Physiology and Biophysics
University of Kentucky Medical Center, Lexington, Kentucky

**Radiographic Studies of the Chest During Changes in Posture and Lower Body Negative Pressure.**
Robert D. Milledge, M.D. ; F. Story Musgrave, M.D., M.S. ; and Fred W. Zechman, Ph.D.
Departments of Radiology, and Physiology and Biophysics,
University of Kentucky Medical Center, Lexington, Kentucky
Published April 1968

**Management of fulminating hyperkalemia in post-traumatic renal insufficiency. Ice packing and peritoneal dialysis.**
Rush, B.F. Jnr., Musgrave, S., Rosenberg J.C.
Published June 1965

**Respiratory mechanics and pulmonary diffusing capacity with lower body negative pressure.**
Fred W. Zechman, F. Story Musgrave, Richard C. Mains and Jerome E. Cohn (with the technical assistance of Roger Shannon)
Departments of Physiology and Biophysics and Medicine
University of Kentucky Medical Center, Lexington, Kentucky
Published May 1966

# *Missions*

**Story Musgrave's Space Shuttle Missions:**
Text source: NASA http://science.ksc.nasa.gov/shuttle/missions/

## STS-6

Space Shuttle: *Challenger.* 6th Space Shuttle mission.
Launch: April 4, 1983, 1:30:00 p.m. EST.
Landing: April 9, 1983, 10:53:42 a.m. PST, Runway 22, Edwards Air Force Base, California.
*Crew:* Paul J. Weitz, Commander; Karol J. Bobko, Pilot; Donald H. Peterson, Mission Specialist;
F. Story Musgrave, Mission Specialist.
*Payload:* TDRS-A,CFES(2),MLR/NOSL(1),GAS(x3)

*Mission Overview:* Primary payload was first Tracking and Data Relay Satellite-1 (TDRS-1). The malfunction of the Inertial Upper Stage booster resulted in placement of the spacecraft into improper but stable orbit. Additional propellant aboard the satellite was used over the next several months to gradually place TDRS-1 into properly circularized orbit. First space walk of Shuttle program performed by Peterson and Musgrave, lasting approximately four hours, 17 minutes. Other payloads included: Continuous Flow Electrophoresis System (CFES), Monodisperse Latex Reactor (MLR) (MLR), Radiation Monitoring Experiment (RME), Night/Day Optical Survey of Lightning (NOSL), and three Get Away Special canisters. This mission used the first lightweight external tank and lightweight rocket booster casings.

## STS-51F

Space Shuttle: *Challenger.* 19th Space Shuttle mission.
Launch: July 29, 1985, 5:00:00 p.m. EDT.
Landing: August 6, 1985, 12:45:26 p.m. PDT, Runway 23, Edwards Air Force Base, California.
*Crew:* Gordon Fullerton, Commander; Roy D. Bridges, Jr., Pilot; F. Story Musgrave, Mission Specialist 1; Anthony W. England, Mission Specialist 2; Karl G. Henize, Mission Specialist 3; Loren W. Acton, Payload Specialist 1; John-David F. Bartoe, Payload Specialist 2
*Payload:* SPACELAB-2, SAREX(1), CBDE, PGU

*Mission Overview:* Five minutes, 45 seconds into ascent, the number one main engine shut down prematurely, resulting in an Abort To Orbit (ATO) trajectory. The primary payload was Spacelab-2. Despite the abort-to-orbit, which required mission replanning, the mission was declared a success. A special part of the modular Spacelab system, the Igloo, located at head of three-pallet train, provided on-site support to instruments mounted on pallets. The main mission objectives were to verify the performance of the Spacelab systems, determine the interface capability of the orbiter and measure the environment induced by the spacecraft. Experiments covered life sciences, plasma physics, astronomy, high energy astrophysics, solar physics, atmospheric physics and technology research. The flight marked the first time the ESA Instrument Pointing System (IPS) was tested in orbit. This unique experiment pointing instrument was designed with an accuracy of one arc second. Initially, some problems were experienced when it was commanded to track the Sun, but a series of software fixes were made and the problem was corrected.

# STS-33

Space Shuttle: *Discovery.* 32nd Space Shuttle mission.
Launch: Nov. 22, 1989, 7:23:30 p.m. EST; 3rd night launch.
Landing: Nov. 27, 1989, 4:30:16 p.m. PST, Runway 4, Edwards Air Force Base, California.
*Crew:* Frederick D. Gregory, Commander; John E. Blaha, Pilot; F. Story Musgrave, Mission Specialist 1;
Manley L Carter, Jr., Mission Specialist 2; Kathryn C. Thornton, Mission Specialist 3
*Payload:* Department of Defense.
*Mission Overview:* Fifth mission dedicated to the Department of Defense.

# STS-44

Space Shuttle: *Atlantis.* 44th Space Shuttle mission.
Launch: Nov. 24, 1991, 6:44:00 p.m. EST.
Landing: Dec. 1, 1991, 2:34:12 p.m. PST, Runway 5. Edwards Air Force Base, California.
*Crew:* Frederick D. Gregory, Commander; Terence T. Henricks, Pilot; F. Story Musgrave, Mission
Specialist; Mario Runco, Jr., Mission Specialist; James S. Voss, Mission Specialist; Thomas J. Hennen,
Payload Specialist.
*Payload:* DSP, IOCM, MODE(2), AMOS(2), MMIS, CREAM, SAM, RME-III, VFT-1, UVPI, BFPT, EDOMP
*Mission Overview:* Dedicated Department of Defense mission. The unclassified payload included
Defense Support Program (DSP) satellite and attached Inertial Upper Stage (IUS), deployed on flight
day one. Cargo bay and middeck payloads: Interim Operational Contamination Monitor(IOCM);
Terra Scout; Military Man in Space (M88-1); Air Force Maui Optical System (AMOS); Cosmic
Radiation Effects and Activation Monitor (CREAM); Shuttle Activation Monitor (SAM); Radiation
Monitoring Equipment III (RME III); Visual Function Tester-1 (VFT-1); Ultraviolet Plume Instrument
(UVPI). Bioreactor Flow and Particle Trajectory experiment; and Extended Duration Orbiter Medical
Project: a series of investigations in support of Extended Duration Orbiter.

# STS-61

Space Shuttle: *Endeavour.* 59th Space Shuttle Mission
Launch: December 2, 1993 at 4:26am EST.
Landing: KSC, Florida, December 13, 1993 at 12:26.25 am EST Runway 33.
*Crew:* Richard O. Covey, Commander; Kenneth D. Bowersox, Pilot; F. Story Musgrave, Payload
Commander; Kathryn C. Thornton, Mission Specialist 1; Claude Nicollier, Mission Specialist 2;
Jeffrey A. Hoffman, Mission Specialist 3; Thomas D. Akers, Mission Specialist 5
*Payload:* Hubble Space Telescope (HST) Repair, IMAX
*Mission Overview:* The first HST servicing mission had three primary objectives: restoring the
planned scientific capabilities; restoring reliability of HST's systems; and validating the HST on-
orbit servicing concept. With its very heavy workload, the STS-61 mission was one of the most
sophisticated in the Shuttle's history. It lasted almost 11 days and crew members made five EVAs:
an all-time record at that time. The mission's major challenge was the amount of work that had to
be completed during the Space Shuttle flight. To minimally satisfy the mission's overall objectives,
astronauts needed to replace one gyroscope pair (either pair #2 or pair #3) and install either an
operational Wide Field/Planetary Camera II or the Corrective Optics Space Telescope Axial
Replacement (COSTAR), the other corrective optics package on the STS-61 manifest. Before launch,
a completely successful mission was defined as replacement of gyro pairs #2 and #3, both optics
packages, the solar arrays, the magnetometer, and the solar array drive electronics. In fact, the STS-
61 crew accomplished all of these tasks plus all lesser priority items such as the Goddard High

Resolution Spectrometer Redundancy Kit, the DF-224 coprocessor, a second magnetometer, fuse plugs for the gyros, an electronic control unit for gyro pair #1 and a HST reboost.

## STS-80

Space Shuttle: *Columbia.* 80th Space Shuttle Mission.
Launch: November 19, 1996 at 2:55:47 p.m EST.
Landing: KSC, Florida, December 7, 1996 at 6:49:05 a.m. EST.
Longest Space Shuttle Mission to date.
*Crew:* Kenneth D. Cockrell, Mission Commander; Kent V. Rominger, Pilot; Tamara E. Jernigan, Mission Specialist; Thomas D. Jones, Mission Specialist; F. Story Musgrave, Mission Specialist
*Payload:* ORFEUS-SPAS-02 (DARA ORFEUS-SPAS), WSF-3, NIH-R4, SEM, EDFT-05, CMIX, VIEW-CPL, BRIC, CCM-A
*Mission Overview:* The final Shuttle flight of 1996 was highlighted by the successful deployment, operation and retrieval of two free-flying research spacecraft. Orbiting and Retrievable Far and Extreme Ultraviolet Spectrometer-Shuttle Pallet Satellite II (ORFEUS-SPAS II) was deployed on day one to begin approximately two weeks of data-gathering. Making its second flight aboard the Shuttle, ORFEUS-SPAS II featured three primary scientific instruments: the ORFEUS-Telescope with the Far Ultraviolet (FUV) Spectrograph and Extreme Ultraviolet (EUV) Spectrograph. A secondary but highly complementary payload was the Interstellar Medium Absorption Profile Spectrograph (IMAPS). Non-astronomy payloads on ORFEUS-SPAS included the Surface Effects Sample Monitor (SESAM), the ATV Rendezvous Pre-Development Project (ARP) and the Student Experiment on ASTRO-SPAS (SEAS). The Wake Shield Facility-3 (WSF-3) – a 12-foot diameter, free-flying stainless steel disk designed to generate an "ultra-vacuum" environment in space in which to grow semiconductor thin films for use in advanced electronics – was deployed on flight day 4. Two planned extravehicular activities (EVAs) to evaluate equipment and procedures to be used during construction and maintenance of the International Space Station, were cancelled when the Shuttle's hatch could not be opened. Due to unfavorable landing conditions at the Kennedy Space Center, the crew were in orbit for two additional days.

# Select Chronology

1931    Percy and Marguerite Musgrave move to Linwood, a thousand-acre dairy farm in the Berkshire mountains of western Massachusetts.

1935    August 19, Franklin Story Musgrave born, second child of Percy and Marguerite Musgrave.

1947    Percy and Marguerite Musgrave's divorce becomes final.

1947    At age 12, Story enters St. Mark's School, at that time a boarding school for boys, in nearby Southborough, Massachusetts.

1953    Story enters US Marine Corps.

1954    Story receives National Defence Service Medal and an Outstanding Unit Citation as a member of the USMC Squadron VMA-212.

1956-58    Story attends Syracuse University, NY and graduates with a Bachelor of Science degree in mathematics and statistics.

1958-59    Story attends UCLA, California and graduates with a Master of Business Administration degree in operations analysis/computer programming.

1959    March 14, Story's older brother Percy, an officer in the Navy, is killed in an airplane accident while stationed aboard the USS Wasp.

1959    Story attends Syracuse University summer courses.

1959-60    Story attends Marietta College, Ohio and graduates a year later with a Bachelor of Arts degree in chemistry.

1960    Story marries Patricia van Kirk.

1960-64    Story earns a Doctorate in Medicine from Columbia University, NYC.

1964-65    Story moves his young family to Lexington, Kentucky, and begins a surgical internship program at the University of Kentucky.

1965    December 21 Story's younger brother Tom commits suicide.

1965-66    After hearing about possible opportunities within the space program, Story resigns from the surgical internship program and undertakes a US Air Force Post-Doctoral Fellowship at the University of Kentucky Lexington, researching aerospace medicine and physiology.

1966-67    Story continues his research with a National Heart Institute Post-Doctoral Fellowship at the University of Kentucky, Lexington, researching cardiovascular and exercise physiology.

1966    Story completes a Master of Science degree in physiology and biophysics at the University of Kentucky.

1967    Story is selected as a Scientist-Astronaut by NASA. The family moves to Houston, Texas.

1968-69  As part of his astronaut training, Story participates in the military jet pilot training program at Reese Air Force base in Lubbock, Texas, where the family relocate for twelve months. He breaks all records at Reese for outstanding performance by a pilot in the program, receiving the Reese Air Force Base Commander's Trophy.

1969    Story and his family return to Houston, Texas.

1971    Story becomes the astronaut representative for spacewalking, leading into the Skylab program.

1973    Story gives a prestigious lecture to the American College of Surgeons.
Story's father Percy Musgrave commits suicide.

1974    Story receives the NASA Exceptional Service Medal and the  Flying Physicians Association Airman of the Year Award.

1981    Story and Patricia divorce.

1982    Story's mother commits suicide.

1983    Story's first space flight STS-6
Story receives another Flying Physicians Association Airman of the Year Award.

1985    Story's second space flight STS 51F/Spacelab-2.

1986    Space Shuttle *Challenger* accident.
Story marries Carol Peterson, a NASA flight engineer.
Story begins studies in the humanities at the University of Houston, Clear Lake.
Story receives the NASA Exceptional Service Medal.

1987    Story completes a Master of Arts degree in literature at the University of Houston, Clear Lake.

1989    Story's son Jeffrey commits suicide.
Story's third space flight STS-33.
Story and Carol separate and divorce a few years later.

1991    Story's fourth space flight STS-44.

1992    Story receives the NASA Distinguished Service Medal.

1993    Story's fifth space flight STS-61– the first Hubble Space Telescope Repair Mission.

1996    Story's sixth and final space flight STS-80.
Story leaves NASA and moves to central Florida.